Effective
Training
Strategies

A PUBLICATION IN THE BERRETT-KOEHLER ORGANIZATIONAL PERFORMANCE SERIES

Richard A. Swanson &
Barbara L. Swanson
Series Editors

Effective

Training

Strategies

A Comprehensive Guide to

Maximizing Learning
in Organizations

James R. Davis & Adelaide B. Davis

Berrett-Koehler Publishers, Inc.
San Francisco

Berrett-Koehler Publishers, Inc.
450 Sansome Street, Suite 1200
San Francisco, CA 94111-3320
Tel.: (415) 288-0260   Fax: (415) 362-2512   Website: www.bkpub.com

ORDERING INFORMATION
Individual sales. Berrett-Koehler publications are available through most bookstores.
They can also be ordered direct from Berrett-Koehler at the address above.

Quantity sales. Special discounts are available on quantity purchases by corporations,
associations, and others. For details, contact the "Special Sales Department" at the
Berrett-Koehler address above.

Orders for college textbook/course adoption use. Please contact Berrett-Koehler Publishers
at the address above.

Orders by U.S. trade bookstores and wholesalers. Please contact Publishers Group West,
1700 Fourth Street, Berkeley, CA 94710; Tel.: (510) 528-1444; Fax: (510) 528-3444.

Printed in the United States of America.

 Printed on acid-free and recycled paper that is composed of
85% recovered fiber, including 15% postconsumer waste.

Library of Congress Cataloging-in-Publication Data
Davis, James R., 1936–
    Effective training strategies : a comprehensive guide to
  maximizing learning in organizations / James R. Davis & Adelaide B.
  Davis.
        p.   cm.
    Includes bibliographical references and index.
    ISBN 1-57675-037-X
    1. Training.   2. Learning.   3. Employees—Training of.   I. Davis,
Adelaide B., 1949–   . II. Title
LB1027.47.D38   1998   98-28368
658.3'124—DC21   CIP

First hardcover printing: July 1998
2001 00 99 98   10 9 8 7 6 5 4 3 2 1

Book Production: Mary Carman Barbosa
Design and Composition: Beverly Butterfield

CONTENTS

ACKNOWLEDGMENTS

WE WANT TO thank Dr. Bruce Hutton, professor of marketing and former dean, Daniels College of Business, University of Denver, for helping to shape the initial concept for this book and for providing for us the first encouragement to venture into this project. Dr. Richard Swanson, professor and director, Human Resource Development Research Center, University of Minnesota, served as Berrett-Koehler's series editor and provided enormous help during the development phase of the manuscript, including a day-long retreat at his summer home and many specific suggestions. Several outside readers encouraged the rewriting of the manuscript in "business style." At Berrett-Koehler we want to thank Valerie Barth, senior editor, for guiding all aspects of the editorial and production work for the book. We especially want to thank the president of Berrett-Koehler, Steven Piersanti, for seeing our manuscript as a "diamond in the rough" when it was still truly a lump of coal.

All of the organizations we visited were gracious in welcoming us and were more than generous with their time and expertise. We want to thank them all, without whose generosity there would be no concrete illustrations in this book. We also want to single out a few people who were helpful beyond the call of duty, sometimes arranging a whole series of interviews or spending up to a full day with us. These include Nancy Birdwell at Boeing Company, Commercial Airplane Group, for guiding us through our very first interview and showing us the magnificent assembly facilities at Boeing; Michael Quinn at Merrill Lynch and Company, who provided housing and chauffeurs for a full day gratis; Christopher Saeger at the American Red Cross; James Buchwald and his wife Maureen, dear old friends at ARIEL Corporation; Anders Stang, Deloitte & Touche Consulting Group, for receiving us at his summer home in Norway; Rajo Palola, ABB, for a full day, lunch, and gifts in Västerås, Sweden; Susan Connally, Eastman Kodak, for arranging interviews with several colleagues; Paul Day for sharing Global 8D at the Ford Motor Company; Bruce Marshall, National Emergency Training Center, for teaching us about simulations; Corporal Donna Morken for setting aside a day for us at the Royal Canadian Mounted Police; Dr. Waleed Abulfaraj, for arranging interviews with Savola and Dallah Group in Saudi Arabia; Atsushi Hamazaki, Sumitomo Metals, his wife Yoko and daughter Yuko, for hosting us in Osaka, Japan; Gene Yokomizo, for showing us the simulations at the United Airlines Flight Simulation Center; Marjo Vuorikoski, for serving as our translator and taking us to Iittala Finland to learn about glass blowing; Barry Wells for arranging a whole day for us at the Foreign Service Institute, U.S. Department of State; Sonia Ferreira Ferraz and Maria Elina Barbassa who organized the interviews done in Brazil; Axel Markert of Tubingen for arranging interviews with BOSCH and Mercedes-Benz in Stuttgart, Germany; and Ken Hou, ELSI Taiwan Language Schools, for hosting our visit in Taiwan.

We grew up in the era of typewriters, white out, and carbon paper, and we stand in awe of the word processing skills of Sharon Irwin, administrative assistant, University of Denver. This book went through some six or eight iterations, with major cuts, expansions, rearrangements, and rewrites. There was never heard "a discouraging word" as Sharon worked skillfully and patiently at the computer from beginning to end of the entire project. Thanks, Sharon!

We especially want to thank Elizabeth Geiser, director of the University of Denver Publishing Institute for providing us with support and guidance during the time we were seeking a publisher. Thank you, Elizabeth, for leading us to Berrett-Koehler Publishers.

There is one more person who deserves credit: our daughter, Marcella, who never spoke of being neglected; who somehow, at age sixteen, seemed to understand the importance of this project to her parents; and who sometimes attended the interviews during overseas travel. Although this book has no formal dedication, we would like to offer her the first copy with the hope that she may be successful in her currently planned career in international business.

INTRODUCTION
Learning About Learning

*T*HIS BOOK is for people who are responsible for formal and informal learning in business, government, or not-for-profit organizations. The intended audience includes managers, planners, and supervisors—people who are in a position to make decisions about how learning takes place—as well as directors of training programs, course developers, and personnel who actually deliver training for the organization. Outside the organization, this includes a host of consultants and facilitators who develop materials and provide training for organizations. Also included are professors in colleges and universities who act as facilitators or consultants, teachers in community colleges who provide customized training in organizational settings, and instructors in proprietary schools who train students for specific occupations in organizations. The audience also includes students of business or education and others who are just entering or aspiring to the field of human resource development. Given the new definition of training set forth in this book, as well as the large number of examples provided, the range of intended readers is very broad. In fact, that is one of our first points: Learning in organizations is more important today than ever before and is being facilitated by people throughout the organization. People who never thought of themselves as trainers are busy facilitating learning.

Many people today are talking about *learning organizations.* Peter Senge describes such an organization as one that is "continually expanding its capacity to create its future." In one sense, the whole organization needs to keep learning about itself, its products and services, its suppliers, its customers and clients, and its environment. On the other hand, no learning organization can survive without the learning that must take place for each individual within the organization. A true learning organization is made up of individuals throughout the system who are continually learning new things and learning to improve old things. *Effective Training Strategies* is a resource for anyone who is involved with or cares about teaching another person how to use knowledge to improve performance or develop capacity.

People responsible for learning in organizations are concerned today about getting results. They know that learning is important and affects greatly the performance of workers and volunteers, but they are worried, as they should be, that they may not have the right organization for training, a focused philosophy of learning, the best approach to planning programs and activities, or appropriate systems for assessing results. The greatest worry is that training may have become a kind of ritual, full of important-sounding terms and acronyms, trendy techniques, and clever activities, all supported by the latest technologies but devoid of *real learning.* This is why Training Strategies are important.

The purpose of this book is to provide well-established, theory-based Training Strategies that can be used to maximize learning in organizations.

Anyone associated with learning knows it is a complex process, full of booby traps and not easily reduced to slogans and formulas.

Many people try to sell easy answers when, in fact, complex thinking and astute professional judgment are needed to facilitate real learning. We are not proposing something easy; we are trying to bring clarity to what is essentially a difficult and challenging activity: maximizing learning in organizations. Our challenge as authors has been to digest the research into seven distinct Training Strategies, to present them clearly, and to illustrate them vividly; your challenge as a reader is to be persistent about developing your understanding of learning.

Using Training Strategies

What is a Training Strategy? Strategies are part of a triad of approaches to getting things accomplished: goals, strategies, and tactics. Strategies are used to carry out plans. Training Strategies are based on proven theories about how people learn.

- When trainers teach skills by setting precise objectives, breaking the task into steps, and using reinforcement wisely— that's a Training Strategy.
- When trainers place people in small groups, provide them with a task, ask them to interact, and then draw lessons from their group experience—that's a Training Strategy.
- When trainers place people in a situation that simulates the real-life performance environment and ask them to act out their role—that's a Training Strategy.

Each strategy has different historical roots, is based on different theories and bodies of research, requires different roles for the facilitator, and produces strikingly different outcomes. Training Strategies are not based on learning styles (individual preferences for visual, auditory, or active learning), although these are described in Chapter Thirteen, "Adapting Strategies to Participants." Training Strategies are based on the solid, well-researched theories about learning that serve as the foundation for effective training. Some Training Strategies have been around for a long time, and others are newer; but, alas, the foundations of most strategies—the basic learning theories—are often hidden in chapters of difficult textbooks or lost in the details of journal articles. We believe that it is time to reintroduce these fundamental well-established learning theories and apply them to the world of organizations. We have assembled them here in one place so that they can be easily understood, compared, and put to work.

The Research

We have studied and written about learning and conducted training for many years. Although our backgrounds are different, together we have accumulated extensive experience training, teaching, and learning. Experience, however, is a necessary but insufficient source for authoring a volume as comprehensive as this. Therefore, we have drawn on two types of research for this book.

First, there is an enormous body of writing on various kinds of learning. We have sought out and synthesized this literature, drawing on many sources from diverse fields—psychology, sociology, philosophy, communications—to describe how learning takes place. Generally, these are not the empirical research studies that establish that one instructional method is better than another method or studies that verify the relationship of particular methods to outcomes. Instead, we have drawn on the literature that describes previously established theories of learning and the things that one must know about them in order to be an effective facilitator. Our task, therefore, is not to prove the theories but to describe them as clearly as possible, saving the reader the trouble of having to look around (as widely as we did) for descriptions of how learning occurs.

Second, we needed to learn more about the variety of learning taking place in organizational settings. To do this, we used what has come to be called *qualitative interviewing* to learn about training in a wide range of business, government, and not-for-profit organizations. We conducted on-site interviews in important organizations scattered across the United States and in many foreign countries from Japan to Germany, Canada to Brazil, and Finland to Saudi Arabia. We wanted to learn about what arrangements organizations make for learning and what philosophies they express, but primarily we were searching for examples, very specific practical illustrations of the Training Strategies presented here. We employed a purposive sample representing various types of industries and service organizations that use quite different arrangements for training. We sought contacts through family, friends, and colleagues, and we also asked to interview trainers in the organizations we wanted in our sample. Whenever either of us traveled over a three-year period, if we could locate trainers willing to talk, we were ready to listen. We also sought *interesting* examples—manufacturers of products and conveyers of services that are familiar, fascinating, and typical of a country or region. In the chapters that follow you will find, among our many examples, illustrations of how people are trained to

- put the doors on a 747 (Boeing—Seattle, Washington, USA)
- make ethical decisions (Motorola—Schaumberg, Illinois, USA)
- become productive new employees (ABB Atom—Västeras, Sweden)
- make tough investment decisions (Merrill Lynch—New York City, USA)
- create new products (Norsk Hydro—Oslo, Norway)
- shoot or hold fire (Lackland Air Force Base—San Antonio, Texas, USA)
- understand basic telecommunications concepts (TELEBRÁS—Brasília, Brazil)
- teach about sensitivity to HIV/AIDS (American Red Cross—Falls Church, Virginia, USA)

- parachute out of airplanes (Fort Carson Army Base—Colorado Springs, Colorado, USA)
- respond to disasters (National Emergency Training Center—Emmitsburg, Maryland, USA)
- blow glass products (Iittala Finland—Iittala, Finland)
- be problem solvers (Sumitomo Metals—Osaka, Japan)
- serve as museum guards (Museo del Prado—Madrid, Spain).

The appendix contains a complete directory of all of the organizations visited. Because the examples were collected over a period of more than three years, we have presented them as they were at the time, recognizing that the organizations have no doubt developed other training methods and that the people we mention may have new titles and duties.

We learned a lot from this research ourselves, visiting the offices of trainers and touring their facilities, and now, through this book, we have created a vehicle for trainers to speak to other trainers about learning and share their methods and examples. Each of the seven Training Strategies described in Part Two is illustrated with examples drawn from our qualitative interviews with trainers. The learning theories are interesting in themselves, but the examples of how Training Strategies are applied in actual organizational settings provide a rich and stimulating set of real-world illustrations.

Learning from This Book

The chapters of this book are grouped in three parts as follows: In Part One, "Preparing for Learning," we address the organizational context of learning. In Chapter One, "The New Importance of Learning," we demonstrate how the place of learning in organizations has been deeply influenced by the new status of knowledge, global market competition, technology, organizational change, and demographic diversity. In Chapter Two, "Reframing Training," we suggest that training needs to be reconceptualized and given new status as a central activity of the learning organization. In Chapter Three, "Learning in Organizations," we explore how organizations of various purposes, types, sizes, structures, and cultures make differing arrangements for learning and how they develop a philosophy of learning that shapes their goals for training. In Chapter Four, "Planning for Learning," basic planning guidelines are offered as well as a technique for establishing learning outcomes. The topics in Part One all provide good reasons for using Training Strategies to maximize learning.

In Part Two, "Understanding Training Strategies," seven effective Training Strategies and the theories of learning on which they are based are set forth and illustrated with examples of actual training done in organizational settings. After extensive research and conceptual wrestling, we designated seven fundamental Training Strategies. A separate chapter devoted to each strategy contains a description of its typical use, the key concepts, its historical origins, the research supporting it, what the facilitator does, appropriate technologies, and the examples of its use in organizations.

In Part Three, "Maximizing Learning," the focus is on how to use the strategies. We begin this discussion of application in Chapter Twelve, "Choosing and Using Training Strategies," where we compare the strengths and shortcomings of each strategy and offer suggestions about how to choose the right strategy for the intended outcomes. In this chapter we also provide a chart for quick side-by-side comparison of the key aspects of all seven Training Strategies. The important characteristics of adults as learners are presented in Chapter Thirteen, "Adapting Strategies to Participants." In the final chapter, "Assessing Learning Outcomes," we discuss how learning can be assessed to determine if maximum learning is being achieved. The focus is on the particular kind of assessment appropriate for each strategy.

Where is the chapter, the reader might ask, on instructional technology? We don't believe that instructional technologies can be understood apart from Training Strategies. A hammer (as a technology) is the extension of the forearm; a fork is an extension of the fingers. It would be a mistake to try to eat with a hammer or pound nails with a fork. We have included some discussion of technologies and media with each of the Training Strategies; thus computer-assisted instruction is with the Behavioral Strategy, video with the Group Dynamics Strategy, and so forth.

We have tried to apply some of what we know about learning to the ordering of topics and the format of this book to make it as user-friendly as possible. It is a book that has been especially designed for self-directed adult learners. Main concepts or words to be emphasized appear in *italic* type. Key ideas, summarizing sentences, and recommendations appear in **bold** type. The examples are set apart and printed in a smaller typeface for quick reference. At the beginning of the chapters describing the seven Training Strategies is a Strategy Overview—a chart that summarizes the basic characteristics of each Training Strategy and serves as an advance organizer. At the end of each chapter is a section called The Bottom Line that contains lists of the important points of that chapter. When appropriate, we have provided charts and diagrams to show the relationships of key concepts.

The Promise

Every book should have a promise, even if it is only the promise of being interesting. The promise of this book is quite simple: You will be better at facilitating learning if you learn more about learning and then practice what you know. Note that we are not providing a money-back guarantee or warranty. Learning isn't like that; training requires skill and professional judgment. As any trainer knows, much depends on the learner as well as on many other factors in the organization's environment. What this book has to offer is the promise of maximizing learning by using Training Strategies.

Best Uses

This book has many uses:

- *Executives and managers* who need to rethink training in their organization can use this book to become better informed about learning. Learning in organizations is too important today to delegate.
- *Training directors* can use this book for staff meetings or training for trainers to provide a common language and set of concepts for thinking about learning. Trainers need to know as much as possible about learning.
- *Trainers* who find themselves stuck in one strategy, using it over and over again, can use this book to explore new strategies. There are many ways to learn.
- *Training providers* can use this book as a solid foundation for selecting and designing training activities and for grounding their work in learning theory. Participants really want and need to learn.
- *Students* who hope to enter the job market can use this book to get an overview of learning in many different kinds of organizations. It is hard to work in a learning organization without knowing about learning.
- *Anyone* who wants to can use this book as a reference and consult it to enhance the use of a particular Training Strategy. Training also needs continuous improvement.

We hope that this book will help to increase the expectations that organizations have for learning, set new standards of excellence for performance, take the guesswork out of training, and raise the overall level of effectiveness of organizations. We also hope that this book will soon have an international readership and that organizations all over the world will be able to move a step closer to becoming learning organizations. The quality of our individual and collective existence, now and in the future, depends on the efficiency, effectiveness, and humanity of the organizations that touch our lives—the ones where we work and those whose products and services we need and enjoy.

PART ONE

Preparing for Learning

*F*OR MONTHS it was the most talked about concept in business: the learning organization. Far from a worn-out cliché, the words still attract attention. What is a learning organization? As Robert H. Waterman Jr. notes humorously in *What America Does Right*, "The phrase 'learning organization' is so catchy that I keep thinking there must be something to the idea."[1] Not all catch phrases describe a reality, but this one appears to do so, and it won't go away.

Where did the idea of the 'learning organization' come from, and why is it persisting? Although the concept is often thought to have originated in the title of Peter M. Senge's 1990 book, *The Fifth Discipline: The Art and Practice of the Learning Organization,* in fact the 1985 classic, *Leaders: The Strategies for Taking Charge,* by Warren Bennis and Burt Nanus contains a section called "The Learning Organization."[2] They describe learning in organizations as follows:

> Organizational learning is the process by which an organization obtains and uses new knowledge, tools, behaviors, and values. It happens at all levels in the organization— among individuals and groups as well as systemwide. Individuals learn as part of their daily activities, particularly as

they interact with each other and with the outside world. Groups learn as their members cooperate to accomplish common goals. The entire system learns as it obtains feedback from the environment and anticipates further changes. At all levels, newly learned knowledge is translated into new goals, procedures, expectations, role structures, and measures of success.[3]

In *The Fifth Discipline,* Peter Senge developed the idea that organizations *as a whole* need to grow and develop and that their forward movement involves disciplined learning of new practices. He defines the *learning organization* as

> an organization that is continually expanding its capacity to create its future. For such an organization, it is not enough merely to survive. Survival learning or what is more often termed adaptive learning is important—indeed it is necessary. But for a learning organization, adaptive learning must be joined by generative learning, learning that enhances our capacity to create.[4]

Senge is also aware, however, that learning organizations are made up of individuals who are willing and eager to learn.

The organization learns as the individuals *within* it learn.

Senge sees learning as a fundamental human activity:

> Real learning gets to the heart of what it means to be human. Through learning, we re-create ourselves. Through learning we become able to do something we never were able to do. Through learning we reperceive the world and our relationship to it. Through learning we extend our capacity to create, to be part of the generative process of life. There is within each of us a deep hunger for this learning.[5]

Since the publication of *The Fifth Discipline* in 1990, a chorus of voices has begun to sing the new importance of learning to organizations. For example, Calhoun W. Wick and Lu Stanton León in *The Learning Edge* describe the importance of learning for companies that want to stay ahead.[6] It is the *learning edge* that gives companies the advantage today. "An organization that relies on learning to enhance its workers' abilities to contribute, produce results, and lead will create a competitive advantage for itself." Furthermore, the authors note, "Employees know when they work for a learning organization. They feel a sense of responsibility to learn how to do things better and improve what they do." Lester Thurow, author of *The Future of Capitalism,* carries the point one step further: "Today knowledge and skills now stand alone as the only source of comparative advantage. They have become the key ingredient in the late twentieth century's location of economic activity."[7]

Some organizations have been learning organizations for a long time, with or without the label. For others it is a relatively new concept, and dramatic efforts are being made to change attitudes and practices. A good example of these efforts comes from a large and successful multinational corporation based in Saudi Arabia.

Dallah Albaraka SAUDI ARABIA

*D*allah Albaraka Group is one of Saudi Arabia's largest and most diversified commercial groups, with investments of over US$ 7 billion in industrial production, agriculture, construction, real estate, transportation, health services, communications, media, and investments. Dallah is actually a group of 160 companies with sixty thousand employees in forty-four countries. "We have been very successful," notes Abdul Hakim Al-Shafei, executive director for training and development, but no one knows how successful we could be. One member of the group, Dallah Group Co., was like many companies fifteen to twenty years ago—preoccupied with growth and without much awareness of the importance of structured learning. Training for management was first organized in 1996 with the goal of transforming people from traditional to strategic managers. "We had to deal with fifteen years of custom, people spending most of their time with the day-to-day job, dealing with an in-basket," notes Hakim Al-Shafei. "Naturally, the upper two levels of management didn't think they needed training, so that's where we put our focus. The results have been amazing. You can actually see them talking and thinking differently in meetings." Training in strategic planning led one group actually to close down a business. Another group recognized it was neglecting its main product. "Now everyone sees that learning is part of continuous improvement." Hakim Al-Shafei is proud and enthusiastic. "The managers are asking about when the next programs will be offered. They are reading. They are using the Internet. They want us to write our own cases. They tell the CEO about the importance of learning. We have come a long way in a short time."

As one might expect, however, *learning organization* means different things to different people, causing confusion. On the one hand, learning organization may refer to the organization *as a whole,* and this may in fact be the way the term was intended to be used by Senge. On the other hand, learning organization can refer to all of the individual learnings and subsystems of learning going on throughout the organization.

The concept of *learning organization* we are using in this book refers to learning within the organization. In this sense, a learning organization is one where all of the individuals in it, in their own place and throughout the system, are learning. We are concerned primarily about the learning within organizations that is necessary for individuals, groups, and teams to do their job effectively, efficiently, and when called for, creatively.

Organizations today are challenged to find ways to maximize learning. If they want to generate more learning within the organization, doesn't that imply that more people in the organization will need to learn more? Doesn't that in turn imply that more people will need to be involved in *planning for and facilitating* that learning? Managers and supervisors will increasingly take on the roles of mentor, coach, teacher, counselor, and general facilitator of learning. It makes sense, then, that more people will need to know more about what learning actually is and how to help make it happen.

Before plunging into the Training Strategies in Part Two, it is important to examine in more detail why and how organizations are preparing for learning. Why has learning come to have this new importance today? How is the new importance of learning reframing the definition of training? What arrangements are organizations making for learning? Why is it important to have a philosophy about learning? What kind of planning do trainers need to engage in to maximize learning? These difficult questions are addressed in the chapters in Part One.

I

The New Importance
of Learning

*T*ALK TO TRAINERS and they will tell you that learning has always been important, but they also recognize that something has happened recently to give learning new importance, a status and urgency that can no longer be denied. Learning is taking place everywhere, within and beyond the boundaries usually associated with training as business, government, and not-for-profit organizations learn how to become learning organizations. Learning in organizations has a new importance because *learning* has a new importance.

In this chapter we provide the reasons why learning has become so important in organizations today. Reading this chapter can help you make the argument for focusing more effort and resources on learning. You will find here the rationale for becoming a true learning organization.

Managers, supervisors, and executives at all levels are getting the message about the new importance of learning. Michael L. Quinn, managing director of Merrill Lynch Capital Management, is in a position to observe and deal with a broad array of businesses. He notes:

> The advance of global competition, coupled with the explosion of information made available through cheaper computer power,

present serious challenges at all levels of industry today. Both small firms and giant corporations are affected. The consequent need for training—or retraining—to adapt to new job demands has never been greater. Classical education, even including advanced degrees, may no longer be enough to ensure success in the new workplace environment. A continuing commitment to learning, and the creation of new methods of investing in its people will be a hallmark of the most successful firms in any industry in the future.

Those who provide leadership in various types of organizations today are realizing that learning is an important activity that permeates the entire organization and is stimulated by many different kinds of people in different roles, including, sometimes, themselves. Today, everyone is teaching someone something somewhere!

Unfortunately, training is often superficial and ineffective. Hank Tarby of the QUANTUM Corporation, a high-growth computer disk drive company based in Milpitas, California, puts it this way:

> We have developed some expressions in the training profession that reflect some cynicism about getting results. We speak of the "spray and pray technique," where you spray out information and pray that some of it adheres to the participants. Or we talk about the "candle-dipping approach" where we dip the person in the candle-wax of knowledge and hang them up to dry, assuming they have it. Even worse, we refer to the "spaghetti-on-the-wall philosophy," you know, where you throw the pasta at the wall to see if it is done, and you hope it sticks. All of this comes from the sense that in training we are working in a kind of "emergency room" situation, where we are always patching up victims and never have time to fix the true social and organizational causes that produce the need for training. So you do the most immediate thing to address the learning gap.

Tarby concludes that organizations can't afford this approach any more. They need to know that training gets results, that learning "sticks." In his view, "The company that will get ahead is the one that learns the right stuff, learns it fastest, and applies it best."

The trainers we interviewed were delighted to see the new importance being given to learning, "as if, after all these years, people finally recognize that what we do is important!" At the same time, trainers are overwhelmed with the scope of what they are now being asked to do and feel intense pressures to get results. They are also deeply disturbed by the superficiality of much that they are offered—the painless panaceas and quick-fix tricks for trainers. Because training is no longer cosmetic and peripheral, just something that every good human resources division needs to do, but is now central and essential, a serious service adding value across the whole organization, trainers all around the world are scrambling to find new ways to maximize learning. Why has learning taken on new importance? What are the broader forces operating in society that make learning so important in organizations today?

Knowledge: The New Raw Material

We live in what has come to be called the *information society,* and although the term may be overworked, the reality it describes greatly affects the activities of business, government, and not-for-profit organizations. Perhaps the best description of the new status of knowledge in the life of organizations is found in Peter Drucker's *Post-Capitalist Society.*[1] He traces the course of three revolutions: industrial, productivity, and management. In each, knowledge becomes increasingly important in different ways, but in the fourth and most recent revolution, the transition to a knowledge society, knowledge takes on an entirely new meaning. Today, Drucker argues,

> Formal knowledge is seen as both the key personal and the key economic resource. In fact, knowledge is the only meaningful resource today. The traditional factors of production—land (i.e., natural

resources), labor, and capital—have not disappeared, but they have become secondary. They can be obtained, and obtained easily, provided there is knowledge. And knowledge in this new sense means knowledge as a utility, knowledge as the means to obtain social and economic results.[2]

Drucker points out that the crucial difference today is that knowledge is not only being applied to the physical world, to production, and to the management of organizations, but to knowledge itself, that is, to create *systematic innovation.*

Lester Thurow makes a similar case in *The Future of Capitalism.*[3] He says that this is an era of man-made brainpower industries that can be located anywhere on the face of the earth. Knowledge is clearly the new natural resource, the iron ore and bauxite of the new millennium. Human capital development is the key to moving from mere survival to success. Those who have the particular knowledge needed for the activity of their organization will prosper or be effective, and those without it will be left behind. One of the most important tasks in organizations today is *knowledge management.* Learning in organizations takes on a new importance as workers are forced to learn new ways to apply knowledge to knowledge.

Not all jobs, of course, require high levels of technical knowledge. Robert Reich, in his useful book, *The Work of Nations,* identifies jobs of the future as providing three types of services.[4]

• *Routine production services* include laborers working with machinery, data management specialists, and routine production workers. Jobs in this category require reading, writing, and computation ability and often involve training to develop basic skills.

• *In-person services* include sales workers, cashiers, hospital attendants, child-care workers, secretaries, mechanics, and flight attendants. Jobs in this category require special skills to function effectively and often require special training in human relations.

• *Symbolic-analytic services* include scientists, engineers, public relations executives, investment bankers, real estate developers, accountants, consultants, and planners. Jobs in this category require knowledge and the ability to manipulate information at high levels of abstraction and often require sophisticated forms of training.

All work today, even routine work, requires some level of skill and knowledge. Much work requires very high levels of knowledge and new understandings of how to apply knowledge to knowledge. Many people work in *learning-dependent occupations*. This gives training a new importance, a new challenge, and a new responsibility.

What does it mean, really, to apply knowledge to knowledge? Here is how one major multinational corporation did it and found itself in the robot business.

──Asea Brown Boveri SWEDEN ──────────

*A*sea Brown Boveri AB (ABB) the world's largest electrotechnical company, manufactures, among other things, turbines and turbogenerators and is capable of delivering whole coal power or atomic power plants anywhere in the world. At the ABB branch in Västerås, Sweden, we saw one section of the plant where the company now manufactures robots. As we walked down the aisle watching new robots being tested, twisting and turning incessantly upon themselves in every imaginable direction like kinetic art gone mad, we asked our host how ABB got into the robot business. "That's an interesting story," replied Reijo Palola, director of university relations. "It goes back to 1974, when we had purchased some of the very first robots made by the Japanese. Our president at the time was impressed with the idea but also by how poorly these particular robots worked. He was sure we could do better than that, so he set his best and brightest on the task of improving them. Today we make six thousand-plus per year, and we are the largest robot producer in the world."

Market Competition:
Economic War in the Global Village

The capitalist system is built on the concept of competition: Whoever provides the best product at the lowest cost will sell the most. Or at least, so it goes in theory. Businesses compete on the national and international levels, government and business often compete as service providers, and not-for-profits often compete with each other—all for market share.

World trade can trace its roots as far back as the sailing ships of the fifteenth and sixteenth centuries, or for that matter, to the camel trains of Marco Polo, but the manner and extent of world trade at its current and projected levels is unprecedented. Paul Kennedy, author of *Preparing for the Twenty-First Century*, notes:

> Given a global market, competition among firms—whether automobile producers, aircraft manufacturers, pharmaceutical companies, makers of computer hardware, or publishing houses—is driving them to sell and produce in all the major markets of the world. Not only does the company benefit from the economies of scale, but it hopes to protect itself from the vagaries of everyday fluctuations, differentiated economic growth, and political interference.[5]

Market competition, stimulated by growing commitments to free trade practices, now drives the behavior of most organizations.

Perhaps the best description of the new state of worldwide market competition is found in Lester Thurow's *Head to Head: The Coming Economic Battle Among Japan, Europe, and America.*[6] Thurow sees a world in which "three economic superpowers, the United States, Japan, and Europe, centered on Germany are jousting for economic supremacy." These three areas will be engaged in head-to-head market competition.

> What was an era of niche competition in the last half of the twentieth century will become an era of head-to-head competition in the

first half of the twenty-first century. Niche competition is win-win. Everyone has a place where they can excel; no one is going to be driven out of business. Head-to-head competition is win-lose.[7]

Thurow suggests that head-to-head market competition among the big three will be fierce. Many things will need to happen to make organizations more competitive, including new process technologies, but surely one important factor is workforce skill and training. Organizations as well as governments will need to invest far more, Thurow believes, in education and training to make sure "that everyone has the skills necessary to participate in the market." Although natural resources, capital, and technology will continue to be key factors in competitive advantage, we believe with Thurow that "the skills of the labor force are going to be the key competitive weapon in the twenty-first century." This puts learning into the spotlight as one of the most important things an organization does.

Globalization is not just a matter of putting company A in the United States in competition with a similar company B in Indonesia; it puts everyone in competition for everything—the cheapest labor, the easiest access to raw materials, the best tools, the lowest cost suppliers, the best markets.

As Rosabeth Moss Kanter notes in *World Class*, globalization has created a "global shopping mall" where world class products and services are bought and sold.[8] As a result of global competition, everything has to be world class. Note, for example, the international quality standards developed in recent years. And what are the implications for learning? Kanter says,

> world-class companies are more *entrepreneurial*, continuously seeking even better concepts, investing in customer-driven innovation. They are more *learning oriented*, searching for ideas and experience through informal inquisitiveness as well as formal education,

holding their staffs to a high performance standard, and investing in their people's knowledge and skills.[9]

One of the companies we visited in Europe provides an interesting example of how it faces international market competition.

— INLAN PORTUGAL

*I*NLAN—Indústria de Componentes Mecânicos, S.A., a small company in the little town of Ponte de Sôr, Portugal, builds rubber and synthetic products for cars and trucks: steering wheels, engine mounts, and weather stripping. How many competitors do they have worldwide in the steering wheel business? At last count it was twenty-six, all trying to build their product better and more cheaply to stay in the market. "Why do cars get more expensive each year when the parts that go into them get cheaper?" asks António Pinheiro, a former law student and now manager of human resources. "We have to build higher-quality, lower-cost parts each year just to stay in business."

Not all competition is international, of course; some of it is domestic, or may involve rivals within one city.

— Massachusetts General Hospital USA

*B*oston is a haven for medical research, teaching, and patient care. Hospitals fill several consecutive blocks, and walking around inside the largest of them, Massachusetts General Hospital, is like entering a small city within a city. In the downtown area alone there are Beth Israel, The New England Medical Center, New England Deaconess, Boston City Hospital, Peter Bent Brigham, Women's Hospital, and Massachusetts General. Although they work together in many ways and some serve as teaching hospitals for Harvard, Tufts, and Boston University, they are also competitors—make no mistake about it. Despite the fact that some are now part of recent mergers and realignments, they still compete to attract patients. In the past when patients required a hospital stay, they would be assigned to the hospitals where their doctors practiced. Now, with a growing number of types of prepaid medical coverage, health maintenance organizations (HMOs) bargain with hospitals, and hospitals must attract HMO group providers to use their facility both for overnight stays and for outpatient services. What are the implications for training? At Massachusetts General, administrators noticed a level of patient dissatisfaction that they found disturbing. It was not that the medical services were poor; they were quite excellent. What patients objected to was attitude, the way they perceived they were being treated. It was decided to reorient the extensive in-house training program and focus for a year on customer service training. Employees needed to learn how to help patients "enjoy" their experience in the hospital. The engine driving the training program was market competition!

Technology: One New Thing After Another

Anyone who has worked for even fifteen or twenty years has seen many new technologies enter the workplace. Technology is the application of the principles of science, or a particular scientific discovery, to some practical use. Technologies can be very simple, like the wheel, or complex, like the computer. New technologies, such as the advent of robots and computers, have often upset the status quo by providing new opportunities to do things in radically different ways. What happens when technologies have greater impact and arrive more frequently?

William Davidow and Michael Malone, authors of *The Virtual Corporation,* note in a provocative chapter entitled "The Upward Curve of Technology" that certain technological breakthroughs have a greater order of magnitude (impact) than others.[10] When technological advance occurs, revolutionary changes in the way people live their lives and conduct business also occur, depending on the order of magnitude of the impact. In weapons technology, for example, the great leap in destructive terror went from bombs of around 2,000 pounds of TNT to 12,500 tons of TNT in the atomic bomb.

What is different about technology today is the rapidity with which advances of great magnitude are made. The advances in technology that came with the computer and telecommunications were of high order-of-magnitude, and the continuing advances have come rapidly, within the span of a few years. The reductions in computer size, cost, and uses of power, and the increases in memory capacity, are all high order-of-magnitude advances, and they have occurred rapidly. Rapid, high order-of-magnitude advances are still occurring in semiconductors, computer hardware, data storage, software and data communications. They are occurring now in other technologies as well such as lasers, xerography, numerical control, speech recognition, computer vision, and liquid crystal and plasma displays. Add to this the technological revolutions in materials science and biotechnology, and we can see that the upward curve of technology will produce frequent, high-impact new technologies accompanied by major adjustments. For many organizations, technology results in one new thing after another, and keeping pace is a serious challenge.

When a new technology appears, someone within the organization needs to understand the technology, examine its relevance, and make judgments about whether, how, and to what extent it will be used. Once those decisions have been made, people have to learn to use it. Much of the training that is done today is about learning how to use new technologies. Usually this involves far more than teaching a worker to use a new machine.

New technologies often involve the revision of whole systems. New technologies usually have high order-of-magnitude implications for learning.

Notice what these companies do to train for new technologies.

—United Airlines USA

*T*he flight attendants who serve United Airlines are capable of working on all of the types of airplanes that United flies. (Pilots are assigned to fly only one.) When a new aircraft is purchased, or when a new technology appears on an aircraft, the attendants need to be trained to operate that technology. When the new 747-400 planes arrived they were equipped with computer touch panels to control many of the cabin systems. What would be the best way to train flight attendants to use the new panels? "We thought about that," notes Michele Manoski, manager of automation for flight operations at the United Airlines Training Center, not far from Chicago's O'Hare Airport. "We developed computer-based instruction with touch screen panels, complete with quizzes, and a sophisticated mastery learning system with branching for remediation. We used technology to teach technology. It worked."

—USIMINAS BRAZIL

*U*SIMINAS—Usinas Siderúrgicas de Minas Gerais, S.A., located in Belo Horizonte, Brazil, is a large, newly privatized, steel company that makes steel slabs, plates, sheets, and coils. Technology is important in all of its production processes, but instead of waiting for technology to happen to it, it is actively involved in discovering new technologies and better processes. The company sponsors its own research center to study the physical and chemical properties of raw materials, metallurgical processes, product performance, new product ideas, and fuel efficiency in industrial processes. In addition to the research center, the company sponsors employees at local universities for advanced study, and through their international program, Technological Development Abroad, they send people to other companies (Nippon Steel, British Steel, and others) to learn about new technologies. "Ours is a business where new technologies are constantly influencing what we do, and when they arrive and we adopt them, we have to train people to use them," says Jarbas de Almeida Krauss, analyst of selection and training. "Sometimes we have to find these new technologies."

Organizational Change: Reengineering, Downsizing, and Outsourcing

Almost every organization today is rethinking its structure, and sometimes the changes are radical and far-reaching. It is hard to determine when *radical restructuring* first began in earnest, but it seems to have grown out of the new business environment that began to emerge more than twenty-five years ago. Rosabeth Moss Kanter identified the new environment as a "transforming era" in her book *The Change Masters*, noting that "an organization can respond to the new era or become a slave of its past—a victim, not a master, of change."[11] The organizational change movement was also stimulated by the work of Tom Peters and Robert Waterman in their book, *In Search of Excellence.*[12] They offered eight characteristics of excellent, innovative organizations, and many "change masters" scrambled to follow their advice. Surely the flames of organizational change were also fanned by the quality movement as organizations tried to establish total quality management (TQM) principles, but clearly the concept that caught everyone's attention—whether it was a new idea or the right label for something they were already doing—was *reengineering*, set forth clearly and powerfully in the book by Michael Hammer and James Champy, *Reengineering the Corporation.*[13] In the authors' own words, reengineering "is the fundamental rethinking and radical redesign of business processes to achieve dramatic improvements in critical, contemporary measures of performance, such as cost, quality, service, and speed." For some organizations reengineering has meant downsizing, outsourcing, reassignment of remaining employees to new tasks, and new organizational structures, particularly the use of teams. What are the implications for learning?

Employees need to learn what the new organization is and how to act in it. The changes need to be communicated, and often this means learning how to behave in new ways in the new structure. More important, however, is how the work is often affected. Workers may have new work, or old work may be done in a new way. They may need to perform their work with new technologies, within new systems, or as members of new work teams.

Today we are witnessing a profound redefinition of the way people work. Organizational change is more than redrawing flow charts; it is getting people to perform work in new ways, and usually that means formal or informal training. The greater the organizational change, and the greater the redefinition of the work, the more training is required to make it actually happen.

Consider how training is affected by reorganization in this example.

— FIAT BRAZIL

"*I*t has been interesting to watch the organizational changes over the years," notes Roberval Brandão Nunes, former director of industrial relations, FIAT Automóveis S.A. "First came the quality movement. In 1989 the company instituted what was called the 'first wave,' and began working seriously on total quality. After that it was the 'rationalized factory' and then 'sixty-five elementary technology units.' Then the 'family system' based on the models (Tempra, Uno). Now it is 'teams.' We believe in change, change, change, and when it starts to get settled, we change it again. Every time there is a new change—a new theme, a reorganization, a new approach—there are huge implications for industrial relations and training."

Sometimes organizational change takes place within a particular unit of the organization and requires a radical restructuring of the work at the same time.

Observe what happened when one subunit of this company reorganized.

─Norsk Hydro NORWAY

Norsk Hydro a.s. is the largest corporation in Norway, and although the government owns 51 percent of the stock, the organization functions as a private company, a huge multinational with a wide range of products including fertilizer, magnesium, aluminum, oil, and salmon, among others. Hydro Data is an internal service unit of the corporation that provides information management services to other units of the corporation, but these units are free to go elsewhere for these services, for example to IBM, or to develop their own. To make Hydro Data more competitive and attractive, a decision was made to reorganize, with the goal of providing service in half the time with half the people. This involved a major reorganization with huge implications for training. The organization, Hydro Data—originally four hundred people in sixty-four units—reorganized its units into fourteen functions with eight critical processes broken into roles and competencies to perform the role, with each of the two hundred remaining employees learning at least two roles and how to report to more than one boss. "It was not easy going from four hundred to two hundred," notes Sigbjørn Engebretsen, vice president for human resources organizational development. "We offered some buyouts, moved some people to other parts of the organization, and chose the two hundred who would swim the river fastest to the new organization. We said that the new structure would not be an organization for reluctant people, so we picked the most promising to train. They would have to learn to *qualify* for the new Hydro Data organization."

Diversity: Multiple Perspectives on Everything

In many organizations, not only are the knowledge and technology new and the structures for getting work done altered, but the people who are doing the work are different. Sometimes they are domestic minorities, sometimes internationals with foreign languages, strange customs, and odd ways of doing business. These new workers have their points of view, their perspectives, and their sensitivities. Not only is the composition of the workforce changing within many countries, the frequency with which workers interface with workers and customers from other countries is increasing rapidly. People are interacting more with people who are different from themselves (hence the buzzword *diversity*), and these interactions are not always smooth. People need to learn how to work with other people, not because they are inept or hateful, but because they truly need new skills for collaboration and for understanding and coping with differences.

What are these differences and how important are they? The differences are obvious: race, language, ethnic heritage, gender, age, sexual orientation, disability, social class, and educational level. These differences imply others, differences in religion, attitudes, and values, and perhaps most important for organizations, differences in how to do business. How will people express their differences in the workplace? John Naisbitt and Patricia Aburdene provide intriguing suggestions in the chapter "Global Lifestyles and Cultural Nationalism" in *Megatrends 2000*.[14]

> The more humanity sees itself as inhabiting a single planet, the greater the need for each culture on that globe to own a unique heritage. It is desirable to taste each other's cuisine, fun to dress in blue denim, to enjoy some of the entertainment. But if that entire process begins to erode the sphere of deeper cultural values, people

will return to stressing their differences, a sort of cultural backlash. Each nation's history, language, and tradition are unique. So in a curiously paradoxical way, the more alike we become, the more we will stress our uniqueness.

Everyone is coming from somewhere with a unique, often deeply held set of cultural values and point of view. These values and points of view influence how people act in the workplace. The implications of cultural diversity for learning are enormous.

Here are two interesting examples of training for cultural diversity.

— Prudential Intercultural USA

𝒜 large electronics firm was opening a plant in Brazil, chiefly to manufacture and sell the electronic products used in cars. They had selected a president, one of their own vice presidents, who was eager to accept the assignment, but they knew that, eager though he was, he needed to learn something about the culture. They wanted him to hit the ground running so he wouldn't have to spend the first six months learning (often the hard way) how you do and don't do business in Brazil. Prudential Intercultural, a division of Prudential Resources Management, a piece of "the rock" well known in the insurance business, specializes in training for cultural diversity. What did they do for the new president? He went to Boulder, Colorado, with his wife for three days of intensive training to learn about geographic and historic roots of Brazilian culture, everyday life in Brazil, key cultural concepts, techniques for cross-cultural analysis, intercultural communication, and cross-cultural business issues. In addition, he was exposed to some background on other South American countries and general north-south cultural differences. At the end of the training, his briefcase was filled with materials and he was better prepared to deal with the diversity he would encounter.

──Deloitte & Touche NORWAY ──────────

*D*eloitte & Touche Consulting Group is the fourth largest management consulting group in the world with ten thousand consultants and over US$1.4 billion in annual revenues. They do extensive amounts of training, some in the U.S. Center in Scottsdale, Arizona, but also in the United Kingdom, continental Europe, and Asia Pacific. We visited with Anders Stang, partner in charge for Norway, at his two hundred-year-old homestead on a lake near Römskog. "In the training in continental Europe, we consciously seek a broad representation of participants. We want people to be fluent in English, so we include several UK participants, even though they have their own center, and we want people from various countries to mix. We want this training to be international, so that people will learn to network. Later they say, oh, yes, you are from Norway; we met at training, right? Because the work can be anywhere, with companies that are involved internationally, the consultants need to be trained to deal with diversity. The best way to do that is to involve them right from the beginning in training that involves an international array of participants."

Other New Influences

We could go on. In addition to these common and well-known influences, others appear almost daily. In the United States, welfare reform legislation has produced an urgent need to train and retrain current welfare recipients. More than five hundred major companies have established a Welfare to Work Partnership to address this issue, perhaps industry's most formidable training task yet. Similarly, organizations are increasingly interested in education that takes place in elementary and secondary schools. Many companies are involved in School to Work programs, many have established internship programs for high school and college students, and some are establishing their own schools. The U.S. Department of Labor is deeply involved in training, as are many labor unions. One of the new movements in adult education is the training of the contingent workforce. Add to this a growing concern about productivity levels, a key to a better economic life even in the most advanced countries, and one can see that learning has a new importance today that simply will not go away.

Perpetual Learning

Any one of these forces alone—the knowledge revolution, market competition, technology, organizational change, or diversity—is sure to have a significant impact on most organizations, but when the forces are combined, the impact is astounding. It is as if these forces are networked (as with computers) and what comes out on everyone's screen all over the world is the same message: "learning . . . learning . . . learning."

Over and over again people are getting the message: No organization today can survive without perpetual learning.

If learning has this new importance in organizations today, who is going to be responsible for it? Who is going to make sure that learning happens? Will traditional training personnel lodged with human resource development divisions take on more and more responsibility for learning? If so, how will they get better at what they do? Will more learning take place informally in organizations? If so, what structure will it take and who will see that it happens? Will other players—managers, supervisors, unit leaders—get involved in delivering training? If so, what roles will they play and how will they become better facilitators of learning? Will more training providers from outside the organization be engaged? If so, how will they be selected and what criteria will be used? Will more training be purchased? If so, to whom will the training be outsourced? What is the role of independent consultants in organizational learning, particularly university professors and community college experts in occupational education and customized training? Perhaps the most important question is, Who is going to referee this new ballgame? Who will make these decisions?

THE BOTTOM LINE

Learning has an incredible new importance in our society, and this has big implications for organizations.

- Organizations exist in the midst of a knowledge revolution, and for many, knowledge is their most important natural resource.
- In the global shopping mall, everyone is in competition with everyone else for everything.
- Rapid high order-of-magnitude advances in technology bring one innovation after another.
- Organizations themselves are changing, reengineering their approaches to the work they do and the structures they create for doing it.
- As individuals in an interconnected world population interface more frequently, human differences take on new importance, setting up a crucial need for better understanding of diversity.

Each of these forces requires learning something new. All of these influences combined give new importance to learning in organizations.

All around the world the message is the same: "learning . . . learning . . . learning"—perpetual learning!

2

Reframing Training

IF LEARNING has a new importance in organizations today, what are the implications for training? What was training and what is it today? How is it related to learning, development, and education? The first step in any professional activity is to become clear—as clear as possible—about what that activity is.

Trainers need to ask, unapologetically: Who are we and what do we do? What is our job? Those questions need to be asked anew in every age in every profession.

Because of the new importance of learning in organizations today, it is necessary to do some reframing of the concept of training.

In this chapter we provide ideas for reframing the concept of training and focusing the profession more directly on learning. Reading this chapter can help you rethink your own concept of training and enable you to understand why a renewed emphasis on learning is so important. If you are seeking a rationale for the value of training as an educational activity, you will find help here.

The idea of training is not new. This is no place for a historical review, and excellent brief histories are available elsewhere.[1] Suffice it to say, beginning around 1750 in England, two conditions made training a necessity: the separation of work from its natural environment, such as farms and shops, and the creation of large-scale organizations. For the first time people had to be trained to do things in an artificially constructed work environment and then learn how to behave in that environment.[2] Training, with great impetus from the exigencies of two world wars, became a *function* within organizations, and its processes became formalized. Like other work, training itself became work and was assigned to the particular people who performed it. This became the basic assumption about the place of training in organizations for almost a century and is still the basic concept that governs how learning takes place in most organizations.

Training is the specific job of specific people.

Sometimes this concept has worked out well and training specialists have been able to organize and provide effective training to develop various kinds of expertise as needed throughout the organization. At other times it has led to an alienation of training from the mainstream areas of organizational functions. Carried to extremes, it has created tension between trainers and the rest of the organization characterized by patronizing attitudes of trainers ("you need to learn this") and suspicion among trainees ("darned if we will"). When a task becomes professionalized, "territory" is created.

Surely we would not argue that training should not be formalized in organizations. As we know, a matter that is everyone's business is no one's business. We wonder, however, whether learning can remain the exclusive domain of training. Won't more people, by necessity, need to get involved?

Trainers have struggled hard within individual organizations and as a national activity to make training a profession, and much credit goes to their professional organizations, the American Society for Training and Development (ASTD) and the Academy for

Human Resource Development (AHRD). Particularly impressive
has been a series of publications for ASTD by Patrick Pinto and
Patricia McLagan that provide descriptions of the professional
roles and competencies of those who work in HRD, definitions of
HRD functions, statements of purposes, and a list of ethical issues.[3]
A particularly useful Human Resource Wheel has been developed
by Patricia McLagan to delineate and define specific HRD functions:
training and development, organization development, and career
development, and to distinguish these from other personnel functions, such as employee assistance, compensation and benefits,
and selection and staffing.[4] Likewise, the AHRD has begun to pub-
lish an annual volume of conference proceedings, a newsletter, a
research handbook, and two journals: a research journal called
Human Resource Development Quarterly and *Human Resource
Development International,* a reflective practitioner journal. AHRD
has taken a strong interest in research and theory building in
human resource development. As Richard Swanson notes, however, theory building is just beginning, and work is badly needed
in the foundational areas of economic theory (the measurement
of economic outcomes of HRD interventions), systems theory, and
psychological theory—particularly theories of learning and motivation.[5]

As HRD moves forward as a profession—and who would not
applaud these efforts to gain greater clarity about roles and functions—the new importance of learning hangs like a thundercloud
over a domain that, oddly enough, has not had much to say about
learning.

Training Without Learning

Something funny happened on the way to the professionalization
of training: Learning got left out. Is that too strong? At least we

could say, learning was neglected or, perhaps more carefully, learning in the context of the HRD profession never became articulated or elaborated as fully as it might have been. What happened?

Training has almost always grown out of some urgent need. Training has usually been a response to a problem—today we call it *performance improvement*—and responding, perhaps, has become a habit. A profession characterized by responding, often under pressures of time and without adequate staff and resources, doesn't have much occasion for reflection, let alone theory building. The immediate job is the task at hand, to improve the performance of *x* through training. Usually that has meant coming up with a workable solution to a specific training challenge—a program or activity that will get the job done.

Furthermore, odd as it may seem, many people who provide training are not trained as trainers and often are not very knowledgeable about learning theories. When would they have had time to learn about learning? Most trainers have come up through the organization; they know cars, airplanes, or breakfast cereal, but they haven't had much opportunity to learn about learning. Recognizing the limits of their knowledge, they often engage training providers, who, ironically, don't know much about learning either.

Training without learning, we are quick to emphasize, is not anyone's fault. It simply is, and the reasons for it are quite understandable. Very few people in the business of training, whatever organization they serve, have had much opportunity to learn about learning. What this does is to make well-intentioned, but often desperate, people vulnerable to false substitutes. Where deeper understandings of learning are missing, superficial ones fill the gap. We do not want to pick on any one provider, because there are many who do this, so we haven't listed the source, but one flyer that crossed our desk offered workshops on the following topics to fill the learning vacuum. We quote the topics word for word:

Tricks for Trainers
Presenter's Survival Kit
First Aid Ideas
Creativity in a Box
Lights, Camera, Action
Wake 'Em Up
Red Hot Handouts
Tinker with Your Thinker
Graphics for Klutzes
Humor in Training
Whole Brain Tools for Today's Learning Challenges
All Aboard! Ride Einstein's Light Beam of Creativity
Know White and the Seven Learners
Quick Stop at the Trainer's Body Shop.

One closing session even offered "key points from the sessions you didn't have time to attend."

Given the new importance of learning, this menu of training opportunities for trainers is not only superficial and inadequate, it is outrageous. Not only is it outrageous, it is insulting to the people who try their best to facilitate learning, sometimes in life-and-death situations. The people we interviewed are far more sophisticated than this. They are all deeply engaged in important and challenging work, and they expressed a sincere desire to learn more about learning. We suspect that even though they are not a systematically drawn sample, they also represent trainers all over the world who would like to learn more about learning.

The HRD movement, on its way to becoming a serious profession, can no longer afford an atheoretical approach to learning. Training must hold forth the promise of maximizing learning.

A New Definition of Training

As learning takes on new importance in organizations today, what will happen to the role of training? Will current definitions and understandings of training and development need to be changed or expanded? Does the new importance of learning require a reframing of the concept of training?

Brenda Sumberg, director of Motorola University, the Americas, sits at her office desk in the Motorola corporate tower on the Schaumberg, Illinois (U.S. campus) and reflects on how the concept of training has changed.

> We have had a commitment to training for a long time. That came with our president, Bob Galvin. That's why we are called Motorola University. Over the years, though, we have had to rethink what we mean by training. We knew it was important for constant renewal. We knew we had to learn new things and that meant we had to teach new things. What happened was that we began to broaden our audience so that we were not only involved with employees but suppliers and customers as well. We had to look at the whole value chain as part of our role. Our credibility has gone up tremendously in the last ten to twelve years. That's the good news. The bad news is that now everybody thinks every problem can be solved with training.

What is training, or to put the question another way: What has been the traditional job description? The American Society for Training and Development provides a useful definition of training in its *Models for HRD Practice:*

> Training and development focuses on identifying, assuring, and helping develop, through planned learning, the key competencies that enable individuals to perform current or future jobs. Training and development's primary emphasis is on individuals in their work roles. The primary training and development intervention is

planned individual learning, whether accomplished through training, on-the-job learning, coaching, or other means of fostering
individual learning.[6]

The strength in this definition is the emphasis on learning and its
focus on planned individual learning. It provides a good starting
point, although the frame of reference appears to be only formal
training in business organizations.

Developing a definition of training is not easy. Because there
are so many different types of training activities today and so
many kinds of organizations, a simple statement could be too
restrictive. Consider these ten examples of training:

- The Savola Company (Saudi Arabia) trains high-potential
  new employees for jobs that don't yet exist.
- United Airlines (USA) trains flight attendants serving
  new international routes in cross-cultural sensitivity.
- Quaker Oats (USA) trains employees in problem-solving
  techniques.
- Grupo Tampico (Mexico) trains women to be more assertive
  and aware of their new role in the world of work.
- Denver Museum of Natural History (USA) trains volunteer
  museum guides for special exhibits.
- Foreign Service Institute, U.S. Department of State
  (USA) trains families of government workers for overseas
  assignments.
- USIMINAS (Brazil) trains marketing personnel to discover
  new uses for its products for specific customers.
- KRESAM (Sweden) teaches the unemployed how to start a
  new business instead of giving them job search skills.
- Royal Canadian Mounted Police (Canada) trains officers
  in community policing through dramatic scenarios.
- Safeway (USA and Canada) trains grocery checkout clerks
  to recognize and recall codes for produce.

- Air Force Institute of Technology (USA) uses distance learning technology to train military personnel in procurement and project development.
- Kodak (USA) expects employees to commit to forty hours annually of informal learning in their personal development plans.

Is there one definition of training that will cover these diverse examples? Here is our basic definition of training. It is explained and elaborated in the list that follows.

> *Training is the process through which skills are developed, information is provided, and attitudes are nurtured, in order to help individuals who work in organizations to become more effective and efficient in their work. Training helps the organization to fulfill its purposes and goals, while contributing to the overall development of workers. Training is necessary to help workers qualify for a job, do the job, or advance, but it is also essential for enhancing and transforming the job, so that the job actually adds value to the enterprise. Training facilitates learning, but learning is not only a formal activity designed and encouraged by specially prepared trainers to generate specific performance improvements. Learning is also a more universal activity, designed to increase capability and capacity and is facilitated formally and informally by many types of people at different levels of the organization. Training should always hold forth the promise of maximizing learning.*

Consider the various components of the definition more closely.

- *Training is always a process, not a program to be completed.* It takes place over time and involves intensity, frequency, and duration. There are no miracles, no instant cures. It is like learning to ski, play golf, or master chess: through a sustained learning process you get better and better at it.

- *Through training, skills are developed, information is provided, and attitudes are nurtured.* This suggests that the content of training can vary widely and may include things that we make or do, things that we know or think, and things that we feel or value.
- *Training is used to help individual workers become more effective and efficient in what they do.* It is usually designed to help workers learn how to do, become better at, become faster at, or become smarter at some specific job or process.
- *Training helps the organization.* The reference point is usually a general or specific need within the organization. The learning that occurs should benefit the organization in some way, its production processes or services, its sales, its management, or its suppliers or customers.
- *Training usually contributes to the overall development of workers.* Significant amounts of training, for several different tasks or increasing levels of responsibility, often have a cumulative effect that contributes to the general enrichment of the organization's employees and the workforce pool.
- *Training helps workers qualify for a job, do the job, or advance.* These have been traditional roles for training and will not diminish in importance.
- *Training is also essential for enhancing and transforming the job.* Training helps workers do their jobs in a different way. Some jobs actually become different jobs through training. Technologically empowered jobs and redefined responsibilities add new value to the organization, but they usually require new learning.
- *Training facilitates learning.* If there is no (or little) learning, there is not much hope for performance improvement or development of capacity.
- *Learning is not only a formal activity. It is also a more universal activity, and it is facilitated formally and informally by many types of people.* Although training is designed to facilitate learning, learning can take place without training. Learning can and should

occur in many ways across the organization today. Many people, sometimes coming from unusual corners of the organization, will get involved today in facilitating learning.

• *Training should always hold forth the promise of maximizing learning.* Training is always conducted with an eye toward efficiency and effectiveness to maximize learning within the limits of resources and time.

Training and Development

From the argument developed for the new importance of learning, almost all of the people in organizations could profit from some form of learning today, but not everyone would agree with that statement. Some would say that training needs to be narrowed, focused, and linked more precisely to performance improvement. The *ASTD Models for Human Performance Improvement* suggests a "shift from training to performance" as the key concept.[7] For some, performance is the issue, and all of the factors that affect performance, including training, need to be accounted for systematically. In another book in this series entitled *Analysis for Improving Performance,* Richard Swanson provides the tools and step-by-step process to "diagnose organizational performance and document workplace expertise."[8] Elsewhere, Swanson describes training and development primarily as "the process of systematically developing expertise for the purpose of improving performance."[9] In some respects this is a welcomed approach, because it increases the chances that training will actually produce results. It also prevents training from slipping into unproductive efforts that can't be measured or assessed. This may, in fact, be the direction that training is moving—toward a sharper focus on learning that improves performance.

On the other hand, many organizations have a long tradition of training as the general improvement of capacity. One can find, for example, in the catalogues of Motorola University, Lockheed Martin Astronautics, and the Ford Fairlane Training and Development Center (and many others), course listings on a huge range of subjects, comparable in some ways to the catalogs—or at least the continuing education catalogs—of major universities. Organizations appear to be willing to invest in the long-range general improvement of employees through courses and certificates and through tuition assistance programs for further study. Notice how this company focuses on the development of general capacity.

—Savola SAUDI ARABIA

Saudi Arabia is well known for its petroleum production, but The Savola Company dominates the Arabian Peninsula in the *edible* oils market. Based in the Red Sea port of Jeddah, Savola began in 1979 as a small manufacturer of edible oils and has become one of the most successful and fastest-growing food producers in the Middle East with interests not only in edible oils but snack foods, dairy products, and confectionery. With emerging interests in packaging and agricultural activities, The Savola Group is active in more than twenty countries in the Middle East, Europe, and North America. "A fast-growing company needs to prepare people to take jobs that don't yet exist," notes Mahmoud M. Khan, senior general manager of human resources. "We may acquire a new company and need a new management team, so we have to have people ready." One of Savola's showcase training programs is designed to develop the capacity of new employees who have been recruited not for a specific job vacancy but because they have demonstrated potential for development. Recruits are screened carefully for general characteristics—persuasiveness, decisiveness, critical reasoning, and skill in English—and are rotated through general management training in presentation skills, time management, finance, quality, team building, and interpersonal skills. "They don't know what job they are training for, but they know that at Savola we reward broad bands of competencies, so recruits had better learn to capitalize on their strengths and work on their weaknesses," notes Khan.

Perhaps the difference between training focused on performance improvement and training as long-range cultivation of capacity is found in the words traditionally used to describe the HRD enterprise—"training" *and* "development." Either way, the facilitators who become involved will need to learn more about learning.

Informal Learning

Performance improvement and the general development of capacity both involve formal training carried out by a unit within the organization with special responsibilities for training—activities that can be quantified and counted. We are impressed, however, with how much informal learning takes place in organizations, where people are learning things on their own, in their own way. Watch for the way informal learning takes place in these examples.

―ARLA SWEDEN

*A*s we ate cheesecake and drank strong coffee in the upstairs offices of one of the milk processing plants at the ARLA Group, a Swedish dairy products cooperative, Birgit Höjer, manager of human resources, described to us what happens when a management vacancy and replacement occurs. "The incoming manager interviews the outgoing manager about his perceptions of how he has performed on the job, his strengths and weaknesses, and what it has been like to hold this job. Meanwhile, the outgoing manager's subordinates are also interviewed, and the anonymous remarks are presented to the old manager in the presence of the new. I don't know if we should call it training, but there is a lot of learning taking place." Often an outgoing manager is incoming to a new position as well, so there is actually a chain of learning going on at ARLA, all of it informal.

—ARIEL Corporation USA

*A*RIEL Corporation, a midsize U.S. producer of gas compressors, is nestled in a low valley on the outskirts of the charming town of Mt. Vernon, Ohio. Factory floor workers are sometimes a little shy about participating in formal training programs. By identifying key workers and training them, largely through question-asking techniques, ARIEL sets in motion a chain of training, whereby the untrained can seek out their peers for informal training. The peers are good at answering questions with questions, because that's the way they were trained.

—Norsk Hydro NORWAY

*A*t Norsk Hydro a.s., a large Norwegian conglomerate with modern corporate offices nestled among the quaint old buildings of downtown Oslo, work teams are composed intentionally of 25 percent "juniors" who know they are there to learn new things and 25 percent "seniors" who know they are there to be mentors, along with others. And team membership rotates; a "senior" could become a "junior" on someone else's project. Work is structured so that everyone is teaching and learning.

Other organizations are making strong efforts to encourage informal learning and are making formal efforts—if that makes sense—to see that it happens. Consider how important informal learning is in this example.

—Eastman Kodak USA

*E*astman Kodak Company has a magnificent training and development center at its River Road site in Rochester, New York, where many formal training programs are conducted; but Kodak has also instituted informal learning as an important part of the employee development process it initiated in January 1995. "There is no way that any amount of formal training could meet all of the training needs of all of its many employees worldwide," notes Catherine Nowaski, supervisor of employee development Initiatives. "That's one reason why we have made informal learning an important part of the employee development planning process." All employees must complete a plan with their supervisors and devote a minimum of forty hours a year to learning. Some of that learning will occur in formal training courses, but the plan also includes activities such as mentoring, engaging in self-study, performing job development assignments, viewing videos, traveling, and reading books from the Kodak libraries. "We have developed a road map for supervisors that gives them suggestions to pass on to employees about vehicles for their informal development," notes Nowaski. "Now we are doing a survey to assess the quality of the plans being developed, and one of the items inquires about whether and to what extent informal learning has been included in the employee development plan."

Informal learning is likely to play a more important role in the learning organization of the future.

Perhaps a new and challenging role for trainers is to work outside of formal training settings to help more employees learn more about learning, so that the employees themselves can become effective facilitators of informal learning.

Training and Education

In developing a basic definition of training it is important to ask, What is the relationship between training and education? For some, the word "training" has come to mean a process that is inferior to education. This is an old prejudice that goes back to Aristotle, who distinguished between *useful knowledge* and *liberal knowledge* and valued the latter more than the former. Although we do not want to take anything away from the importance of liberal education as a foundation for many vocations and professions and as a valuable process in its own right, it appears to us that through the years Aristotle's hierarchy has been damaging to the concept of training and is counterproductive in a modern high-tech society. When you get on an airplane to fly to your next meeting, you want the pilot to be well trained. Furthermore, you want the workers who put the airplane together to be well trained. If you should ever require medical surgery, you want the doctor performing the surgery, not to mention the lab technicians whose tests showed that you need surgery, to be well trained. For many tasks, employees need to be not only well educated to make good decisions but well trained to do their jobs perfectly, without error. In a high-tech, information-based society, how can we afford to think of training as a second-rate form of education? Many forms of training today involve high levels of intellectual and communication skills usually associated with education. The pilot and surgeon have to be trained to make complex decisions and to exercise good judgment, especially in an emergency. In other words, the old distinction between training as learning to perform mindless routines and education as learning higher-order thinking skills doesn't hold up.

Moreover, it is no longer possible to distinguish education from training on the basis of where it occurs. Some training takes place today in educational settings, and much education takes place in training settings. Furthermore, it is inappropriate to suggest that education implies high-quality experiences and training implies low-quality ones. Sophisticated efforts with outstanding results can occur within educational settings *and* in training programs in organizations; and, alas, muddled efforts with mediocre results can occur in both settings as well. Neither has an exclusive claim to quality when the criterion is maximal learning.

We want to take the tarnish off the word *training* and restore the validity and status of training as an important aspect of the educational enterprise, wherever it is practiced.

The status of training is a serious issue, not only for educational institutions, but also for organizations. As most educators and trainers realize, there is a need for a high level of collaboration between educational institutions and organizations today, both for planning and for implementing education and training. Collaboration works best among equal partners where status hierarchies don't exist, and neither party comes to the table with a sense of superiority. The status of training is also important *within* organizations, and we have found that many trainers perceive that their leaders, sometimes unwittingly, give a negative value to training. Even worse, trainers, having heard the negative message, often go about their work with a sense that they are second-class citizens in organizations where training isn't really valued.

We would like to declare peace on these old status battles. Training is a different kind of education, but as we have seen, learning has a new importance today that makes training indispensable in most organizations.

Given the new importance of learning, the old status battle between education and training is silly. Training is a special type of education that has no preconceived limitations as to purpose, place, or quality.

Learning-Centered Training

Perhaps the most important goal to accomplish in the reframing of training is to shift the emphasis from training to learning. Depending on your involvement with learning in organizations, you will need to make your own definition of training and decide whether what you do is more like training, development, or education. The important question to raise, however, is whether and to what extent training activities have anything to do with learning. The job description for trainers, no matter how you write it, is to *facilitate learning.*

How can learning-centered training be an effective process unless those who are facilitating the learning—managers, supervisors, trainers, consultants—know about learning? How can you be a chef if you don't know cooking? Learning is a process—actually many different processes—and if you don't know about each of the processes, you will never be very good, or as good as you could be, at facilitating learning.

Learning-centered training requires many people who are good at maximizing many kinds of learning.

What exactly is learning? This is surely a difficult word to define. A large dictionary usually lists several meanings for the noun, which is our first clue that learning is not just one narrowly defined process. How interesting that learning should be so many different things! Is it not natural, therefore, that there should be several ways of going about learning, that there should be several different theories about the way people learn? Our definition is as follows:

> *Learning is that varied set of processes whereby individuals and groups of individuals acquire knowledge or skill, change attitudes, become better informed about something familiar, or discover, inquire about, or become aware of something new.*

Furthermore, we believe that in training settings learning involves behavior change based on new understanding—a better, faster, smoother, more reasonable way of doing something, or at least an improved capacity for doing so. Training involves helping people reorganize their heads so that they can reorganize their work. It is new understanding transforming action. We might add to this definition Peter Vaill's terse observation that learning in organizations involves *know-how, know-what,* and *know-why.*[10]

Because learning within the organization takes place at many levels and occurs in many forms, those who facilitate learning need to know not just one aspect of learning, or even a few, but many aspects. This is not cause for despair, however, because learning about learning is fascinating, and the essentials of learning can be reduced to seven effective Training Strategies.

THE BOTTOM LINE

Trainers need to ask, Who are we and what do we do?

As training became professionalized, learning, ironically, got left behind.

The content of many workshops for trainers is outrageous and insulting.

The definition of training needs reframing.

- A broader definition of training emphasizes learning as a process and includes informal as well as formal learning facilitated by many types of people at different levels of the organization.
- Training is aimed at both improving performance and developing capacity.
- Sometimes training transforms the job.
- Training is a special type of education that has no preconceived limitations as to purpose, place, or quality.

The job description for trainers, no matter how you write it, is to facilitate learning.

Learning-centered training requires many people who are good at maximizing many kinds of learning.

3

Learning in Organizations

THE NEW IMPORTANCE of learning provides the impetus for reframing training. Even if there is general agreement on the point that learning has a new importance and that training needs to be reframed, each individual organization is still confronted with the task of articulating how learning will take place within its walls. What kind of learning is most needed? Where is it most needed? What structures are needed to facilitate it? A key aspect of getting ready for learning is making decisions about the *organizational arrangements* for learning.

It is also important for an organization to have a *philosophy of learning*. What do the leaders of the organization believe about learning? What do they value? Because the resources to be devoted to learning are limited, what kind of learning takes priority? As the nineteenth-century philosopher Herbert Spencer put it, "What knowledge is of most worth?" Organizations that have a philosophy of learning are better able to focus their efforts.

It is easy to become a prisoner of the organizations we serve, taking for granted their arrangements and philosophies and forgetting that there are alternatives. Perhaps we even lose sight of the fact that well-established traditions were once choices and that

current arrangements have no real claim on the future unless they are effective.

In this chapter we provide some conceptual lenses for looking at organizations and several examples of how organizations make arrangements for learning and establish a philosophy of learning. Reading this chapter can help you become more conscious of the arrangements for learning in the organization where you work, the assumptions behind those arrangements, and the spoken or unspoken philosophy about learning in that organization. If you are reexamining the arrangements for learning in your organization, the examples presented here will stimulate your thinking about options. Being clear about organizational arrangements and philosophy are important parts of the process of getting ready for learning.

The Organizational Arrangements for Learning

All organizations need to make some arrangements for learning, and many organizations today are reexamining what these should be. Consider this description of the reengineering of training from Katie Weiser, global director of education for Deloitte & Touche Consulting Group, one of the big five international consulting firms:

> In 1995, we decided that we needed to reengineer our approach to education. It was time to take a look at ourselves, and because we didn't have the answers, we drew in some consultants—we who usually *provide* consultants—to help with that process. What was our motivation for this reexamination? It began with feedback from students, who reported that training was really fun but not as rich in content as they were anticipating. Our service lines were also changing, and our clients were becoming more sophisticated. We also discovered in our recruiting that candidates were asking about training, and we knew that providing good training was a

competitive advantage in attracting and retaining the people we wanted to hire. Add to this that our business is global and that we now want to involve employees from other countries, and it became evident that we needed to reexamine everything: the content, delivery, timing, instructors, and location.

Many organizations, even those with model structures for training, are rethinking what they are doing about learning. This is not always an easy task, however, because sometimes training gets caught up in larger reengineering efforts. Figuring out what to do about learning is a key part of the reorganization problem. What should an organization keep in mind as it begins to establish or undertakes to rethink arrangements for learning?

The first step toward making new arrangements for learning is to understand clearly the organization itself. What kind of organization is this and what business is it in? We all know what organizations are, or we should know at least; as Edward Gross and Amitai Etzioni point out, "We are born in organizations, educated by organizations, and most of us spend much of our lives working in organizations."[1] In their book, *Organizations in Society*, Gross and Etzioni provide a classical definition of *organization* that has worked well through the years: "Organizations are social units (or human groupings) deliberately constructed and reconstructed to seek specific goals." Organizations, the authors note, are also characterized by deliberately planned divisions of labor, one or more power centers to control their efforts, and interchangeability (removal and replacement) of personnel.

As we noted earlier, however, organizations today are changing, sometimes radically. The classical definition implied a fixed identifiable unit with established goals and boundaries, but most would argue that organizations don't work that way any more. Rosabeth Moss Kanter, the author of *The Change Masters*, pointed out in the early 1980s that organizations are open systems where singular and clear goals are impossible, where individuals work in contexts where coordination may be the most critical problem.[2] At about the same time, Tom Peters and Robert Waterman Jr. proclaimed the "fall of the rational model" for organizations, and laid out a new set of principles in *In Search of Excellence*.[3] They suggested looser, leaner, more people-driven arrangements, at least for business organizations. Now, more than a decade later, one of the authors, Tom Peters, suggests that crazy times call for crazy organizations and that most organizations need to abandon everything and *disorganize* to unleash imagination.[4] Peter Vaill suggests that most organizations today live under conditions of turbulence he calls "permanent white water."[5] Although we are aware that some organizations need to self-destruct and "dis-organize" (cut, decentralize, regroup) the resulting arrangements, probably more responsive, fluid, and creative, will still be organizations with some sort of goals and structures for reaching those goals. Even reorganized organizations will need to make arrangements for learning.

Organizations vary tremendously in purpose, type, size, structure, and culture; and these characteristics influence the kinds of arrangements that they make for learning.

A systematic approach to rethinking the arrangements for learning involves careful consideration of each of these characteristics one by one.

Purpose

Organizations can be divided into three categories by *purpose:* business, government, and not-for-profit. We used these three fundamental groups as a starting point for thinking about the place of learning and the process of training in different types of organizations.

• *Business organizations* are entrepreneurial, and their purpose, even their responsibility, is to make a profit. Most are driven by a need to maintain a competitive edge in a global market, and this often shapes how they organize for learning and why they are pre-occupied with results. Although profit shapes the bottom line, most of their interest and activity, however, focuses on the services or products to be consumed—how to make them better, faster, and cheaper and how to invent new ones. They are interested in learning that supports entrepreneurship.

• *Government organizations* do not make a profit, but they are held accountable for outcomes in the administration of programs, agencies, and laws. Governments operate at national and local levels and are subject to changes (often decreases) in funding levels today. Their purpose is to administer programs, ranging from diplomacy to the military, from police to social services. They are interested in learning that improves their programs or services.

• *Not-for-profit organizations* usually are set up not to make money but to spend their resources wisely (usually fees and gifts but sometimes other revenues) for the purpose of providing services. They often work with volunteers who need training. They are interested in learning that makes their work in the community well received and effective.

The organizational arrangements for learning will be different for Motorola, the U.S. State Department, and the American Red Cross.

Organizations have different fundamental purposes, and the learning that is valued most depends on their basic purpose.

Type

Organizations also vary by *type*. Sociologists J. Eugene Haas and Thomas Drabek classify organizations into the following categories:[6]

- *Rational*—scientific in their pursuit of specified goals, usually bureaucratic in their management
- *Classical*—preoccupied with efficiency and formal structures to achieve desired results
- *Human relational*—composed of human beings who are social creatures that work best together as their needs are met
- *Conflict oriented*—driven by internal conflict, which is seen as natural and essential, and concerned with maintaining equilibrium through balances of power
- *Interactional*—characterized by simple trades or complex interactions, where exchange, reciprocity, and mutual dependence are important
- *Technological*—structured by the technologies used to shape raw material into a product or deliver a service
- *Holistic*—operating as systems within systems to be seen not as parts but as one open system, fluid within and open to its larger environment

These seven "lenses" are useful for looking at types of organizations, and although some organizations combine more than one type, usually every organization has a dominant way of behaving. A classical business organization such as Sumitomo Metals in Osaka, Japan, may emphasize aspects of learning, such as hierarchical levels of management training that are different from a technological business such as Motorola, where technical skills are important. The focus on learning for an interactional government organization such as the Foreign Service Institute of the U.S. State Department may be quite different from a human relational not-for-profit entity such as the American Red Cross.

Different types of organizations will single out particular kinds of learning as most useful.

Size

Another factor that influences the arrangements for learning is *size*. How big is this organization? Is it a small business such as a local Coors beer distributor, or a big national government agency such as the U.S. Air Force? It makes a difference. Robert Heilbroner and Lester Thurow, in a valuable book entitled *Economics Explained*, provide in Chapter Three, "A Birds-Eye View of the Economy," a description of what they call "the two worlds of business," one made up of the very small proprietorships and partnerships that gross less than $100,000 a year, the other the large, often huge and increasingly multinational, corporations.[7]

• Small businesses are small farms, mom and pop stores, restaurants, dry cleaners, and retailers. They make up 80 percent of U.S. businesses and employ one-third of the labor force.
• Large corporations range from medium-size companies to huge multinationals. They employ two-thirds of the workforce, and the 17 percent that generate more than $1 million of revenue annually take in 93 percent of the receipts of all corporations.

What is true of business is true also of government organizations, which range from small municipal service agencies to the U.S. Department of State, and for not-for-profits, which range from the local shelter for battered women to the American Red Cross. Organizations vary tremendously in size, and these differences affect the arrangements for learning and the place of training within the organization. Some large organizations have huge training facilities, comparable to a university campus. Some centralize their training functions; others decentralize them in smaller units. Some set training apart as a separate and highly visible function; others connect it to other activities and infuse it throughout the organization. In many small organizations, most training is informal.

In making decisions about arrangements for learning, size is usually an important factor and affects how much can be done and who will do it.

Structure

Organizations take on a *structure*, and there is great variety in the way they are structured. Susan and Allan Mohrman Jr., writing about "Organizational Change and Learning" in *Organizing for the Future*, an edited volume produced by scholars at the University of Southern California's Center for Effective Organizations, provide a useful description of organizing:

> Organizing is the arranging of the organizational *elements* (people, tools, and information) required for the ongoing transformation of organizational *inputs* into products and/or services that constitute the organizational *outputs* . . . The arrangement of organizational elements and the recurring patterns of organizational activities constitute the organization.

One might say, then, that a business, government, or not-for-profit organization not only is an organization but it has organization.[8]

Without delving into all the interesting classical works on organizations, it may be valuable here simply to note some of the current trends in thinking about organizational structure. These trends are well-elaborated in *Organizing for the Future* in the chapter "Effective Organizations: Using the New Logic of Organizing" by Jay Galbraith and Edward Lawler III.[9] The trends are:

- *Decentralized organizations*—where decision making is pushed down into organizational units that are closer to customers and products

- *Distributed organizations*—where traditional corporatewide functions are distributed to the units with the most volume, experience, and expertise to carry them out
- *Large-small organizations*—where the advantages of small-scale units (trust, cohesiveness, involvement) are supplemented by the benefits of large-scale coordination (capital, research and development, new technologies)
- *Nonhierarchical organizations*—where rank and status are played down and lateral cooperation and creativity are emphasized and valued
- *Fluid and transitory organizations*—where static organizational charts and fixed reporting relationships are replaced by evolving, self-designed structures in which competencies of individuals and teams are stressed over fixed job descriptions
- *Information-rich organizations*—where large amounts of information are moved cheaply and in multiple directions throughout all levels of the organization

The authors suggest that "the overall direction of change represents significant movement away from the traditional, hierarchical command-and-control model" to emerging structures, such as these others.

These new ways of structuring organizations also suggest new ways of structuring learning.

Culture

Organizations also have different types of decision-making processes and cultures. The older literature speaks of decision styles.[10] Rensis Likert, now famous for his *Likert scale,* but also one of the early insightful writers on organizations, divides organizations into participative and authoritative decision styles and further subdivides authoritative styles into exploitive, benevolent, and consultative.[11] Without going into the distinctions here, we want to note and emphasize that organizations have a different feel internally and that much of the impression that one gains about an organization, even on a single visit, derives from the way its decisions are made. More recently, those who write about organizations describe that internal "feel" of the organization as *culture*, which derives in part from its manner of decision making, but from other factors as well.

The term *culture* comes from anthropology, where it was applied to whole societies, but now the term is frequently applied to all types of organizations. Rosabeth Moss Kanter effectively describes the culture of an organization as follows:

> Out of the design and structure of the organization arises a set of patterns of behavior and cultural expectations that guide what people in the system consider appropriate modes of operating . . . . Such expectations or cultural "norms" guide behavior in a holistic sense.[12]

Peters and Waterman made "organizational culture" a key concept in *In Search of Excellence* and noted that "without exception, the dominance and coherence of culture proved to be an essential quality of excellent companies."[13] Peters and Waterman favor strong cultures, but as Kantor points out, cultures can be strong and also negative and dysfunctional; in fact, an organization can have strong "cultures of mediocrity."[14] If the organization already has a strong culture, where creativity and continuous improvement are valued highly, learning will no doubt be given a prominent place in that organization. Clearly, the decision processes and cultures of some organizations are more hospitable to learning than are others. What is possible in one setting may not work at all in another for cultural reasons.

The arrangements that an organization makes, or would like to make, for learning depend considerably on the culture of that organization. Sometimes the culture needs to change for learning to thrive.

Self-Analysis and Comparison

Now we have some tools for analyzing systematically how specific organizations build their structural arrangements for learning. The matrix provided in Figure 3.1 can be used to analyze any organization. What words would you place in the boxes of the matrix to further describe the organization(s) you are involved with where you may have responsibilities for providing leadership for learning or facilitating learning? Once you have described adequately the organization that you serve, the key question to ask is, How do organizational characteristics affect the arrangements for learning?

The matrix in Figure 3.1 also can be used to analyze the organizations described in the examples of creative arrangements that follow. Our objective here is to provide, uninterrupted by commentary, several positive examples drawn from the organizations in our interview sample. Compare these examples to the organization where you work and with each other. What useful ideas do the examples provide? Can you apply the matrix to them? What are the arrangements for learning?

Paychex USA

*P*aychex Inc. is a midsize business with 4,500 employees and one hundred offices spread around the United States. They offer payroll services to 275,000 clients, most of whom are small companies that outsource their payroll functions to Paychex. Even though Paychex is widely dispersed,

Figure 3.1 Analyzing Organizations: A Characteristics Matrix

Key question: How do organizational characteristics affect
the arrangements for learning?

| | Purpose | | |
Dominant Characteristics	Business	Government	Not-for-Profit
Type rational			
classical			
human relational			
conflict oriented			
interactional			
technological			
holistic			
Size small			
medium			
large			
Structure traditional			
emerging			
Culture dominant values			
strong			
weak			

its training functions are centralized at the home offices in Rochester, New York. Most new employees (around 90 percent of new hires) come to the Rochester offices for initial training. The average age of Paychex employees is thirty-three, and they are there to learn how to do payrolls the way Paychex does them and to drink deeply of company culture. The owner, Tom Golisano, who started the company, has high standards and wants employees to feel that they are responsible for their own success and for solving their own problems. He is not afraid to talk about attitudes, expectations, competition, and ethics. To get everybody "off on the right foot" and "reading from the same page," new employees are brought to the beautiful corporate headquarters in suburban Rochester. "What is the first thing the new employees see on the first floor when they enter the door?" asks training director Roberta Goheen. "Training classrooms. That sends a powerful message from the CEO about learning and development. It was set up this way on purpose."

—Motorola USA

 Motorola, with more than 142,000 employees worldwide and net sales (in 1995) of more than $27 billion, is among the fifty largest industrial companies in the United States. As a huge company with a technical emphasis, Motorola brings its training efforts together under the designation "Motorola University," but the university is not so much a place as a concept, the structure for organizing Motorola's $120 million annual investment in training and education. There are facilities with classrooms and specialized laboratories in Schaumberg, Illinois, home to the largest training facility, the Galvin Center for Continuing Education, and the Motorola Museum of Electronics, but there are also centers in Australia, China, England, Japan, Korea, Singapore, as well as additional regional centers in the United States in Texas, Arizona, Massachusetts, and Florida (for Latin America). Motorola University is organized for instruction into units for key competencies, management and executive education, customer and supplier services, quality and evaluation, and has a special unit that conducts research on its own education efforts. Motorola also has specialized units for its education partnerships, its huge involvement in K–12 education, its ties with universities, and its other corporate alliances. Additional information services are provided through a marketing and communications unit, a customer relations unit, an electronic publishing unit, and Motorola University Press. Motorola University functions like a modern multiversity system with certain centralized functions and a huge range of activities scattered over its campuses. As a company, Motorola takes advantage of centralization and decentralization, distributed functions, and the economies of scale of small and big, but learning is held together and coordinated as Motorola University.

—INLAN PORTUGAL

*I*n the small town of Ponte de Sôr, Portugal (population 9,000), in a broad upland valley east of Lisbon, is a small factory that produces rubber automotive parts—steering wheels, motor mounts, and weather stripping. INLAN—Indústria de Componetes Mecânicos, S.A., has only 640 employees, but most of these are permanent, and under European labor laws and with strong unions, it is difficult to release anyone. "We often have more people than we need," says António Pinheiro, director of human resources, "so we spend a lot of effort on training and retraining. Many people know how to do more than one job." Training is lodged in the human resources department, but everyone gets involved in planning for and carrying out training. The company sets annual goals and the department uses those goals to set the focus for training that year. Managers and first-line supervisors are drawn into the process of identifying needs, and through frank and open human resources meetings the balance is struck between needs, wants, and budgets. "Over the years we have tried to address everything—quality, safety, absenteeism, career paths." An amazing characteristic of Inlan is the way training seems to permeate the entire operation. A walk through the plant reveals setup and operating instructions posted for most manufacturing functions and models of high quality (perfect) products. Quality standards are set and posted for each part. There are mirrors posted with a sign "You are responsible for quality. Look in the mirror. It's you." Workers are trained to maintain their own tools. At one corner of the factory is a small training school for sixteen- to twenty-year-olds who may become part of the pool for new employees (only around twenty per year). The teachers are the employees who train others as part of their regular work hours three days a week. At the end of the year the same committee that planned the training assesses what went well and identifies what has been left undone. "We have some advantage in being small," notes Pinheiro, "but our main advantage is that we don't separate training from the work environment. Here training is like breathing."

— American Red Cross USA

The American Red Cross is a large not-for-profit organization that trains huge numbers of volunteers to work in armed services assistance, disaster relief, blood services, and a wide range of health and safety education programs. A member of the International Federation of Red Cross and Red Crescent Societies, the American Red Cross is nonetheless relatively autonomous and conducts training as a national operation, although increasingly shares materials with other countries. The Red Cross is made up of local chapters, which are (excuse the pun) the lifeblood of the national organization. The organization is similar to a franchise operation. "At the national level, we charter and support the local franchises (Red Cross chapters)," notes disaster services senior training development associate, Christopher Saeger. Contributions sent to local chapters help support, among other things, the training efforts at national headquarters in Falls Church, Virginia. "To help ensure a consistent product, course design and development and instructor training is coordinated by the national organization, but the key to our success," says Saeger, "is dissemination." We are organized to train the trainers who train the paid and volunteer staff in the local chapters." A typical local chapter might have a paid executive and a few staff members. The number of volunteers is usually ten times the number of paid staff. Chapters have disaster action teams that respond to house fires and other disasters every day, as well as to the big disasters that get more visibility. All of the chapter volunteers need training for their roles—providing disaster services, blood services, or HIV/AIDS education. The organizational structure is designed to produce efficient design and dissemination of training for paid and volunteer staff.

— Air Force Institute of Technology USA

Some organizations spend very little time on training, but for others training is almost all they do. One might say, without much exaggeration, that *most* of what takes place on military bases around the world is training. The armed services are government organizations, and they are a huge and widely dispersed effort that provides mostly services, although increasingly much of the work is technical. Setting aside the specialized functions of institutions such as the U.S. Air Force Institute of Technology (AFIT) or the U.S. Air Force Academy, the Air Force, as one branch of military service, focuses training through the Air Education and Training Command at five major bases (Lackland, Kessler, Shepherd, Goodfellow, and Vandenberg) and authorizes training programs at 151 affiliated schools. Many training programs award academic credit, and to assure transfer and comparability of effort, the Community College of the Air Force serves as an umbrella institution, with its five campuses and 151 programs, fully accredited by the Southern Association of Colleges and Schools. Lackland Air Force Base in San Antonio, Texas, just one of these campuses, is home to the 37th Training Group, with various training squadrons (341st–345th) assigned to different types of training tasks. In a recent year (1995) the 37th Training Group served more than thirty thousand students with more than 250 courses. "One mark of the scope of the operation at Lackland," says training administrator Robert L. Koger, "is that seventeen people work full time on assessment of learning outcomes."

— Sumitomo Metals JAPAN

S umitomo Metal Industries, with corporate offices in Osaka, is the tenth largest steel producer in the world. (Oddly enough, Japan has neither iron ore nor coal.) The 22,000-plus employees are scattered across several "works" that produce the various kinds of metal products that add up to over US$ 9 billion of net sales annually. The blue collar workers are mostly trained in the works, largely through the informal sharing of knowledge between older experienced workers and newer workers, and through *jishu kanri* (voluntary group activities) teams that stress solving problems on their own. Atsushi Hamazaki, general manager of automotive materials, notes, "Much of the *kenshu* (in-service training) is dispersed and quite informal." On the other hand, the training for managers is centralized in the Osaka headquarters and follows a very formal series of steps for each level of management. "It is definitely a matter of working your way up the steps of the ladder," notes Hiroshi Tsubouchi of the personnel department. New hires will get intensive training for a month and will be supervised closely for three years. Advancements are related to years on the job (six to eight years, or nine to eleven years) and are carefully graded: ordinary staff, qualified staff, senior staff, assistant manager, manager, general manager. Training is specifically designed for each level and is offered at the right time so that aspiring managers can qualify for advancement. "The training is formal," notes Tsubouchi, "and focuses on progressive development of problem-solving skills."

Foreign Service Institute USA

The Foreign Service Institute of the U.S. Department of State trains government workers and their dependents overseas. Established by an act of Congress in 1948, the institute now carries on its work in the new and remodeled National Foreign Affairs Training Center in Arlington, Virginia. Designed at first to provide language and cross-cultural training for Foreign Service workers—primarily the diplomatic corps—the institute now serves more than forty U.S. government agencies, including the CIA and FBI, but also the overseas work of the Department of Agriculture and Department of Commerce—even the Internal Revenue Service.

Over 60 percent of the activity is intensive instruction in 65 foreign languages, but there is also cross-cultural training for families, regional area studies, high-level policy roundtables, and gaming on volatile policy issues. There are now also overseas language schools in Yokohama, Seoul, Tunis, and Taipei. "The mission of the Institute has evolved," notes Barry Wells, associate dean of the senior seminar. "In the past we served primarily State Department employees and our resources were focused there. As a bureau of the Department of State, we receive our funding there, but now another forty agencies are paying direct and indirect costs to us for our services. It is much more complex because we have to manage our resources carefully and still provide high-quality services to an expanding population of users with differing needs."

Companhia Vale do Rio Doce BRAZIL

Companhia Vale do Rio Doce (CVRD) is a true conglomerate that has enterprises throughout most of Brazil. Its operations include companies involved in iron ore and pellets; steel products; aluminum and bauxite; railroad transportation and shipping; wood, pulp, and paper; potassium chloride and fertilizers; gold; port operations; manganese; and others. It has been said that when the company needed to get ore to the coast they got into railroads, and when they needed to ship it, they got into shipping and port operations. In 1992 training was decentralized, largely because human resources, which had been centralized, became the responsibility of individual companies. Now there is a central training office with only eight people in Rio de Janeiro, and regional training support centers in Belo Horizonte, Vitória, São Luís, and Rio. "We help with programs, and we plan and contract," says Virgínia de Abreu of the general training office in Rio, "but our main job is to stimulate and facilitate training. We work with the support centers on regional needs. But the real responsibility for training is in the human resource divisions of the companies. It is natural, then, that training is very much linked to the personnel system."

—Coors Distributing USA

*A*lthough there are six hundred Coors Beer distributors nationally, only four are owned directly by the Coors brewery. Coors Distributing Company in Denver, Colorado, is one of these. The company distributes Coors Beer and other brand name beverage products to supermarket chains, convenience stores, restaurants and taverns, and concessionaires, such as Coors Field, Denver's new major league baseball stadium. Sounds easy enough—just take the beer around, right? Actually, it is more complicated than that and, you guessed it, it involves training. The sales training specialist, Robert Jiron, works with seventy-two people. "I run some workshops, but my goal is to spend 60 percent of my time on the road, in the trucks with my drivers. As for structure, it's just me, and I report to the sales manager."

What is interesting to note about these examples is how varied they are. Paychex (a medium-sized business with a strong culture) centralizes learning and brings employees in from around the country. Motorola (a large, multinational, technological company) has huge far-flung operations and regional centers but coordinates learning through Motorola University. INLAN (a small, classical company with a traditional organization) embeds learning everywhere in the work environment. The American Red Cross (a large, not-for-profit, human relational organization) uses a franchise system and a dissemination model. The Air Force (a large, holistic, government organization) uses its traditional command, base, and squadron structure for learning and generates a community college for transferability and accumulation of credits. Sumitomo Metals (a large, classical organization) uses both informal and formal structures for learning. The Foreign Service Institute (a large, rational, government organization) trains its own State Department employees and contracts out learning to other government agencies. Companhia Vale do Rio

Doce (a large, interactional organization) decentralizes learning and makes it a personnel function. Coors Distributing (a small, classical business) has a one-man operation.

There is no one best set of arrangements for learning; each organization, therefore, should devise the arrangements that best serve its purposes. Every organization, however, needs to evolve some structures, formal and informal, for maximizing the learning that is most important to that organization.

Arrangements for learning grow out of the characteristics of the organization and set the broad framework within which other important decisions about learning are made. Ultimately, arrangements for learning also affect, to some extent, the choice of Training Strategies.

A Philosophy of Learning

Most organizations that do effective work in training also have a philosophy of learning. We use the less formal meaning of *philosophy* here: a system of principles to guide practical affairs. Most of the people interviewed in our study could identify and express a philosophy of learning that helped guide what their organizations were trying to do with training to give it focus, emphasis, impact, and coherence.

Perhaps you can identify already the philosophy of learning in the organization you serve. If you are trying to develop a philosophy of learning, or rethink your organization's philosophy, these examples should help.

The key words in these examples, which appear in italics, provide insight into the emphasis given to the philosophy for learning in that organization.

—Museo del Prado SPAIN

*W*e wondered why the museum guards at the Museo del Prado in Madrid were not very friendly. "The guards you see in each of the galleries are trained to spot danger signs and deal with emergencies," said D. José Manoel Hernando, director of organizational procedures. "Our philosophy is that the training has to *fit the job*. We begin first by analyzing the job. We could train our attendants to be friendly and informative, like a tour guide. But that is not their job. They need to look for someone who might take out a knife or spray can and damage a valuable painting. Guards need to know exactly what to do if there is an emergency. We train them to be watchful and suspicious. That's why they won't talk to you. They're busy watching."

—Organizações Martins BRAZIL

*M*artins, Comércio e Serviços de Distribuição Ltda., is a large variety store wholesaler based in Uberlândia, a growing service center to a prosperous agricultural area of western Brazil. Martins subscribes to the *gap philosophy* of training. "It's fairly simple," says Ricardo Rezende, director of human resources. "There is a job to do. The guy has this, the guy needs that. In between, there's the gap. Our job is to find and describe the gap for that job. Whatever the job is—truck driver, accountant, manager—it can still be described as the gap. Then we design programs to help people bridge the gap."

—FMC USA

*F*MC Corporation is a large conglomerate with businesses in industrial and performance chemicals, precious metals, defense systems, and machinery and equipment. On the sixty-seventh floor of the Amoco Building at the home offices in downtown Chicago, Illinois, we talked about FMC's comprehensive, three-cornered philosophy of training. "We see training as involving three areas," says William O'Brien, director of organization excellence, "and these areas, *knowledge, skills, and relationships,* are interrelated like the three corners of a triangle. For any job there are certain skills an employee must be able to do, but the skills fit into a larger universe of knowledge about the marketplace and the business we are in. The skills and knowledge are enhanced, however, by how we behave and communicate with each other. All three go together in each job, and we believe we have to keep working on all three all the time."

Sumitomo Metals JAPAN

Sumitomo Metal Industries, Ltd., a huge steel and metal products corporation, has a very focused philosophy of training that emphasizes problem solving. Certainly, they train for specific skills, too, but the emphasis at all levels is on *problem solving.* "The philosophy," says Personnel Director Hiroshi Tsubouchi, "is closely related to the larger structure of the organization, to our philosophy of employee relations, and to the culture of Japanese business. You don't invent a philosophy of training; it grows up out of the kind of organization you are."

Blue Cross/Blue Shield USA

Blue Cross Blue Shield of Massachusetts, a major U.S. health care insurer, also ties training to organizational goals. When you come in the door at the elegant downtown Boston offices, you are welcomed by a Statement of Operating Guidelines posted on the wall. It includes admonitions such as "serve the customer," "prevent error," "admit and fix mistakes," "simplify where possible." "Our training philosophy," says Sandra Casey Buford, manager of employee relations, "grows out of our organizational philosophy. We train people to *follow the operating guidelines.*"

——Safeway USA

Safeway Inc., a large supermarket food chain in the western United States and Canada, trains people for a variety of jobs, among them the checkout clerks. "Our philosophy is very simple," says Linda Hawkins, training instructor for Safeway, located in the modern tech center south of Denver, Colorado. "We want *success*. We want the people we are training to succeed, and we do whatever we have to do in supporting them on the road to success. We screen, of course, looking for people with the right aptitudes, but we stick with them until they can do it. If that means some retraining, we do it. If it means going out to the store for a couple of days to support them, we do it. If it means one-on-one, we do it. Hey, some are teenagers, and it is their first job. You can ruin their self-esteem, or you can build confidence. We're not just training checkers, we are building basic, lifelong attitudes about work. So we want them to be successful."

——Companhia Vale do Rio Doce BRAZIL

Companhia Vale do Rio Doce (CVRD), a major corporate conglomerate in Brazil with operations ranging from mining to railroads, links training closely to its *performance evaluation systems*. Training is dispersed across many units, but it is held together with a central philosophy about learning. "We start with our performance evaluations," says Virgínia de Abreu, general training director, whom we talked with at the central training center in downtown Rio de Janeiro. CVRD has a sophisticated two-by-two model for employee appraisal, using present performance and potential as key factors. People can be rated as high or low on each dimension, as illustrated in Figure 3.2. Workers who are low in performance and low in potential (lower left square) may be candidates for dismissal, and those with high performance but low potential tend to get transferred laterally to keep life interesting. Those with high potential

Figure 3.2 Potential-Performance Matrix

	POTENTIAL	
	Low	**High**
Low	L Performance L Potential	L Performance H Potential
High	H Performance L Potential	H Performance H Potential

PERFORMANCE

and low performance are good candidates for focused training, and those with high performance and high potential are seen as a major corporate resource. The main input for ranking is by managers and employees themselves, not by formal tests. For the shorter range, training focuses on performance, general desired skills, but the longer range development of employees, particularly for those with high potential, involves a career path plan. In either case, the philosophy of learning is to focus on performance and potential.

─Asea Brown Boveri SWEDEN

*A*sea Brown Boveri AB (ABB), a huge multinational conglomerate (atomic power plants, robots) with home offices in Sweden and Switzerland, puts at least some emphasis on, among other things, *succession training.* "We believe that we need to know each other's jobs. We can't let ourselves become dependent on one person being the only one to know what to do," says Reijo Palola, coordinator of university relations. "Someone needs to be ready to step in, even at the top. It is a sad story to tell, but the president of one of our divisions, ATOM, died in a bizarre accident with his family as they were driving their car onto a ferryboat in Denmark. Someone had to be ready to take his place. We always have a 'crown prince' waiting to do the job if necessary."

As the examples illustrate, there is a great amount of variation in the way organizations develop a philosophy about learning. There are also some very interesting options.

An organization needs a philosophy of learning, expressible in a few key words, to help focus and prioritize its efforts to maximize learning. The philosophy of learning grows out of organizational characteristics and provides a framework for other important decisions about learning in the organization. Ultimately, the philosophy of learning also influences to some extent the choice of Training Strategies.

THE BOTTOM LINE

Organizations have goals, a reason for being, and they organize human activity around these goals. They also organize learning around these goals. The structural arrangements for learning in organizations are important and being aware of these arrangements and reexamining them periodically is necessary.

- The first step is to understand the characteristics of the organization according to its purpose, type, size, structure, and culture.
- These characteristics influence the arrangements for learning, which should be regarded as choices.
- Different types of organizations generate differing kinds of arrangements for learning.
- Many creative options exist. The issue is appropriateness.
- An organization needs a philosophy of learning, expressible in a few key words, to help focus and prioritize its efforts to maximize learning.

The structural arrangements for learning and the philosophy of learning both grow out of organizational characteristics and help to frame other important decisions about learning. Ultimately, they also influence, to some extent, the choice of Training Strategies.

4

Planning for Learning

ORGANIZATIONS HAVE GOALS. Even very diffuse organizations that operate as open systems have goals. Sometimes goals shift or get altered during restructuring, and sometimes they are recombined with new goals. Some organizations are so large, diverse, and complex that they need several sets of goals for different units. Organizations also have *goals for learning*. Sometimes these goals are set forth formally in goal statements. More likely they are expressed less explicitly through the structural arrangements and through the philosophy of learning.

These larger *organizational goals for learning* frame the way people within an organization think about learning and often become an important consideration in selecting Training Strategies. These organizational goals are the big goals for learning.

On the other hand, organizations need to make specific plans for particular kinds of learning. These specific plans are the little goals more familiar to trainers—the goals for a particular workshop, course, or event.

These *immediate goals for learning* also become an important consideration in selecting Training Strategies. Goals operate at both macro and micro levels.

In this chapter we provide useful techniques for planning for learning. We put learning in the larger context of human resource development and emphasize the importance of careful planning. Reading this chapter can help you to identify and use rational models for planning, understand how to negotiate interests among those involved in planning, and clarify the role of subject matter experts. The most important thing you will learn is how to establish desired learning outcomes that will guide you in selecting appropriate Training Strategies. You will also learn about the relationships of goals, strategies, and tactics.

Limits to Learning

The purpose of planning is to develop opportunities to learn that will eventually improve performance or develop capacity. That sounds simple enough, but experienced trainers know that there is not always a direct route from a particular learning experience to improved performance or expanded capacity. Many other factors can affect this link—participant motivation, relevance to job need, workplace arrangements, peer attitudes, equipment or resources, and pay scales. We want to acknowledge that these, and many other factors like these, can and do influence the outcomes of training efforts. In other words, many influences can come along to knock learning off track. This is why people who are responsible for learning need to work closely with others in the organization who can impact these influences. We would be the first to acknowledge that there are limits to learning and that learning takes place in the broader context of human resource development.

In the language of research, learning is just one of the variables that influences performance and capacity. There are many books in the field of human resource management that address these complexities. We have not written one of those books. This book is about learning, the neglected variable. Our thesis is that learning itself can be maximized but in waving the flag for learning, we have not forgotten that this is just one vegetable in a complex, multivariate stew.

Planning

If it is true that learning is just one factor in a set of factors that influence performance and the development of capacity, is it not even more important that efforts to facilitate learning be as effective as possible? Everything directed toward maximizing learning needs to be done well. This includes planning, the subject of this chapter, and facilitation, the topic of the chapters in Parts Two and Three.

Planning involves all of the functions that take place before the training is actually delivered. Planning is also necessary to set the scene for informal learning. There are some useful techniques for planning, and without careful planning, training usually does not produce learning. Somewhere within most successful organizations there are people who have the responsibility for maximizing learning, whether these are managers, supervisors, or personnel designated to conduct formal training. At some point, someone in the organization must take hold of the training task and begin to develop plans for providing experiences that help people learn.

Over the years, trainers have accumulated and developed useful *rational models* for planning and implementing training.

Rational models go back at least to Charles R. Allen's four-step method: show, tell, do, check. That is the beginning of a rational model. Examples of more elaborate models can be found in Cyril Houle's *The Design of Education* and Malcolm Knowles's *The Modern Practice of Adult Education.*[1] As Jerald Apps has indicated, most of the rational planning models involve steps, usually these five:[2]

1. Assess learners' needs.
2. Define objectives based on these needs.
3. Identify learning experiences to meet those objectives.
4. Organize those learning experiences.
5. Evaluate the program in terms of its objectives.

Models with steps are usually called linear models, where completing step one is necessary before addressing step two.

Rosemary S. Caffarella has presented what she calls an *interactive model* in *Planning Programs for Adult Learners.*[3] The interactive model has components, things to be attended to, but not necessarily in linear order and not all components must necessarily be addressed for all programs. She sees her model as an open system. The components of Caffarella's interactive model are

Establishing a Basis for Program Planning
Identifying Program Ideas
Sorting and Prioritizing Program Ideas
Developing Program Objectives
Preparing for the Transfer of Learning
Formulating Evaluation Plans
Determining Formats, Schedules, and Staff Needs
Preparing Budgets and Marketing Plans
Designing Instructional Plans
Coordinating Facilities and On-Site Events
Communicating the Value of the Program

This is a valuable checklist of things to think about and is more flexible and, perhaps for that reason, more valuable than linear models. Caffarella recognizes that in working with adults it is important to focus on learning outcomes and change, that planning is both systematic and spontaneous, that program planning involves interaction and negotiation (a cooperative as well as operative process), and that by using models planners can become more proficient. Caffarella also provides some reasons for using a rational model: Outcomes can be predetermined and insured, resources can be used more effectively, daily work is made easier, teamwork is fostered, a basis for control is provided, and better programs are developed.

To maximize learning it is useful to begin with a rational model for planning training.

Experienced trainers often complain, however, that rational models don't work; they are good in theory but break down in practice. Planning for training is much more complicated than the models suggest. Often a great plan is developed and then someone says you can't do it that way. Or even worse, the training is planned and carried out, and the very audience it was developed for finds it boring or irrelevant. What happens?

In an insightful book by Ronald Cervero and Arthur Wilson, *Planning Responsibly for Adult Education*, the suggestion is made that the role of the planner is not so much to create the perfect rational plan but to be "responsible for negotiating the interests of all people who may be affected by the educational program."[4] Planning, they suggest, "is always conducted within a complex set of personal, organizational, and social relationships of power among people who may have similar, different, or conflicting sets of interests regarding the program." What needs to happen is "to move planning out of the minds of individual planners and into the social relations among people working in institutional settings." Planning is always done in a context where people have interests (predispositions, values, expectations) and power (capacity to influence or act), and the main task that effective planners do is *negotiate* among various interests. This is not to say that planners do not have ideas or plans themselves. But planners "act in and act on their settings through negotiation." In the later chapters of the book, the authors make a strong case for employing democratic planning processes to bring all the players to the table to negotiate interests openly.

There is something refreshing about these ideas, something that rings true for experienced trainers. They know that the workers involved in the training can often make important suggestions about the training, that their supervisors ought to be able to describe what is needed, that the boss needs to be satisfied, and that the people who conduct the training need to hear all of these interests and adapt the training to the specific needs and concerns expressed. Notice how NOVA International, a large gas company of nearly 5,700 employees and $4.5 billion in annual revenues makes plans for learning.

──NOVA Corporation CANADA

NOVA Corporation, prior to splitting into two companies, was a worldwide natural gas services and petrochemicals company headquartered in Calgary, Alberta. NOVA operates through three principal businesses: NOVA Gas Transmission Ltd., NOVA Gas International Ltd., and Novacor Chemicals Ltd. About 80 percent of Canada's marketed natural gas and 15 percent of North America's gas flows through NOVA's pipelines. NOVA is developing sophisticated procedures for planning for training across its main business units. Joy Halverson, organizational effectiveness specialist, provided this overview of planning. First NOVA conducted the Hay Group Employment Climate Survey. From the results NOVA executives identified nine areas where the company could benefit from improvement. They set up nine task forces (corresponding to the nine areas) composed of ten persons, each from a different business background, work area, and level of responsibility. Their task was to research best practices and make recommendations. Based on the reports from the task groups, the nine areas of concern were consolidated and reduced to three priority areas: Leading and Learning, Rewards and Recognition, and Resourcing. To facilitate further planning in each of the three areas, new teams, called People Networks, were formed consisting of business representatives, human resource persons, representatives of service users, and people exterior to the company with a valuable outside perspective. Each of the People Networks now works with the individual businesses to develop the programming they most need. "Let's assume one Network wants to generate programs on diversity," says Stella Cosby, senior consultant. "Maybe Gas Transmission wants to explore differences in thinking styles, while NOVA Gas International wants cross-cultural training. They can do that, and we encourage individualizing. We don't think everyone needs to get dipped in the same training, but we want to coordinate it through an overall planning process. The People Networks set priorities and suggest strategies, but the separate businesses design and deliver the training they need." Even the three networks are coordinated by a senior coordinating body called the People Council with human resources personnel and one vice president from each company to keep an eye on how the planning of training meets company goals and priorities. This carefully planned and highly coordinated effort is now called the People Leadership Program.

NOVA's process may seem long, involved, and cumbersome to some, but NOVA is taking what they believe are the necessary steps to get a high level of involvement and support through an established process for negotiating interests and priorities. To NOVA it is worth the time and effort.

Results-driven planning involves balancing interests and power through people-centered negotiation. This suggests that more people need to be involved from the beginning in thinking through what the training is for and how the results will be supported in the workplace and used on the job.

Knowing the Subject

Although most of this book is about the process of learning, we want to recognize that training has its subject matter. Subject matter includes the *material, topic,* and *content.* Educators are frequently accused of being long on method and short on subject knowledge. Without entering that debate, we will state that someone needs to be the subject matter expert and be drawn into the planning and delivery of training. Sometimes the trainer is also the subject matter expert, but often the trainer works with subject matter experts in defining the subject and making decisions about how to shape and deliver it.

Subject matter is important because it is part of the goal, indeed, it may be the very foundation of the goals for a particular type of training. Many examples of training will appear in the Training Strategies in Part Two. They all have subject matter:

- At Boeing the subject matter for training in how to attach the doors to a 747 is called door rigging.
- At Merrill Lynch the subject matter for training financial consultants is the information on the General Securities Representative Examination (Series 7).
- At Lackland Air Force Base the subject matter for the training of military police about when to use their weapon is called decision-making protocols.

Decisions about which Training Strategy to use depend, in part, on how the subject is defined. In schools and universities, the subject often follows along the lines of academic disciplines such as math, history, or biology. In training settings, the subject may grow out of the traditional curriculum for a business degree, such as management or marketing, but usually subject matter emerges from the business of the organization. Thus, subject matter and the idea of subject matter experts are derived from the general topic or content area of the training. The ability to describe the subject matter and express it clearly is very important. Useful concepts borrowed from the field of curriculum planning are valuable for analyzing subject matter.[5]

- *Scope.* Where does the subject begin and end? If the subject is management or computer technology, what are the boundaries for these fields?
- *Breadth.* How much of the defined subject can be covered in the allotted time? Given a well-defined subject, such as financial planning, which topics and how many different topics within that subject can be covered?
- *Depth.* How deeply should the training go into each topic? Decisions need to be made about extent of coverage and detail.
- *Centrality and balance.* Of the many topics agreed to be covered, which ones are the most important and deserve the most emphasis? Not all topics are equal, and some will get more time than others.
- *Sequence.* Which topics or skills should be taught first and which second, and does it matter? Are certain topics or skills prerequisite to others? Is there a particular order?
- *Gap.* What is being left out? Are the gaps unconscious or intentional? Are certain topics being skipped or left for another time, or are they being forgotten?
- *Intention.* What is intended, and what actually takes place? What does the facilitator sometimes unwittingly or unintentionally teach? For example, if the topic is rules and regulations, does the trainer unconsciously teach an unintended attitude about this topic?

There are two ways of knowing the subject: one is to know the content of the subject matter; the other is to know how to select, define, order, and package it for presentation. Choices about Training Strategies depend partly on how the subject has been conceptualized.

Establishing Learning Outcomes

Knowing subject matter, as we shall see, is not the same as being able to describe learning outcomes. Most trainers know that they should establish learning outcomes, but often they are unclear about how to do this. It is tempting just to repeat details about the subject matter, usually cast as what people should know. Participants need to know, for example, about this organization, about our products or services, about how this process works, the three types of effective communication, the five steps to being happy and productive team members, and so forth. No, these are not learning outcomes. If you find yourself making a list of what people need to know, don't throw it away, but realize that these usually are not learning outcomes.

Learning outcomes move beyond the subject matter. They are about what the learner is supposed to get from or do with the subject. Consider again the three previous examples.

- At Boeing the participants in training will be able to rig doors so that they close, latch, and lock properly.
- At Merrill Lynch the participants in training actually will be able to pass the General Securities Representative Exam (Series 7).
- At Lackland Air Force Base the military police trainees will be able to demonstrate that they can always use their weapons appropriately.

It is important to step back from the subject matter and ask more generally: What are the intended learning outcomes? What kind of learning are we involved with here? Learning isn't one process,

it is many processes, so what kind of learning is desired in this training situation?

Different types of learning can be identified and described and the differences made clear. Different learning outcomes derive from different goals. In the technique described below, we have related a series of questions about learning to each of the Training Strategies. If you apply the questions to a particular kind of training, and you try to answer the questions in some detail, you will get learning outcomes. The questions can be used as a useful checklist for determining the types of learning outcomes associated with different kinds of learning.

• Is this learning that involves a skill? Is this something concrete and observable that someone performs? Is it a routine (though not necessarily easy) set of mental or physical operations that can be tested or observed? Is this a task that someone does and can get better at how he or she does it? These are learning outcomes that are well served by the *Behavioral Strategy.*

• Is this learning that involves information? Does it involve new ideas, new terminology, or useful theories? Does it require understanding of how something works or functions? Is this information that might be presented through an explanation? Is it possible to identify key concepts, main ideas, or points to be understood and remembered? These are learning outcomes that are well served by the *Cognitive Strategy.*

• Is this learning that involves thinking? Does this involve criticizing information, evaluating arguments and evidence, or reasoning to conclusions? Does this learning involve creative thinking— actually producing unusual but relevant new ideas? Does it involve appreciating what other people think? These are learning outcomes that are well served by the *Inquiry Strategy.*

• Is this learning that involves solving problems or making decisions? Do the people involved need to learn how to find and define problems, how to generate solutions, and how to evaluate and choose among solutions? Does this learning require people to deal with issues where they need to make choices, weigh the values of different options, and predict outcomes as probabilities? These are learning outcomes well served by the *Mental Models Strategy.*

• Is this learning that involves changing opinions, attitudes, and beliefs? Does it deal with feelings? Does it build speaking and listening skills? Does it cultivate empathy? Are teamwork or collaboration being addressed here? These are learning outcomes that are well served by the *Group Dynamics Strategy.*

• Is this a kind of learning that needs to be practiced in a safe environment? Does this learning involve activities that could cause damage, expense, or even loss of life? Will participants feel more confident and be more competent if they have been able to work first in a simulated environment before going into the real world? These are learning outcomes that are well served by the *Virtual Reality Strategy.*

• Is this a kind of learning that bubbles up out of experience? Is this learning that occurs when you go out and get immersed in a new experience? Could people learn something from the experience they are in if they had a chance to reflect on it and make meaning of it? Is there a potential here for learning to see something in a new way? These are learning outcomes that are well served by the *Holistic Strategy.*

The answers to these questions provide the material needed to express learning outcomes.

The generic question underlying all of these questions is, What kind of learning is the goal of this training? If the learning outcome can be identified, then the appropriate Training Strategy can be selected to maximize that kind of learning.

Using Strategies

All of the discussion in this chapter has been about planning, the process of getting ready for learning. Planning is mostly about clarifying goals. The arrangements the organization wishes to make for learning express broad goals. A philosophy of learning focuses and sharpens these goals. The planning process is essentially about establishing and negotiating more specific goals. Clear thinking about the subject matter results in clearer goals. Establishing learning outcomes provides a set of very specific, concrete goals. Is it possible to reach all these goals? Assuming that the goals are harmonious and well established, they should be reachable, but the only way to reach goals is to pursue them systematically.

Goals are part of a triad of approaches to getting things done: *goals, strategies,* and *tactics.* We have described how the goals for learning emerge. The way to reach them is by using strategies. We have purposely selected the word *strategy* to refer to the Training Strategies that are the subject of each chapter of Part Two of this book. *Strategy* is originally a military term going back to Sun-Tzu's famous *Art of War* written in China around 550 B.C.[6] One interesting point about ancient Chinese warfare, which makes it somewhat different from Western models, is that it was based heavily on deception, as opposed to direct confrontation. Thus, strategy takes on central importance and involves careful review of options, with the recognition that "no single principle can ever dominate or be applicable in every situation."[7]

We are surely not suggesting that training involves warfare or deception, only the use of strategies to achieve goals. Strategies involve not only the development of a plan of operations but also the carrying through of that plan. Think of some board games that involve strategy—chess, Chinese checkers, and Go. In military affairs *tactics* generally are referred to as the art of handling troops in combat whereas *strategy* is the science and art of planning and executing large-scale military operations. The famous Prussian military philosopher, Karl von Clausewitz, defined the relationship of the two: "Tactics is the art of using troops in battle; strategy is the art of using battles to win the war."[8] To maximize learning, Training Strategies are necessary for reaching desired goals.

Figure 4.1 portrays the relationships of goals, strategies, and tactics. Too much training, we believe, operates at the level of tactics, the use of activities, materials, and media to achieve short-term outcomes. Too much time is spent with tactics; too little time is spent on strategies. Tactics without strategies seldom achieve goals. For training to be effective, goals need to be well established, and a strategy for reaching those goals needs to be selected. Tactics come later. Obviously, effective training also depends on the alignment of goals, strategies, and tactics, and training can fall apart when this congruence is not achieved. We believe, however, that where training is concerned, it is the middle term of the triad, *strategies,* that gets neglected. To be more concrete, group activities are good tactics for achieving certain learning outcomes, and trainers use them all the time, not necessarily knowing how or why. Group activities in the hands of a master strategist, however, who truly understands how the Group Dynamics Strategy works, will be used effectively and powerfully to maximize the desired learning.

Most important to maximizing learning in organizations is to engage in careful planning and then use theory-based Training Strategies to reach established goals.

Figure 4.1 also portrays how this book is organized. In Part One are the concepts needed to establish goals; in Part Two are the Training Strategies, and in Part Three are suggestions for how to select, adapt, and employ the strategies, as well as techniques for

Figure 4.1 Goals, Strategies, and Tactics

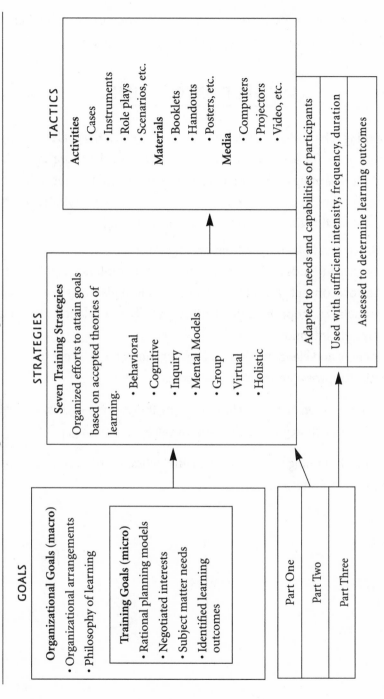

GOALS

Organizational Goals (macro)
· Organizational arrangements
· Philosophy of learning

Training Goals (micro)
· Rational planning models
· Negotiated interests
· Subject matter needs
· Identified learning outcomes

STRATEGIES

Seven Training Strategies
Organized efforts to attain goals based on accepted theories of learning.

· Behavioral
· Cognitive
· Inquiry
· Mental Models
· Group
· Virtual
· Holistic

TACTICS

Activities
· Cases
· Instruments
· Role plays
· Scenarios, etc.

Materials
· Booklets
· Handouts
· Posters, etc.

Media
· Computers
· Projectors
· Video, etc.

Adapted to needs and capabilities of participants

Used with sufficient intensity, frequency, duration

Assessed to determine learning outcomes

Part One

Part Two

Part Three

assessing outcomes. By examining the figure you can tell where we have been, where we are now, and where we are going.

THE BOTTOM LINE

Planning is basically an attempt to establish and clarify goals—organizational goals for learning at the macro level and the more immediate goals for learning at the micro level. Because learning is just one factor among other personnel and workplace variables, everything directed toward maximizing learning needs to be done well.

- Use rational planning models and checklists.
- Balance interests and power through people-centered negotiation.
- Borrow concepts from the field of curriculum planning to analyze the subject: scope, breadth, depth, centrality and balance, sequence, gap, and intention.
- Identify and elaborate desired learning outcomes in order to select appropriate Training Strategies.

Among the triad of approaches to getting things done—goals, strategies, and tactics—strategies are the most neglected in training.

Too much training is preoccupied with tactics; more attention needs to be given to strategies.

PART TWO

Understanding Training Strategies

*A*LL OF THE elements of effective training discussed in Part One are necessary and important: having a clear definition of training, knowing how learning is to be structured within the organization, developing a clear philosophy of learning, and engaging in sufficient and appropriate planning for learning. The key to maximizing learning, however, is in understanding and using Training Strategies.

At some point, no matter how clever the arrangements or profound the philosophy, no matter how elegantly designed or carefully planned the programs, someone needs to set the environment for learning and interact with those who are to learn. This is where Training Strategies become important.

The problem with training, as with other kinds of teaching, is that it is easy to get by but difficult to be an expert. The temptation for facilitators of learning is to operate at less than full capacity, to learn enough about learning to survive the next training session, without ever developing the critical expertise to maximize learning. A good analogy is buying a microwave with all the fancy controls but only using it to boil water. We suspect that is the situation with many facilitators of learning—they have significant underdeveloped potential that could be enhanced simply by learning more about learning. In this book we have gathered together in one place the essentials of what is known about learning and presented them as seven theory-based Training Strategies.

As we outlined in the last chapter, strategies are part of a triad of approaches to getting things done: goals, strategies, and tactics. A Training Strategy is a theory-based effort to maximize a particular kind of learning. Don't be put off by the word *theory*. One simple definition of *theory* is "a statement of the relationship between two or more phenomena."[1] For example, the theory of supply and demand suggests that when goods are in low supply but high demand, the price will go up. A dictionary definition suggests that theory is a more or less well-established explanation that accounts for certain facts or processes. A good theory makes a convincing argument for how things work and is often used as a basis for further research. A famous saying, attributed to Kurt Lewin, the well-known theorist of group behavior, tells us, "Nothing is as practical as a good theory."[2] We agree. A good theory is useful in several ways. It helps to *describe* a set of phenomena, like supply and demand, but it also helps to *explain* the relationship of the phenomena. People who use theories are better able to understand what they are doing; they know how the parts fit together, and they understand why something works or doesn't work. Above all, theories help to *predict* what is likely to happen. If you have a good theory, you can predict that if you do certain things, you are likely to get predictable results. No serious professional today can operate without theory; life is just a jumble without it. Theories provide the lenses that help us to see more clearly things that would otherwise be a blur.

Theories come in different sizes. They have been labeled *substantive, middle-range,* and *grand.*[3] Substantive theories are the "small *t*" theories that grow up in specialized fields, such as the theory of supply and demand in economics. Middle-range theories cover more and explain more. People who work in organizations are familiar with the theory of bureaucracy, with change theory, or with conflict theory. These theories help to describe how a whole set of phenomena works, and they provide a broad framework for planning and action. Grand theories are the "capital *T*" theories, such as the Theory of Evolution or the Theory of Relativity. They are used to cover a wide range of phenomena and may bring together a number of middle-range and substantive theories into a larger configuration.

Learning theories are middle-range theories. They include substantive theories, such as "behavior is affected by its consequences," within the behavioral theory, but they are big enough to describe how particular types of learning take place. Learning theories provide a focus for understanding how a given type of learning works. Consider two examples:

• When a trainer needs to teach a skill, a useful theory is the behavioral learning theory, which can provide guidance on how to operationalize objectives, measure present performance, break learning into steps, and reinforce correct approximations of those steps.
• When the training calls for helping people reconsider their opinions, attitudes, or beliefs, group dynamics theory is useful. Group dynamics theory will help the facilitator to compose the groups, set the tasks, develop the instruments or design the apparatus, manage the process, and describe the outcomes.

If the facilitator understands and employs a theory-based Training Strategy, real learning is more likely to take place. It is possible to do some training without theory, but when we understand the theory and use it, learning can be maximized.

Theory serves as a foundation for and organizer of each of the Training Strategies. An important reason why the Training Strategies presented here hold forth the promise of maximizing learning is that they are based on theory.

As we explained earlier, training in organizations is often atheoretical, which is a fancy way to say that people operate with tactics, a bag of clever techniques and activities, and they don't take the time and effort to learn about and use the theory. Doing training without theory is like trying to do surgery without understanding anatomy. One might, by luck, cut in the right place, but perhaps not. When we use theory we know what we are doing, and we markedly improve the chances that we will get the intended results.

Our main purpose in Part Two of this book is to name, describe, advocate, and illustrate seven theory-based Training Strategies that hold forth the promise of maximizing learning. What is the case for using Training Strategies? We summarize this discussion by providing six reasons:

1. *Getting beyond tactics.* To avoid superficiality, it is important to get beyond the tactics of learning—activities, charts, acronyms, videos, materials—to the psychological basis of learning. Training Strategies provide the psychological foundations for selecting the appropriate activities, media, and materials. Training Strategies are an antidote to random selection of activities that look good and sound good but are not directed to specific outcomes.

2. *Grounding learning in theory.* People who study learning conduct research, and over a period of time they are able to assemble an accumulated body of evidence and construct theories about how learning takes place. Training Strategies are based on theories

about what works and why it works. People who use Training Strategies know what they are doing and why they are doing it.

3. *Getting significant results.* Learning ought to result in significant and lasting changes in behavior. Training Strategies provide the strategic tools for helping people to change what they know, change how they regard what they know, and change how they behave. Using Training Strategies will increase the likelihood of bringing about desirable changes in what people know, believe, and do.

4. *Organizing communication.* Learning involves some form of communication about the subject matter to be learned. Training Strategies provide a basis for selecting communication models, technologies, and activities. People who use Training Strategies design patterns of communication based on what they hope to achieve.

5. *Clarifying roles.* In all learning there are things the teacher performs and things the students perform. Training Strategies help to clarify the roles of the learner and the facilitator of learning. When Training Strategies are used, everybody knows what they are supposed to be doing and how to proceed.

6. *Making deliberate choices.* Because not all learning is the same and every method has its strengths and weaknesses, facilitators of learning need to choose what kind of instruction will best achieve the desired learning. Training Strategies provide options that can be placed side by side and compared, so that the right strategy can be selected deliberately to bring about the designated outcome.

Who can use these Training Strategies? Certainly trainers, supervisors, or managers, but really anyone who cares to learn about Training Strategies and practice them can use them.

Anyone who wants to maximize learning can profit by using Training Strategies.

Although there is a logic to the arrangement of the Training Strategies in Part Two, they can be read in any order. Select those that interest you most, but read both the theory and the examples. Note that we play the role of advocate for each strategy. Surely you will have your concerns and criticisms, but begin with an open mind and sympathetic outlook. That is why this section is called "Understanding Training Strategies."

5

The Behavioral Strategy
Skill Development and Coaching

While technology creates man-made comparative advantage, seizing that man-made comparative advantage requires a work force skilled from top to bottom. The skills of the labor force are going to be the key competitive weapon in the twenty-first century. Brainpower will create new technologies, but skilled labor will be the arms and legs that allow one to employ—to be the low-cost masters of—the new product and process technologies that are being generated . . . skilled people become the only sustainable competitive advantage.[1]

— LESTER THUROW, *Head to Head: The Coming Economic Battle Among Japan, Europe, and America*

BEHAVIORAL STRATEGY OVERVIEW

BEST USE
Beginning or advanced skill development, when a motor or cognitive skill needs to be learned as accurately and as efficiently as possible.

LEARNING THEORY
Behavioral learning theory—learning by moving from present performance level through successive approximations toward a goal.

HISTORICAL ROOTS
Research by Watson, Thorndike, and Skinner on operant conditioning during the first half of the twentieth century.

APPLICATIONS
Developing essential workplace skills and abilities.

PARTICIPANT ROLES
Involves participants at cognitive and psychomotor levels in active exploration and practice of approximations while adjusting to feedback from consequences.

NATURE OF MOTIVATION
Stimulates motivation extrinsically through consequences: reinforcement, feedback, knowledge of results, and success with the task.

PARTICIPANT FIT
Best for participants who may lack intrinsic motivation, who need immediate success, and who like a step-wise, hands-on progression toward a concrete goal.

FACILITATOR'S ROLE
Sets clear and measurable behavioral objectives, analyzes the task, sequences learning experiences, provides well-timed and appropriate feedback, and uses appropriate technologies.

STRENGTHS
Provides clear and specific goals, high level of control of the process, efficient procedures, and observable outcomes. Allows complex tasks to be simplified and teaching to be extended through technology. Makes possible individualized learning whereby participants can proceed at their own pace.

WEAKNESSES
Lacks emphasis on thinking and other cognitive processes. Is inattentive to the learner's feelings and social needs. Allows reinforcement to become a preoccupation and the structure to become rigid and confining.

Skill Development

What we need is skilled workers—that is the plea of nearly every organization. Trainers as well as those who work more informally with learning as supervisors or managers are often called upon to teach skills. Some of these skills involve physical movements and are what psychologists call *psychomotor skills.* Other skills involve the ability to make routine calculations or follow procedures. They are called *cognitive skills* because they require mental effort. Sometimes psychomotor and cognitive skills are combined. Skills can also be simple or complex. In any case, the following definition applies: A skill involves a patterned set of operations requiring routine—though not necessarily easy—physical activity or mental activity, or both.

Consider the following:

- The master glassblower at Iittala Finland teaches would-be glassblowers the refined skill of making hand-blown glass.
- U.S. Army Special Forces often work behind enemy lines on very specific missions. One of their special skills, for which they need to be well trained, is jumping out of airplanes and landing safely.
- Many of the people who work on airplanes at Boeing, including those who mount the doors, need to be certified to show that they have the skill to do the job. In order to be certified, they have to be trained.
- When FIAT opened a new car production plant in Brazil, the workers they were able to hire lacked even the most basic mechanical skills and had no experience working on cars. These workers were trained to work on a high-speed production line.
- TELEBRÁS, the large holding company for twenty-seven statewide telephone companies in Brazil, trains workers across the country in basic telecommunications skills.

All these examples draw on what we know about learning through the Behavioral Strategy. Although many people who conduct training in organizations are familiar with this strategy, it is important to understand the learning theory behind the strategy in order to use it most effectively.

Shaping Raw Behavior into Skills

Psychologists first learned about behavioral learning and elaborated it as a theory through a series of very clever experiments performed with animals in laboratory settings. Just as new medicines are tested first on animals, so were some of the earliest approaches to learning, and we should be grateful for, not offended by, these early efforts to establish the principles of behavioral learning theory. There is no better way of understanding how to teach simple skills, through a process known as *shaping,* than to return to these early laboratory experiments.[2]

Suppose that the objective is to train a pigeon to turn clockwise in a complete circle. First the trainer must clearly describe (operationalize) the objective as observable behavior so that everyone can agree that the pigeon is doing the job. In this instance turning circles is comparable to the skill to be learned in the training environment. Next, the pigeon is put into a specially designed box and observed to see whether it is already able to turn in clockwise circles. Psychologists call this *measuring the operant level* or *taking the subject's base rate.* Trainers call it *measuring present performance level* or *seeing what the employee already knows.* Assume that the pigeon does not turn in circles and that it just walks around poking its beak into every nook and cranny of the box. How will the trainer get it to turn in clockwise circles? How does the trainer move from raw behavior to skills?

The answer is to break the objective into a series of small steps called *tasks*—successive approximations of the objective. Thus, when the pigeon makes its first move—it may simply shift its weight to the right foot—it is reinforced with food dropped into the box at just the right moment through a device controlled by the trainer. Next the pigeon steps to the right and leans to the right. Accidental? Who cares? More food appears. Then the pigeon takes two steps to the right and twists its neck back and to the right. Food drops into the tray again. The shaping process continues over time through a series of successive approximations, one step after another, until the objective is attained.

The pigeon learns through a shaping process by making connections with the reward, and this process is called *operant conditioning*. Additional research shows that the process of shaping works for many kinds of human learning.

A similar shaping process is now adapted for various forms of training involving people in organizations. The procedures are relatively simple:

1. A clear agreed-upon observable skill (objective) is identified and described.
2. A base rate measure of existing skill or present performance level is taken.
3. The skill is broken into tasks of appropriate size and difficulty.
4. Successive approximations of the goal are reinforced, providing incentive and feedback until the skill has been shaped.

A simple model of the shaping procedure is presented in Figure 5.1.[3]

The Behavioral Strategy has its foundation in this theory drawn from laboratory experimentation. The theory works, and the strategy can be used for very simple or highly complex skills.

Here is a fascinating example of how the Behavioral Strategy works when a master glassblower teaches a new trainee how to blow glass.

Figure 5.1 The Shaping Procedure

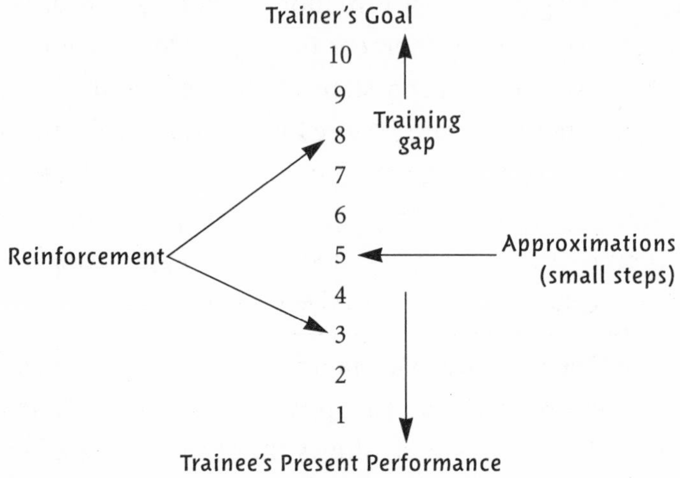

Iittala Finland FINLAND

*L*ocated between Helsinki and Tampere in rolling lake-filled country-side is Iittala Finland, a company of about two hundred employees that produces and sells high-quality glass products created by Finland's finest designers. Harri Jokinen, a fourth-generation descendant of Swedish glassblowers, has been blowing glass for nearly forty years. Now he teaches that skill to the next generation. "It is not really so hard," he said to us, "but it takes much practice. There are steps. We teach the steps, and the workers practice under supervision." Harri has also coached sports, and he makes that comparison. "You go forward in small steps, encouraging the right moves, like coaching."

The first step is to learn how to take the glass from the oven. Harri shows us how. The glass-blowing tube is inserted into the molten glass in a small furnace. It is important to get just the right amount of glass for the project and to turn it so the blob of molten glass forms a teardrop shape. "A lot has to do with cooling. Turn it too soon, and you lose it; tip it too late and there is no teardrop," says Harri. This first step is practiced under supervision more than a hundred times until the trainees get it right. The second step involves getting the molten glass into its particular form and to begin to shape it by rolling it across a little shelf. The feedback comes both from Harri and from the success of doing it right. The third step involves shaping the glass to a particular form: long, short, thin, whatever. Up to this point there has been no blowing through the tube, just working with the blob of molten glass on the end of the tube. In the fourth step, a *posti* (little post) is created inside the blob of glass to make a space for the air. Now it can be blown into a particular shape, but this is tricky, too, because the air pressure differs depending on the temperature of the glass, and the shape may vary. All of this is one-on-one instruction—the novice tries things, the master provides feedback. The skill is shaped in small approximations, and the early steps are automatically reviewed and practiced each time to get to the more advanced steps.

Does Harri use the Behavioral Strategy? Yes, of course. Does he know he is using it? Probably not, but he is drawing on two hundred years of experimentation with the best way of blowing glass. He shapes the skill of his trainees just as he shapes the glass itself, almost by instinct now.

The Behavioral Strategy is there working, whether we know it or not. When we understand it, we can use it consciously to improve results.

Like most ideas that have become second nature to us, someone had to get the insight, develop the theory, and put it into a usable form. For behavioral learning theory, we can thank B. F. Skinner.

Origins of the Behavioral Strategy

Next to Sigmund Freud, Burrhus Frederic Skinner is perhaps the world's most famous psychologist. Behaviorism became completely identified with B. F. Skinner, and before his death he was its foremost spokesperson.[4]

Skinner did not invent behaviorism, nor did he discover it. He described it so thoroughly as one of the ways that people learn, that we can now call it a theory.

Skinner is indebted to John B. Watson for establishing psychology as a science of human behavior, hence, the term *behaviorist* applied to B. F. Skinner and his colleagues. Skinner is perhaps even more indebted to E. L. Thorndike, who at the beginning of the twentieth century had already outlined the basic relationship (connection) between response and consequence that is the foundation of operant conditioning. By examining behavior, Thorndike was able to identify the relationships between rewards and learning.[5] Thorndike is remembered for his Law of Effect. If the consequence (reinforcement) that follows a response is satisfying, the behavior is likely to be repeated. If the *aftereffect*, as he called it, is annoying, the behavior is not likely to be repeated.

Skinner followed through on the work of Watson and Thorndike by conducting extensive research on animals and humans to establish the principles of operant conditioning experimentally.[6] He investigated how the rate and persistence of learning are affected by different schedules and types of reinforcement. He wrote extensively about the implication of his ideas for education, developed a method for teaching handwriting, authored a text on operant conditioning, developed teaching machines, coauthored a programmed text on conditioning techniques, and in his later years, began to speculate on how behavioral principles could be used to form a more just and humane society.

Specifying Behavioral Objectives

When the Behavioral Strategy is used for teaching skills, it is necessary to get very specific about learning outcomes, and these outcomes are usually called *objectives*. Where do objectives come from?

They are derived from the competencies needed to do a given job. In the Behavioral Strategy, training cannot begin until the trainer has worked out and usually written down an adequate list of *behavioral objectives*. Objectives need to be stated as behavior that can be observed, described, and measured. Behavioral objectives by themselves won't take you very far if you don't use the rest of the Behavioral Strategy. But without them, you probably won't even get started.

Behavioral objectives have been formally defined as "relatively specific statements of learning outcomes expressed from the learner's point of view and telling what the learner is to do at the end of instruction."[7] Note that the emphasis in the definition is not on what the trainer does, but on what the learner is able to do when the learning has been completed. The classic specifications for formulating behavioral objectives were developed by Robert F. Mager, whose name is now well known in training.[8] To help teachers write objectives that were precise and specific, Mager developed two lists of verbs, one vague and one specific, shown in Figure 5.2.

Note that the words in the righthand column describe behavior. Mager advocates that behavioral objectives be expressed in

Figure 5.2 Mager's Verbs

Words Open to Many Interpretations	Words Open to Few Interpretations
to know	to write
to understand	to recite
to really understand	to identify
to appreciate	to differentiate
to fully appreciate	to solve
to grasp the significance of	to construct
to enjoy	to list
to believe	to compare
to have faith in	to contrast

very specific language. He also suggests that a well-written behavioral objective should contain a statement of *terminal behavior* (what the learner will be doing when the objective has been achieved), a statement of the *conditions* under which the behavior will be expected to occur, and a statement of *criteria* (the standards of acceptable performance). This is how a behavioral objective might be written for a skill training task at Boeing Commercial Airplane Group:

> Given a four-day training course with verbal instruction, practice sessions on a sample door, and regular feedback, the trainee will pass written tests and demonstrate the ability to rig cargo and passenger doors for the Boeing 747 so that they close, latch, and lock perfectly.

Consider the component parts of this behavioral objective:

- The *terminal behavior* is the skill to rig cargo and passenger doors for the Boeing 747.
- The *conditions* are the four-day course that combines verbal instruction with practice sessions on a sample door and regular feedback.
- The *criteria* are close, latch, and lock perfectly, as measured by written tests (the cognitive skill) and demonstration (the psychomotor skill).

Well-stated behavioral objectives contain all three components: terminal behavior, conditions, and criteria.

Consider another attempt at stating a behavioral objective:

> Employees need to really appreciate the importance of rigging doors well.

The terminal behavior? *Really appreciate.* The criterion? *Rigging doors well.* The point is clear. The language needs to be very specific so that all aspects of the behavioral objective are operationalized.

For trainers using the Behavioral Strategy, well-written behavioral objectives are beneficial in planning instruction and essential in designing and evaluating instruction. For trainees, they are useful as a guide to what to learn and how to study.

When behavioral objectives are used effectively, they link the goals of instruction with the means of evaluation, and the trainer with the learner, so that everyone is clear about the desired outcome. The case for clear behavioral objectives is hard to refute. An effective behavioral psychologist would never think of asking a pigeon to really appreciate circles, but the equivalent often shows up in training when not enough time and energy have been devoted to operationalizing the intended outcomes. We don't want to fly in an airplane where workers have learned to really appreciate doors.

Measuring Present Performance Level

Once the objective is clear, the trainer needs to find out whether a trainee can already perform the skill. The nice thing about the Behavioral Strategy is that it usually is easy to establish *present performance level* simply by asking the trainee to perform the skill. If trainees can do it perfectly, send them on their way. The chances are, however, that they will give a less than perfect performance. In some cases they won't be able to do it at all and will need to start from the beginning. But where is the beginning? If the person to be trained can't learn the first step needed to achieve the objective and has little success with the initial stages of training, there may be some prior learning—some *prerequisite skills*—that must be learned. Airplane mechanics, for example, need certain prerequisite mechanical skills. A trainee might need to go back and learn the prerequisites before proceeding with the scheduled training.

Knowing the present performance level—where the learner is initially—helps the trainer to prevent repetition of things already known and avoid beginning at a level that is too high. Establishing present performance level can save time, money, and frustration for everyone.

Performing Task Analysis

It is important to specify the objectives of instruction, but an objective is seldom achieved in one leap. As a destination or end an objective is also logically distinct from the means of getting there. The objective may be to rig doors, but the steps involved in actually performing the skill are something different. Rigging an airplane door so that it will close, latch, and lock, involves a multitude of tasks and subtasks. Thus anyone learning new skills must advance in small steps toward the objective. The process used to break a skill into its parts is called *task analysis*.[9]

For some skills there are several ways of reaching the objective. The learner takes the lead, and the approximations that the learner presents are reinforced. In teaching a new employee to go to your favorite restaurant several blocks away, it doesn't matter whether the route the employee takes is west three blocks and north two, or north two blocks and west three; either route will lead to the destination. When the objective is the key, the route for getting there is often unimportant. The tasks involved in attaining such objectives are called *variable sequence tasks*. But sometimes the route is important, and in those cases the objective can't be reached unless the steps are followed in the exact order. In cooking, for example, recipes often must be followed step by step—sift the dry ingredients together *before* adding the liquid. These tasks are called *fixed sequence tasks*.

Task analysis is employed to break learning into its component parts so that steps can be identified and, when necessary, learned in sequence.

Task analysis involves four steps:

1. Define the skill as a behavioral objective.
2. List all the component parts of the objective—the tasks and subtasks.
3. Arrange the tasks in sequential order and identify the prerequisites.
4. Test the routine for correct order and any omissions.

The key to task analysis is in gathering up all of the tasks and subtasks and getting them in the right order. The tasks can be collected in several ways: by talking with subject matter experts who know how to perform the skill, by watching people who are proficient at the skill perform it, by consulting manuals and books that describe the skill, and by logically analyzing the steps needed to perform the tasks leading to the objective. The trainer may or may not be an expert in performing the skill, and likewise, an expert may be able to perform the skill automatically without being able to describe the tasks that go into it. Note how task analysis is used in training and retraining U.S. Army Special Forces Green Berets in parachute jumping.

─U.S. Army Special Forces USA ─

*T*he U.S. Army Special Forces are assigned a variety of unusual missions, such as direct action (going in to blow up a radio tower), special reconnaissance (watching troop movements behind enemy lines), foreign internal defense (protecting a government against insurgents), unconventional warfare (aiding guerrillas), and antiterrorist activities (preempting a bomb attack). Most of these activities involve special deployment accomplished by a parachute jump from a C130, C140, or helicopter.

Basic parachute jumping techniques are taught at the U.S. Army Training Command at Fort Benning, Georgia, but refresher courses are often taught at other bases. One of the headquarters for Special Forces is Fort Carson in Colorado Springs, Colorado, and to keep their jumping skills in top form, the Green Berets take a regular refresher course known as Sustained Airborne Training. The course is designed for review of the Five Points of Performance in a safe and effective jump.

The materials for the course are found in a thick training manual that includes objectives and a detailed task analysis of the successful jump. The Five Points of Performance are, in fact, the basic steps in the task analysis. They include the following:

1. *Exiting the aircraft*—all of the procedures leading up to and including the jump
2. *Gaining canopy control*—checking risers, suspension lines, and toggles to make sure everything is functioning properly
3. *Looking below for fellow jumpers*—avoiding collisions with or taking the air from other jumpers
4. *Preparing to land*—getting into proper position at 200 feet above landing surface, releasing combat gear, and getting unhooked if the landing is on water
5. *Landing*—using the Five Points of Contact procedure and getting free of the parachute

There are also emergency procedures, all listed by task, for total or partial malfunction of the parachute and for landing in wires, trees, or on the water.

"It has all been worked out as a series of routines and subroutines," notes Captain David Bruce, one of the commanders of the 10th Special Forces Group at Fort Carson. The task analysis for landing—the fifth performance point—is very detailed. "We call it the *Five Points of Contact*," says Bruce. They are:

1. Make contact with the ground with the balls of the feet, legs together.
2. Begin roll with the calf of the leg making contact with the ground.
3. Continue the roll onto the side of the thigh.
4. Make contact with the ground with the buttocks.
5. Roll on to the push-up muscle of the back of the shoulder.

Bruce stands up and the next thing we know he is rolling on the ground, just having demonstrated the task analysis in one sweeping motion. Captain Bruce has landed.

When the task analysis has been completed, decisions still need to be made about which parts of the skill to teach first and how to coordinate the various parts of the task into one smoothly functioning whole. The order for teaching the task may not be the same as the order for performing the task. The order for teaching is sometimes referred to as a *learning hierarchy*.[10] The development of a learning hierarchy involves asking, What do students have to know first in order to perform X, and what do they need to know next in order to perform Y? One skill may come before another, like steps on a ladder.

Once a task analysis and learning hierarchy have been developed, it is sometimes useful to demonstrate or *model* the task to be performed and to talk about it. For example, with the Five Points of Landing, it can be useful to demonstrate how to do a landing roll, just as Captain Bruce did it for us. The common-sense inclination to demonstrate and describe the activity is supported by research on modeling.[11] The classic studies, reported by Albert Bandura, suggest that learners who watch a task being performed actually benefit simply from having been able to watch. Of course, this does not mean that a novice watching a Green Beret will suddenly be able to perform perfect landing rolls. It does mean that some gains in learning may occur that might not happen in the absence of the modeling. Variously known as *imitation, observational learning,* or *vicarious learning,* modeling tends to augment the shaping process through visual and verbal mediation that takes place within the learner. Furthermore, it has been found that by watching others who are being reinforced for learning a task makes learners not only more likely to do better with the skill, but more able to overcome their fearfulness of the task.

Trainers who use the Behavioral Strategy become proficient in breaking complex instruction into its component parts through task analysis and the development of a learning hierarchy that can be used as the basis for the shaping process. They also find appropriate ways to describe and model the skill.

Using Feedback

After the behavioral objectives have been determined, a baseline has been established, and the skill has been analyzed into its tasks, it is time to have the trainees try the skill. As indicated, this may involve some explanation and modeling, but the essence of the Behavioral Strategy is action, having the trainee practice the actual task involved. That's how learning occurs in the Behavioral Strategy: The learner tries something and the trainer provides feedback. This is the point in the training where the coaching comes in.

What is feedback and how does it work? Recall the pigeon learning to turn in clockwise circles in a laboratory setting. The pigeon tries something, actually many things, but only certain things bring food. Only certain efforts bring positive consequences. It is at that crucial moment, when a specific action gets linked with a particular consequence, that learning occurs. The process of linking behavior to consequences is called *reinforcement*. In training, where people are involved in making their first awkward efforts to learn a skill, for example, blowing glass, we simply call it *feedback.*

Managing feedback, as a sensitive and observant coach, is one of the most important things a trainer does within the Behavioral Strategy.

Feedback can be divided into two basic classes: *rewards* and *punishments.* Behavior that precedes a reward is likely to be repeated, hence a reward is often referred to as a *positive reinforcer.* Positive reinforcers are anything that an individual is willing to put forth effort to obtain. Punishments, on the other hand, are those things that an individual is willing to work hard to avoid. But how do we know what people find rewarding? It varies, and behaviorists know that. The process of feedback does not depend on the *intrinsic properties* of the reward or punishment itself. In fact, a reinforcer probably has no intrinsic properties. Consider why. When people have just pushed back from the holiday dinner table, they probably will not find food to be rewarding. The degree to which something is reinforcing depends on the internal state of the organism, its relative hunger and satisfaction. Furthermore, there will be considerable variation in tastes. For a consequence to work as a positive reinforcer, it must be satisfying to that particular individual. What works as feedback for some won't work for others. It is not accidental, therefore, that behaviorists define feedback in terms of the behavior it produces. If the behavior is repeated (learned), the feedback that brought about the repetition of the behavior can be regarded (then and only then) as reinforcing.

Feedback brings about learning, but it is the occurrence of learning that defines whether it is feedback.

There are four types of feedback—two simple methods to initiate, speed up, or maintain desired behavior: *positive reinforcement* and *negative reinforcement,* and two simple methods to slow down or stop undesirable behavior: *extinction* and *punishment.* (Negative reinforcement is often confused with punishment, but the differences between the two will become clear as they are further defined.)

To keep these simple feedback methods in mind, refer to the chart in Figure 5.3. Uses of the four types of feedback are described in the next sections.

Positive Reinforcement

This method of feedback is used as a reward for tasks to be learned. Depending on the age or personality type of the trainee, positive reinforcers are likely to be things such as:

- praise, attention, and recognition
- confirmation of right answers
- positive comments on a test or assignment
- free time for social interaction
- points, stars, trophies, certificates, or awards
- various types of food
- promotions or pay increases

Positive reinforcers are anything that might convey approval or generate satisfaction. The best positive reinforcement comes

Figure 5.3 Four Types of Feedback

Methods for Initiating, Speeding Up, and Maintaining Desirable Behavior	
Positive Reinforcement	*Negative Reinforcement*
Giving a reward	Threatening something unpleasant

Methods for Slowing Down and Stopping Undesirable Behavior	
Extinction	*Punishment*
Withholding all reinforcements	Doing something unpleasant

naturally from the task itself—when the trainee gets things right, finds out how something works, or successfully performs a skill. Sometimes this is called *knowledge of results*. Positive reinforcement may take the form of a grandmother's incentive: If you do this, then . . .[12] The trainer's role in using positive reinforcement is to provide incentive for the trainee to do each task and to reward correctly performed approximations of the objective.

Negative Reinforcement

This method of feedback involves setting aversive conditions that an individual will work hard to avoid. It is like punishment in that the prospect is unpleasant, but it is unlike punishment because it is never applied. It is best thought of as the *threat* of punishment, because the emphasis is on avoidance. Like positive reinforcement, it can be used, or it can occur naturally. Typical types of aversive conditions are those things trainees will work hard to avoid, such as:

- doing things wrong
- having to repeat the task
- becoming unhappy with poor performance
- working longer at the task
- failing a test or checkpoint
- critical remarks on papers or assignments
- reprimand or embarrassment
- not getting the job, getting a demotion or pay cut, or losing one's job

Although negative reinforcement is unpleasant, it is the possibility of avoiding it that controls the behavior. Working hard in a training program is often motivated by the threat of negative consequences. The problem with threats, of course, is that they are negative, and sometimes they must be carried out, at which point they turn into punishment, with all its problems.

Extinction

A third method of feedback is the process of withholding reinforcement selectively. *Extinction* is a somewhat outdated term and
trainers today are more likely to say that the behavior is simply
being ignored. Behavior is neither punished nor rewarded, but is
passed over with the hope that it will slow down or go away. Sometimes a trainer will ignore certain mannerisms associated with a
particular skill, knowing that wasted motions will cease when the
trainee discovers they are nonfunctional. Not all behaviors need to
be provided with consequences. Any of the things normally used
as rewards or punishments can be withheld. Extinction functions
as the absence of positive reinforcement.

Punishment

A final method of feedback is the direct application of an unpleasant stimulus. Most people need no further definition of punishment.[13] All the forms of aversive feedback listed above under
negative reinforcement become punishments when applied. The
basic research on punishment shows that it works, if by work one
means that it will stop the behaviors with which it is associated.
A behavior that is punished is not likely to be repeated. In certain
situations a sharp reprimand or warning may be used in training,
especially when matters of safety, basic rights, or human dignity
are involved. This kind of feedback may occasionally be used
where something must be stopped, but in most training the goal is
not stopping behavior but getting it started in the right direction
and continuing it. The research is clear; punishment is good for
stopping behavior but not for establishing it.[14] Positive reinforcement, in generous quantities, is needed to establish new patterns
of behavior, such as learning new skills.

With the exception of punishment, which poses a special
problem, the four types of feedback can be mixed and used gener-

ously. The effects of punishment are not easily contained. Punishment has a way of generalizing and escalating, and it produces a conditioned (associated) emotional response in the learner. Although the trainer may have meant to provide a carefully targeted punishment to stop a specific behavior, the trainee will often associate other things with that punishment. A trainee who is punished can learn quickly to dislike the trainer, the workshop, the topic, and the entire organization, because each has become associated with the punishment.

Effective trainers use punishment sparingly, if at all, and focus their energies instead on imaginative ways of using positive reinforcement.

After all, most trainees are adults, and they respond better to the carrot than the stick.

It is important to remember that a lot of feedback should be given—much more than usually is given in typical training situations—and it needs to be well timed, that is, as close as possible to the occurrence of the desirable behavior.

Immediate feedback is what makes learning take place because it reinforces the *connection* between the task (effort) and the feedback (reward). Without appropriate, well-timed feedback, the trainee just stumbles along, never sure whether anything is right or wrong. When the person who is learning to rig airplane doors finally gets it right, the door falls into place and fits. Immense satisfaction (feedback) is derived just from getting the door to work. The feedback would be much better if the trainer (or coworker) is there to say, "Hey, nice job, all right, you got it." And at the end of the course, though it may seem a little awkward, maybe even a bit embarrassing for some, most trainees like to get that certificate, that moment of personal recognition, those few words of praise for learning the sum total of all the tasks that make up the skill. Don't forget, though, feedback is important all along the way as the learner works through each task and subtask in the task analysis.

The shaping process functions by providing appropriate, timely feedback for small steps accomplished, as well as for the overall goal.

Making It Work

Now we can put the whole Behavioral Strategy together. Let's find out how they train the workers at Boeing to put those doors on a 747. Watch for all the components. How is the entire process managed? What does the facilitator do?

— Boeing USA

On the east bank of Puget Sound, north of Seattle, Washington, with the Cascade and Olympic Mountains in view in either direction, sits the Everett plant of the Boeing Company, Commercial Airplane Group, where the famous Boeing 747, 767, and the new 777 are built. "Assembled," might be a better word, they told us, because the parts are made all over the world. How do you train someone to assemble a Boeing 747? It is not someone, of course, but thousands of someones, and the training involves many skills and an endless array of tasks and subtasks that must be done perfectly.

An airplane is assembled in sections. The fuselage, depending on the model, has several sections that are built separately, then hooked together. The assembled fuselage is wheeled to another place to have the wings, also being assembled separately, attached. After the wings are on, the airplane gets its General Electric, Pratt and Whitney, or Rolls-Royce engines. The plane is customized to the specifications of the buyer. The process for assembling the fuselage takes six days; that is, every six days another 747 is ready for its wings. During those six days what goes on is more like building an apartment complex than rolling an auto along an assembly line. There is a bar chart checklist of everything to be done each day, which is keyed to a reference for the task, the specifications, and the functional performance test. When the fuselage is nearly assembled, someone has to rig (put on) the doors. Rigging doors means putting them on so that they will close, latch, and lock. Those are also the basic names that are used for the training performance objectives. The airplane door, besides opening and closing smoothly (and quickly in emergencies), has to seal tight, not only against the weather but also the air. It cannot leak, even when the pressures inside and outside are different. It cannot spring open. The pilot also needs to be able to read the control panels in the cockpit, which display information from the sensors on the doors that tell when and whether the doors are closed, latched, and locked. The rigging process itself needs to work smoothly; it needs to be done on time and without damage to the door or the body of the aircraft. If you trim the door wrong while making minor adjustments with a disk sander, for example, it costs about $125,000 per door, and there are ten of them on a 747.

Door riggers need to be certified, which means that the trainer agrees that riggers and the inspectors who work with them know how to rig doors perfectly. Rigging doors is a skill, and the tasks can all be operationalized. Differences exist among doors: there are plug doors and inward/outward translating doors, as well as passenger doors and cargo doors. But basically "doors is doors." The objectives are the same: all doors need to close, latch, and lock. To rig a door so that these objectives are met, the workers focus on six rigging points, three on the door and three on the body.

"Because these tasks can be operationalized into observable behaviors—the outcomes of training—the trainer can actually watch them being done by the worker, right or wrong," says Nancy Birdwell, course developer. The course developers get together with the engineers and the trainers (experienced riggers who are going to do the teaching. The engineers work up a specifications manual with an appropriate set of standards, which are used to establish the behavioral objectives. The job of training is to translate that material into usable formats, that is, to relate the objectives to specific tasks, the things the rigger needs to do to, and with, the door to get it hung. "Door rigging, depending on the door, has approximately eighteen clearly defined tasks," says Birdwell, "and for each of these there are subtasks ranging in number between five and seventeen. The course developer and trainer do a task analysis to verify the steps indicated in the specifications. This is done in the usual painful way—observe, write, check, try it, test, rewrite." The task analysis is used to clarify the rigging document. The trainer and course developer then have to design the course, with plans for lessons, supporting materials, tests—everything that is going to be done hour by hour. A two-and-a-half day course involves (ideally) two workers and two inspectors, but there can be as many as eight people altogether in a course.

The training unfolds primarily through step-by-step shaping. Brief explanations are given to describe how to go about each step. Then the process is demonstrated. "We used to have to go out on the floor and do a lot of looking," notes Jeff Nelson, industrial skills trainer. "But now, at last, we have our own door, right here in the classroom. There is a tell-and-show part, but eventually the workers have to do it. As they try it, of course, they are given immediate corrective feedback: a little more of this, a little less of that, that's good, next time watch out for . . . , if you do that, then it will . . . " The feedback is direct and well timed, and delivered in such a way that the workers begin to develop their own feedback cues, knowing what to look for to tell them how they are doing. The feedback also focuses on helping the workers *understand* what they are doing. "They get a lot of questions, and they had better know the answers," notes Nelson. "At the same time that they are doing it, they need to be able to explain why they are doing it that way." If they get stuck, they have a written job aid. They can look it up, and they learn how to get feedback that way, too. The trainer takes them step by step through the process of rigging doors, shaping perfect behavior in small increments.

This example is interesting because it illustrates how the Behavioral Strategy functions as a total system. All of the elements have to be in place to make the strategy work. Perfectly written objectives are worthless without a good task analysis. The tasks won't be learned without appropriate, well-timed feedback. The effective facilitator knows behavioral learning theory and plans for and executes each element of the system, from present performance level to final goal.

Making the Behavioral Strategy work often depends on adjusting the size of the steps, the time allotted for learning, or the strength and frequency of the feedback. The effective facilitator needs to be good at managing all of these elements.

Consider how the Behavioral Strategy was made to work under rather adverse circumstances in Brazil.

— FIAT BRAZIL

*F*IAT Automóveis S.A. is a large multinational manufacturer of automobiles ranging in size and price from the Uno to the Alfa Romeo. FIAT, with home offices in Italy, now has operations in many countries, including, among others, Russia, Poland, Turkey, Algeria, and Brazil. They are also a large holding company with operations that involve many things other than cars.

When FIAT first opened its automobile manufacturing plant in what was then a rural area outside of Belo Horizonte, Brazil's third largest city, it had a problem attracting workers who had even the most basic prerequisite skills for working on automobiles. "We attracted mostly farmers," notes Roberval Brandão Nunes, director of industrial relations. "When we finally found a guy who had experience painting cars, it was like locating a Ph.D. The problem is the guy was accustomed to painting one car in three days, and when we tried to show him how to paint more than one car a day, he quit. We knew right then we had a

huge training problem: How were we ever to get these workers to function on a fast-moving production line?"

FIAT set up two lines, one a regular production line and right beside
it, a very slow, and sometimes stopped, training line. Workers with very
limited backgrounds were shown how to do a carefully analyzed, highly
operationalized task. They were given plenty of time—so they wouldn't
feel stressed to the point they wanted to quit—and were given direct, on-
the-job, one-on-one instruction with lots of feedback and coaching. As
they learned the task, they got faster at it, and as they got faster the line
could be speeded up. Gradually the instruction and the coaching could
be faded out. Eventually the work of the training line was equal to the
production line. Then came the big surprise. The quality on the training
line was higher than the quality on the regular line. "The quality control
people reported it with their eyes all bugged out in amazement, notes
Nunes, that these farmers could do such good work. I think this was one
thing in training we did where we were having real certainty about the
effectiveness of the training."

There are several lessons in this example that illustrate important points about the facilitator's role with the Behavioral Strategy.
One point is that workers often do not have even the prerequisite
skills, and if that problem is not faced and addressed, everyone is
going to be unhappy—workers as well as trainers. Moreover, the
behavioral model calls out for one-on-one instruction with lots of
well-timed feedback. That's expensive and time consuming, but it
gets results. In addition, limited time is often a key negative factor
in learning. Often it is necessary to slow down the learning process,
to remove the pressure of time, in order to allow learners to move
at their own speed. The greatest instruction in the world fails
unless the participant is given enough time to learn what needs to
be learned. Furthermore, learning takes practice. There is very little one-trial learning even with a well-engineered behavioral
approach. It is often necessary to repeat the process several times.

Finally, training can be phased out in in a clever and timely way. There is no need to teach something after it has been learned. Gently remove the support. As with teaching a child to ride a two-wheel bicycle, take off the training wheels as soon as possible.

An effective facilitator stands ready to fine-tune any element of the Behavioral Strategy as needed.

Computer-Assisted Instruction

The Behavioral Strategy has modern, high-tech computer applications. Unfortunately these applications are not always associated with their roots, and the power of the Behavioral Strategy is often lost in the excitement over the technology. Today the Behavioral Strategy is used on the computer, but it took several years for the hardware, software, and learning technology to come together.

In 1961, B. F. Skinner published an article in the *Harvard Educational Review* entitled "Why We Need Teaching Machines."[15] This article marked the beginning of efforts to use various forms of technology to extend the principles of behavioral learning theory. Skinner's teaching machines drew upon a format for carefully developed textbooks called *programmed instruction,* a system for presenting lesson materials through small steps called *frames,* to which the student responds by selecting from answers provided or by filling in a blank. By referring either to the bottom of the page or the back of the book for the right answer, students are able to get immediate confirmation of right and wrong answers and are able to move through the material at their own pace.[16] The statements in the frames contain clues, technically known as *thematic prompts,* which are like the hints a theater prompter gives to aid the actors in remembering their lines.[17] A good program utilizes these techniques to ensure that the proper information is systematically embedded within the frames.[18] Skinner and his colleagues developed the frames of programmed instruction into sequences of visual materials stored on disks, cards, and tapes (mechanical as yet, not electronic) and fed them into teaching machines that presented the material one frame at a time. The student made a trial guess about how to fill in the blank, then turned the material in the machine upward for comparison with the correct answer. Teaching machines are no longer used, but programmed instruction still shows up occasionally in training materials. Then one day someone put this instruction on the computer.

There are many ways to use computers in training, including techniques for supporting presentations and conducting group activities (to be discussed with other strategies), but one common use is still *computer-assisted instruction (CAI)*, the drill-and-practice and tutorial applications growing out of the Behavioral Strategy. Anything a teaching machine could do, a computer can do better. As with Skinner's crude teaching machines, trainees are presented with frames that display information and prompts on a screen with questions that call for a response. When the trainee responds, the computer replies either with a confirmation of the right answer, accompanied by appropriate praise (reinforcement), or with some suggestions about how to get the right answer. Because the computer can be programmed, it can be ready for a range of typical trainee responses and make decisions about the reply. For example, a trainee might choose any of five answers to a single question; the computer can be programmed with five different responses, including where to look for help, how to try again, or brief instructions on how to correct what went wrong. Some CAI incorporates an *expert system* that catalogs and analyzes student responses and offers appropriate help based on the analysis.[19] The expert system can branch the learner back for review or forward for more challenging material.

Tremendous advances in computer technology and software are made each year. It is now possible to move beyond the frame-oriented CAI described here with techniques known as *generative CAI.* The computer constructs questions as it goes, based on what it "knows" about the subject matter through sophisticated algorithmic descriptions of classes of problems. This type of CAI is called generative because the program can operate on the lesson content in such a way as to generate forms of output that are structurally similar but functionally unique, thus producing the appropriate content for lesson material.[20] Generative CAI has the obvious advantages of using more varied and interesting material and increasing the opportunity for individualization of learning.

Another recent application to computers is in the linking of visual materials to CAI. A CD-ROM can store thousands of frames of visual information, including slides, films, videotapes, and graphics, as well as large libraries of text. Real images, not just computer graphics, appear on the screen. It is possible to jump forward and back through this information very rapidly and with precise control. The implications for branching CAI are tremendous. For example, it is possible to present information in a film and to ask questions about it, and it is possible for the learner to move in and out of the text or graphics to seek definitions, to review information previously presented, or to seek new visual material on a related topic or subtopic.

Authoring software is now available for generating sophisticated learning materials by linking media with computers via CD-ROM. Trainers can now learn to create their own lesson materials without extensive technical background.

The most powerful teaching technology ever created is now available to trainers on computers, and it is usually received enthusiastically, especially by younger workers. We forget, however, that CAI is really just an electronic extension of the Behavioral Strategy.

Employing Instructional Design

The ultimate application of the Behavioral Strategy is in large-scale instructional systems that control as many of the variables in the learning process as possible: objectives, tasks, materials, reinforcement, and tests. The goal is to guide the learning process completely from beginning (objectives) to end (evaluation). Such efforts are sometimes referred to as *instructional design* or a *systems approach* to learning.[21]

Some years ago a specific form of instructional design known as Personalized System of Instruction (PSI) emerged at the college level. PSI originated in a psychology course at Arizona State University and was developed by Fred Keller, one of B. F. Skinner's graduate students.[22] At first PSI was used primarily in psychology courses, but it has been widely adapted by people who provide training materials and course designers. A PSI course can have many variations, but most involve a precise set of objectives and a series of self-paced learning modules designed to help learners reach the objectives. Trainees are expected to work through the course one unit at a time, progressing at their own pace. Before moving on to the next unit, they must pass a readiness test to demonstrate that they can perform the objectives of the past unit, which is the prerequisite to the next unit. Instruction is provided in many forms—reading, laboratory work, presentations, demonstrations, discussions, software, films, videotapes, audiotapes—and is made available as a majority of the class is ready for it or on an individual basis. Variations of the PSI approach are used in many organizations today.

Instructional design courses are developed to maximize success, reduce failure, and allow some learners to take more time or to finish early.

Notice how both computer-assisted instruction and instructional design are combined in a large telecommunications company in Brazil.

—TELEBRÁS BRAZIL

*B*rasília, the capital of Brazil, rises from the rolling green high plains of the State of Goiás. A short distance from downtown, not far from the campus of one of Brazil's several federal universities, is the TELEBRÁS National Training Center, occupying an impressive campus of its own with auditoriums, classrooms, high-tech laboratories, computer centers, a television studio, and a library. TELEBRÁS—Telecomunicações Brasileiras S.A. is the holding company for a conglomerate of twenty-seven statewide local telephone companies and EMBRATEL, the company responsible for long-distance services. How does such a vast, highly decentralized telecommunications company provide training? By using computer-assisted instruction to reach employees throughout the system. At the National Training Center, courses are developed using a systems approach along with highly sophisticated computerized training materials. Drawing on its earlier experience with modular systems, the training center now uses a method called SINTA—Integrated System of Training—for most course development. SINTA is essentially an instructional design model using systems theory as an extension of the Behavioral Strategy.

Using the SINTA model, trainers focus first on the performance needs of individual workers, that is, the accumulated data about the competencies for the job. Working now with sets of courses across the organization, course developers invite specialists from the local companies—the technical consultants who are really the experts on the job—to help develop objectives, select content, validate materials, and choose instructional methods and assessment procedures. From skill prerequisites to evaluation items, the team guides the instructional process using a SINTA flowchart to ensure that every step in instructional design is covered systematically, including post-course feedback after three months to see if employees actually are using their new skills effectively.

The TELEBRÁS National Training Center uses technology as a natural extension of the systems approach to instructional design and is now working in computer-based interactive video, distance learning, and local-area networking. Courses designed to build basic skills and introduce fundamental concepts include "Introduction to Telecommunications" (now translated from Portuguese into Spanish and used in other South American countries), "Concepts of Digital Transmissions," "Concepts of Digital Switching," and even a course called "How to Develop Computer-Based Training." Computer-based training courses, now available at seven hundred computer stations in phone companies across Brazil, are designed for highly dispersed populations in high-demand areas (where many trainees need to be served), on topics where the technology is fairly stable, and where sound and image combined add power to the instruction. "Computer-based training," notes José Moreira, systems analyst with the human resource development department, "in addition to individualizing instruction, decentralizes it and results in enormous economies of time, travel, and use of instructors. We can send out the discs to the companies all over Brazil, and they can make as many copies as they want to use throughout the organization. The computer has become the coach."

THE BOTTOM LINE

Some work requires high levels of skill. Skills can involve movement (psychomotor skills) or routine mental operations (cognitive skills) or both combined. Skills can be simple or highly complex. This kind of learning takes place best through skill development and coaching.

Skill development can be done more effectively by drawing on what is known from behavioral learning theory. Facilitators do the following:

- State <u>objectives</u> and clearly define them as observable behavior.
- Establish <u>present performance level</u> and identify prerequisite skills.
- Break complex learning activities into their component parts through <u>task analysis</u>.
- <u>Shape</u>, through steps, successive approximations of the goal.
- Use various forms of well-timed reinforcement as <u>feedback</u>.
- Model and allow sufficient time and opportunities for <u>practice</u>.
- Employ appropriate <u>technologies</u>.

The Behavioral Strategy is also used in very sophisticated ways with detailed training manuals, instructional design, and computer-assisted instruction.

The power of the Behavioral Strategy for building skills has been established through almost a century of research.

Feedback operates on behavior whether we are aware of it or not. It is best to be aware of feedback and manage it to maximize learning.

6

The Cognitive Strategy
Presentations and Explanations

*T*he first time I heard the term "Information Age" I was tantalized. I knew about the Iron Age and Bronze Age, periods of history named for the new materials men used to make their tools and weapons. These were specific eras. Then I read about academics predicting that countries will be fighting over the control of information, not natural resources . . . It sounds nonsensical because information isn't as tangible and measurable as the materials that defined previous ages, but information has become increasingly important to us. The information revolution is just beginning.[1]

— BILL GATES, *The Road Ahead*

COGNITIVE STRATEGY OVERVIEW

BEST USE
Conveying important information and explaining how things work or came to be.

LEARNING THEORY
Cognitive learning theory—learning that involves attending to, processing, and remembering information.

HISTORICAL ROOTS
Research by verbal learning theorists, linguists, and systems analysts that after 1950 gave birth to the new subfield of cognitive psychology.

APPLICATIONS
Transmitting information, stimulating interest in ideas, introducing new terminology, and explaining concepts used in the organization.

PARTICIPANT ROLES
Involves participants visually and auditorially in a highly individualized cognitive effort to attend to, process, and remember information.

NATURE OF MOTIVATION
Derives from the internal need to find patterns in and make sense of verbal and visual stimuli so that they can be understood and remembered. Presupposes some background and internal disposition toward the subject.

PARTICIPANT FIT
Best for participants who are intrinsically motivated and skilled in listening, watching, and dealing with abstractions conveyed in words and visual symbols.

FACILITATOR'S ROLE
Selects, orders, and presents information with appropriate visual support, so that the essence of the subject can be attended to, grasped, and remembered.

STRENGTHS
Provides an efficient arrangement for presenting a body of information. Stresses cognitive activity in learning and acknowledges variation in processing across different individuals. Is useful for conveying information to large groups. Allows outcomes to be readily tested.

WEAKNESSES
Lacks emphasis on thinking and problem solving. Is inattentive to the learner's feelings and social needs. Invites passivity. Tends to ignore present performance level and postpones evaluation of outcomes. Separates learning from real-world experience.

Essential Information

In the Information Age, having the right information, understanding it, and being able to remember it is of prime importance. Although information is available at our fingertips through a multitude of electronic sources today, sometimes the information needs to be in our head. In short, there are aspects of many jobs people perform where they need to know something. Sometimes the information we need is basic and uncomplicated, but more often the essential information in organizational settings today is quite complex, involving technical language, difficult concepts, and complex relationships among ideas. Presenting essential information is one of the key training tasks in many organizations today.

The problem begins with selecting. Bill Gates, chairman and chief executive officer of Microsoft Corporation, describes a "global information market" in which "your workplace and your idea of what it means to be 'educated' will be transformed, perhaps almost beyond recognition." He predicts that "the information highway will transform our culture as dramatically as Gutenberg's press did the Middle Ages."[2] Easy access to information sets up a difficult selection problem: What do people really need to know?

Consider how essential information functions in the following organizational settings:

- At the Denver Museum of Natural History, volunteers learn about a special exhibit so they can explain important information to visitors and answer their questions.

- At Safeway, checkout clerks are trained to recognize and remember more than one hundred produce items, know the code number for each one, and know whether it is sold by the item or by weight.

- At INLAN, in Ponte de Sôr, Portugal, workers are taught to know why quality needs to go up and prices need to come down each year and what it means to be a competitor in a world market.

- At Organizações Martins, a wholesaler marketing all over Brazil, sales managers are given information about company trends and are expected to know consumer marketing techniques to become effective supervisors of their three thousand–member sales staff.

- At Paychex, new employees learn the Paychex way of processing payrolls for their clients, who outsource their payroll functions to one of Paychex's ninety offices around the United States.

- At Merrill Lynch, financial consultant trainees need to have the essential information to pass the General Securities Representative Examination (Series 7) and are taught the Merrill Lynch approach to dealing with clients.

- U.S. Air Force personnel, and now those in many other government agencies as well, are given basic information on project management, including fundamentals of planning, budgeting, acquisitions, control, and logistics.

In all of these examples, essential information is important for understanding products, processes, or services.

Presenting Information

When people within the organization have identified and selected the information they regard as essential to some function to be performed, they must then make decisions about how to *present* that information. A vast array of technologies is available today for presenting information—videos, teleconferencing, satellite broadcast, computer displays, slides, films, overhead images—and it is natural to get caught up in the excitement about selecting the proper media to support a presentation. Before a media selection can be made, however, there are three important questions to be answered: Why will people want to pay attention to this information? How will they process it? What should they remember? Without a clear understanding of how people *receive* information, the media frenzy is premature and superficial.

Every participant in training knows from prior experience that a presentation can be brilliant or dull, involving or boring, enlightening or deadly. What makes it so? Some would say it is the personality of the presenter. Others say it is the content or the media.

We believe that where learning is important, the most important factor in an effective presentation is the way the Cognitive Strategy has been employed in designing the communication process.

How is it that people come to learn when they are listening to or watching a presentation? What kind of learning is this? What actually takes place when participants attempt to pay attention to, process, and remember information? You will see how presentations are used in the following two rather different examples.

— Paychex USA

*A*t the Paychex Inc. training center in suburban Rochester, New York, new employees are brought in for training on how to develop and provide payroll systems for client companies who are outsourcing their payroll function. "We put a lot of emphasis on presentations," says Roberta Goheen, training director, "because this work involves complex procedures that need clear explanation." Presentations are developed for each training module, and the explanation is supported with appropriate use of slides, videos, and computers. "We tell them and show them, but we also ask them to apply it and do their own presentations where they teach each other," says Goheen. "The presentations include a high level of information set forth in the most effective ways we can devise. The payroll process is a detailed system, and we have to present the information in such a way that they can remember the details."

Presentations are only one form of training at Paychex, and even these are highly interactive and supported by other forms of learning. Paychex uses its own trainers and some outside presenters, who are also trained. The development and delivery of presentations is supported by forty-three people who work on design in training and development. These are product and sales trainers, management developers, performance consultants, instructional designers, publishers, and support staff.

── Denver Museum of Natural History USA ──────

The Denver Museum of Natural History in Denver, Colorado, is the fourth largest natural history museum in the United States and has the largest volunteer program of all the museums, one that serves as a national model. In addition to the two thousand volunteers who work regularly in various capacities, the museum also trains specially recruited volunteers for blockbuster events, such as a special archaeological exhibit on the imperial tombs of China. For this exhibit more than four hundred volunteers were trained as guides and interpreters through specially designed lecture sessions to prepare them to talk about artifacts in the exhibit and answer visitors' questions. Although they are assigned to a specific station for their four-hour shift, they could be assigned to any station and must know the entire exhibit. Among other training activities, including a complete walk-through before opening day, is a series of presentations on the historical background and aesthetic influences of the dynasties represented in the exhibit. Volunteers receive an outline of background information for each session, listen to and view several slide presentations, read various articles and texts, and complete a take-home exam. "The volunteers receive something like a graduate course in Asian studies in exchange for their four hours per week of volunteer time," notes Beth Steinhorn, anthropology educator. "We provide them with a lot of information in eight sessions."

The Information Processing Model

Picture the typical training classroom: a trainer speaking in a strong voice and using overheads or showing slides; the participants sitting in rows and taking notes, trying to process what is being shown and said. What is known about this kind of learning? The processes we use for communicating through presentations have been investigated extensively by cognitive psychologists, scholars who study the mental activity of attending to, processing, and remembering information. After nearly thirty years of research, they have reached agreement on the outlines of a basic information processing model. Figure 6.1 is a composite and simplified version of models that appear commonly in the literature.[3]

According to these models, information comes in through any of the five senses and impinges on a *sensory register*. Filters are activated and let pass or screen out what a person will pay attention to

Figure 6.1 Information-Processing Model

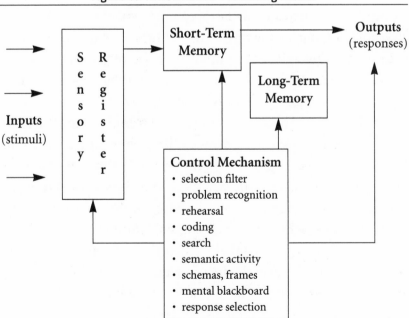

based on interest. The main features of the information are analyzed, abstracted, and encoded. They are held in *short-term memory* for a few seconds while a decision is made about what to do—respond directly, think about them, integrate them with new information, or store them in *long-term memory*. Perhaps the new information requires a search for old information held in long-term memory. Although the process is enormously complex, there appears to be general agreement about the functions called attention, processing, short-term memory, and long-term memory. These are not places in the brain, of course, but rather sets of interrelated processes that go on in the mind to facilitate the symbolic manipulation of information.

Origins of the Cognitive Strategy

Cognitive psychology has no B. F. Skinner, no single figure who can be said to be its foremost spokesperson. The study of mental processes has its roots in the work of Willhelm Wundt, William James, F. L. Bartlett, and the European movement known as *Gestalt* psychology, but from the turn of the century until the end of World War II, the behaviorists dominated psychology, insisting that human consciousness was a "black box" and that behavior—both animal and human—was the only appropriate subject of scientific psychology.[4] What occurred in the period from 1950 to 1980 in the area of cognitive psychology was nothing short of an intellectual revolution.[5] An area that had been beyond the proper domain of study for psychologists—human consciousness—now became the focal point for an outpouring of scientific investigation and theory building. Although some psychologists continued to study communication processes in animals, such as the fascinating work on apes and sign language, the focus of the research was on human information processing. The field attracted some of the best scholars and became an area of intense and exciting activity.

Behaviorism had reached its zenith. But more important, an increasing number of psychologists found the behavioral theory inadequate for fully describing human learning. Although learning is certainly influenced to some extent by connections and consequences, human beings, they argued, tend to act upon and reorder the stimuli that constitute their environment, largely through the uniquely human instrument of language. Through language and other symbolization processes, humans engage in complex, covert mental activity called *mediation*. A new breed of psychologists became convinced that the behaviorists were wrong about not being able to study the black box of the human mind. They came to believe that covert mental processes—the things that go on in the mind—were the key to understanding human behavior. It was as if the behaviorists were leaving out the most important aspect of human behavior just because it was hard to study.

Other forces combined to stimulate new interest in cognitive psychology. A science of human engineering was emerging from military applications of psychology. Verbal learning theorists and linguists were developing new models to explain language behavior.[6] Communications engineering developed as a new science, and systems analysts began to describe what took place between *input* and *output* in a computer. As cognitive psychologists began to speculate about the processes that occur between human input and output, it was only a short leap from thinking of the computer as a *complex information-processing system* to conceptualizing the human mind as a complex symbol manipulation system.[7] If one were to attempt to assign a date for the emergence of cognitive psychology as a recognized field, the year would probably be 1958, the date of the now-famous conference sponsored by the Rand Corporation, a meeting of the leading psychologists of the day, from which emerged the influential *metatheory* of Newell, Shaw, and Simon.[8] Their work stimulated a flurry of research.

Attention Mechanisms

First a presenter must get the attention of the participants. Why should the participants pay attention? For that matter, why does anyone pay attention to anything? How many things can we pay attention to at the same time? Is it possible to help participants focus on the most important aspects of a presentation? What about distractions?

Some of the earliest experiments on attention were designed to examine what happens when people try to listen to more than one thing at a time. Cherry called this the *cocktail party phenomenon.*[9] Most people have had the experience of standing around at a party listening in on one conversation but then being drawn off to another. What does a person hear in another conversation that tends to make them lose what they hear in the first? Cherry and others simulated the party situation by having subjects listen to two separate but comparable messages through earphones, one message in one ear, another message in the other ear. In these *dichotic presentations* the subjects were directed to shadow (repeat aloud) the message they were hearing in the designated ear. It is not surprising that subjects usually could report in great detail afterward what they heard in the designated ear, but when asked what they heard in the unattended ear, they floundered. Sometimes they could not even tell if the message had been switched to another language or played backwards. In other words, their attention was relatively undivided.

Experiments like these became the basis of *switch theories of attention.* If two messages arrive at the same time, one will get through and the other won't, as if there were a switch to turn one channel on and another off.[10] Apparently when attention is focused on something, it is focused there almost exclusively. Notice the word *almost.* More recent studies suggest that attention is not so much like a switch that is on or off but is instead like a filter that selectively lets through the important information while screening out most (but not all) of the rest.[11] Additional dichotic listening experiments confirmed this view—subjects heard at least some things (like their own name) in the unattended ear or would cross channels to follow an interesting story.[12] But in general, attention tends to be highly focused.

Other experiments on attention have dealt with the amount of attention required (and available) for different kinds of activities. Some activities simply require more attention than others, and when that is the case, more mental energy is used for paying attention. Capacity for attention, though limited, is not a fixed entity; it varies with the difficulty of and familiarity with the activity. Some activities, when sufficiently practiced, are almost automatic; others are deliberate.[13] It may be possible to carry on a heated debate while driving on an open highway but nearly impossible to speak at all while negotiating a car through a crowded intersection.

The bad news is that our capacity for attention is limited, perhaps far more limited than intuition would suggest or multimedia-oriented adolescents would admit. The good news is that when it is necessary to attend closely to something, we have a rather remarkable capacity for focusing on what we want and need to see or hear.

The lessons for presenters, described in Rules 1 through 5, are clear.

Rule 1: Whatever it takes, get their attention.

Participants won't learn anything from a presentation unless they are first inspired to pay attention to it. This may mean beginning with something sensational—a fascinating story, a strong visual image, or three good reasons why the participants will not survive without this essential information.

Rule 2: Tell participants what to focus attention on.

It is encouraging to know that participants can be well focused and single minded in their attention if they know what to pay attention to, so it helps to tell them directly to focus on certain things, such as the three main points, the essence of the model, or the key process. An effective presenter helps participants to distinguish between the trivial and the important.

Rule 3: Don't overload the system.

Because participants have a limited capacity for attention, effective presenters use media serially, that is, one at a time. If they distribute a handout, they know participants will read it, so they give them time to do so. If they show a slide, they talk about that slide and then take it away. They never talk, pass out handouts, and show slides at the same time.

Rule 4: Slow down and regain attention when necessary.

Effective presenters also know that some things are harder to pay attention to than others. They recognize that they may need to slow the pace, cover material more than once, or refocus attention for difficult concepts. The harder the material, the more likely the mind will wander.

Rule 5: Don't try to compete with distractions.

Most presenters know that when someone comes in late, continually asks irrelevant questions, or starts a private conversation, the other participants will lose their focus. If the distraction is a strong competitor, the presenter may need to stop, wait, and repeat what was being covered at the time the distraction began.

Attention is a limited resource, and effective presenters work to create sustainable learning environments. If attention is never gained or breaks off, all else is lost.

Sometimes the topic itself is naturally interesting or can be cast in a way to gain attention. Notice in this example how workers on the shop floor have become interested in broader aspects of the business as a result of information-sharing sessions.

—INLAN PORTUGAL

*I*NLAN—Indústria de Componentes Mecânicos S.A., in Ponte de Sôr, Portugal, is a small company in a small town in a rural area east of Lisbon. INLAN produces rubber automotive parts and has to increase quality and lower prices each year. "That's easy for us to say in management," notes António Pinheiro, director of human resources, "but the guys on the shop floor don't really understand that. In fact there were a lot of things, we discovered, that they did not understand about the business. It was no fault of theirs; we just never told them." Now INLAN has monthly meetings in the company cafeteria where presentations are made about interesting aspects of the business. "We have no trouble getting their attention. It turns out that this is information they really wanted to know," notes Pinheiro. The presentations describe the situation of the company, the business, who the competitors are, the trends in prices (down) and salaries (up), and why the times are made difficult by global competition. "We use a lot of charts and graphs to present the actual data. We show other data from other companies and some of the trends in Portugal and the European Union. We talk a little about wages and benefits in the broader economic context and, of course, that gets their attention. "If they are interested, it is amazing how much they understand," notes Pinheiro. "They will come up a few weeks later to say thanks or to follow up on some point, and you know they are getting a lot out of it."

Information Processing

Assuming that the presenter has captured and focused the attention of the participants, what can be done to help them comprehend what is being said and shown to them? Once information has begun to come in through their senses—usually sight and hearing in a presentation—how is it processed?

A traditional, commonsense view of perception is that a person simply sees or hears what is out there. Philosophers have struggled for centuries with this problem—the relationship of the mind to the real world. Cognitive psychologists have joined those in this debate who emphasize the importance of what the mind does in information processing.

Cognitive psychologists today say that there is no one-to-one correspondence between what is out there and one's perception of it; rather, perceptions involve a highly complex mental *interpretation* of what is being said or shown.

Think about it: What is the "real world" interpreted by a dog, or for that matter, a butterfly? Doesn't it depend on the equipment the organism has for making perceptions and interpreting them?

What is involved in this process of interpretation? How does a person come to recognize and make meaning of the sounds, words, sentences, and images that are the building blocks of communication? As with many other breakthroughs in cognitive psychology, the story begins with the computer.[14] In developing the technology for scanning, now widely used to read zip codes and bank checks, it became necessary to learn how to develop programs that would "read" letters and numbers. A process known as *template matching* was developed to search for and match a predetermined shape. Thus, an electronic template for the number 3 was created to correspond to the shape of the number 3 used in the account number on the check. It is not surprising that this crude model of template matching was proposed as a way of thinking about how people process information, and there is, indeed, some support for it in lower animals, like the insect template possessed by a frog.

The template-matching process works well for what are called *invariable* sets, that is, when the pattern to be registered is always the same. But the problem becomes more complex when the scanner must read a variety of stimuli, known as *variable* sets, and make correct discriminations of letters and numbers. A scanner could read the type from many different printing styles—even handwriting.

For example, what does a scanner have to do when it is asked which of the following figures are *A*'s:

$$A \triangle V A_a F_a$$

In this situation the electronic device does not have a template but rather a bank of features, all of which have characteristics of *A*'s. For example, *A*'s have some of these typical features:

$$/ \; / \; ^\wedge \; _\circ \; \gamma\ell$$

This more complex scanner looks for features, not an exact template; it looks for the abstract characteristics of *A*, not just a specific *A*. Selfridge and his colleagues developed an electronic scanner for hand-printed characters that employed what came to be known as the pandemonium system, which could identify key features, count them, and "decide" whether the letter had enough characteristics to be called an *A*. Not surprisingly, the pandemonium system became a useful model for describing human information processing as well. If this system was what was necessary for electronic intelligence to read the features of a stimulus, something very similar must occur in the minds of human beings.

Humans apparently have a highly complex, feature-based pattern recognition system for information processing.

Up to this point, this description of information processing has centered on what cognitive psychologists call bottom-up processing, those aspects of the system that are data driven and guided by the features of the stimulus coming into the system. Operating simultaneously with this *bottom-up* system is a *top-down* system, which is more concept driven or hypothesis driven and seems to come more from within the individual than from outside stimuli.[15] While processing outside stimuli, the individual simultaneously marshals ideas, thoughts, and meanings from prior knowledge and tests the new inputs against experience.

Top-down theorists emphasize what the individual brings to the information during processing. These researchers have found that *context, meaning,* and *prior knowledge* affect information processing directly and deeply.

Drawing on the work of the Gestalt psychologists who preceded them, cognitive psychologists have been able to establish that perception is greatly influenced by context. For example, groups of dots, five rows of four, will tend to be perceived as rows or columns, depending on the way they are arranged.

```
•   •   •   •
•   •   •   •
•   •   •   •
•   •   •   •
•   •   •   •
```

Here they tend to look like columns, especially if you cover up the last column, thus reducing the length of the rows. In the diagram below, like elements tend to be grouped together (even though they are all the same distance apart) so that the rows tend to dominate.

```
X   X   X   X
O   O   O   O
X   X   X   X
O   O   O   O
```

The legacy from Gestalt psychology is that individuals organize their perceptions according to the whole configuration (gestalt), and context is, therefore, very important.

The perceiver puts individual perceptions into the big picture and sees things as part of a larger whole.

Top-down processing theory also emphasizes the importance of meaning making in the processing of information. Individuals work hard to discover the meaning of what they are seeing and hearing, especially semantic meaning, and then process that information as part of an overall pattern of meaning. For example, for processing the word *ice*, in the sentence, "The car slid on the ice," a great deal of help is provided by the earlier part of the sentence, "The car slid on the . . ." That part of the sentence almost cries out for the word *ice*. Less help is provided if the sentence ends with the word *banana*. Even though a person might slide on a banana, a car usually would not, and the statement begins to border on nonsense, causing the reader to slow down and take a second look. Research bears out the importance of semantic meaning in information processing. Word pairs that are meaningful, such as *nurse-doctor,* are processed and pronounced more rapidly than nonmeaningful pairs such as *nurse-tree*. Similarly, lists of words presented in a meaningful order, such as *dog, chased, cat, tree,* are more rapidly processed than unrelated words presented in random order such as *tree, boat, pickles, sheep.*

The place of semantic meaning making has been widely examined by cognitive psychologists interested in the study of reading. Although reading surely involves, to some degree, the bottom-up functions of learning the alphabet and certain phonic rules, there is growing evidence that readers also depend, to a large extent, on context for establishing meaning. For example, it is not necessary to have every letter of every word to read a sentence:

Thix example xhould proxe xhe poixt.

Sometimes the reader makes the same symbol into different letters as needed according to the context, as in the next example:

TⱯE CⱯT

Clearly, when people read, they process words, groups of words, and phrases—chunks of information, not individual letters. In fact, once one has learned to read and practiced it considerably, it is very difficult to process individual letters accurately. Consider the point by counting the number of *F*'s in the following passage:

> Finished files are the result of years of scientific study combined with the experience of many years.

A count of less than six requires more careful reading. As most writers know, proofreading goes much slower than reading for meaning, and most cognitive psychologists would agree that different processing activities are involved.

In most processing of information, an attempt is made by the individual to make sense of what is being processed, but not all individuals will arrive at the same meaning at the same time.

Meaning, of course, does not come out of thin air; it comes from *prior knowledge.* What the person knows already about the information being presented has a great effect on the speed and ease of processing. For example, when subjects are given a very brief glimpse of a flash card containing three rows of nonsense letters, such as:

G B Y
Q D P
L Z V

they have a great deal of difficulty in processing the information quickly and accurately. They may get one row or a few letters in a couple of rows. But when exposed for the same length of time to another set of letters:

```
I   B   M
S   O   S
I   O   U
```

the processing is rapid, easy, and accurate. In the second set of letters, of course, most subjects would have a high degree of familiarity—previous knowledge of the letter sets.

Cognitive psychologists have tried to describe how previous knowledge is stored and called forth to assist in information processing. What previous knowledge does it take, for example, to understand a simple passage like the following:[16]

> Jack was invited to Jill's birthday party. He wondered if she would like a new pail. He went to his room and shook his piggy bank. It made no sound.

The reader of this passage must understand what a birthday party is and what the expectations are about presents. In addition, the reader must know something about "real" pails and "play" pails, not to mention piggy banks, coins, the sounds of coins, and so on. Obviously, if none of this information is in place, it will be difficult to understand the passage. If it is in place, what place is it in, and how does it come into play in processing?

Cognitive psychologists (with some help from linguists) suggest that individuals organize their prior knowledge into *scripts, frames,* and *schemas* and that they call up this knowledge in preorganized knowledge packets when they encounter new information.[17] For example, when a person is learning about going to a Chinese restaurant, the "restaurant script" is called into play. It already contains information about general restaurant experiences such as getting seated, reading a menu, ordering, being served, and paying the bill, as well as the proper sequence for doing these things. When one learns something new about how this is done in a Chinese restaurant, the basic restaurant script is used and serves quite well for making sense of the new learning that takes place. If there is no restaurant script to begin with, then there will be problems in learning about sharing main dishes, about eating with chopsticks, and about limiting dessert to a fortune cookie. Effective information processing involves relating new information to old (previously known) information.

Processing information is not a passive process for the participant. To "get it" the learner needs to be actively involved—fully engaged in trying to perceive and understand the information being presented.

Utilizing their abilities to understand context, to make meaning, and to draw on previous knowledge, participants who are actively involved can receive and understand impressive amounts of new information from effective presentations.

Rules 6 through 11 address the question, What does the presenter need to do to increase the likelihood that information will be processed as intended?

Rule 6: Recognize that interpretation will always occur.

It is important to remember that there is no one-to-one connection between what the presenter says and what the participant hears or sees. What participants process is not the information but their *perception* of the information. In this sense, it is never possible to tell anyone anything directly, because it is always being acted upon by the learner.

Rule 7: Help participants discover the overall patterns in the information being presented.

Participants never process individual pieces of information—sounds, words, images—as isolated bits, but as parts of larger patterns. If participants are searching for overall patterns, why not offer them some? The trees are always part of a forest, so give the participants the forest, name it, and then look at the trees. Details take on importance when they fit into overall patterns.

Rule 8: Present information in context.

Because context makes processing smoother, information should always be presented in its larger context. Where did this information come from? How is it related to similar or different information? How can this information be used? How does this information improve operations or services?

Rule 9: Help the participants with meaning making.

Because the participants are trying to find meaning in order to process information more effectively, the presenter needs to provide interpretations of the meaning of the information along with the information. How do things work? Why do they work? What are the best words and phrases to carry the meaning? Is there a good story that can be used to illustrate a key point? Recognizing that different people make meaning in different ways, the presenter does not assume that the meaning is obvious but states explicitly the meaning of the information.

Rule 10: Build strong bridges from prior knowledge to new information.

Because new information needs to be understood through prior knowledge, the presenter needs to have a good grasp of the prior knowledge that most participants have. If participants have little prior knowledge to use as a base for the processing of new information, the presenter may need to go very slowly or back up and build that knowledge base. Assuming adequate prior knowledge, the presenter then needs to make connections to that prior knowledge. The presenter can remind participants that they already know certain processes, techniques, and procedures and that they already have the scripts for certain activities. The new information draws on and fits that prior knowledge.

Rule II: Devise ways to ensure that participants are actively involved.

Because this kind of learning requires active participation (not passive acceptance) from the learner, the presenter finds ways to engage the participants with activities and exercises interspersed in the presentation to stimulate involvement. Presenters may ask for volunteers for an experiment, may ask each individual to think through his or her own response to a question, or may ask pairs of participants to summarize a key point in their own words and share it with each other. Presenters may stop to ask participants what point is still muddy or unclear.

Sometimes trainers will go to extremes to try to help participants process the key points of a presentation, as you will see in this example:

──Organizações Martins BRAZIL ───────────

The headquarters for Martins Comércio e Serviços de Distribuição Ltda. is in Uberlândia, an inland city in the western part of the State of Minas Gerais. Although Organizações Martins has no outlet stores, they wholesale products from over 900 suppliers—more than 11,000 items from bar soap to computers—to *varejos,* small retail convenience stores, at 140,000 points of sale all over the country, including a few remote areas where they know they lose money. They employ some 3,000 sales reps and over 150 sales supervisors. The biggest retail company in Brazil, Organizações Martins was founded by a simple country-store owner, Alair Martins, in Uberlândia in the 1960s. Today, his wholesale dream has sales of over US$ 1.2 billion.

Each year the sales managers are brought in for four and a half days of training, using presentations to bring them up to date on company trends and sales techniques. Well-known speakers present new ideas on consumer marketing and the interpersonal aspects of sales. Company speakers present crucial information on the areas that interface with sales, such as purchasing, logistics, and finance. Participants need to get actively involved in the material, and they know they will be given brief quizzes on important points. "To get them involved," notes Ricardo Rezende, director of human resources, "we bring in some *animadores*—professional actors who listen to the presentations along with the participants. It is the job of the actors to provide humorous dramatizations of the key points." The *animadores* will act out certain typical situations, often drawing on familiar television programs, such as "The Little School of Professor Raimundo," which every Brazilian knows. "Sometimes the sales managers get drawn in to play certain roles, and it gets quite funny. The purpose of the *animadores* is to fix certain key points," notes Rezende, "to help the processing of the dry information and underscore the main ideas."

Memory

Most presenters would like participants to remember what they said, but, oddly enough, they seldom identify what to remember or how to remember it. Retaining information over long periods of time involves memory. How do we remember things, and is it possible to improve our memory or the memory of others?

After many years of research, cognitive psychologists have made a distinction between *short-term memory* (STM) and *long-term memory* (LTM).[18]

Short-term memory, as the term implies, doesn't last very long, and it doesn't hold very much. It is used to keep information temporarily in mind in order to act on it.

In looking up a phone number, a person uses short-term memory to keep the numbers in mind long enough to dial them, and, alas, even then it is often necessary to take a second peek at the phone book, especially if there has been an interruption. How short is short-term memory? Estimates vary on the exact length of storage time. Visual images last in the sensory register for less than one-half second and sounds last only one-fourth second, but their features can be extracted and retained in short-term memory for somewhere between fifteen and thirty seconds.[19] Unless the information is rehearsed (repeated over and over mentally) or unless something else is done with the information to fix it in long-term memory, rapid decay sets in. Hence the name short-term.

Short-term memory is also limited in capacity, that is, it doesn't hold very much. In a now famous and influential paper entitled "The Magical Number Seven, Plus or Minus Two: Some Limits on Our Capacity for Processing Information," G. A. Miller established that most people are limited to retaining between five and nine bits of information in their short-term memory.[20] In the experiments that he did, and in those done subsequently by others, the magical number seven kept popping up. In tests of the number of sounds, digits, or words people could retain in short-term memory, the results were always similar—somewhere around seven, plus or minus two. People then forget what they have in short-term memory unless they do something with the information to establish it in long-term memory. Usually this means taking a longer string of information and grouping it into a smaller number of *chunks*.[21] It would be difficult, for example, to remember the number

100101110

as a single number, but it can be "chunked," as shown below, into

100 101 110

It is more likely that these three chunks of three numbers will be retained, but this is no longer short-term memory. The material has, in fact, been transformed, encoded, and sent on its way to long-term memory.

What is the purpose of short-term memory, with its demonstrated lack of staying power and capacity? Short-term memory plays an important function in holding information temporarily in mind while other monitors and control mechanisms get to act on it. It is like hanging a picture. One person holds the picture in place, while another takes a look and tries to decide whether to move it up or down, left or right, or whether to hang it, put it in another room, or put it in storage. In hanging pictures it is not wise to go too fast or to look at too many pictures all at once. Similarly, short-term memory provides a necessarily limited mechanism for holding up words, images, ideas, and sounds to look at briefly while a decision is made about what to do with them next. This is why short-term memory is sometimes called *working memory.*

Long-term memory, on the other hand, is what most people mean when they refer to memory, and it is this kind of memory that is usually the concern of trainers and participants. It picks up where short-term memory leaves off—after a few seconds—and goes on for weeks, months, and years.

Cognitive psychologists have described various types of long-term memory and recognize that somewhat different processes are at work for remembering different kinds of things.[22] Remembering the event of walking to school as a child is different from remembering what was learned about Pilgrims in sixth grade. Remembering images, such as the international driving signs, is different from remembering movements, such as skiing or riding a bicycle. Most trainers deal primarily with semantic memory, the memory for information, ideas, and concepts mediated by words.

How does long-term memory work and what can be done to assist it in its work? One commonly expressed view is that the mind records everything perfectly, like a human camcorder, but the trouble comes in playback. When individuals representative of the general populace are surveyed and asked how they think their memory works, three-fourths believe that all the information is in long-term memory; they just can't retrieve it.[23] This idea of a complete but inaccessible memory, while widely held, does not bear the scrutiny of research. Research suggests that the mind does not record everything and that what is recorded is subject to inaccuracy, distortion, and serious decay.[24] Recent attempts to unlock the memory with hypnosis, truth drugs, and electrical stimulation result in as many false reports, fragments, and distortions as accurate memories. If long-term memory is not a videotape of experience, how does it work?

Memory works somewhat like a computer. There are places where information is stored, like files, and it is necessary to enter that information in a systematic way so that it can be retrieved. Similar kinds of information seem to be stored in the same "files." Thus, *animal, bird, feathers, wing,* and *fly* are arranged in a hierarchy on networked files.[25] The structure of these networks has been mapped and tested, and we know that some things are easier to call up than others, for example, the concrete image of *zebra* is easier than the abstract concept of *justice.*[26] Putting things into long-term memory and retrieving them involves associations among words, concepts, and ideas, and usually, but not always, semantic associations. The best models of long-term memory currently available focus on the importance of word associations, hooking up one word with another word (or image or sound) to produce meaningful and memorable connections within the networked filing system. The human computer, with its potentially enormous and complex storage and retrieval system, relies heavily on language and the associations of meaning conveyed by language and image for its smooth functioning.

If it is known that memory depends on building associations between and among words, images, concepts, and ideas, what are some of the ways that an individual might go about storing information with the hope that it might be retrieved as needed?

Five categories of techniques are especially useful for enhancing the storage and retrieval of information in long-term memory: rehearsal, encoding, imagery, method of loci, and semantic association.

• *Rehearsal.* The most frequently used and least effective memory technique is rehearsal, sometimes referred to by educators as *rote learning.* Rehearsal involves repeating information over and over again (out loud or to oneself) until it "sinks in." It is possible, for example, to memorize a difficult list of words if sufficient time for rehearsal is allowed between the presentation of each word.[27] Rehearsal, however, is not very efficient, and when it does work there is often another technique being used (perhaps unconsciously) besides pure repetition.

• *Encoding.* Far more efficient and productive is the memory technique known as *encoding.* At its simplest level, encoding means associating a key word with the word to be remembered; at its more complex levels encoding means transforming the information to be remembered into a new semantic unit or form. Using a synonym is a form of encoding, so is placing a word in a meaningful and memorable sentence. More complex encoding involves developing mnemonic devices known as acronyms—such as HOMES to remember the Great Lakes (Huron, Ontario, Michigan, Erie, Superior)—or catchy sentences, such as "Every good boy does fine," to remember the lines on the treble clef (E, G, B, D, F,). Research on encoding suggests, oddly enough, that more elaborate and distinctive devices work best.[28] One of the more useful forms of encoding is *chunking.* Long strings of information can be subdivided or transformed into chunks, so that the number of individual units to be remembered is smaller and more manageable.

• *Imagery.* Images are mental pictures. Research has shown that people generally find it easier to remember pictures than words.[29] When subjects were shown 1,000 vivid pictures, 1,000 ordinary pictures, and 1,000 words, on the average they remembered (identified correctly from test pairs) 830 vivid pictures, 770 ordinary pictures, and 615 words. One picture may not be worth 1,000 words, but vivid images may be useful in storing information in long-term memory. Associating words with vivid images is the main technique set forth in a popular best-seller of some years back by Lorayne and Lucas entitled *The Memory Book.*[30] Unlike some popular psychology books, this one advocates techniques that are in harmony with research. The authors explain step by step how to remember a new piece of information by associating it with vivid, preferably ridiculous and even bizarre images. Suppose, for example, that a person is asked to learn a list of words that includes "airplane," "tree," and "envelope." You may wish to picture an airplane with trees growing from the wings and with envelopes hanging from the trees like leaves. Apparently bizarre and elaborate visual associations work well as memory devices.

• *Method of loci.* Another memory technique involving the use of imagery is known as the *method of loci,* or the *place method.* The object is to place items to be learned into a pattern of familiar locations, such as the rooms of a house, the corners of a classroom, or the shops along a familiar street. A grocery list, for example, might be learned by placing each item on the list mentally at a different place in the kitchen: the milk in the refrigerator, the paper towels on their rack, a can of soup at the stove, and so forth. While shopping, one mentally walks through the kitchen and retrieves the items to be purchased.[31]

• *Semantic association.* Information that has meaning is remembered more easily than nonsense. Language has both what linguists call *surface structure,* properties of the words themselves, and *deep structure,* the underlying meaning the words convey.[32]

What people do when they read a passage or listen to a presentation is look for the underlying message of the information, the gist of the content. What people often put into long-term memory are not the exact words, but the message, and the message, in turn, is also what they recall. When subjects were given a passage to read about the performance of exploratory surgery, they later recalled a host of words, such as "doctor," "nurse," and "scalpel," that weren't in the passage at all. Apparently they remembered the general theme of the passage and made decisions on the basis of what words should have appeared in such a passage.[33] Other studies show that people remember exact wording in sentences only when the sentence itself is particularly noteworthy; otherwise they have trouble distinguishing the actual sentence from a paraphrase. Long-term memory is facilitated by associations derived from the underlying meaning of the information.

If this is how people remember, why do they forget? There are many explanations for forgetting. Forgetting can involve interference from previously learned material; repression, as in the classical Freudian sense; failure in the retrieval system, as with tip-of-the-tongue forgetting; or actual memory decay, as with aging.[34] More likely than not, however, what is called forgetting is really a matter of not learning the information in the first place. People don't forget names; more likely they don't learn them initially. Memory usually involves active processing that requires significant intentional effort. When subjects were asked to recall the head of a penny, most could not describe what was on it, or where, and could not distinguish real pennies from fake pennies that were presented, even though they dealt with pennies every day.[35] Did the subjects forget? Unlikely! One must learn something before it can be forgotten. When trainees say "I forgot," a more accurate admission usually would be "I didn't learn it."

Rules 12 through 15 address the question, What does the presenter need to do to increase the likelihood that the information presented will be remembered by the participants?

Rule 12: Allow time for short-term memory (STM) to function.

It is important for presenters to move slowly enough to allow time for participants to deal with new information. Those in the audience need to be able to project the words and images on their own private short-term memory screens long enough to decide what to do. It takes some time for the raw material of the presentation (as spoken words, overheads, slides, computer images) to register, and, as soon as it does, beware, it will start to be lost. The listeners/watchers have to scramble to decide what to do with this material—whether to take notes, relate the visuals to the spoken words, or search the memory for something familiar—and they are busy trying to decide what to do with it all before they lose it.

Rule 13: Explode the myth of automatic memory/ faulty recall.

Let participants know that they need to get actively involved in trying to remember. To facilitate long-term memory (LTM), it is useful for presenters to stop acting as if the participants were so many camcorders, remembering what took place because they were so fortunate as to have been in the same room at the same time with the presenter. It is also valuable if presenters share one important little piece of information with participants: You won't remember it just because you were here and heard it and saw it.

Rule 14: Provide the participants with mnemonic devices.

Because we know that information will be lost unless it is actively transformed into something memorable, the presenter should play a role in facilitating the storage and retrieval process. One can, of course, take the position that presenting is the presenter's job and remembering is the participant's problem, but it makes for a huge difference in learning if the presenter assumes at least some of the responsibility for helping participants to remember the material. This means being selective in telling participants what is essential—if you don't know, how can they?—and creating the actual mnemonic (memory) devices for them or with them.

Rule 15: Let participants know that rehearsal doesn't work.

Work with participants to use the techniques of encoding, imagery, and semantic association to remember essential information. Usually this means providing a synonym, an acronym, a set or chunk, a diagram, a bizarre image, a simple routine, or sharp metaphor for remembering the material.

In the next example, look for what trainers do to help participants remember the information they need.

—Safeway USA

Safeway, Inc., is a big supermarket chain with stores in large western U.S. cities such as Denver, Phoenix, and Seattle, as well as stores in Vancouver, Calgary, and Winnipeg, Canada. The work of checkout clerks has been greatly simplified, in some respects, with the electronic bar code system, but most produce is still sold by the item or weight and needs to be identified and charged separately. To train checkout clerks to recognize and remember the produce, Safeway has developed training presentations supplemented by study materials. "We have a good presentation on the various types of produce," notes Linda Hawkins, training instructor, "complete with color slides. It is amazing how many exotic types of produce there are now—kale, rutabaga, starfruit, jicama." The problem is to teach the trainees how to associate a name with the image and then a code number with the name. They also need to know whether the produce is sold by weight or item. "We try to present this in a way they can remember it. We give them memory devices, like 'hello, yellow' onion and 'jicama hiccups.'" To supplement the presentation, and as a follow-up to it, a picture book is made available to review identification, and flash cards are used to practice linking the names and code. "We keep working on this presentation to make it as effective as possible, because eventually the trainees must pass a hundred-item test and get all the items correct. We think it is our job in training to help the workers remember so they can be successful on the exam.

Presentations in Other Media

Although the focus of this chapter has been on live presentations, where someone delivers information in spoken form to an audience of participants, almost everything we have discussed can be applied also to information presented in written form (texts, booklets, or manuals) or through audiotapes, video presentations, computer and CD-ROM programs, and informal explanations. In all of these media, the learner presumably still needs to attend to, process, and remember the information. Observe how training information is presented by this large, far-flung, investment company.

——Merrill Lynch USA

$\mathcal{M}$errill Lynch & Co., Inc., is a holding company that through its subsidiaries and affiliates provides investment, financing, insurance, and related services on a global basis. Although one may think of Merrill Lynch primarily as a securities firm, the business of the subsidiaries extends to many types of financial activity. With total client assets of over one trillion dollars (October 1997) and almost fifty thousand employees, Merrill Lynch is a huge company with many types of training activities, some of which focus heavily on the transmission of information. This transmission does not always need to be done in person in a conventional presentation, and although Merrill Lynch owns and operates a state-of-the-art training center near Princeton, New Jersey, much of the introductory level training done by Merrill Lynch is through written materials, teleconferencing, audiotapes, videotapes, and computer. Presentations and explanations employing these media are used to provide basic information for financial consultant trainees.

To become a financial consultant, promising candidates must be able to pass the General Securities Representative Examination (Series 7), an SEC mandate, and that requires having an understanding of a lot of basic information. Merrill Lynch has developed a course that combines written text, telephone tutoring, and computer-aided testing to help trainees over this initial hurdle. Using a sophisticated understanding of how trainees are likely to attend to, process, and remember information, Merrill Lynch has developed a series of specially prepared booklets that contain the needed information laid out in a clear format using short paragraphs and bold print for key concepts—an information processing dream. Trainees work on Book 1, for example, on *Equity Securities,* on their own and call into the training center at an assigned time on a regular telephone from their own desks. Thus the class, scattered around the country, meets two or three times per week by telephone with an instructor who is specialized in that material and is prepared to give additional brief explanations and answer questions. If some trainees are having problems understanding some aspect of the material, a special teletutoring class can be composed around that need, with brief "lecturettes" on more complex concepts. How do students know if they are understanding? "They take sample tests," notes Priscilla Corielle, vice president for curriculum planning and education, "through a computer-based testing system that provides feedback and an error analysis report that suggests where they may be having difficulty. The results on practice tests predict probable scores on the actual exam, and it is not surprising, then, that Merrill Lynch trainees have a 90–95 percent pass rate on the exam." Once the General Securities Representative Examination has been passed, trainees move into more advanced work, and once again it is information laden. The next level, which has come to be known as the "Live from Princeton Course," focuses on the information a financial consultant needs in order to work with clients, beginning with making contact, meeting face to face, gathering information, drafting financial plans, and making investment recommendations.

As before, concise, user-friendly materials have been developed to convey the information in a form that can be easily processed and remembered. The written materials are supplemented with videotapes of experienced financial consultants telling their stories and interacting with clients. Only after seven weeks of this serious information downloading does the trainee, under supervision, begin to deal with the public. "It would take a big auditorium to hold the trainees from the more than five hundred branch offices who sit at their own desks, working through the materials we prepare with such care for them," notes Corielle.

Sometimes a live presentation is combined with video satellite transmission in what is being called *distance learning*. The armed services and other U.S. government agencies are linked by satellite to accommodate presentations. Here is how it works.

──Air Force Institute of Technology USA ────

*T*he course, "Systems 200: Acquisition Planning and Analysis," is offered in a three-week block by the School of Systems and Logistics at the U.S. Air Force Institute of Technology (AFIT) at Wright-Patterson Air Force Base near Dayton, Ohio. The course includes information on how to manage large-scale projects, including topics such as planning, budgeting, acquisitions, control, and logistics. The instructor, after receiving counsel on distance-learning techniques, teaches the course simultaneously to a live class at AFIT and through one-way video and two-way interactive voice communication to students at bases literally all over the world via satellite. AT&T helped develop the system, called Telstar 401, which uses a classroom equipped with remote video cameras. In an adjacent room, an engineer operates the cameras and mixes the images for a professional television presentation. Students at the remote classrooms kick back and listen, and if they have questions they get on the microphone (one for every two students), sometimes getting into some lively discussions that bounce from site to site. "Students like it and learn from it," notes Philip Westfall, director of the AFIT Center for Distance Education, "with students at remote sites slightly outperforming those at AFIT. Maybe the students at the remote sites spend more time interacting, checking the information with their classmates, and reviewing together what they think is important." One important aspect of distance learning is its cost effectiveness. "We once delivered courses to around three hundred students per year," notes Westfall, "at a cost of $1,800 per student. Via satellite we reach three thousand students annually at about $65 per student—or a maximum of $150 if you count the amortization of equipment." With savings like that it is not surprising that plans are underway to use distance learning more widely. The Army, the Air National Guard, and the Coast Guard are already on Telstar 401, and several other government agencies, such as the Department of Energy, the FAA, and the EPA, have joined together under AT&T facilitation to form the Government Education Training Network. The technology to support distance learning is advancing every year, which is wonderful, but obviously the course is still only as good as the presenter.

What the Facilitator Does

If the facilitator is the presenter, obviously the thing to do is to follow rules 1 through 15 as closely as possible. Knowing the subject, of course, is essential; but knowing the theory derived from cognitive psychology and applying it can greatly enhance any presentation and get better results.

The facilitator is not always the presenter, however, and sometimes the trainer's role is to work with other presenters to help them improve what they do. This is not always easy, because presenters are usually focused on content and coverage.

What the facilitator needs to do in this case is to upset the preoccupation with content—sometimes it is an obsession or fixation—by asking disturbing questions about outcomes. What is it, after all, that participants are expected to take away from this presentation and remember? What is the learning that is supposed to take place?

The facilitator who works with presenters can also play a key role in helping them to organize their thinking. Brilliant people do not always have organized minds, and a trainer can help them reduce their ramblings to a few well-organized points. The trainer can help the presenter think about the participants as learners and can encourage structuring the presentation in such a way that it can be attended to, processed, and remembered. The best way to encourage this structuring is to ask persistently tough questions: What do you need to do to get participants' attention? What do you want them to focus on? What are the main ideas and concepts? How can you relate new material to what is already known? What do you want them to remember?

In addition, the facilitator can provide guidance in selecting supportive media. Many presenters are inclined to rely entirely on the spoken word, believing, perhaps, that teaching is talking because they were taught that way. The facilitator encourages the use of Powerpoint, overhead transparencies, slides, software, or video clips to support or augment the main points of the presentation. Sometimes making decisions about supporting media helps the organizational task described above. There is no better exercise for shaping and ordering a presentation than having to design the handful of overheads or Powerpoint frames used to support the main ideas. The message should determine the medium, but the medium can be used as a vehicle for becoming clearer about what the message actually is.

Above all, the facilitator, whether working as the presenter or a consultant to presenters, needs to keep in mind that heavy, formal presentations, done in the traditional manner without benefit of cognitive learning principles, do not work. Formal speeches are like throwing the shot put.[36] The speaker spends a lot of time getting together a very heavy message, usually a written script. When the athlete flings the shot, no one would think of trying to catch it. Onlookers may admire the form or measure how far it went, but they would be crazy to try to catch it. Formal speeches are usually received the same way. On the other hand, an effective presentation is like throwing a Frisbee: The presenter has a lighter message, one that is attention catching, relevant, and understandable, and throws it in such a way that it can be caught, examined, and thrown back.

THE BOTTOM LINE

Most jobs require that people know something. Having the right information, understanding it, and being able to remember it is important. This kind of learning takes place best through presentations and explanations. Presentations and explanations can be designed and delivered more effectively by applying what is known through cognitive learning theory in three critical areas:

- Attention. Get their attention. Help people focus. Don't overload the system. Slow down for new or difficult material. Don't compete with distractions.
- Information Processing. Realize that interpretation is always taking place. Help people discover patterns. Present information in context. Explain the meaning. Link new information to prior knowledge.
- Memory. Allow time for short-term memory to function. Get people actively involved in remembering. Provide mnemonic devices. Introduce people to rehearsal, encoding, imagery, method of loci, and semantic association as memory aids.

The Cognitive Strategy is used to design and guide formal presentations, but its principles also apply to presentations in written form (booklets, manuals) and other media, including distance learning arrangements.

Sometimes the facilitator's role is to work with other presenters to help them maximize learning.

The well-established principles for the Cognitive Strategy grow out of the research begun by cognitive psychologists in the 1950s.

Presentations can be dull, boring, or deadly. They are better if they are brilliant, involving, and enlightening. Your presentation should be a Frisbee, not a shot put.

7

The Inquiry Strategy
Critical, Creative, and Dialogical Thinking

*W*e need as much information as we can get. But we also need thinking. We need thinking to decide what information we should seek and where to look for it. We need thinking to make the best use of the information we have. We need thinking to set up possible ways of putting information together. The traditional notion in education that information is sufficient is old-fashioned and dangerous.[1]

—EDWARD DE BONO, *De Bono's Thinking Course*

INQUIRY STRATEGY OVERVIEW

BEST USE
Developing and refining critical, creative, and dialogical thinking skills.

LEARNING THEORY
Philosophical and psychological theories of different thinking processes and theories of creativity. Learning by engaging directly in one or more types of thinking by asking questions.

HISTORICAL ROOTS
Ancient and modern philosophy and recent psychological investigations of thinking and creativity.

APPLICATIONS
Anywhere in the organization where analyzing and critically evaluating information, generating creative ideas, and understanding opposing arguments may be important.

PARTICIPANT ROLES
Involves participants in asking questions, analyzing arguments and assertions, and actively discovering new ideas and opposing viewpoints.

NATURE OF MOTIVATION
Stems from posing intriguing questions that arouse curiosity and inspire the desire to provide rational and creative responses.

PARTICIPANT FIT
Best for participants who have high levels of natural curiosity, are good at verbal expression, and are well prepared to engage in sustained investigations using linear reasoning or creative thinking.

FACILITATOR'S ROLE
Selects appropriate tasks for inquiry and establishes a climate where participants are encouraged to engage in thinking. Facilitates discussion by asking questions, probing assumptions, examining assertions, and asking for evidence, fresh ideas, or opposing viewpoints.

STRENGTHS
Is useful for engaging participants directly in tasks that require thinking and answers to open-ended questions. Can be spontaneous and free-flowing. Focuses on the processes whereby questions are framed, evidence is evaluated, and knowledge is established.

WEAKNESSES
Can be slow, cumbersome, and difficult. Allows digressions that can bog down discussion. Can be frustrating due to failure to find satisfying answers. Presupposes in participants some base of knowledge and a willingness to search for understanding.

The Inquiring Mind

Having the right information is important, but what do we do with it when we have it, and how do we know if it is right? Organizations need people who possess the ability to think clearly and creatively. Richard Paul, a major leader in the international critical thinking movement describes the work increasingly required in industry and business as intellectual. This work requires thinking and must be coordinated with, and must profit from, the critique of fellow workers.[2] Intellectual work requires an inquiring mind, an approach to information that involves asking a lot of questions.

The new importance of learning in most organizations today provides a privileged place for thinkers. They are the ones who generate new ideas, develop or analyze proposals, invent new products, devise new services, suggest quality improvements, or simply sift through the deluge of information flowing into and through the organization to determine its importance. Most of the organizations we visited were eager to get their hands on good thinkers, and some went out of their way to try to increase the human capacity for thinking through training. Consider the following examples.

- At the ARLA dairy cooperative in Sweden, one hundred new board members are trained by helping them learn to ask the right questions about how their dairy cooperative works.
- At COBE BCT, new employees are taught to become members of a question-asking culture.
- General Mills uses cross-functional creativity teams to develop new food products.
- SHARP gets new employees to begin thinking creatively about new electronic products in their initial training.

- The Foreign Service Institute of the U.S. Department of State sponsors policy roundtables that teach high level foreign service personnel critical thinking about hot-spot foreign policy issues.
- Norsk Hydro, Norway's biggest company, uses an inquiry process to develop creative new business ideas from within.
- KRESAM worked with the Värmland County Labor Board in Sweden using an inquiry process to help unemployed youth create their own jobs.
- Motorola executives use dialogical thinking to discuss ethical issues in a cross-cultural context.
- At ARIEL machine tool operators teach their coworkers about computer numerical control (CNC) by helping them to ask questions.
- ReliaStar combines critical, creative, and dialogical thinking for envisioning its future.

Thinking About Thinking

What is thinking? The random thoughts that pass through our heads as we shower or drive along the highway are called *non-directed thinking,* which is different from purposeful *directed thinking.*[3] Directed thinking includes asking questions, analyzing arguments, identifying reasons, formulating hypotheses, seeking and weighing evidence, distinguishing facts from opinions, judging the credibility of sources, classifying data, making definitions, using analogies, making value judgments, and weighing alternatives. Directed thinking also involves certain dispositions or habits of mind, such as trying to be well informed, being open-minded, being willing to consider opposing viewpoints, respecting evidence, suspending judgment, tolerating ambiguity, being curious and skeptical, and revering the truth.[4]

There are three types of thinking that are very important in organizational settings: critical thinking, creative thinking, and dialogical thinking.

• *Critical thinking* has been defined broadly as "judging the authenticity, worth or accuracy of something, such as a piece of information, a claim or assertion, or sources of data."[5] Critical thinking focuses on the *justification,* or set of reasons to support a *conclusion.*[6] A justification is usually set forth in an *argument.*

The emphasis in critical thinking, whether in building an argument or in criticizing the arguments of others, is usually on analyzing the way evidence is used to support a point of view.

Key elements to look for in analyzing arguments can be learned and skillfully applied through practice.

• *Creative thinking,* on the other hand, is "thinking guided—indeed driven—by a desire to seek the original. It involves mobility; it revels in exploration; it requires flexibility; and it honors diversity."[7] Instead of following rules, creative thinkers break them.

Creative thinking usually results in creative products or services, inventions, or new processes. Creative outcomes stretch or break boundaries, but they are also well suited and relevant.[8]

Creative thinking has several characteristics, such as *ideational fluency,* the ability to generate large numbers of appropriate ideas easily and quickly; *remote association,* the ability to call forth and link together ideas that would ordinarily not be associated; and *intuition,* the ability to generate sound conclusions from minimal evidence.[9]

• *Dialogical thinking* involves seeing and being able to evaluate different points of view at the same time. Some points can be "settled within one frame of reference and with a definite set of logical moves," and they usually have a "right" answer.[10] Other matters, however, are not so easily settled, and depend upon some arguable choice among alternative frames of reference, so that not only the evidence but the whole way of looking at the issue must be tested. Such matters usually have more than one "right" answer, and to deal with them, one needs to enter into a dialogue with another thinker. Dialogical thinking is based on the assumption that we tend to be egocentric in our thinking. To put the matter bluntly, people tend to think they are always right, and it takes some strong effort even to consider another point of view.

Through dialogical thinking—a kind of role playing of the thinking of others—we are able to enter empathetically into opposing arguments and viewpoints, thereby examining our own thinking and recognizing its strengths and weaknesses.

Origins of the Inquiry Strategy

Unlike the Cognitive Strategy with its rather recent origins, the Inquiry Strategy has roots in classical antiquity. One of the great contributions of philosophers has been their effort to clarify, each for their own age, what is meant by thinking. Thinking did not mean the same thing to Aristotle, Bacon, Descartes, Locke, or Russell. Philosophy, as a way of thinking about thinking, preceded science by almost two thousand years, and many of the things that writers today have to say about thinking—the difference between inductive and deductive reasoning, the procedures for examining syllogisms, and the nature of dialogue—go back to Plato and Aristotle.

The modern history of thinking begins in the early twentieth century with *A Compendium of Human Reasoning,* an important joint effort of Bertrand Russell and Alfred North Whitehead, based on the earlier work (1854) of the mathematician George Boole.[11] Another important classic work is Edward Glaser's *An Experiment in the Development of Critical Thinking* (1941) and the Watson-Glaser tests of critical thinking.[12] Studies of creativity, on the other hand, emerged somewhat later. One of the early studies of "men of genius" was produced by Galton in 1869, but the turning point for research on creativity was the 1950s with the work of J. P. Guilford on the factors of human intelligence related to creativity and the work of E. P. Torrence in making tests of creativity.[13] The great-grandfather of dialogical thinking, of course, is Plato, who gave us the famous dialogues of Socrates.

Facilitating Inquiry

As with other Training Strategies, the Inquiry Strategy requires a particular set of skills for facilitators and a different role for participants. In some ways the Inquiry Strategy poses special problems in its use because it emphasizes behaviors that are exactly the opposite of those found in the Cognitive Strategy. It is hard for teachers to give up telling and students to get beyond listening. Unfortunately, most training in critical, creative, and dialogical thinking involves workshops where experts are brought in to tell people what thinking is and how to do it better. What could be worse for actually cultivating thinking skills than having to listen to a presentation where there is no chance to speak, to make arguments, to generate and test ideas, or to see what others think! For training in thinking to be effective, participants should be able to practice thinking under the guidance of a skilled facilitator. Sharing some of what is known about thinking along the way can be helpful, but this is done, not by a presentation on thinking skills, but by describing and labeling what is happening when participants are actually thinking. The facilitator, therefore, needs to understand thinking—develop expertise about the process—but the main activity is to involve participants in thinking.

How is this done? Primarily by asking questions—the right kind of questions—to involve learners in productive inquiry. By emphasizing asking rather than telling, the facilitator systematically assaults typically passive classroom behavior—what Paulo Freire has called the "culture of silence."[14] For the facilitator this is often a battle, and resistance is sometimes stiff because habits are hard to break and thinking is usually hard work. Inquiry is seeking truth through a process of asking questions.

If there is a bottom-line behavior for all types of thinking, it is asking questions.[15] Inquiry is the foundation of all training that involves the cultivation of thinking skills, hence, the Inquiry Strategy.

Notice how important question-asking is in the next three examples.

— ARLA SWEDEN

*A*RLA Group is a large dairy cooperative of 10,500 milk producers who join together to make and sell dairy products. Although there are other cooperatives, ARLA gathers in and distributes 60 percent of the milk in Sweden. The board consists of 500 selected members, and every other year 100 members are new. How can they be trained quickly and effectively for their new duties? "We once brought them in for a series of lectures on how the company works and what its various divisions and products are about," notes Ingrid Bäckmann-Persson, training manager for members and elected members. "Now we use an inquiry process where they learn by asking questions. We give them training on how to conduct a telephone interview, and then we send them out in small groups to do these telephone interviews with the managing directors of subsidiaries." What the new board members find out from their interviews is important, because they must return and explain it to the others. Piece by piece, the company comes into full view. "We believe that this inquiry-based training is more effective than just telling them."

—COBE BCT USA

COBE BCT, Inc., a high-tech producer of blood component technology equipment based in Lakewood, Colorado, incorporates inquiry into many aspects of its training, including basic orientation for new employees. "We want to create a question-asking culture right up front," notes Kathe Burke, director of human resources. COBE puts people into groups and asks them to generate questions for the speakers. The facilitator puts their questions on flip charts and organizes them into topics. For some of the participants, having to come up with questions is a new experience. Then they see the speaker actually responding to their questions and asking for even more questions from the floor. "We tell them," notes Burke, "that this is a place you can stop any time to ask questions, and the people around you have time to answer them. And you can ask each other questions; you don't need to seek out the authorities." Asking questions carries over into the assembly environment, where people work in small teams. Workers learn how to ask: Should we stop the line? Are the materials good? Are the bonds of high quality? Are there gaps, voids, occlusions? Is there a better way to do this? "We teach them to be questioning on the job and to use each other's ideas. We tell them, hey, please don't check your brains in the clean room when you come in; we need you to make some important judgments about the work you do." COBE trains workers to ask questions.

—United Methodist Church USA

The United Methodist Church believes in the importance of having an educated laity (nonclerical members), and there are many training programs for church members at the conference, district, and local church level. One of the biggest efforts in the training of laypersons has been in the area of Bible study. Methodists, like other Protestants in the Reformation tradition, believe that understanding the Bible is an individual matter, but they also believe that the important influence of modern scholarship needs to be brought to bear on the process of interpretation. They seek to cultivate in lay members a deeper understanding of the context of the Bible—when it was written, how it was written, the various genres of literature it contains, and what it means. Getting the typical layperson involved in this process was seen as a significant challenge. To meet this challenge, a specially developed study program entitled Disciple Bible Study was developed, and a system of training was prepared for facilitators at United Methodist Publishing House, in Nashville, Tennessee. Participants in local churches committed themselves to nine months of rigorous study in two-and-a-half-hour sessions. "The study manual itself is designed for inquiry," notes Timothy Moss, director in the Discipleship Ministries Unit of the Regional Board of Discipleship and a leader in his own congregation's Disciple Bible Study effort. "It is full of questions and difficult issues. The facilitators have this manual, as well as their own guide, full of even more questions for each lesson. The training is all based on asking questions." Those who receive training take classes in which certain sections of the text are modeled by the facilitator. They learn that the facilitator does not lecture them but instead asks important questions that lead to dialogue. "This whole thing is about dialogue," notes Moss, "serious exploration based on asking questions. Participants learn to raise their own questions and reach their own conclusions." Laypersons in groups of ten to fifteen have now been trained through this inquiry process in thousands of churches. For United Methodists, understanding the Bible involves clear thinking. "The best way to cultivate this kind of thinking," notes Moss, "is to get people asking questions."

Is it really possible to train people to ask questions and to become good (or at least better) thinkers? Are not good thinkers born, and would it not be better to focus on finding them rather than training them? Is not thinking just a matter of intelligence? Well, yes and no. Evidence for the view that intelligence and thinking ability are not the same thing is mounting. As Raymond Nickerson points out, "intelligence relates more to the 'raw power' of one's mental equipment. Raw power of intelligence is one thing, the skilled use of it is something else."[16] Researchers have come to see that thinking involves other important elements as well: knowledge (the subject one is thinking about), operations (the steps and processes used), and dispositions (attitudes or habits of mind about thinking).[17] All can be improved through learning. If thinking is something that can be done well or poorly, efficiently or inefficiently, then "how to do it better is something that one can learn."[18]

Three things are necessary for training designed to cultivate thinking skills:

• *The facilitator needs to know about thinking processes—the elements, the concepts, the rules, and the fallacies—and should be able to use that knowledge to guide inquiry.* The facilitator is on the alert for problems in the discussion and keeps in mind, as much as possible, all the points where thinking gets off track. The facilitator has mastered the common techniques for making assertions and arguments, the methods for analyzing an argument, the most common reasoning fallacies, the characteristics of creative thinking, and the aspects of dialogical thinking described below, and uses that knowledge to craft the discussion.

• *A safe environment must be created where participants can learn and practice the process of thinking without the fear of appearing foolish.* The facilitator creates an atmosphere where thinking can actually take place, by listening to participants actively, appreciating different viewpoints, encouraging open discussion, promoting participation, accepting unusual ideas, permitting mistakes, allowing time for participants to think, building their confidence, and truly valuing what they have to say.[19] The facilitator avoids making presentations.

• *The facilitator must be an active manager of the discussion.* The facilitator paraphrases, reflects back an idea, asks for a clarification, seeks agreement or disagreement among the participants, asks for another viewpoint, suggests what people seem to be agreeing or disagreeing about, and above all, raises more questions. In a classic work with a marvelous title, *Teaching as a Subversive Activity,* Neil Postman and Charles Weingartner suggest that teachers who manage a successful inquiry are reluctant to accept a single statement as an answer to a question; they encourage student-student interaction; they rarely summarize conclusions, and they usually let the lesson develop from the students' responses to a problem that has been posed.[20] The facilitator, therefore, walks the fine line between directing the discussion and letting it flow. Too much management closes down an open discussion; too little management results in a frustrating free-for-all. A good inquiry centers around debatable issues and goes somewhere. An effective facilitator knows what questions to use to launch the discussion, knows when and how to change course, and is comfortable traveling toward an undetermined destination.

Critical Thinking

What is critical thinking? How does it occur in organizational settings, and how do people learn to do it? Notice in this example how critical thinking is used and modeled at the U.S. Foreign Service Institute.

——Foreign Service Institute USA

*T*he Foreign Service Institute of the U.S. Department of State sponsors policy roundtables at its center in Arlington, Virginia, on various critical issues in foreign policy. A particular set of issues, for example, U.S. strategic interests in Caspian Baisin energy, is the focus of one session. Senior State Department policy makers and analysts take part along with senior officers from other agencies, such as the Department of Defense, the Central Intelligence Agency, and the Treasury Department, along with a number of leading experts outside government from academic circles, business, and think tanks. Some of the observers, for example, may be going to a new embassy post or to other assignments in the region, and although this is not a training program, as such, it gives diplomats and others headed to a particular region a chance to sit in and become familiar with how the issues are debated. "The format is carefully worked out in advance not to exceed three to four hours," notes Fred Hill, director of special programs, "and participants, even leading national experts, are under direction not to lecture. The purpose of the sessions is to stimulate open inquiry and to generate interagency consensus where possible."

Critical thinking employs a series of seven steps, and those who facilitate inquiry should master them.

Step 1. Assertions

What assertion is being made? Someone says or writes something, and someone else says, "Is that so?" Raymond Nickerson, the author of *Reflections on Reasoning,* provides this definition: "An assertion is a statement that asserts (states positively) something to be true. It is a claim about reality."[21] What are we to make of assertions?

Step 2. Opinions and Beliefs

Is this assertion an opinion or a belief?[22] An example of an *opinion* is "Pepsi tastes better than Coke." A skilled facilitator notes immediately that this is an opinion, a matter of taste, and that nothing will settle this dispute. A belief, on the other hand (used here as philosophers, not theologians, use the term), is different from an opinion because evidence can be called on to support a belief. If we rephrase the statement about soft drinks to read "More people in Ohio prefer Pepsi to Coke," we now have a belief, and it is possible to gather evidence (a poll of soft drink consumers would provide one kind of evidence) to support the belief. For assertions to be beliefs they need to be clear and explicit, to have some relation to a reality about which evidence can be supplied, and to be capable of being believed or disbelieved, depending on the evidence.

Step 3. Warranted Beliefs

Can the belief be supported? Warranted statements have evidence, something to back them up. When a belief has a lot of good evidence to back it up, we can call it a *factual statement.*[23] When the statement corresponds to a state of affairs, and there is good evidence for it, we are more inclined to believe it. That is why we call it a belief—a statement we believe is warranted. The facilitator looks for evidence.

Step 4. Arguments

What is the argument? In everyday use, an argument is a verbal disagreement. We say, "Alas, I had a bad argument with my spouse last night." Critical thinkers use the word *argument* a little differently: "An argument is a sequence of assertions, some of which are premises and one of which is called a conclusion."[24] More simply, an argument is a chain of statements designed to support a conclusion. Nickerson suggests some points we ought to remember about arguments: they have a purpose (to convince); they can be strong or weak; they have parts; they can be taken apart, changed, and put back together; they can have steps missing; they can be simple or complex; and they can be evaluated.[25] A skilled facilitator listens to a discussion and asks, What kind of argument is being built here? What is this person trying to prove?

Step 5. Conclusions

What is the conclusion? The first element to look for in an argument is the last one, the conclusion. What is it we are supposed to believe? Usually some words serve as clues to finding the conclusion, such as "therefore," "thus," "proves that," "as a result," or "we can conclude that . . ."[26] *Descriptive conclusions* are statements about the situation as it currently exists; *prescriptive conclusions* are statements about how the situation ought to be.[27] The argument—this company is in poor financial health—is a descriptive conclusion. The argument—this company ought to downsize by three hundred workers—is a prescriptive conclusion. A skilled facilitator listens for conclusions, the part of the argument that the maker of the argument wants you to believe.

Step 6. Premises

What are the premises? A premise is simply a statement that provides evidence.[28] Premises are warranting statements used to support conclusions, usually several. To support the conclusion—this company is in poor financial health—we would look for statements that seem to be providing evidence about financial health, such as sales, gross revenues, profits, market share, and productivity. Premises contain the facts and figures of the evidence. Note, however, that premises are debatable—they can be questioned—and because the evidence is being assembled to support a conclusion, some perfectly good evidence that might support a different conclusion can be left out. Arguments, we need to remember, are designed to support conclusions, and when we have different and opposing conclusions is when we have an old-fashioned argument, a verbal disagreement.

Step 7. Assumptions

What are the assumptions? Assumptions are statements that people already believe and are obvious, or they are statements that no one has questioned.[29] They may be used as evidence, and often are, without having been examined carefully. Sometimes assumptions are identified and labeled, and the clue is usually wording such as, "for the purposes of our argument, let's assume that . . ." Or assumptions may not be identified so that we have to find them and label them. Or, even worse, assumptions may be missing completely, not having been identified at all, and yet the conclusion depends heavily on them. Facilitators watch for assumptions because they are dangerous; they often operate as evidence and go unchallenged or unidentified.

The elements of critical thinking discussed above are easier to spot in writing, where we have a chance to go back to review and analyze the statements, but in a discussion they can go by fairly fast, and sometimes it is hard to tell what is going on.

A skilled facilitator using the Inquiry Strategy knows how to listen for the structure of the argument—its conclusion, premises, and assumptions. While participants are expressing their ideas, the facilitator is silently asking, What is being sold here? What are the reasons offered for buying it? What is being assumed?

Types of Arguments

Arguments can be inductive or deductive. They can use metaphors, or they can take the form of a legal argument. Skilled facilitators also help participants discover what kinds of arguments they are making and how to make them well.

Inductive Arguments

Inductive arguments are the easiest to understand and are probably most widely used in organizational settings. An inductive argument uses several pieces of evidence and draws a conclusion from that evidence. Edward Corbett, the author of *The Elements of Reasoning,* offers Thomas Huxley's example of green apples to illustrate induction.[30] If you pick up a hard green apple and find it sour when you bite it, you form a hypothesis: Maybe hard green apples are sour. If you find several hard green apples sour (a way of testing your hypothesis) you are ready to make a generalization (to conclude) that hard green apples are usually sour. If you try to find hard green apples that are sweet (to counter your hypothesis), but you don't find any (you miss the Granny Smith), then you are ready to conclude that all hard green apples are sour. Inductive arguments are the very foundation of most scientific research. The evidence in inductive arguments can be strong or weak depending on how it was gathered, how much of it was gathered, how it was analyzed, and what efforts were made to test the hypothesis or alternative hypotheses. Inductive arguments tend to pile up evidence, and a skilled facilitator listens to see what is being tossed in the evidence pile and how deep the pile is. Is there enough of the right kind of evidence to support this particular conclusion? Inductive arguments use evidence to lead up to a conclusion.

Deductive Arguments

Deductive arguments work the other way around. They start from an assertion and work backward. To use the green apple example again, we start with the statement about hard green apples (which serves as a premise now) and reason out from it toward a conclusion.[31]

> All hard green apples are sour.
> The apple you are offering me is hard and green.
> Therefore, this apple is sour.

The conclusion has been reasoned out from the content and arrangement of the premises. I do not have to taste the apple to know it will be sour; it is a logical conclusion. Logicians have elaborated a whole system of rules for the arrangement of deductive arguments, and these are useful, but even Aristotle, the originator of the syllogism (the form of the green apple argument above) recognized that this is a somewhat artificial construction. As a facilitator, it is unlikely that you will see people building arguments in a discussion by hurling syllogisms at each other, but you may see them using pieces of a syllogism in their arguments, what Aristotle called an *enthymeme*. An enthymeme employs just one premise and a conclusion, the other premise being implied. For example:

> Diane must be a happy employee because she's smiling all the time.

The full syllogism would be

> A worker who smiles all the time is happy.
> Diane is a worker who smiles all the time.
> Therefore, Diane must be a happy worker.

The skilled facilitator learns to spot these fragments of deductive arguments and knows how to raise the right questions about them.

Analogies

Analogies are comparisons, and an argument that uses analogies trades on the similarities of the items being compared.[32] For example, one might hear people say—being a good manager is like being a good parent. The comparison being made is between managing and parenting, and it is the manager about which conclusions are being drawn. The evidence in this case grows out of the similar characteristics, such as wisdom, experience, deep concern, ability guide, and so forth. The analogy works to the extent that illuminating similarities are found, but the analogy breaks down (as all analogies will eventually) over crucial differences. The hierarchy implied in parenting, with its potential for paternalism or maternalism, may be seen as a serious enough difference to begin to spoil the analogy. The skilled facilitator learns to spot the analogy in the argument and to tease out the similarities (which make it a good analogy) and the differences (which make it a weak analogy).

Above all, the facilitator knows that "an analogy never really proves anything . . . and can only be persuasive, never conclusive."[33]

Legal Arguments

Legal arguments employ the form used in a legal case, often referred to as the *Toulmin system*.[34] Stephen Toulmin, a twentieth century British philosopher, published a book in 1958 entitled *The Uses of Argument,* in which he laid out a system of argument that prevails in the legal profession. In every legal case there is a *claim*. A *datum* is a fact or reason that supports the claim. The datum needs *backing,* the supporting evidence needed to warrant the claim. The claim is usually not *absolute,* and it is possible, therefore, that one can take exception to the claim in the form of a *rebuttal.* The Toulmin System is interesting in that it deals with *degrees of proof.* As Corbett notes in describing the system, "the logic of the courtroom is that often cases are decided not by proven facts but by argued probabilities."[35] A skilled facilitator will note when an argument has taken on a courtroom tone.

The Building Blocks

The facilitator of inquiry also looks for the four important building blocks of critical thinking: definition, type of language used, categories, and relationships among ideas.

Definitions

When people think, they think about something, and they usually use ideas to describe what they are thinking about. Naturally, ideas are learned, and people bring with them their own understanding of an idea. For a concept like "dog," people will have a high degree of shared similarity, but their concept of "leadership" may be quite different, depending on their understanding and experience. A facilitator can help the participants become clearer about the ideas they are talking about by making definitions. The participants may not all be talking about the same thing, although they may think they are. A skilled facilitator can spot when people differ in their understanding of an idea and help them to resolve or at least understand these differences. Sometimes this means arriving at a working definition for the purposes of discussion. Making definitions involves agreeing on words that represent adequately the phenomenon being described, its *general attributes* and its *critical attributes*.

Language

Sometimes language is used metaphorically, as a poet would use it, full of image and emotion. At other times language needs to be used in a precise way, with as much direct correspondence as possible between the words being used and the reality being described. Language is the carrier of ideas, the vehicle of concepts, and the conveyer of meaning. Unfortunately, language is also often the source of misunderstanding and muddy thinking. Language can be slippery. Consider this humorous example provided by Nickerson.[36]

> Nothing is better than eternal happiness.
> A ham sandwich is better than nothing.
> Therefore, a ham sandwich is better than eternal happiness.

Note how the word *nothing* changes its meaning from the first to the second premise, thus leading to the ludicrous conclusion. Or to take the point further, how do the meanings get confused with this imprecise use of language?[37]

> He cooks carrots and peas in the same pot.

Does he cook two vegetables, or does he cook one vegetable and urinate? Critical thinkers are careful about how they use language, and skilled facilitators are alert to how problems in language usage can derail a discussion.

Categories

Clear thinkers often have to put ideas into larger bundles called categories. This involves sorting out and classifying ideas, the "what-goes-with-what" task. For example, in thinking about a new product, a planning group may need to consider market niche, materials, production factors, human resource concerns, and so forth. It may be useful to group these concerns by category, perhaps even making lists or charts. The categories are not always known in advance, and sometimes they emerge in the process of making the lists. A skilled facilitator recognizes when a group needs to use categories and provides help to participants in establishing and naming categories and then getting the particulars into the right category.

Relationships

Clear thinking also involves gaining clarity about the relationship of one idea to another or one category of ideas to another. Does one set of factors cause another so that it makes sense to think of causes and effects? Or is one set of factors simply correlated with another without a causal relationship? Is the relationship temporal or spatial, linear, circular, or spiral? Can the ideas be put into a matrix or a web? Often the participants in a discussion are too close to the material to see how it needs to be organized. A skilled facilitator can point out the importance of trying to describe the relationships among the ideas being expressed and may make some suggestions the group can test. Sometimes it is useful to make drawings to illustrate the relationships of concepts.

Logical Fallacies

Critical thinking also involves certain hazards. Scholars who write about critical thinking call these hazards *logical fallacies*. A good facilitator knows these logical fallacies very well and can spot them quickly. Usually they can be identified for the group and corrected by talking about them. This list of fallacies is not exhaustive nor is this an extensive discussion of them, but these are some of the things to anticipate and avoid.

Fallacies Involving People

Ad hominem—attacking the person, name-calling. The Latin phrase meaning "to the man" suggests an attack on the credibility or trustworthiness of the person who supports a particular position.[38]

Ad populum—appealing to the people. The argument is shaped in such a way as to appeal to the fears, prejudices, or emotional needs of the people involved, which usually puts them in an unthinking state of mind where their emotional needs take over.[39]

Association—credit or discredit by association, testimonials, or guilt by association. The argument is strengthened by associating it with the views of close friends or famous people or weakened by associating it with someone disreputable.[40]

Fallacies and Outside Support

Appeal to authority—using an expert, increasing the strength of the argument by associating it with the name or words of an authority.[41]

Appeal to tradition—justifying the present by the past. A case is made for the status quo by arguing, "we have always done it that way" or "we have a long tradition here of . . ." Although valued traditions should not be discarded lightly, neither should they interfere with examining new evidence openly.[42]

Appeal to numbers—mass support. An effort is made to show that large numbers of people approve of or disapprove of a particular idea or position. Of course, the fact that a view is widely held does not make it best or necessarily true.[43]

Fallacies Involving Language

Stereotyping—using labels. Labels are used to cover the need for deeper explanation, such as "she's uncooperative" or "he's having a midlife crisis."[44]

Glittering generalities—using showy terms, fancy jargon, or clever phrases. They may sound good but usually cloud understanding.

Equivocation—changing the meaning. Sometimes the meaning of a term is changed as a discussion proceeds, as in "nothing" in the ham sandwich example or when "blue" starts out as a color and ends up as a mood.[45]

Begging the question—restating the conclusion. Sometimes evidence is not really evidence; it is just a restatement of the conclusion, a clever way of avoiding the question.[46]

Red herring—changing the subject. Sometimes another issue is thrown in that takes the discussion off track. The term derives from an old folk custom where a fish is dragged across the trail to mislead the pursuing hounds.[47]

Fallacies and Frameworks

False dilemma—setting up only two alternatives when, in fact, there may be several.[48]

Simple explanation—failure to admit rival causes or multiple causes. Sometimes the desire for at least some explanation overrides efforts to explore and provide explanations sufficiently complex for the situation.[49]

Confusing "should" and "is"—mistaking actuality for expectation. It is a fallacy to assume that what should take place has, indeed, taken place.[50]

Fallacies and Evidence

Biased information gathering—seeking only data that support a position, rather than examining all the evidence in an unbiased way.[51]

Selective use of evidence—using only data that support a position, while contrary evidence is ignored or dismissed.[52]

Irrelevant evidence—extraneous information; information that has nothing to do with the point being argued.[53]

Fallacies and Conclusions

Overgeneralization—concluding too much from limited evidence, for example, drawing definite conclusions from one study using a small sample, the informal opinions of a few close friends, or one or two good or bad personal experiences.[54]

Hasty closure—jumping to conclusions. Some conclusions lacking enough evidence may need to be regarded as tentative, serving best as hypotheses for further exploration.[55]

Seeking the perfect solution—rejecting partial solutions. Some solution may be better than no solution at all, even though it addresses only part of the issue or may work less than perfectly. Partial solutions keep many organizations alive.[56]

Contrary conclusions—rejecting the conclusion of a poorly made case. Just because an argument is poorly made or the evidence is not the best does not mean the conclusion is not true. It may be true and just needs better support.[57]

Although critical thinking may appear to be somewhat complicated, the essence of the process is really quite simple.

In plain language, critical thinking is knowing what point of view is being presented and how it is being supported. Critical thinking is learned by having opportunities to do it under expert guidance.

Creative Thinking

What is creative thinking, and how does it fit within the larger concept of creativity? Consider this fascinating example of an effort to cultivate creativity in a corporate setting. What does it tell us about the nature of creativity?

─Norsk Hydro NORWAY

Norsk Hydro a.s. is the biggest company in Norway, and although the government owns 51 percent of the stock, it functions as a private company. With interests in magnesium, aluminum, oil and gas, petrochemicals, and salmon fishing, Norsk Hydro has been a producer and seller of commodities that someone else finishes or develops into a final product. Now there is increasing interest in products that are closer to the end user. "For example, with salmon," notes Sigbjørn Engebretsen, vice president for human resources, "the basic price of salmon is not very high and won't go up much, but if you smoke it and package it in fancy little boxes, you can sell it for a small fortune." Norsk Hydro is on the lookout for new business ideas and creative new products. To foster creativity, as part of their International Management Program, divisions establish teams for developing new business ideas or taking old businesses into a new market. Teams of five to eight people are handpicked to explore a new opportunity or challenge. "These are high-potential, talented people," notes Engbretsen, "and they are intentionally mixed together across divisions. We usually run five teams in parallel. The idea is for the team to explore seriously new business ideas." It starts with a workshop, where people get acquainted, learn methodologies for the creative process, and explore the basic parameters of the challenge. Often in defining the challenge, they redefine the challenge. Then people go back and work on this challenge for one or two months. Then they go to Lausanne (Switzerland) for a week to get some consulting help from the Institute for Management Development (IMD International). They learn to generate many proposals, select the best, and converge on one for development. After another working period they come together again for a two- to three-day workshop that ends with a presentation of their ideas. By now the ideas have been refined into a plan with goals, activities, milestones, time limits, cost proposals, and names of responsible persons. Other division chairs listen to and challenge the proposals. Then it is up to the team's sponsoring division chair to decide what to do about the proposal. Obviously, not all of the proposals can be put into effect, but some are. "This is real planning for a potentially real new business venture," notes Engebretsen, "but at the same time it is training for an organizational culture that supports adventure, risk, and creativity."

Definitions of Creativity

Each of the following definitions of creativity emphasizes something slightly different.

- "The ability to bring something new into existence" (Frank Barron, one of the earliest writers on creativity)[58]
- "The process of becoming sensitive to problems, deficiencies, gaps in knowledge, missing elements, disharmonies, and so on; identifying the difficulty, searching for solutions, making guesses, or formulating hypotheses about the deficiencies; testing and retesting about the deficiencies; testing and retesting those hypotheses and possibly modifying and retesting them, and finally communicating results" (E. Paul Torrence, respected creativity theorist and developer of the most widely used tests of creativity)[59]
- "Unforeseeable novelty" (Henri Bergson, French philosopher)[60]
- "Oppositional thinking—the capacity to conceive and utilize two or more opposite or contradictory ideas, concepts, or images simultaneously" (Albert Rothenberg, research psychiatrist)[61]
- "Cognitive activity that may result in a creative production that is perceived as new and useful" (John Feldhusen, leader in education for gifted children)[62]

We like best the definitions found in a recent book-length report of a five-year interview study of creative people whose contributions have been widely recognized. The book, by the University of Chicago psychologist Mihaly Csikszentmihalyi, is entitled *Creativity: Flow and the Psychology of Discovery and Invention*. The author notes different usages of the word *creativity* as it applies to

- persons who express unusual thoughts, who are interesting or stimulating—in short, people who appear to be unusually bright
- people who experience the world in novel and original ways, whose perceptions are fresh, whose judgments are insightful and who may make important discoveries that only they know about
- individuals who, like Leonardo, Edison, Picasso, or Einstein, have changed our culture in some important respect.[63]

The definition that grows out of Csikszentmihalyi's interview research is: "Creativity is any act, idea, or product that changes an existing domain, or that transforms an existing domain into a new one." His definition of a creative person is: "Someone whose thoughts or actions change a domain, or establish a new domain."

Clearly, Csikszentmihalyi emphasizes creative products and suggests that public recognition of these products is important. Creativity is not just a personal trait, and, in fact, the author suggests, "a creative person must convince the field that he or she has made a valuable innovation."[64] A problem exists, of course, with recognition, because recognition depends on context, taste, and the times, and it was the fate of many artists that they had to die before their work was recognized. We must distinguish, therefore, between a *novel* work, the *value* of the work as assessed by the members of the field, and the actual *influence* the work has had as evidenced by its use and incorporation into the work of others.[65]

We prefer Csikszentmihalyi's definition of creativity because it fits well with the place of creativity in organizations, where the goal is not simply to have a lot of bright and interesting people on the payroll but to hire and nurture people who will be creative by producing creative outcomes that are recognized as valuable to the organization.

The following are two examples of how creativity is cultivated for new product development:

General Mills USA

General Mills, Inc., a well-known food products company famous for its breakfast cereals and Betty Crocker baking products, uses high-level cross-functional teams to create new products. "We provide them with background on the creative process," notes Scott Weisberg, director, employee and organizational development, and then we ask them to design plans for a new product that include marketing, sales, distribution, research, and manufacturing. That's how we came up with Frosted Cheerios, and it has been a winner. Once we had the creative process in place, we were able to act quickly on a number of new products and themes related to the Olympics using our Cheerios process.

SHARP JAPAN

At SHARP Corporation, a well-known electronics company based in Osaka, Japan, even the newest employees are asked to begin thinking creatively about new products. As part of their initial orientation, they are given the challenge of creating a new electronic product that would fit SHARP. Small teams are formed to define the product, develop the marketing and advertising plan, and devise a method of explaining the product to other participants when the group reassembles. Sometimes strong competition develops among the teams to win the prize for best product. "It is just an exercise," notes Asanori Fujita, manager, overseas personnel, "but it sends the message that all employees at all levels can learn to be creative."

Theories of Creativity

Where does creativity come from and how does it work? There are numerous theories about creativity, beginning with the ancient Hebrew belief in divine inspiration and the Greek concept of the Muses, goddesses of song and the arts.

The Genius Theory

Among the earliest studies of creativity are Galton's studies of "men of genius." The idea of inherited genius dominated theories of creativity for almost a century, so much so that many people still think of creativity as a matter of genius—having it or not. Robert Weisberg argues that "the genius view is in fact a myth," a perspective that assumes "that truly creative acts come about when great individuals, on their own and independently of what has been done before, produce some great achievement in a burst of inspiration." Individuals who produce creative works may not be just the same as ordinary individuals, "but the thinking processes are not different," argues Weisberg.[66] In other words, the opportunity to do creative thinking is initially open to all; what matters is how one builds on the past yet goes beyond it.

The Association Theory

Another theory stresses *associations,* the putting together of ideas in a systematic way, especially in ways that ordinarily might not occur. The associative theory of creativity is the basis of a test developed by Mednick and Mednick called the Remote Associations Test, known affectionately in the field as the RAT. One section of the test provides three seemingly unrelated words and asks the respondent to find a fourth word related to all three. Thus for

out   dog   cat

the associated word would be "house." According to this theory, creativity involves the way associations are made, the number of associations that can be made, the selection of appropriate associations, and the organization of these in an associative hierarchy.[67]

Divergent-Thinking Theory

J. P. Guilford was interested in testing for factors involved with creativity and differentiating them from the characteristics usually used to describe intelligence. He devised a complex cube of variables called the Structure of Intellect Model (SOI). By using a statistical technique called factor analysis, he was able to study the 150 combinations of variables and reduce them to clusters of variables (factors) that appeared to be about various aspects of creative thinking.[68] Guilford named and described these factors:

- *Sensitivity to problems*—the ability to notice that a problem exists: being aware of the odd and unusual, seeing that something needs to be done, and knowing what questions to ask about it.
- *Fluency of ideas*—the number and complexity of ideas produced, particularly the ability for divergent production, that is, generating ideas that go off in new directions yet still seem plausible.
- *Flexibility*—adaptability to changing conditions, freedom from inertia, and ability to change directions; ability to reinterpret information and change meanings; spontaneity in changing one's mental set to do things differently; and ability to make transformations of a given thing into something else.
- *Originality*—the uniqueness of a response compared to the typical responses of others.

- *Redefinitions*—the ability to redefine something and change its meaning.

Guilford's original work has been refined and elaborated (by himself and others), and the factors are now generally referred to as *fluency, flexibility, originality,* and *elaboration,* the latter including the ability to flesh out the details of an idea.[69] Guilford's categories were developed into a full-blown theory of creativity by E. Paul Torrence, who also produced a series of tests of creativity that have become the most widely used measurement device for creativity.[70] Guilford's theory and Torrence's tests provide an up-to-date list of the kinds of skills, abilities, and habits of mind associated with creative thinking.[71]

The Creative Process

The idea that the creative process involves certain steps goes back to Wallas in 1945, who described them simply as "preparation, incubation, illumination, and elaboration."[72] Alex Osborn, the inventor of the brainstorming technique, lists the steps as "orientation, preparation, analysis, ideation, incubation, synthesis, and evaluation."[73] The recent research study by Csikszentmihalyi sets forth a five-stage process based on what the interview subjects described and is perhaps the best modern description of the creative process.[74] Keep in mind that Csikszentmihalyi has already expressed a strong bias toward creative products being recognized as creative by peers. The author's five categories and his descriptions of them are quoted directly as follows:[75]

- *Preparation*—becoming immersed, consciously or not, in a set of problematic issues that are interesting and arouse curiosity.
- *Incubation*—during which ideas churn around below the threshold of consciousness . . . when ideas call to each other on their own, without our leading them down a straight and narrow path.

- *Insight*—the Aha! moment when the pieces of the puzzle fall together.
- *Evaluation*—when the person must decide whether the insight is valuable and worth pursuing . . . when the internalized criteria of the domain, and the internalized opinion of the field, usually become prominent.
- *Elaboration*—working out the details, which takes up the most time and involves the hardest work . . . what Edison was referring to when he said that creativity consists of 1 percent inspiration and 99 percent perspiration.

Csikszentmihalyi warns that the steps should not be taken too literally and that the process is "less linear than recursive. How many iterations it goes through, how many loops are involved, how many insights are needed, depends on the depth and breadth of the issues dealt with."[76]

Csikszentmihalyi's position supports the old adage, "Creativity favors the well-prepared mind." He places considerable emphasis on becoming well grounded in a domain or a field as a prerequisite to creative insights. Although he is sympathetic to unconscious processes—taking time out and sleeping on it—he also points out, "A new solution to quantum electrodynamics doesn't occur to a person unfamiliar with this branch of physics."[77] The preparation and elaboration stages also appear to draw heavily on *critical thinking skills*. As Csikszentmihalyi states in describing the elaboration phase, "Under the cold light of reason, fatal flaws appear."[78]

Creative People

What are creative people like? Certainly there are stereotypes, such as deviance or madness. Earlier research produced a list of characteristics so long that it lost its usefulness. Csikszentmihalyi's interviews produced a list of characteristics full of curious con-

tradictions:[79] Creative people, he notes, have a "great deal of physical energy, but the energy is under their control." They are an odd
combination of "smart and naive at the same time." They exhibit a
combination of "playfulness and discipline," and they are "original
without being bizarre." They are a curious combination of "introvert and extrovert," capable of working for long stretches alone but
knowing "the importance of seeing people, hearing people,
exchanging ideas, and getting to know another person's work and
mind." They are "psychologically androgynous" and are "likely to
have not only the strengths of their own gender, but those of the
other one, too." They tend to be "traditional and conservative" but
also "rebellious and iconoclast." They are "very passionate about
their work, yet they can be extremely objective about it as well."
The are open and sensitive and are exposed to "suffering and pain
yet also a great deal of joy." Above all, notes Csikszentmihalyi, creative people are distinguished by their complexity, so that "instead
of being an 'individual,' each one of them is a 'multitude.'"[80]

Cultivating Creative Thinking

As with critical thinking, the cultivation of creative thinking takes
place best when people are given the opportunity to think creatively.

**Although there is a growing belief that creativity can be developed,
too much is promised by brief exercises in so-called out-of-the-box
thinking. Creativity is a complex matter and not something that
can be established in an ongoing way through a few workshop
activities.**

A report on the experience of the Creativity Research Unit of the
Manchester Business School in England suggests that one-day
programs rarely lead to follow-up work and three-day programs
produce valuable results. However, ten-day programs—where
people are adequately prepared through prior contact and formal

and informal networking and where real problems and opportunities are addressed—may produce more tangible products and changes of behavior.[81]

Based on what is known about creativity, trainers should focus on the following:

- *Preparation*—spending more time on nurturing the well-prepared mind in the subject matter field where creativity is desired, recognizing that this nurturing process is also creativity training.
- *Acquaintance*—letting participants know about and experience the components of creative thinking, particularly the skills identified by Guilford and Torrence: fluency, flexibility, originality, and elaboration.
- *Concrete projects*—having participants work on concrete projects potentially useful to the organization.

The key to creative thinking is the same as for critical thinking—asking questions. Although critical and creative thinking are quite different, employing different forms of inquiry, they are both learned by asking questions. Fluency, flexibility, originality, and elaboration are all learned through inquiry, and the facilitator's role throughout the training is to ask questions and help participants ask questions, the same kinds of questions they will ask all along the way at the various stages of the creative process: What is the issue or opportunity here? Why is it interesting or intriguing? Are any of these ideas worthwhile? What would it take to develop this?

Consider this fascinating example of how creativity training was used in working with a group of unemployed youth in Sweden. Why was the creative process so difficult, and what did the facilitator have to do to get the participants to believe that they could be creative?

—KRESAM SWEDEN —————————————————————

The Värmland County Labor Board in the region of central Sweden, contracted some years ago with KRESAM, a training provider, for job training for unemployed youth. Bengt Gustavsson said he would take the contract if it could be agreed that his job was not to help these young people find existing jobs but to create new jobs for themselves. The authorities in Karlstad found this an interesting idea, worthy of experiment, so they agreed. Bengt called together his twelve subjects, warned them that this was not school, and told them, "Start with your dream and maybe we can help you work it out." Unfortunately, they had no dreams, so Bengt's job was to help them dream. He and his colleagues gave them every creativity exercise they could think of, and every day the young people came faithfully to "play the games." Soon the young people started to get very angry with Gustavsson because he wasn't helping them to find jobs. The twelve pairs of eyes stared at him week after week, and he stared back and told them that it was not his role to find them jobs. When he told them they would have to create new jobs, they didn't believe him. After a while he wanted to tell them, "You are like they say you are." For six weeks they played the games and explored business ideas. Then one day when they were putting their creative ideas on a flip chart, the group stumbled onto the concept of selling mushrooms. Aha! (In Sweden, lingonberries and blueberries are public property and may be picked by passersby on farmland or in the forests, so why not mushrooms?) Mushrooms had never been thought of as particularly valuable—they make the milk taste bad when cows eat them—so who would want them? Some of the participants liked the mushroom idea, though, and they wanted to learn about what the market would be. Through Bengt's help they found a buyer in Italy, then another in Germany. Then they needed money. Bengt taught them about banks. They borrowed fifty thousand Kroner, and soon they had three trucks and a cooler. Then they had to locate good sources of

mushrooms and train people to pick them. After twenty weeks of training they had delivered twenty-seven tons of mushrooms to their customers. Four participants left the project to do something else, but of
the remaining eight, two immediately became by far Scandinavia's leading mushroom exporters. Last year (1997) the gross sales totaled fifteen
million Crowns. "Obviously," says Bengt, "the participants weren't very
well prepared to be creative. In fact, what I had to deal with was deeply
ingrained 'learned helplessness.' It is hard for people to have a dream if
they have never dreamed."

Dialogical Thinking

Critical thinking requires carefully reasoned steps moving systematically toward a conclusion. Creative thinking involves long
preparation, bursts of insight, the ability to see things in a new
way, and the persistence to elaborate. A third type of thinking, dialogical thinking, is necessary to reach a better understanding when
people disagree.

People who care deeply about thinking are concerned that
thinking skills can be misused. Critical thinking, in particular, can
be used for selfish purposes by those who are good at it. In Plato's
time in ancient Athens, the "Sophists taught young citizens the
social skill of how to get along in law courts and other public
forums," that is, how to reason well and get the better of the argument.[82] This use of critical thinking, to achieve one's own purposes, carries a name with ancient roots: "sophistry."

Egocentric Thinkers

Richard Paul, one of the leaders of the Critical Thinking Movement in the United States, provides interesting descriptions of the
human tendency toward egocentric thinking.[83] We all have "a side
of us willing to distort, falsify, twist and misrepresent." Paul sug-

gests that "our egocentric side never ceases to catalogue experiences in accord with its common and idiosyncratic fears, desires, prejudices, stereotypes, hopes, dreams, and assorted irrational drives."[84] Lacking extensive dialogical practice, "people from different ethnic groups, religions, social classes, and cultural allegiances, tend to form different but equally egocentric belief systems and use them equally unmindfully." We "superimpose adult belief systems on top of unreconstructed but still highly activated infantile ones." We take our "inert knowledge" and turn it into "activated ignorance," and perhaps, notes Paul, this is part of the reason why so many adults, including those in high positions, often seem to act or talk like egocentric children.[85] At the very moment when we could most profit from hearing another point of view, we get defensive and "dig in our heels," "stick to our guns," "shoot off our mouth," and do the least amount of thinking. The corrective to this egocentric tendency is to make conscious efforts to understand how other people think.

Fair-Minded Thinkers

Elsewhere, Richard Paul describes three types of thinkers: the uncritical person, the self-serving critical person, and the fair-minded critical person. The fair-minded person has worked hard at developing a set of moral virtues that accompany critical thinking skills:

- *Intellectual humility*—understanding the limits of one's own knowledge
- *Intellectual courage*—facing beliefs about which we may have initial negative emotions
- *Intellectual good faith*—being consistent and honest and trying to practice what one expects of others
- *Intellectual perseverance*—willingness to struggle with unsettled questions

- *Faith in reason*—believing that in the long run reason is best
- *Fair-mindedness*—treating all viewpoints fairly[86]

Fair-minded thinkers are dialogical thinkers. Dialogical thinking involves "dialogue or extended exchange between different points of view or frames of reference . . . Dialogue becomes dialectical when ideas or reasonings come into conflict with each other and we need to assess their various strengths and weaknesses."[87] Most of us would profit from a full remedial crash course in dialogical thinking, but, short of that, training experiences designed to help people understand another's point of view can be valuable in cultivating fair-minded thinkers.

Encouraging Dialogical Thinking

The essence of dialogical thinking is in truly experiencing the inner logic of alternative points of view.

At a minimum, this means being able to present sympathetically more than one side of an issue. This sympathetic presentation can be achieved by role playing the thinking of another. What would he or she say? How would he or she make the argument? What issues would receive the highest priority? The challenge is to become willing to enter sympathetically into opposing points of view and to recognize weaknesses in one's own point of view. In such a discussion, "people learn to experience the dialogical process as leading to discovery, not victory." To do this, participants learn to argue for and against opposing views and to critique their own views as well as the viewpoints of others. Furthermore, it becomes important in dialogical thinking to let emotion resurface as an important component of, and perhaps deterrent to, thinking and to analyze the role it is playing. The goal is to learn how to make reasoned judgments, knowing that most issues are not just a search for the facts nor are they only matters of opinion.[88] Dialogical thinking is especially well suited to ethical issues, where matters of good or bad, right or wrong, are at stake. As Richard Paul notes,

> The world does not present itself to us in morally transparent terms. The moral thing to do is often a matter of disagreement even among people of good will. One and the same act is often praised by some, condemned by others. Furthermore, even when we do not face the morally conflicting claims of others, we often have our own inner conflicts as to what, morally speaking, we should do in some particular situation. Considered another way, ethical persons, however strongly motivated to do what is morally right, can do so only if they know what that is.[89]

Ethical issues call out for dialogue—inner dialogue as well as dialogue with others. Notice how a major corporation engages its top managers in dialogical thinking about ethical issues.

—Motorola USA

Motorola has among its stated key beliefs "Constant Respect for People" and "Uncompromising Integrity," but it is not always clear how to act on these beliefs, particularly in other cultures. "As we move around the globe," notes Brenda Sumberg, director of Motorola University, The Americas, "knowing what is ethical or not may not be so black and white." To address this issue, some of the former (but still active) executives put together a pilot program on how ethics can be taught and modeled by executives. With help from Motorola's own Cultural Competency Center and the Harvard Business School, cases were developed that were rich in cross-cultural issues, for example, "Motorola-Penyang," a case about business operations in Malaysia. "When a particular event occurs," says Sumberg, "it does not necessarily produce a dilemma for the home culture, but when people from outside come into that culture and see these things happening, then, yes, this poses a dilemma for us and for the corporate culture. So then we have to ask why this takes place and what action is appropriate." The challenge for the experienced staff who lead these cases is to engage the participants in dialogical thinking about cultural differences, to get into the shoes of the people in the other culture in order to experience what they experience, and then to try to define what is "right" for Motorola in light of this.

What does the facilitator do in a discussion where the goal is dialogical thinking? Perhaps the facilitator has now met the most difficult challenge of all: to help the participants engage in a true Socratic dialogue not with the facilitator but with each other. Richard Paul suggests that the facilitator's role in this kind of Socratic inquiry is to keep raising "root questions and root ideas." Noting four types of root questions that can be asked of all beliefs, Paul provides this useful framework, quoted in its entirety:[90]

- *Their origin.* How did you come to think this? Can you remember the circumstances in which you formed this belief?
- *Their support.* Why do you believe this? Do you have any evidence for this? What are some of the reasons why people believe this? In believing this aren't you assuming that such and such is true? Is that a sound assumption do you think?
- *Their conflicts with other thoughts.* Some people might object to your position by saying . . . How would you answer them? What do you think of this contrasting view? How would you answer the objection that . . . ?
- *Their implications and consequences.* What are the practical consequences of believing this? What would we have to do to put it into action? What follows from the view that . . . ? Wouldn't we also have to believe that . . . in order to be consistent? Are you implying that . . . ?

Such discussions don't move forward in a linear way from question to question. Paul suggests more of a "criss-crossing, back-and-forth effect." Another writer on dialogical thinking, Matthew Lippman, calls it *thinking in community* and likens it more to walking, "where you move forward by constantly throwing yourself off balance. When you walk, you never have both feet solidly on the ground at the same time. Each step forward makes a further step forward possible; in a dialogue, each argument evokes a counter argument that pushes itself beyond the other and pushes the other beyond itself."[91] To practice dialogical thinking in your next meeting, try this technique: Take the side that is losing until it appears to be winning; when that side is winning, switch then to the side that is losing.

How the Facilitator Models Inquiry

As we have demonstrated, there are different kinds of thinking, and what the facilitator does will vary depending on what kind of thinking processes are taking place. The facilitator first needs to ask, What kind of thinking is this? What are the intended outcomes of this thinking process—critical analysis of assertions, creative new ideas, or better understanding of different points of view? Where is the thinking going, and what kinds of thinking skills are being cultivated through the training being used?

Having recognized these differences, however, the facilitator is best served by returning to the standard technique for any form of inquiry: asking the right questions and getting participants to do the same. But what are the right questions, and of all the questions that could be asked, how does the facilitator select the best ones? Drawing on the work of J. T. Dillon, author of *The Practice of Questioning*, and other works on inquiry, we offer these guidelines.[92]

• *Avoid recitation.* Distinguish between inquiry and recitation. Recitation usually involves asking a question for which there is a right or wrong answer. Nothing will shut down genuine inquiry like recitation.

• *Choose questions carefully.* Focus on the goal of the question. What will people learn from the inquiry, and how will a particular question move them toward that understanding?

• *Anticipate answers.* Project likely answers and what to do with them. Reexamine questions. Ask how the question worked. Would another question have been better?

• *Look for assumptions.* What are the assumptions behind a question? Assumptions force certain kinds of responses.

• *Avoid dichotomous questions.* Questions that allow two alternatives—either/or questions—will not foster inquiry. These questions can be rephrased as, Some people think X, but others think Y; what do you think?

• *Use open questions.* Open questions provide for a wide range of responses.

• *Use narrative questions.* Some questions invite a narrative response as opposed to a direct response. For example, "Where were you last Thursday?" invites a direct response, as opposed to, "Tell us what happened last Thursday."

• *Phrase questions carefully.* Questions will get different responses depending on the wording and ordering of terms.

Effective facilitators think carefully about the types of questions they ask, the structure of the question, the wording of the question, the ordering of terms, and the kinds of potential responses that can be given, and they know that the way a question is framed will have an effect on the discussion.

Questions also have answers, but answers are not, by definition, "something said in response to a question." Instead, it is better to think of *responses* to questions. Some questions get a *nonresponse*. Other questions get a *nonanswer response*. Therefore, in an inquiry it is best not to look for answers, but to look for useful and honest responses that add to the discussion. What one hopes for are responses that enrich or elevate the dialogue, including additional questions. The facilitator looks for responses that provide valuable information, definitions and redefinitions, clarifications, ground rules for evidence, identified values, workable hypotheses, creative insights, other viewpoints, and tentative conclusions.

Effective facilitators carefully monitor the answers they hear and are alert to nonresponses and nonanswers. Although they rely heavily on questions, they are not so much seeking answers as responses that contribute to understanding.

The inquiry process depends not only on carefully constructed and well-formulated questions but also on the sequencing of questions and the productive flow of the discussion. The attitude of the facilitator and the presumption and tone of the way the question is expressed will greatly influence individual responses as well as the overall climate of the inquiry. Equally important is the flow of the discussion—the pace at which questions are asked, the wait time for answers, and the time between questions. Facilitators tend to move too quickly in an inquiry and in their impatience do not provide enough time for participants to think. If thinking is as complex and difficult as it has been described to be, it will surely take time, even under expert guidance, to do it.

Effective facilitators work hard at framing and pacing questions, listening to responses, and identifying and summarizing valuable comments in order to develop a discussion that has direction, momentum, and outcomes.

To the extent that the facilitator is skillful, a model is provided for participants to try out and use in what is essentially their inquiry. The facilitator wants to train inquiry skills, hoping gradually to give the facilitator's job over to the participants, who themselves get better and better at asking the right questions and providing insightful responses. Consider this marvelous example of how question-asking spreads once people learn how to do it.

──ARIEL USA

*A*RIEL Corporation in Mount Vernon, Ohio, makes gas compressors. An important aspect of the work at ARIEL involves machining (cutting and shaping) parts. At one time machine tools were run by hand to machine each part, but today the machine tools are computerized. The process is called computer numerical control (CNC), and inside each machine tool there is a computer able to accept and remember complex orders for routines and subroutines. "They are capable of doing really amazing things," notes Skip Parker, ARIEL's training director, "and they are quite friendly once you know what you are doing." ARIEL management had to learn about each new machine, and they got some training from suppliers. They decided then to train two groups of machinists, fifteen in each group, and chose to do it largely by inquiry to help employees get into the spirit of figuring things out for themselves. Now the training is one-on-one and side-by-side, because there is a critical mass of people who know CNC and how to ask questions. Listen in to the expert training a new worker: "Okay, think about it. What happened? How did you get here? Try something else. What do you think? It is right there, read it to me now. What are you missing?" Parker adds, "It's all done by asking questions, and we don't give the answers out freely. It is amazing that when we train them that way, that's how they train the others."

Technology that Supports Inquiry

Because we have emphasized so strongly the facilitator's role in asking questions, perhaps we have forgotten what this does to participants—it increases their need for answers. Thinking is not always a matter of sitting alone in a room waiting for the lightbulb to come on; sometimes it involves actively seeking out more, better, or new information. As we have seen, assertions need to be warranted, and that means having good evidence. If creativity favors the well-prepared mind, part of the creative thinking process is gathering the information that makes the mind well prepared. If dialogical thinking involves understanding other viewpoints, sometimes it may be necessary to seek out what those other viewpoints are.

The most valuable technologies for supporting the Inquiry Strategy, therefore, are those that assist in locating relevant information—the so-called information technologies. These capabilities have increased greatly over the last fifteen years, and we can already begin to predict how these will emerge in "the road ahead." The facilitator of inquiry needs to be prepared to suggest to participants some of the many ways of finding relevant information for the topic at hand. These suggestions include the vast computerized library search mechanisms now available for books and periodicals as well as internet capabilities with the World Wide Web. Although this book is not the place for a lesson on how to search for information, facilitators should remember to suggest to their participants that the data they need may be easily accessed. A stimulating question for a facilitator to ask is: Where would you look for that? Although formal search mechanisms are valuable, many summaries of research have already been completed and are easily found in encyclopedias, handbooks, directories, and review articles. The answers to questions are sometimes also found by networking—identifying experts and contacting them by phone or e-mail. Except in cases where proprietary information may be involved, most people who know something are usually glad to share it or provide leads to other sources or colleagues.

Modern information technologies provide up-to-date resources for the information and evidence needed to conduct serious inquiry. The Inquiry Strategy is not about pooling ignorance; it is about finding out.

Combining Critical, Creative, and Dialogical Thinking

Although the three types of thinking described in this chapter can be separated for analytical purposes, they are essentially complementary, not conflicting, processes. The three types of thinking may take place side by side, intermittently, and mixed together in a particular training experience. Note, in one final example, how critical, creative, and dialogical thinking are intermingled in a single inquiry.

──ReliaStar USA

ReliaStar Financial Corporation, with home offices in Minneapolis, Minnesota, is a family of companies that provides a diversity of financial security products and services, earning major income through individual insurance, employee benefits, and life and health reinsurance. Clearly not as large as Aetna or Prudential, ReliaStar is nonetheless a major player, and one of the questions constantly before its leaders is, What do we need to do to accomplish our vision—to become a lifetime partner with our customers delivering integrated financial solutions? To address that question systematically, ReliaStar put together a SWOT team to explore Strengths, Weaknesses, Opportunities, and Threats and to envision ReliaStar's future in 2007. The company assembled a group of twelve of their most creative and visionary people to think about a set of difficult questions: What will be the characteristics of the environment in which we will be operating? What must we look like and how must we function to be successful in that environment? What actions will contribute to closing the gap between where we are and where we want to be in the year 2007? Who will our customers be? Who will our competition be? What will we sell? How will we sell? "We do some very serious critical thinking about where we are and what we have been saying about ourselves," notes Dean Hoppe, second vice president of human resources and facilitator of the inquiry, "but we also try to think creatively, to go beyond the traditional paradigms. We create a certain level of discomfort for the participants. The company is doing very well financially, but our president has said that that's when we are most vulnerable. So we take this task of creating our future very seriously. We also have to get beyond our own way of thinking and ask how the competition thinks and, most important, what the customer thinks and wants." What came out of this critical, creative, and dialogical thinking went to the eighteen most senior executives of the company, where it received another round of inquiry. "This work produced action," says Hoppe, "which included the formation of follow-up teams to address recommendations generated by the SWOT team. One of the most impressive outcomes, however, going beyond the valuable recommendations, was the education and training benefit for the participants. They learned strategic thinking processes and developed relationships of candor and trust that have led to new forms of collaboration. It was a broadening experience for the SWOT team to do this thinking together."

THE BOTTOM LINE

Organizations need clear thinkers—experts in critical, creative, and dialogical thinking. These skills can be learned, and this kind of learning is fostered through the Inquiry Strategy.

- <u>Critical thinkers</u> are good at examining arguments, and they know how to look for assertions, conclusions, premises, and assumptions. They know how inductive, deductive, metaphorical, and legal arguments work, and they understand the importance of definitions, language, categories, and relationships of ideas in doing critical thinking. They are also on the outlook for a host of logical fallacies.

- <u>Creative thinkers</u> are well prepared in a specific field and produce creative products recognized as valuable. Factors related to creative thinking are fluency, flexibility, originality, and elaboration. They know that the creative process has steps—preparation, incubation, evaluation, and elaboration.
- <u>Dialogical thinkers</u> move beyond egocentric thinking patterns and try to become fair-minded thinkers by understanding how other people think. They carry on productive dialogue with others, or an internal dialogue with themselves, to understand opposing points of view.

This kind of learning involves practicing thinking under the expert guidance of a facilitator who understands thinking processes and knows how to ask the right questions.

The Inquiry Strategy is based on philosophical writings about building supportable arguments and the process of dialogue. Theories of creativity are well established by psychologists.

Effective facilitators ask well-chosen questions, and they carefully manage the flow of the discussion through the pacing of questions. The best response to some questions is a question.

8

The Mental Models Strategy
Problem Solving and Decision Making

Complex systems tend to produce novel problems ...
Novel problems are those that are not only not
anticipated but also not even imagined by those
concerned with the system ... We might hypothe-
size that the large macrosystems of modern society,
with their innumerable delicate interdependencies
and closely calibrated operating specifications, are
actually novelty generators, that it is in their nature
to throw up problems no one has seen before or
even imagined.[1]

—PETER VAILL, *Learning as a Way of Being:*
Strategies for Survival in a World of Permanent White Water

MENTAL MODELS STRATEGY OVERVIEW

BEST USE
Developing and refining problem-solving and decision-making skills.

LEARNING THEORY
Classical and modern problem solving and decision theory.

HISTORICAL ROOTS
Newall and Simon's basic problem-solving model and
Pascal's expected utility-decision theory.

APPLICATIONS
A wide variety of problem-solving and decision-making situations
in organizational settings.

PARTICIPANT ROLES
Involves participants in selecting, using, and monitoring various mental models
to manage cognitive overload and applying them to cases or projects.

NATURE OF MOTIVATION
Intrinsic desire to resolve problems satisfactorily and make decisions
that have positive consequences.

PARTICIPANT FIT
Best for participants who are analytical and persistent and have a
good capacity for monitoring their own cognitive processes.

FACILITATOR'S ROLE
Provides familiarity with problem-solving and decision-making techniques
and uses cases and projects to allow participants to practice.

STRENGTHS
Provides sufficient complexity and challenge to engage participants in
lively discussion and genuine search for solutions. Often provides opportunity
to work on real cases or projects of some realizable value.

WEAKNESSES
Is time consuming and potentially frustrating. Suffers from breakdowns
in participation and "let me out of here" avoidance. Requires analytic ability,
patience, and persistence not always in good supply.

Problem Solving and Decision Making in Organizations

Most organizations have recurring problems, but problem solving in organizations can be thought of in much broader terms than the short list of nettlesome difficulties that occur day to day. Organizational life may be thought of as "an ongoing process of problem finding, problem solving, and solution implementation activity. Problems can be current or future changes, trends, challenges, and opportunities as well as things that are going wrong."[2] Problems can be ordinary or novel. Seen in this way, problems—big and small—are everywhere in organizational settings, and problem solving and decision making can be used in a wide range of activities.

Consider how problem solving and decision making appear as areas for training in the following organizations:

- At Sumitomo Metals, workers in *jishu kanri* (self-control) groups learn problem-solving techniques, and upper-level managers are trained in problem solving through cases and projects.

- At Ford, problem solving and decision making is taught through the Global 8D Model.

- Military police trainees at Lackland Air Force Base use high-tech laser equipment to practice decision making about when to shoot or hold fire.

- Workers at BOSCH develop problem-solving skills and apply them to real problems in project settings.

- Marketing cells at USIMINAS use problem-solving skills to learn how to help customers to buy USIMINAS products.

- At Deloitte & Touche, new recruits learn problem solving and decision making through cases based on real clients.

- At Quaker Oats, participants are given extensive training on problem-solving techniques and use these on problems they bring from their work settings.

Problems and Decisions

A problem is a question proposed for solution or discussion, usually a matter involving doubt, uncertainty, or difficulty.

Diane Halpern cites a classic example of a problem:

Suppose you are driving alone at night on a long, dark stretch of freeway that is infrequently traveled when you suddenly hear the familiar "thump-thump" of a flat tire. You pull onto the shoulder of the road to begin the unpleasant task of changing a tire, illuminated only by the light of the moon and a small flashlight. Carefully, you remove the lug nuts and place them in a hubcap by the roadside. A speeding motorist whizzes past you hitting the hubcap and scattering the lugnuts across the dark freeway and out of sight. Here you sit, spare tire in hand, a flat tire propped against the car and no lug nuts, on a dark and lonely stretch of freeway. To make matters worse, a cold rain is beginning to fall. What would you do?[3]

The problem is classic in many respects. There is a *desired outcome* at the center of it: Get the spare tire on the wheel. There is *information given* in the problem—some of it relevant, some not. The loss of the lug nuts makes the situation *problematic,* and the problem may have to be *recast* or worked on *systematically* to arrive at a *solution.* How can the problem be solved? What kind of problem is it? Have we seen any problems like this before?

Halpern reports that one of her students claims to have had this problem occur in another setting, during the daytime, with the following resolution:

The flat tire occurred alongside a large mental institution near our college. While the hapless motorist sat pondering his problem, he attracted the attention of several residents of the institution, who gathered near the motorist along the chain link fence that separated them. One resident offered this solution to the motorist's problem: Remove one lug nut from each of the other tires and use the lug nuts to attach the spare. Each tire should hold securely with three lug nuts until the motorist reaches a gas station. The grateful motorist thanked the institution resident and then asked, "How'd you think of such a good solution to this problem?" The resident replied, "I'm not dumb, I'm just crazy."[4]

And so it is with us who work in organizations—we may be crazy, but we are not dumb. There are ways to solve our problems by using mental models.

Problems are different from decisions. People make decisions by selecting among choices about what course of action is best. Because decisions involve values and feelings, it is natural that people will disagree about them. Decisions arouse partisan feelings, and, in fact, that is usually a good test of whether something is a decision or problem.[5]

Problem solving is focused on generating solutions that will make a change for the better. Problem solvers make recommendations; they say how they think a particular problem can be addressed with a particular solution. Then it is up to decision makers to decide what to do.

Once the solution to the lug nut problem has been offered, someone still has to decide whether that is the preferred solution and what probability it has of succeeding.

Why Use Mental Models?

Most problem solving and decision making gets complicated. The more influences (variables) relevant to the situation, the more difficult it is to keep them all straight. Picture the juggler keeping all the tenpins in the air, or the circus performer spinning ten plates simultaneously. Such a sight "boggles the mind" we say, and *boggle*, the dictionary tells us, is to alarm, astound, shock, or stagger. So our mind must find some alternative to getting boggled. Psychologists call this boggling *cognitive overload*. Our mind needs some system for dealing with complexity. That is why we turn to *mental models*.

We operate with mental models all the time in our daily life. Usually these are fairly simple pictures of how things work. Thomas Ward, Ronald Finke, and Steven Smith have described the concept well:

> We actively construct mental models to comprehend complex phe-
> nomena, and we use our general knowledge about the workings of
> the world to do so. We might want to understand the nature of the
> digestive process in humans, how a clutch or brake system operates,
> or why the sun, moon, and stars appear and disappear in a consis-
> tent sequence. The mental pictures we form of the component
> parts of these systems and how those parts interact are called men-
> tal models.[6]

For all kinds of complex phenomena, we develop mental models of how they work. When we use mental models, "they allow us to set up hypothetical situations, make predictions about outcomes, and mentally 'run' the model to test those predictions."[7]

Most expert problem solvers use mental models to proceed through the various steps involved in solving the problem. Decision makers use mental models to weigh the factors in a decision and to predict likely outcomes.

The first step in making a mental model is to generate some sort of mental image of the situation. Consider what is meant by "making mental images." Which of the following dogs have ears that stick up above the head: German shepherd, beagle, cocker spaniel, or fox terrier? When people are asked how they think about that, they report that they try to picture the dogs and visualize the ears. People generally do not approach this question verbally because no one has ever had to memorize a list such as shepherd-up, beagle-down, and so on.[8]

This simple process of making and manipulating images is the foundation of the Mental Models Strategy.

What we are calling mental models are sometimes referred to by other names. They may be called *mental tactics, languages, programs, strategies* or even *tools.* The important point is not what they are called but how they function as tools for problem solving and decision making. As David Strauss notes, "Just as we use physical tools for physical tasks, we employ conceptual tools for conceptual tasks. To familiarize yourself with a tool, you may experiment with it, test it in different situations, and evaluate its usefulness."[9] Mental models are also referred to sometimes as *heuristics* or "rules of thumb." From the Greek word *heuriskin,* meaning "serving to discover," heuristics are general rules, guidelines, or models that may be useful in discovering solutions to problems. No one can guarantee that using mental models will help people solve problems, but at least the likelihood is increased. One might say, mental models are better than a boggled mind.

Origins of the Mental Models Strategy

The mental models theory has a fascinating history. As with behavioral psychology, some of the early research was done with animals. The classic experiments were done by Wolfgang Köhler with monkeys. Köhler devised a series of ingenious experiments with a caged chimpanzee named Sultan. The experiments involved

Sultan's solving the problem of reaching a banana tied high in his cage. Sometimes he was given two sticks that needed to be fitted together, sometimes boxes had to be piled on top of each other, and sometimes he was given a combination of sticks and boxes. As Köhler observed the behavior closely, he noticed that after some period of puzzlement and frustration, the chimp appeared to be "thinking it out." Some insight would come, and then he would pile up the boxes, climb up, and use the stick to reach the banana. After many observations of this behavior with Sultan and other chimps, Köhler concluded that problem solving, even in animals, involves some "mental manipulation of operations toward a goal solution"—an insight that goes beyond trial and error.[10] Were Köhler's chimps using mental models?

The modern history of problem solving begins with the work of Karl Duncker in 1945. Following the approach of Köhler and other Gestalt psychologists in Germany, Duncker asked his subjects to think aloud as they attempted to solve problems so that he could trace their reasoning processes and cognitive states. Duncker discovered that there was a close connection between the way subjects represented the problem to themselves and the accuracy of their solutions.[11] One of the classic treatises on problem solving, also from the 1940s, is the work of George Polya, entitled *How to Solve It*.[12] Polya was a famous mathematician born in Hungary in 1887, who began teaching at Stanford University in 1940. He brought into common use the term *heuristic*.[13] Perhaps the most cited contribution to the theory of problem solving is Allan Newell and Herbert Simon's general model of problem solving, first published in 1972 in their book *Human Problem Solving*. They coined the terms *goal state*, *initial state*, and *problem space*, now referred to in almost every text on problem solving.[14]

Decision making involves weighing choices and predicting outcomes, and it depends to some extent on probability theory. Decision making in the formal sense goes back to the philosopher and mathematician Blaise Pascal (1623–1662), who developed what some consider to be the first decision-analysis technique, which he used to weigh the consequences of living or not living the Christian life without knowing whether God exists.[15] The idea of decision worksheets for weighing the pros and cons of a decision is said to go back to Benjamin Franklin. Modern decision theory is complicated and often mathematical. A general theory of decision making, now known as *expected utility theory,* was developed by John von Neumann and Oskar Morgenstern in 1947.[16] Their theory set the basic directions for psychological research on decision making.

Training for Problem Solving and Decision Making

As with critical, creative, and dialogical thinking, there is a growing awareness that the skills needed for problem solving and decision making can be learned. Perhaps the first challenge is to convince people who think they are no good at problem solving that they can improve. Frustrated by years of struggling with homework problems, and because there was no school subject called "problems in general," many people have come to hate problems and have developed the self-image that they are not good at solving them. Without workable problem-solving strategies, they experience high levels of frustration. What they learn from their frustration is to *avoid* problems, what John Bransford and Barry Stein call the "let me out of here approach."[17] Trainers need to be able to spot the "let me out of here" participants and make sure that they experience incremental successes that will rebuild their confidence so that they can learn to be good problem solvers and decision makers.

At the very minimum, sound approaches to teaching problem solving and decision making involve a clear understanding of what those processes involve and the theory behind them.

There is no other area, except perhaps creativity, where people are so eager to provide packaged, formulaic training programs full of easy answers. It is important to let participants in training know how problem solving and decision making actually work: what the basic processes involve, what the steps are, what the theories are, and what mental models are useful for generating good problem solutions and satisfying decisions. It is also important for participants to know that problem solving and decision making, like creative thinking, are improved through domain-specific knowledge, that is, knowing well a particular field, process, product, or service. The best thing trainers can do is to provide people with situations where they can practice problem solving and decision making.

As Alan Lesgold concludes in his chapter on "Problem Solving,"

> Practice is necessary if learning is to occur. One should invest one's effort in problem solving and not just listening to a teacher talk about it . . . The best instruction involves the student in actual problem solving, with the instructor making the process more efficient by preventing the student from pursuing wild goose chases and providing hints if no progress is being made . . . To learn to solve problems, one has to solve some problems successfully.[18]

If this is so, the role of the facilitator in training is to provide problems—either real problems or the next best thing, cases and projects—to give participants sustained opportunities to work on problems.

The role of the facilitator is to provide expert guidance to keep the pursuit of solutions on track. The facilitator gains this expertise by learning about problem solving and decision-making theories.

You will see how training in problem solving is used throughout this large Japanese company.

—Sumitomo Metals JAPAN

Sumitomo Metal Industries, with home offices in busy downtown Osaka, is a major producer of steel and steel products. As with many other Japanese companies, *kenshu,* the training of workers, is a high priority, and problem solving is an important theme around which much of their training is organized. Workers, for example, hold *kenshu kai* (training meetings) where they identify and work on problems confronting their work groups and receive training in problem-solving techniques. Problem solving is integrated into the way workers at Sumitomo Metals think about their jobs. They practice a philosophy of *Jishu Kanri* (JK) using voluntary workers' groups aimed at solving various problems. Following the principles of JK, workers meet together with their team leader, sometimes including their supervisor, to decide what problems to solve and how to approach them. "Consider, for example, a production problem of reducing the repair time of products to 50 percent of the current level," notes Atsushi Hamazaki, general manager of automotive materials. "A JK group would address this issue and try to generate solutions to the problem on its own." Workers in JK groups get training on problem-solving techniques, and sometimes staff members may give hints and clues. "All of this is part of our *kaizen katsudo,* or voluntary continuous improvement activity," notes Hamazaki, "and sometimes there is a bonus prize or a simple remembrance cup or trophy awarded to the team that achieves good results."

Problem solving is a theme that reappears in management training in other parts of the company. Entry-level personnel meet regularly in groups of ten with facilitators from two or three ranks above to consider real problems they have brought for consideration by the group. For others, those in their eighth year or more, training focuses on problem solving through cases and projects. "Managers are given problems to work on, usually not the same as their job, but related, and they are assigned advisors to guide them in their problem-solving projects," notes Hiroshi Tsubouchi of the personnel department. Managers in their ninth or eleventh years are given intensive training through cases specially developed and led by professors from Keio University, a well-known private university in Tokyo. At the very upper levels, a small group of twenty to thirty candidates are organized into problem-solving teams of six to eight members to work on projects. They do research on real management problems for six months. It is considered 10 percent of their work assignment, and they meet twice a month as a team. "What they produce is considered very seriously," notes Tsubouchi, "because upper management and the board is watching their problem-solving behavior carefully so they can pick future executives."

Steps and Stages

As with creativity, there appear to be certain standard steps that occur in the problem-solving process. Perhaps the most widely used description of the problem-solving process is the IDEAL Problem Solver developed by John Bransford and Barry Stein.[19] IDEAL is the acronym formed by the first letter of each of the steps paraphrased as follows:

- I—Identify problems and opportunities. Instead of assuming that problems are given, go out and find them, and when you do, treat them as opportunities.
- D—Define goals. Get clear about the goal or desired outcome. Different goals can lead to radically different outcomes, and clarifying goals often leads to redefining the problem.
- E—Explore possible strategies. Use general and specific strategies to generate a broad range of possible solutions.
- A—Anticipate outcomes and act. Solutions need to be weighted in terms of their possible consequences, but eventually they need to be used and tested.
- L—Look and learn. Look closely at the effects of a particular solution and learn about its effectiveness.

Some aspects of the model deserve further explanation. One of the first steps identified in most of the writing about problem solving is *problem finding*. This needs to be brought to our attention because our general orientation in life is avoiding problems, not finding them. Our parents told us to stay out of trouble, and part of the folk wisdom of our culture is "Don't go looking for trouble; it will find you."[20] Problem finding is an especially foreign concept in organizations. People tend to wait for others to find problems for them to solve rather than taking the initiative to seek them out. Important problems that cross departmental lines are often avoided ("that's not our problem").[21] The case can be made, however, that the first step in effective problem solving is to find the right problems to work on in the first place.

The middle stages of the process—define goals and explore strategies—will be discussed in detail next and are at the heart of the Mental Models Strategy. The last two stages in the IDEAL model—anticipate outcomes and act, look, and learn—appear to us to be processes more generally associated with decision making and will be discussed in that section of this chapter.

It is important to recognize that there is a process with steps and that problem solving exists within a larger context of problem finding and using and evaluating the results.

Consider a problem-solving process designed and used at the Ford Motor Company.

—Ford USA

*T*he Ford Motor Company uses a well-developed model for problem solving and decision making. In fact, the process is now so clearly defined and well-respected that other companies contract with Ford's Fairlane Training and Development Center for training in this area. The model is called the Global 8D Process—"global" because it is used all over the world in Ford plants and "8D" for disciplines. Originally sponsored by Marvin Baker, the Global 8D Process was designed to deal with problems growing out of frequently expressed customer concerns. Although Ford has many quality control systems in place and participates intensely in the quality standards movement, sometimes some aspect of a product, either manufactured or from a supplier, does not work as intended and complaints begin to surface. To give an example, an otherwise perfectly good exhaust converter system might produce a bad odor. "Now we have a problem for Global 8D," says Paul Day, program manager for North American education, training, and development at the Fairlane Center.

Without going through all eight steps, we can note that the process begins with establishing whether the problem needs an 8D review. If it does, an interdisciplinary team is assembled using people with varying kinds of appropriate expertise for addressing the problem. They use a set of worksheets and work hard at describing and defining the problem. They also ask whether it is necessary to develop an interim containment action before moving to a consideration of long-term solutions. The next step is to diagnose the problem further and define root causes and the place where the problem should have been detected. After that various corrective actions are considered and related back to root causes, and the best corrective action is selected. Plans for implementation and monitoring long-term results are produced. Interestingly, the process does not stop there. The next step is to identify how to prevent recurrence. Ford does not want to have this problem happen again. Finally, the team members are thanked for their individual and team contributions.

Each step in the 8D Process is carefully worked out with systematic models. "Rather than just doing this in your head," notes Pat Timmons, Global 8D trainer, "the process is all laid out with charts and steps. People like that because it is logical and rational and the models are appealing." For example, at the step where the problem is being described and defined, there is a chart that needs to be completed. Down the side are the words "What, When, Where, How Big," and across the top are "Is/Is Not." Thus, in describing the problem it is necessary to say what the problem is and is not. Another sheet is used to define the type of problem: Is it a special-cause (change-induced) problem where something went wrong with a process that was working well, or is it a common cause (never-been-there-before) problem where the goal is not so much to fix something as to improve it?

Actually there is one final procedure after the Global 8D Process has been completed. Ford is now developing a computerized system for recording solutions called the Lessons Learned Data Base. "It is a way of documenting the problem we have already solved," notes Day. We now have a global computer system, so that in a matter of seconds someone from Brazil, for example, could check to see whether anyone at any other Ford location has faced this problem before and solved it." The step after the last step, therefore, is to record the solution, and the step before the first step is to see whether the problem has already been solved by someone else.

"We teach the Global 8D Process where we can throughout the organizations because we like to have trained problem solvers on hand," notes Paul Day, "but we also train the members of a particular team and the facilitators." What is interesting to note about the process is that it has steps and uses mental models.

A Basic Problem-Solving Model

The classic study of problem solving, as noted previously, is Newell and Simon's *Human Problem Solving*. They provide the theory and a general approach to problem solving now represented in various texts and outlined briefly here.[22]

• *Goal state.* Most problems call for a solution. In the flat tire problem, having the spare tire on the wheel is the goal state, or even more generally, driving the car again. It is possible to observe people in organizations engaged in a flurry of problem-solving activity without first having arrived at a clear concept of the goal state, some idea of what things will be like when the problem is solved.

• *Initial state.* The conditions that are given along with the statement of the problem describe the initial state. They are what the problem solver has to work with initially. In an organization the initial state includes all the givens that people bring to the problem: conditions, boundaries, and information currently available.

• *Problem space.* The distance (gap) between the initial state and goal state is the problem space, the area within which the problem can be worked out.

• *Solution paths.* Within the problem space a number of options can be generated. Options are the potential solutions or the steps within the process that might add up to a solution. Solution paths are the ideas that people in the organization generate as possible solutions or steps toward a solution of the problem. This simple, but very useful, mental model for thinking about a problem can be diagrammed as shown in Figure 8.1.

• *Operations.* Also within the problem space, certain operations must be performed to move from the initial state to the goal state. Mental models become very useful in performing operations, because usually the operations are quite challenging.

• *Barriers.* The problem space is filled with barriers. It is not so easy to move from initial state to goal state; if it were easy, there would not be a problem. If there are no barriers, these operations might best be referred to as tasks, the algorithmic activities for which the

Figure 8.1 General Problem-Solving Method

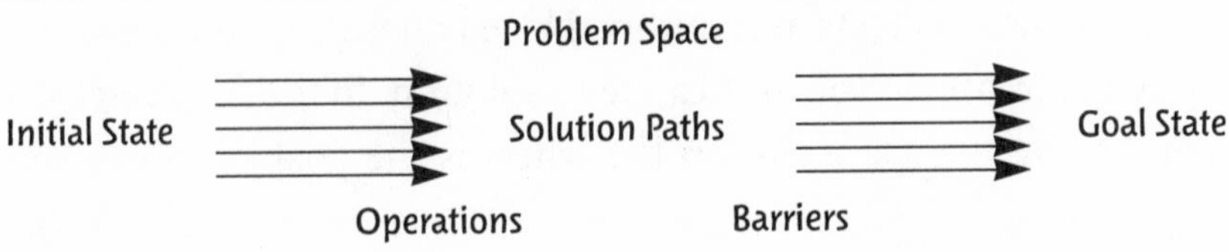

solution methods are already known. If there are no barriers, there is no problem.[23]

Newell and Simon's general framework for thinking about problem solving provides a useful model into which more specific mental models fit. Where they fit is in the problem space, and they are used for performing operations to generate solution paths.

Several rules can be applied in using the general model effectively:[24]

1. *Define the goals.* Problems seldom are stated clearly. Most problems require further definition, redefinition, and clarification of goals before seeking out solutions.

2. *Decide whether the problem should be solved.* Ian Mitroff and Harold Linstone offer this good advice in *The Unbounded Mind: Breaking the Chains of Traditional Business Thinking.* "Question whether a problem is to be 'solved,' 'resolved' or 'dissolved.' To solve a problem means to produce an exact or optimal solution to it. To resolve a problem means to seek a solution that is 'good enough.' On the other hand, to dissolve a problem is to realize that there may be some other problem that is more important to focus one's attention on."[25] Is this problem worth solving?

3. *Identify the givens.* Givens are the facts and figures, whatever information is available, as well as the factors that define the problem and constrain solutions. What part of this information is valuable, and what is really just extra, useless, or maybe even misleading information?

4. *Manage the solution paths.* The object is not to generate large numbers of solution paths, but only the right and best ones. As Wayne Wickelgren notes, "Highly skilled problem solvers . . . often have too many ideas and are forced to choose among a variety of possible approaches to a problem."[26] Which solution paths have the most promise?

5. *Do not confuse problem solving and creativity.* Problem solving, contrary to popular ideas about it, does not involve pushing the envelope or out-of-the-box thinking. "Creative problem solving" is probably a misnomer, and brainstorming is probably not the best technique for it. Generating solution paths is not so much a matter of creativity as the skillful use of mental models to produce the most promising solution.

6. *Identify the type of problem.* A crossword puzzle provides challenges that are different from a jigsaw puzzle. *Analytical* problems contain the evidence needed within the problem; *synthetic* problems require reaching outside the problem to gather new information and possibilities.[27] Some problems involve *rearrangement,* as with anagrams, where the task is to take a series of letters, ISTSCTSITA, and arrange them into a new word, STATISTICS. Other problems involve discovering a *structure* or *relationship,* as with analogy problems. Problems are classified as *transformational* when objects must be rearranged within a fixed set of rules, as in move the coin to . . . without . . . [28] *Prohibitive problems* have too many possible solutions, like the Rubik's Cube, and the challenge is to reduce the number of solution paths, hoping that the correct one can be found.[29] As Barry and Rudinow note, "Problems come in an extremely wide variety of shapes, sizes, and kinds. The specific strategies and skills one needs to be an effective problem solver are equally diverse."[30]

In the following example these rules are applied well. Note how the problem is clarified and defined, how participants are prepared, and how specific usable solutions are generated and developed.

—USIMINAS BRAZIL

*U*sinas Siderúrgicas de Minas Gerais, S.A. (USIMINAS) is a large steel-producing company with headquarters in Belo Horizonte in the state of Minas Gerais. Founded in the late 1950s with federal support under the Kubitschek Development Plan, state support from Minas Gerais, and as a joint venture with Japan under the organization name of Nippon Usiminas K.K., this big and highly successful company has now been privatized. "There was a time," notes Jarbas de Almeida Krauss, analyst of training and development, "when marketing was a matter of taking orders, and orders took up all the production." Today USIMINAS finds itself in a highly competitive international market. "We realized we had to change our concept of marketing completely," notes Krauss. "We got some help from consultants and our colleagues in Japan and developed a totally different approach. Naturally, it required training."

USIMINAS formed what it calls *marketing cells* composed of people associated with a particular client. Each cell was assigned the problem of figuring out how to increase business dramatically with that client. The training involved sixty hours of workshops on problem solving and decision making, case studies, human relations, and the latest ideas on marketing. All of this was to prepare participants for the projects to be carried out in their cells. The cells had to define the problem with their particular client, generate solutions, and make decisions about a new marketing plan. "They began to bring forward real cases from the marketing cells, which were subjected to deep and profound analysis. The solutions people began to generate were incredible," notes Strauss. The FIAT cell, for example, realized that the problem was not just to get the client to buy more but also to assist the client in some way. They discovered that FIAT could use the product better if it was already stamped out, and when USIMINAS agreed to do that, naturally FIAT wanted to buy all its steel from USIMINAS. The MANGELS cell had to show the customer how to sell its tractor wheels to a much broader South American market. "It seems a little obvious now looking back; if we could help them sell more, then they could buy more from us," notes Krauss. "But that's the way it goes with problem solving—it doesn't seem like a problem after you have solved it."

Using Mental Models to Generate Solutions

What happens within the problem space is crucial, of course, and this is where mental models come into play directly. This may be, in fact, the most important part of the process. Expert problem solvers monitor their thinking and use *normative models,* which provide the "best thinking for achieving the thinker's goals."[31] These are some of the mental models that can be used to attack problems.

Random Search

Random search is sometimes called *trial and error.* Random search works when the number of options is small. An exhaustive search involves examining every possible option on the solution path. For example, in working with the anagram THA, there are only six possible solution paths for arranging these letters: THA, TAH, ATH, AHT, HTA, and HAT. The problem solver will arrive at HAT as the solution, eventually and inevitably, even if it is last, through trial and error. This mental model works well for certain problems with few options and may even require less time and energy than a more sophisticated model, but when there are many potential solution paths and the solution paths themselves are complex and branching, something better is needed. Under these conditions exhaustive search methods become highly inefficient.[32] Think of some organizations trying one thing and then another in rapid succession, testing an idea, withdrawing it, trying another, learning primarily through trial and error. One might go so far as to say exhaustive search is not an intelligent approach to problem solving and is not really a mental model. Köhler's chimp probably did better than this when he solved the banana problem. Being aware of random search is important, however, if only to know that we are still using it when the situation calls for something better.

Systematic Random Search

This mental model consists of classifying the random search efforts, writing them down, and noticing the degrees of effectiveness that certain options may have.[33] If a large number of options are available, it may be possible to link a whole group of similar options. Some of these efforts take the randomness out of random search and make it more systematic. A systematic search is more like what we are calling a mental model.

Hill Climbing

Picture yourself blindfolded on a hill. Your goal is to get to the top. You start out in some direction, and you get some feedback from your legs that this is downhill. You try again and move in the other direction. You start moving up. The steps are small, but you can tell that you are getting closer to the goal, even though you do not know exactly where the goal is.[34] Physicians sometimes use hill climbing in arriving at the right dose of medicine for a chronic patient. The drug can be increased in small doses until the unspecified goal has been reached. In organizational settings, this is like trying to get the optimal use out of equipment without wearing it out or in arriving at just the right size sales force or the optimal number of volunteers. Unlike trial and error, there is at least some feedback in this situation as the goal is approximated.

Means-Ends Analysis

If the goal is the end, and the means for getting there are not clear, it is sometimes useful to find subgoals and then devise the means for reaching these. One might say more simply that this is a way of dividing a problem into subproblems in order to work on the easier parts first. A frequently cited example, known as the Tower of Hanoi Problem (shown in Figure 8.2) illustrates means-ends analysis.[35] The object is to move three coins of one stack (quarter, nickel, penny, with the quarter on the bottom) from the first site

Figure 8.2 Tower of Hanoi Problem

and restack them in the same order at a third site by using only an intermediary second site and moving only one coin at a time.

In this problem the goal state looks exactly like the initial state, but the rule that one may move only one coin at a time makes it a problem. The idea of an intermediary site suggests that coins can be moved there for staging. The solution to the problem is not difficult if it is taken in steps. One step toward the solution, then, is to seek a subgoal. One subgoal is to get the quarter to the third site. Another subgoal is to get the nickel and penny off the quarter so it can be moved. That can be done by moving the penny to the third site, the nickel to the second site, and the penny back to the nickel. At this point, the third site is vacant and the quarter can be moved to it. The next subgoal is to get the nickel back on the quarter. This can be achieved by moving the penny temporarily back to the first site, thus freeing the nickel to move back on the quarter at the third site. Then the penny goes back on the nickel. The point, of course, is that the mental operations required for solving the problem can be managed better by working on subgoals one at a time. Comparable types of problems in organizations, such as moving railroad cars around, scheduling flights, or working out the logistics of various manufacturing processes—might all be easier when the means-ends analysis model is applied.

Working Backward

The natural question for all of us to ask is, What should I do first? With certain kinds of problems, it may be best to ask, What should I do last? next to last? and so on, back to the beginning. The paper-

and-pencil mazes that children enjoy working are usually more easily solved by starting at the goal and working backward.[36] Working forward, each turn in the maze is a decision point, but working backward the decision points turn into inevitabilities. Once again, Diane Halpern provides a marvelous illustration:

> Water lilies on a certain lake double in area every twenty-four hours. From the time the first water lily appears until the lake is completely covered takes sixty days. On what day is the lake half covered?

Try working backward. On the sixtieth day the lake is covered. What is it like on the fifty-ninth day? Well, if the growth doubles every day, it is half covered on the fifty-ninth day. In organizations, instead of projecting out to solve a problem, it might work well to set a target date and project back. If a museum is planning to host a blockbuster temporary exhibit, working back from opening day—backward through the maze of supporting activities, publicity, and volunteer training—may be the best way to figure out what needs to be done.

Split-Half Method

Diane Halpern illustrates this mental model with a game she has invented. It is possible to guess the age of anyone under one hundred in seven guesses using this method. First, one asks the subject if he is under fifty. If the answer is yes, the next question is whether he is older than twenty-five, and so on. The next question always splits the remaining amount in half until the answer is found.[37] In organizational settings, this method is often used as a technique for locating a difficulty, such as a power outage, a cut cable, or a blocked drain pipe. To avoid tearing up the whole line, it is best to check out sections of it and, by the process of elimination, determine the spot that needs to be fixed. Some problems can best be solved through a narrowing-down process.

Figure 8.3 The Reverse Tenpin Problem

Given	Goal
•	• • • •
• •	• • •
• • •	• •
• • • •	•

Simplification

Some problems are complicated, and simplifying them, by temporarily suspending the rules or cutting down on the details, may help. Consider, for example, what Wickelgren calls the *reverse tenpin problem*, shown in Figure 8.3.[38] Assume that Susie has a bowling set, and she has set the pins backward at the end of the hall. The pins need to be rearranged from the (given) backward arrangement to the (goal) correct arrangement. Susie may have set them up wrong, but she knows how to fix it by moving only three pins.

Several actions can be taken to simplify this problem. First ask yourself if the pins have to remain in the exact same horizontal rows, or can the configuration move forward or back a row or two? If only a small number of pins need to be moved, then consider which will remain in place. Think about what pins will stay instead of which pins will move. Perhaps you can visualize a central core of pins that need not be moved. Consider what new arrangement will keep the maximum number of pins in place. Now the problem has been greatly simplified, and it may be possible to consider which pins to move. (If you still need a hint, try moving the left and right pins in the row of four back to the row of two. Then what?) In organizations, complicated problems often need to be stripped down to manageable terms.

Using Actual Data

Many problems are hard to deal with in the abstract, but they sometimes become more manageable when actual numbers or objects are used.[39] For example, consider this abstract problem:

Prove that all six-place numbers in the form of *abcabc* are evenly divisible by thirteen. It may be best first to try it with numbers

$$416416 \div 13 = 32032$$
$$258258 \div 13 = 19866$$

This example does not *prove* the relationship. Proof takes some factoring and algebra to show that the relationship will always hold, but using numbers shows that it works at least in some instances. Problem solving in organizational settings often involves plugging in the numbers to see whether a proposed solution will work or not work. A good approach to many problems is to try out a solution using real data to see how it works.

Contradiction

For some problems it is easy to get overwhelmed with the number of solution paths, and it may be necessary to eliminate some of them.[40] One way to do this is to see if the potential solutions are contradictory to the givens in the initial state or incompatible with what might be reasonably expected in the goal state. In some cases an eyeball comparison or an estimate will generate the awareness "It *couldn't* be that!" Some of the potential solutions can then be rejected, and one's mental efforts can be focused on more promising solution paths. The method of contradiction, therefore, is very much like estimating and is used to sort out impossible or absurd solutions from plausible ones. Unfortunately, not everyone is good at estimating.

When students were asked to estimate the answer to 3.04 x 5.3 and were given these responses,

a. 1.6   b. 16   c. 160   d. 1,600   e. don't know

only 20 percent of the thirteen-year-olds and 40 percent of the seventeen-year-olds got the right answer. When asked actually to compute the problem, however, 60 percent of the thirteen-year-olds and 80 percent of the seventeen-year-olds got it right.[41]

One of the best questions we can ask about potential solutions is, Could this possibly be the answer or should it be discarded?

Graphs and Diagrams

No rule says that all problem solving has to take place exclusively in our heads. Although we may enhance problem solving through the use of mental models, we might also enhance the use of the mental models by writing things down. Diane Halpern provides a good example of a problem where it is useful to make a written, visual representation.[42] We have adapted the problem as follows:

> Melvin, Brock, Marc, and Claire decide to form a babysitting cooperative. They agree to babysit for each other's children with the understanding that when one of them stays with another's children, the recipient will repay some member of the pool. The problem is that the number of babysitting hours are not always equal. They decide to tally hours at the end of the month to see who owes the pool. During the month, Melvin sat with Brock's children nine hours, Marc sat with Melvin's children three hours and Claire stayed with Melvin's children six hours. Marc babysat nine hours with Claire's children, and Brock babysat five hours with Claire's children. Who owes the cooperative hours, and who has earned extra hours that should be received?

You get the feeling immediately that this is not a problem that you can solve in your head. There is too much information—the mind will be boggled—and it looks like a diagram or chart would be useful. There are many ways to chart the information. A simple bar graph, with the name of each person and a bar showing how many hours each gave to whom, is a good start. We found it useful to create a simple diagram, shown in Figure 8.4, to show the hours given and received.

While the diagram helps, something more may be needed to get a useful answer. It is possible to tell from the chart what the

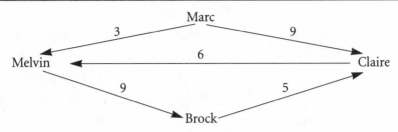

Figure 8.4 Babysitting Hours Given

Figure 8.5 Account of Babysitting Hours

	Gave	Received	Due	Owe
Melvin	+9	−3, −6	0	0
Marc	+3, +9	0	12	0
Claire	+6	−9, −5	0	8
Brock	+5	−9	0	4

giving and receiving patterns are and from there develop a simple matrix, as we did in Figure 8.5, to show who owes the pool what.

At this point, Marc is due to receive twelve hours, and Claire owes eight while Brock owes four. The basic mental model is one of debit and credit, similar to that in an accounting system. What complicates the situation and makes it a problem is the idea of a cooperative. Putting this on paper takes the mental model out of the head and helps portray individual debits and credits from the time pool.

Analogy

Perhaps the problem at hand is analogous to another. This does not mean that the two problems are similar necessarily; in fact, they can be quite remote from each other, but something can be learned from one problem that might be applied to another. In a series of clever experiments, psychologists Gick and Holyoak tested students to see whether an analogous situation in a story would provide a model that might suggest possible solutions not otherwise generated.[43] They used Karl Duncker's famous radiation problem involving a doctor faced with treating an inoperable stomach cancer. They then provided an analogous military problem of a general who needs to capture a fort. The results of the analogy experiments showed that 75 percent of the participants come up with new solutions when exposed to the analogy, but only 10 percent of the students not exposed to the analogy did so. The trick, of course, is to generate good analogies (they will not always be provided) and to have the ability to learn from them and apply them to the problem.

Selecting the Right Mental Model

Effective problem solvers think carefully about what kinds of problems they are dealing with and what models apply. It is helpful to be able to say, "Oh, this is like the Tower of Hanoi problem, and we need to work on subproblems," or "This is one of those maze problems where we need to work backward," or "This is just the babysitting co-op problem all over again."

Within organizations, certain types of problems will occur frequently, and effective problem solvers learn from previously solved problems which mental models work best. Effective problem solvers become good at spotting the similarities and differences among problems and knowing which mental models to select.

During the problem solving process it is also important to know whether the selected model is working or not and when it is time to switch to another model. As Wayne Wickelgren notes in *How to Solve Problems:*

> you may repeatedly think of the inadequate methods for solving
> the problem and get the feeling that you are going around in circles
> ... thinking of the same inadequate ideas over and over again ...
> An excellent first step in getting out of a loop and doing something

different is to analyze what you have been doing . . . rather than think about the problem itself.[44]

At a certain stage it may be important, as Wickelgren suggests, to back away from the problem itself to engage in some careful reexamination of the mental model being used, to reassess the effectiveness of a particular mental model, and to consciously select another. Effective problem solvers monitor their selections and uses of mental models—the term for such monitoring is *metacognition*—and they know how to switch effectively from one model to another.

Avoiding Pitfalls

There are certain common pitfalls associated with problem solving, things to watch out for and avoid.

Misunderstanding the Problem

Rushing to find solution paths can lead to confusion about the goal state or an inadequate reading of the initial state. Two things happen with initial-state information: when one rushes the search for solution paths, good information gets ignored or irrelevant information is regarded as valuable. The following example illustrates how important it is to get clear about the goal state and to sort out the essential from the irrelevant information in the initial state.[45]

> If you have black socks and brown socks in your drawer mixed in a ratio of four to five, how many socks will you have to take out to make sure of having a pair of the same color?

Participants do all kinds of interesting things with this simple little problem. For some reason they have trouble seeing that the goal is to get one pair of socks of the same color guaranteed with the fewest picks. They think they need two pairs or that the goal is to get the owner to reorganize his sock drawer so this problem will not exist. They make up all kinds of worries (are the socks the same size?) and rules (do I have to put each sock back in after I have taken it out?). They want to know if they can look, and then they sheepishly recognize that if they can, it will not be a problem any more. They tend to ignore the most important piece of information in the initial state (that there are only two colors), and they tend to focus on the irrelevant and misleading information (that the ratio of black to brown is four to five). The solution comes fairly quickly once the problem is understood: With some luck (and without looking into the drawer) one may draw two socks of the same color in two picks, but to be sure, one needs to make only one more pick, for surely then two socks of the same color will have been drawn. Problem-solving efforts are doomed when the problem is misunderstood.

Unrecognized Presuppositions

Presuppositions are the constraints imported to the problem from general knowledge (or lack thereof) usually without the individuals being aware of them. Presuppositions tend to narrow down the number of options within the problem space. Consider how this well-known example illustrates the narrowing effect of presupposition:

> A man and his son were away for a trip. They were driving down the motorway when they had a terrible accident. The man was killed outright, but his son was alive, though badly injured. The son was rushed to the hospital and was to have an emergency operation. In entering the operating theater, the surgeon looked at the boy and said, "I can't do this operation. This boy is my son." How can this be?

The boy can be the son if one sheds the presupposition that a surgeon must be a male; the female surgeon could indeed be the boy's mother.[46] Recognizing and discarding presuppositions allows more potential solutions to flow into the problem space.

Functional Fixedness

The tendency to employ the labels we have learned for the use of certain objects or concepts in such a rigid way that we cannot think of using them for anything else is called *functional fixedness*. A screwdriver is for twisting in screws, and it is hard to think of using a screwdriver for anything else because that is what it is for. But if we stop thinking of it as a "screwdriver" and call it a "gadget" or "doohickey," that rethinking opens up many more possible functions for it. "When the name of a thing is left open, the possibilities for using the device seem also to remain open."[47] The same is true for abstract concepts, such as "accounting" or even "training."

Expert and Novice Problem Solvers

Here is what we know from studies conducted to compare expert and novice (beginning level) problem solvers.

• Problem-solving ability, like creativity, presupposes a high level of domain-specific knowledge. As John Bransford and Barry Stein note, "research conducted during the past two decades shows that problem-solving abilities often depend on specialized knowledge in a discipline. Our ability to solve problems is not simply equivalent to a set of problem-solving skills."[48]

• Experts approach problems by structuring the knowledge needed from principles drawn from the relevant domain and from vast amounts of knowledge previously organized into chunks; they are more efficient at searching the solution space for options; they tend to construct physical models or diagrams to represent the problem, and through these representations they use complete, coherent, and specific schemas to think through the problems.[49]

• Expert problem solvers are also good at figuring out what kinds of problems they are dealing with. They have a repertoire of mental models in their head, so that when they confront a problem, they are able to represent it as a mental model and begin to compare it with other mental models they have. Expert problem solvers can represent and classify problems correctly even when they have only one-fifth of the problem, long before they have enough data to actually formulate a solution.[50]

• Expert problem solvers become very proficient at monitoring their own problem-solving efforts. Nickerson, Perkins, and Smith summarize this point well: Experts are more likely than novices to conduct an executive review of a process in which they are engaged, perhaps especially when the process seems to be getting bogged down. It is almost as though the expert has developed the ability to assume simultaneously the roles of doer and observer. He works on solving the problem and watches himself critically as he does so.[51]

Although most research on expert problem solvers suggests that they have more background in the subject at hand, studies also confirm that they handle their mental resources better than novices.

From Problem Solving to Decision Making

People in organizations are called upon frequently to make decisions about hiring and firing personnel, whether to develop a new product, when to launch a new marketing campaign, or whether to change the organization's basic purposes. Whereas problem solving requires moving through various solution paths to get to the desired goal state, decision making involves weighing various pros and cons and selecting the best (or lesser of the evils) often among many alternatives. Decision making differs from traditional problem solving in that there is usually no one correct decision; there are only options, and the task is to select the best. Furthermore, in problem solving the choice is usually known to be good or bad at the time as a result of the logic that relates the givens to the solutions; but in decision making usually some time must pass to tell whether the decision was a good one or not. Consider the Global 8D Process example from Ford once again.

—Ford USA

*T*he Global 8D Process described earlier at the Ford Motor Company actually combines problem solving and decision making. At the step where permanent corrective actions are selected, the process actually shifts over to decision making—deciding which of the proposed solutions is best and predicting how it will work. "We may change the composition of the team as we go along," notes Paul Day, program manager, "and at the decision-making phases we may pull in new people with different kinds of expertise." Because there may be a tendency to push solutions out to another department or settle on something that creates a problem for someone else, it becomes very important to weigh all aspects of the options and project the implications of selecting a particular solution.

What problem solving and decision making have in common is that they both use up cognitive capacity, the ability to juggle all the mental activities needed to solve a problem well or make a good decision. Most decisions involve many different variables and require *multidimensional comparison.*[52]

The central challenge in decision making, therefore, is to decide which and how many dimensions are going to be taken into consideration and how to weigh them. This decision-making process is where mental models again become advantageous, and this is why decision making and problem solving are considered together in this chapter: They both can boggle the mind.

Decisions can be made without the use of mental models, of course, but usually they are improved when a model is used. As John Mullen and Byron Roth note in *Decision Making: Its Logic and Practice:*

> Sometimes when you make a decision in a slipshod way, with little thought or analysis, it turns out well. That's when you thank your lucky stars. More often than not, decisions that are made badly produce bad results. This points up the fact that there is a difference between the process of making a decision and whether or not the decision produces favorable outcomes. When we say of a decision that it was smart, or reasonable, or rational, we should be referring to the thinking that went into the decision, not to its favorable outcomes.[53]

Good decisions that result from a poor process might be called guesswork. When we make decisions in organizations, there are often many other people who are the beneficiaries (or victims) of our choices, and we are acting as trustees or fiduciaries as we make decisions.[54] In organizations, therefore, it is important to follow a decision-making model and to evaluate regularly the results that model is producing.

Basic Decision-Making Model

The mental model for decision making has ten key steps:[55]

1. *Determine values.* Begin at the end of the model with values and work backward. Values are simply statements of what is desirable or has utility, and "there is no reason to think that, as a class, value claims cannot be well reasoned."[56] In decision theory, values have to do with what the organization believes is desirable—more desirable than something else—and these values drive the decision process. To avoid the word *values,* some decision models use the term *utility.* What values will this decision address? What utility will it have?

Figure 8.6 Outcomes and Values

Choices	Have Outcomes	That Fulfill Values
1	A	X
2	B	Y
3	C	Z

2. *Determine outcomes.* What outcomes will fulfill the values? The important part of this step is to align choices with outcomes that fulfill values. We have expressed this arrangement in a simple diagram, shown in Figure 8.6.[57] Some decisions are easier, and this type of decision making is referred to as *decision making under certainty.* The decision rule for these situations is simple: "Select the choice that leads to the outcome with the greatest value."[58] If you want to select the vans for a fleet and there is only one top value—best mileage—then select the van with the best mileage. On the other hand, most decisions in organizations involve several desirable outcomes and many values.

3. *Weight the outcomes.* If several outcomes are possible, they may not all be equally desirable. Some outcomes may be assigned greater weight than others. Outcomes can be ranked, or they can be assigned numerical weights to reflect importance (most important gets assigned the number 1, with lesser outcomes assigned decimals such as .80, .75, and so forth.[59] With or without numbers attached, the weighting process establishes the relative importance of different outcomes.

4. *Generate options.* Decisions involve choices among options. Options can be plans, scenarios, products, services, or personnel. Someone needs to generate the best options available. Sometimes options grow out of effective problem solving. Not all decisions have good options, and some choices are among the least damaging options. Naturally, decision making is enhanced by having a large number of suitable options.

5. *Identify attributes of options.* Options always have attributes. For example, in personnel selections the candidates all have their strengths and weaknesses. Some of these attributes may be viewed as compensatory, which means that a weakness in one area can be made up for with strengths in another.[60] Years of experience may compensate for fewer years of education, or vice versa. Other deficiencies may be regarded, however, as noncompensatory, thus providing a rule: Candidates with no college degree may not be considered.

6. *Match attributes to outcomes.* Next, the decision maker wants to examine what attributes appear to fit the outcomes. This arrangement is expressed in Figure 8.7. In a rational decision, the attributes of the options are matched to the weighted characteristics of outcomes.

7. *Make a choice.* Consider carefully the attributes of various options and how they will produce desired outcomes. Make a choice and frame the choice as a decision rule, a recommendation for action.

8. *Cast the choice as a probability and consider the consequences.* No one knows for sure how a decision will work out. That is why prediction is part of decision making, and decision rules are usually cast as probabilities. Writing in the seventeenth century, Blaise Pascal posed the essential dilemma of all decision making under conditions of uncertainty.[61] Because Pascal found it difficult to prove through philosophical arguments that God exists, he saw the decision to live

Figure 8.7 Choices, Attributes, and Outcomes

Choices	Have Attributes	That Match Weighted Outcomes
1	A, B, C ⟶	A = 1
2	A, C ⟶	B = .80
3	A, D* ⟶	C = .75

*D is a nice attribute, but it does not correspond to listed outcomes.

a Christian life as a kind of bet (now known as Pascal's Wager). If you live a Christian life and wager that God exists, you can be saved. If you don't live a Christian life, you can be damned, and so on. What is important to remember from Pascal's Wager is not the theology but how he set up the decision in terms of *probable outcomes* and *consequences*. Because outcomes are uncertain, one must ask how uncertain they are and then consider the consequences. Thus, a tension is set up between the choice and probable consequence. Decision theorists call this *expected utility theory.* How much usefulness (or potential disaster) is there in the consequence?

9. *Predict the likelihood of outcomes.* In most decision making people think the work is done when they come up with options. The hardest work may lie in trying to predict outcomes. Probability has been described as a "willingness to bet." If you are willing to bet, is the bet a sure thing or is there some risk? If there is risk, how much? That is where numbers may again come in.[62] In most decisions several variables (the attributes of options) combine to produce likely outcomes. These are the things you bet on. In making a prediction, a person looks to see which characteristics of the options are present and what their strengths are. Predictions can be made through careful measurement and use of statistics or through more subjective impressions, but the point is that somehow someone has to predict the outcomes of a decision and base those predictions on something.

10. *Align the steps.* Check the alignment of values, outcomes, the attributes of options, and actual choices. We have provided a simple mental model that portrays decision making as a loop, shown in Figure 8.8. Begin with values and work back to values.

The tendency in using the model is to focus too much on one aspect of the process, such as laying out goals and objectives or generating creative options. For the model to work, all of the steps need to be brought into play and kept well aligned.

Figure 8.8 Decision-Process Loop

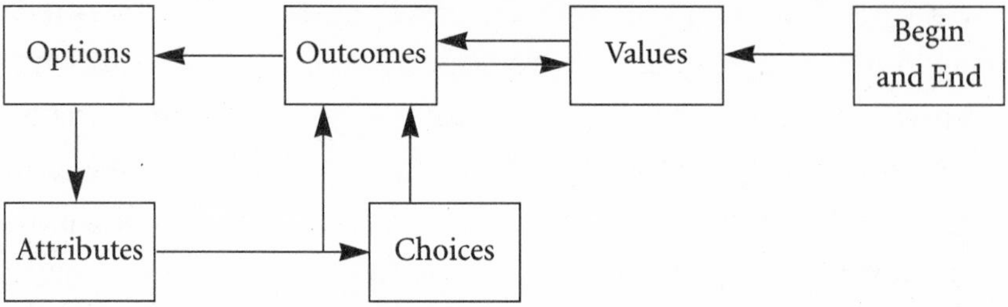

In other words, we do not get good decisions just from generating a large supply of creative options. A large applicant pool does not necessarily ensure a good hire.

Decision Protocols

Some decisions are being faced for the first time and may never occur again. Other decisions are the kind that appear again and again, and the decision process can be refined and tested. For such decisions, the process has been worked out carefully in advance and a *decision protocol* is used. Is someone using a decision protocol really making a decision? We think so, because those who use the protocol still have things to decide as they apply it. Expert decision makers use mental models to design decision protocols. How do you teach the decision protocol for shooting someone? Consider this fascinating example.

——Lackland Air Force Base USA ——————————

*S*ometimes decision making involves life-or-death choices employing the best judgment possible, and the mental models have to be worked out very carefully in advance and established as protocols. At Lackland Air Force Base—37th Training Group in San Antonio, Texas, military police from all the service branches (as well as other contracted federal agencies such as the FBI and Customs) are taught how to make decisions about when and when not to use their weapons, usually a 9 mm pistol or M-16 rifle. Participants are first taught protocols for the uses of minimum and intermediate force, the rungs of a ladder that include physical presence, voice persuasion, escort (removal from the scene), pain compliance (physical restraint), intimidation (drawing the line), and high-impact striking—all of the things to do when there is no threat of deadly force. Participants learn to make decisions about the use of each of these alternatives. When a weapon appears, however, the rungs of the ladder are no longer relevant, and a new set of decision-making procedures comes into play. "We impress upon the trainees," says Staff Sergeant Steve Delorey, "that they are now in a very different situation, and they have to shift quickly to their decision-making model for deadly force."

The trainees are taught to recognize three decision criteria for using their weapons: opportunity, capability, and intent. *Opportunity* signifies the ability to cause harm. The perpetrator's weapon is most likely a gun or knife, but could also be a hammer, crowbar, or other tool that could cause physical damage. A person with a knife, standing twenty-five feet from another person, does not have opportunity; on the other hand, someone armed with an M-16 four hundred meters away has opportunity. *Capability* signifies the size, power, and know-how to use the weapon. A small female, for example, may not have the capability to wield a large crowbar, nor will a blind person shoot accurately. *Intent* signifies demonstrated action toward carrying out a violent act. Waving a gun in the air and making threats is not intent, but arcing the arm downward toward a shooting position is. Holding a knife is not intent, but lunging forward at someone with it is. The protocol for using deadly force requires the presence of all three decision criteria.

"The decision criteria are very clear," notes Sgt. Delorey, "but it takes practice to learn to apply them, because every situation is a little different. We provide many examples and talk the students through each example so that they learn to apply the rules." After the trainees have demonstrated intellectual understanding of the decision rules, they are ready for the FATS (Firearms Training System) training room. Working in teams of four, rotating in and out of the decision-maker position, trainees watch computerized, video scenarios of actual situations where they may or may not need to use their weapon. An actual 9 mm pistol with special laser equipment is used by the decision maker, who is required to shoot or not shoot at the screen depending on the situation. "We play them sixty scenarios that cover every imaginable situation from domestic violence to snipers. Each individual is at bat for twenty examples (an optimal number derived from experience), and the computer records the performance variables: if they shot, when they shot, how well they shot, and whether they were on time and effective. For each decision there is an estimated window of one to one-and-a-half seconds of decision-making time. After each scenario, the participant has to explain and justify his or her decision. The other three members of the team join in the discussion as they review the decision protocol rules and applications. After the practice decisions, each trainee takes on five new scenarios. The trainee must shoot (and shoot effectively) when all of the decision criteria are present, and must not shoot if some of the criteria are absent. Passing is a perfect score with correct decision making and correct explanation on all five trials. "The whole system runs about $100,000," notes Sgt. Delorey, "but it really teaches good decision making."

More Pitfalls

As with problem solving, decision making has its pitfalls.

Wishful Thinking
Sometimes known as the *Pollyanna Principle,* wishful thinking is the tendency to overestimate the chances of being successful, to see the wonderful things that could happen from a particular decision, and to minimize or deny the risks.[63] Expert decision makers evaluate risk realistically, and they ask what the consequences will

be if the decision proves to be wrong.[64] It is possible to be wrong, of course, in choosing a certain option, but it is also possible to be wrong in not choosing it. Risks show up both as opportunities missed as well as blunders made. In terms of the general decision-making model, wishful thinkers tend to overvalue the attributes of particular options, exaggerate the way the options will attain outcomes and fulfill values, or overproject the utility and probability of a particular option.

Entrapment

Most decisions exist within the context of other decisions, and one decision, especially a bad decision, can affect another.[65] Sometimes previous decisions that have turned out badly have already cost a great deal in time, money, and effort. If a person, or collectively the persons in an organization, has already made a big investment, he or she constantly becomes trapped in previous decisions such that a free, fresh, rational choice becomes difficult in the decision at hand. The best way to avoid this pitfall, of course, is to separate decisions and view each on its own terms.

Trade-Offs

Trade-offs occur when we are willing to give up one outcome for another, or we forget about a weak or missing attribute because it is compensated by another.[66] The questions to be asked include these: What is being given up and how important is it? Is the trade-off truly compensating? There is also a tendency, once one trade-off has been made, to engage in others. Sometimes known as the slippery slope tendency, engaging in a series of compromising trade-offs can eventually lead to a collection of bad decisions. The *slippery slope tendency* can be countered with guidelines that set limits about what is important. In the case of a personnel decision, for example, rules can be made about characteristics of applicants that will not be traded off, even if it means starting the search all over again.

Aversion to Loss

Aversion to loss refers not to the prospect of losing, but to the loss we suffer when we have to give up something we already have. Consider the following example:[67]

> Mr. Smith buys a case of wine for $5 a bottle. Several years later he is offered $100 a bottle. Although he never buys wine for more than $35 a bottle, he refuses to sell.

Why? Mr. Smith would have to give up his wine. Even though this is a terrific opportunity and would no doubt pass through any decision-making model with flying colors, aversion to loss gets in the way. Offer Mr. Smith (before the above situation has occurred) a choice between $2,400 ($100 x 24) or a case of wine valued at $35 per bottle. Is there any question in Mr. Smith's mind now? Probably not, because he doesn't have to give up anything.

Missing Information and Uncertainty

A particular option will sometimes not be selected because important information is missing.[68] That makes sense; we want to postpone the decision to get the information, but what happens when the information is truly missing and unavailable? The tendency is still not to select that option, even though it may otherwise be a good option. At times, then, we can be unduly concerned about missing information. Lack of information and uncertainty tend to move us toward conservative decisions or postponement.

Gambler's Fallacy

In so-called wheel-of-fortune games, there is a tendency to say, "If number seven has come up twice already, it is unlikely to come up again," or "If number seven hasn't come up lately, it is about time for it." In a truly random situation, however, every number on the wheel has a chance of coming up on every spin because the wheel has no memory. Over a very large number of spins the random distribution will play itself out, but in any limited period, there is no memory for what has been played or not. This irrational tendency to impute memory in situations involving chance has been called *Gambler's Fallacy*. In organizations, probable outcomes are not likely to be random, as with spinning a wheel, but people may still think in terms of the Gambler's Fallacy.[69] Watch out for symptoms of irrational decision making, as in phrases such as, "We're due," "It's our turn," or "We've had our share of bad luck."

Misinterpreting Trends

Another pitfall associated with predicting outcomes relates to understanding trends. Trends are tricky because the trend can always change as new factors come into play. Trends are true only if all the factors producing them stay the same. Sometimes, however, trends are shaky to begin with because they are based on a limited data pool.[70] For example, there can be a trend toward 60 percent female births in a small rural hospital because the number of births is too small to average out as they would in a large metropolitan hospital. Sometimes trends are part of larger trends. There may be a trend for older women to buy more sneakers, but is that part of a trend toward more exercising in the population, part of a trend toward more informal dress, or are there simply more older women as a proportion of the total population? Projecting probable outcomes of a decision includes careful use of trend data.

Facilitating Learning Through Cases and Projects

Although some time may be spent productively in providing explanations of what mental models are and how they work, the key to unlocking the Mental Models Strategy is practice.

There is no better training in problem solving than solving problems, no better training in decision making than having to make decisions.

Although people have opportunities to solve problems and make decisions all the time, they may not get any better at those processes in the midst of the daily pressure of their job. This is where training comes in—by providing the opportunity to develop these problem-solving and decision-making skills through systematic consideration of cases and projects under expert guidance.

The idea of using cases for educational purposes, though common in the Jewish Talmudic tradition, goes back to the 1880s when Christopher Langdell introduced cases at the Harvard Law School, and Lawrence Lowell, the president who founded Harvard's Graduate School of Business in 1909, made this amazing observation about how to teach business:[71]

> The case method of business training is deemed the best preparation for business life, because the discussion of questions by the banker, the manufacturer, the merchant or the transporter consists in discerning the essential elements in a situation and applying to them the principles of organization and trade. His most important work consists of solving problems, and for this he must have the faculty of rapid analysis and synthesis.[72]

Harvard appears to have been the originator of the case method for learning about problem solving and decision making in organizations, and to this day Harvard is a leader in teaching through the case method and producing cases.[73]

Originally known also as the *laboratory method* or *problem method,* the case method is an "active, discussion-oriented learning mode, disciplined by case problems drawn from the complexity of real life."[74] Consider the definition provided by Michiel Leenders and James Erskine in *Case Research: The Case Writing Process.*[75]

The case method refers to the use of cases as educational vehicles to give students an opportunity to put themselves in the decision maker's or problem solver's shoes. Through repeated personal analysis, discussion with others, definition of problem, identification of alternatives, statement of objectives and decision criteria, choice of action and plan for implementation, the student gains an opportunity to develop analytical and planning skills in a laboratory setting. In medical analogy, the case provides the corpse for the student to practice on.

The essence of the case method is problem solving and decision making. The reason for this focus is that cases require the learner to specify solutions and courses of action. This requirement is why the case method involves discussion, analysis, and a case report.[76]

In the academic world professors have to go into organizations, find problematic situations, gather up the material, and write cases that represent the real thing. The advantage of training settings in organizations is that organizations do not need to go out looking for cases; they *are* the cases. Organizations are surrounded all the time by real material rich in problems or calling out for decisions.

Although organizations may at times turn to prepared (off-the-shelf) cases, the more real and relevant the case material, the more likely there will be significant learning.

Notice how real case material is used in the next two examples.

—BOSCH GERMANY

*R*obert Bosch GmbH (BOSCH) is a large manufacturing company well known for its automotive equipment but now also very much involved with communications technology, consumer goods, and capital goods (machinery and equipment). BOSCH has fifty-five sites scattered across Germany and numerous subsidiaries, affiliates, and foreign representatives in 128 countries. We visited with Peter Gutzan, director of training at the Feuerbach facility, on the northwest edge of Stuttgart. "We focus on solving real problems in our training at BOSCH," notes Gutzan, "and although we send people to workshops prepared by the central office on problem solving and decision making, the key to the learning is that participants return to the work setting to transfer those skills and apply them to actual problems. Eight weeks later they go back to training to report on how it worked. We try to avoid throwaway cases and projects."

Deloitte & Touche USA

The Deloitte & Touche Consulting Group is one of the world's largest auditing, management consulting, and tax service firms. They employ over 10,000 consultants and work in more than 100 countries. Their clients include more than 20 percent of the world's businesses with sales or assets in excess of US $1 billion, as well as thousands of other national and international enterprises, public institutions, and fast-growing smaller businesses. Not surprisingly, a major focus of the training of new recruits is on problem solving and decision making, and the company has available many actual cases to use in training. Of the approximately 250 to 350 new hires in any particular session, 60 to 75 percent have M.B.A. degrees and work experience, but many have no prior consulting experience.

"We want them to be 'market- and job-ready' consultants," notes Katie Weiser, global director of education, "and much of the focus is on problem solving and decision making." The training begins with data-gathering techniques—learning how to build rapport with the client and listening to what they are telling and not telling. Trainees learn individual- and group-interviewing techniques, but they also learn how to gather data about the company from external sources. They learn to do problem diagnosis and situational analysis. Trainees learn problem-solving techniques to maximize their own individual abilities, but they also learn how to pull on the strengths of others in the group. These skills are then refined and practiced on cases. Actual cases, usually with a strong financial data component, are drawn from experience with clients the company has served. Sometimes videotapes of actual clients are used. Trainees are required to draw out conclusions about the case and shape recommendations. In addition, they are taught how to sell their recommendations. "We also teach trainees about the implementation phase. We don't just write a report and leave; we have to live with our recommendations," notes Weiser. Although much of the new hire training is about company processes and culture, initial training in problem solving and decision making through the use of real cases provides a solid baseline for learning to be a consultant.

Facilitators may draw on several types of cases:

• *Traditional cases.* The traditional case provides a detailed summary of background and current information, includes descriptions of key decision makers, poses problems or asks for recommendations, and may unfold through time over several stages. In a traditional case, participants are expected to read the case ahead of time, be prepared to analyze and discuss it, and eventually report recommendations.

• *Live cases.* Another type of case, originated by Walter B. Murphy at the Wharton School of Finance and Commerce (University of Pennsylvania), is known as the live case and involves a brief written statement and a live presentation by an actual representative of the organization, someone who has lived through the case.[77] Participants provide reports on the case, which the live presenter reviews, before returning for another visit to share with students how the case actually turned out.

• *Key incident cases.* Another type of case, known as the *Pigors Incident,* involves the presentation of a key incident that stimulates questions that the discussion leader (the person with the facts) answers in some detail, thus providing the factual basis for the case.[78] Participants are asked to focus the key elements and diagram the issues, to present reasoned opinions, and then to reflect on the case as a whole, coming back to it to reconsider certain aspects.

Because some prepared cases are quite long and require much preparation time, trainers in organizational settings may prefer to supplement more traditional cases with live cases, abbreviated cases, single-problem cases, and critical incidents—all growing out of actual organizational problems and decision points.

It is only a short step from cases to projects. A project may begin like a case with a description of a problem, incident, or issue to be decided. Participants usually work together in teams on projects, going out to gather data, seeking input from key people, generating and testing solutions, and reconvening from time to time to check progress. A project in an organizational setting usually involves a real problem or preparation for a real decision, and the task takes on added seriousness because the results matter. Some projects may take several weeks to complete. Usually project teams designed for problem solving and decision making will have a project leader, a fixed schedule of deadlines, and the opportunity for regular consultation with a facilitator.

What is the role of the facilitator with cases and projects? Paul and Faith Pigors provide a list of roles that are summarized, reordered, expanded, and modified here to include work with projects as well as cases:[79]

- *Planner*—develops or selects the case or project, provides materials, and makes sure that resources are available.
- *Host and supervisor*—orients participants to the case or project goals, introduces techniques and procedures, sets guidelines, and establishes time frames.
- *Representative of group purpose*—defines and redefines the group purpose throughout the case or project.

- *Provider of factual information*—serves as a resource on the details of the case, provides additional information, or locates sources of further information.
- *Communicator*—models the communication process through effective listening, questioning, summarizing, and reflecting, and encourages others to write, speak, and think clearly.
- *Manager*—helps participants to work together, facilitates participation, and guides people in finding a useful role.
- *Technical consultant*—makes available the equipment, technologies, and resources needed to address the case or project, and presents solutions or recommendations.
- *Pinch hitter*—steps in when there is an emergency to deal with unavoidable absences or delays, or picks up someone else's role to keep the case or project moving.
- *Perennial student*—is willing to learn through the case or project along with the other participants and demonstrates a willingness to improve the case or project content and process.

The case facilitator must juggle all of these roles, playing them well and at the right time. Observe how Angie Karesh plays the facilitator role at Quaker Oats.

—Quaker Oats USA

*I*n her office in the thirty-four-story Quaker Tower, overlooking the Chicago River in downtown Chicago, Illinois, Angie Karesh, senior manager of training and development, has a cabinet full of materials developed to address specific training needs at The Quaker Oats Company, a large international producer and distributor of food and beverage products. She has a big notebook containing course materials on problem solving. "When people come for training in problem solving, we tell them to bring a real problem with them. We present some techniques for solving problems, but our basic goal is to empower them to solve their own problems," she notes. What kinds of problems do people have at Quaker Oats? "It covers a wide range," notes Karesh. "It could be process problems, such as leftover corn in the rice cake maker or crumbly tops on the biscuits. Or it might be communications problems, such as getting non–core team members to provide input to the core team or getting the big-picture perspective down through the organization."

The participants are introduced to a five-step process involving problem definition, problem verification, analyses, solution generation and selection, and solution implementation and evaluation. The training is set up in two parts, allowing participants a break for the analysis section to go back to their units for several days to gather the specific information needed to conduct the analysis, before going on to the generation of solutions. Participants are given specific exercises to complete and discuss, for example, a list of tough questions designed to bring focus to the problem definition phase: What are current symptoms of the problem? What are the desired outcomes? Who is responsible for and/or adversely impacted by the problem?

To prepare for the analysis phase, participants are introduced to two key reasons for collecting data: verification of the problem and quantification of its dimensions. They are taught to distinguish between data that measure performance (number of oatmeal tubs or Gatorade® jars per thousand with misaligned labels) and data that help in understanding causes (percent of misaligned labels resulting from poor adhesion). After a data collection plan has been developed, more tough questions are asked in order to evaluate the plan. The process continues in a similar way for the solution and implementation phases of problem solving. "We present some concepts in the beginning," notes Karesh, "but most of the training is facilitation, getting people to solve problems in a systematic way. So we set the context and give them some procedures, but they spend most of their time within their groups doing problem solving. They ask me questions, but I usually throw it back to them. They are a little uncomfortable with that at first because they are so accustomed to being told things. Also, as facilitator I just fill in the blanks from a process standpoint. They present their work to the other problem-solving teams for evaluation, and sometimes they can be tough." Angie Karesh recognizes that teaching problem solving has involved her in some new roles. "Before, I think I wanted people to believe that I was an expert; now I try to transfer this expertise back to them. I recognize them right away as experts and that sets the right climate for productive problem solving."

The role of facilitator might be likened to an orchestra conductor. After Anatol Dorati's three-year-old daughter watched her first orchestra rehearsal, she explained the mysteries of conducting to her father: "Daddy," she said, "you are the only musician who makes no noise."[80] We would not say that case facilitators and project directors make no noise, but they are very careful about the noises they make. Because their role is primarily to orchestrate the contributions of others, their task is "not so much to teach students as to encourage learning," to shed the "role and status of a center-stage, intellectually superior authority figure" and become "a member of a learning group, albeit one with a unique position."[81]

What is that unique position of the facilitator? To be the behind-the-scenes expert on problem solving and decision making. The difference between the violinist and the conductor is that the conductor knows the whole score and from it derives the tempo, the crescendos and diminuendos, the phrasing, and the color. The conductor is also able to see all of the parts in context and has a vision of how a symphony is to be played and how this particular symphony might be interpreted.

The facilitator of cases and projects also knows the score with regard to the processes used for problem solving and decision making. The facilitator of cases and projects knows about problem-solving and decision-making theory and is skillful in employing the Mental Models Strategy described in this chapter. Cases and projects are good tactics, but they become even more powerful for

learning when orchestrated by a facilitator who knows the Mental Models Strategy.

Using Computers and Telecommunications for Cases and Projects

Participants who work on cases and projects often need some way to communicate their ideas outside of the formal workshop or classroom session. Networked computers provide an excellent medium for this communication. The case can be assigned initially via e-mail as an attachment. Case participants can be asked to write their initial reactions to a case and communicate them via e-mail even before the first workshop session. Participants may be networked by a listserve so that they can communicate with the members of the group. After a class discussion, they can also communicate their insights to each other or the facilitator, raise additional questions, or offer tentative solutions to the case problems. Networked computers provide an excellent means of sharing fresh insights that may not have occurred on the spot in a training session. The same kind of networking is valuable for projects. One complaint frequently voiced by participants in projects is that they have trouble arranging times to get together. Internet communication or conference calls may provide the answer. Face-to-face group work can be supplemented with other forms of communication, which can be used to share ideas, dig out information, and provide the groundwork for a subsequent meeting.

The ultimate technological application is to put the case on the computer. This is how a well-known computer software company does it.

— J.D. Edwards USA

With corporate headquarters in Denver, Colorado, J.D. Edwards World Source Company now grosses over half a billion dollars in revenues, employs more than three thousand people worldwide, and translates its software into twenty-one language versions to serve its clients in over ninety countries. Its training activities are extensive and include three tiers of participants: its own employees, its clients or end users, and its business partners and others involved in strategic alliances with the company. The software is for big jobs, for example, tracking inventories and financial data at a pharmaceutical company or monitoring international sales across currencies for a gas company. "It's not just buy it off-the-shelf, load it, and run it," notes Susan Daly, manager of worldwide translations. "We have to work with the client, adapt it, help them to do more with it." Much of the training for implementation teams involves problem solving and decision making.

Although the training includes many aspects, the centerpiece in one program is a case, the ABC Corporation, run on computers using real software with real programs. Participants are paired on terminals, and they see such things as charts of accounts, journal entries, spreadsheets, and data bases—a lot of frames of things very much like what they will see when the software is being implemented with a client. "We throw them some data they don't know what to do with, some things that pose a problem, and they have to find a way to get unstuck. It's not just 'follow these ten steps.' They have to find solutions, and what they often discover is that there is more than one way to get there." The participants not only work in pairs on the case but also as a total team. "A synergy develops among them as they talk in the halls and share their solutions," notes Daly. "They are modeling complex reporting systems with the software, but what they are really learning through the case is how to deal with bugs, errors, and problems."

Problem solving and decision making have traditionally worked best in face-to-face groups, but the new possibilities for communication made possible through networked computers and telecommunications suggest that participants can also build these skills outside the classroom and from remote sites.

THE BOTTOM LINE

Organizational life is filled with problems, challenges, and opportunities to make good decisions. Organizations need people who are good at problem solving and decision making.

Effective problem solvers and decision makers use mental models to deal with cognitive overload—when too many ideas collect all at once and boggle the mind.

• A basic <u>problem-solving model</u> is useful for identifying the goal state, initial state, problem space, and solution paths. In the problem space other mental models are useful, such as random search, hill climbing, means-ends analysis, working backward, split-half method, simplification, using actual data, contradiction, graphs and diagrams, and analogy. Effective problem solvers avoid the pitfalls of misunderstanding the problem, unrecognized presuppositions, and functional fixedness.

•   A basic <u>decision-making model</u> is useful for describing desirable values, identifying and weighting important outcomes, generating options, noting the attributes of options, and matching these options back with outcomes and values. Choices are made and decisions are cast in terms of their probabilities of attaining outcomes and fulfilling values. Effective decision makers avoid the pitfalls of wishful thinking, entrapment, trade-offs, aversion to loss, uncertainty, Gambler's Fallacy, and misinterpreting trends.

The best training for problem solving is solving problems, and the best training for decision making is making decisions. This kind of learning is facilitated best through cases and projects.

Facilitators share with participants the useful theories on problem solving and decision making, but their main work, drawing on these theories, is to orchestrate opportunities for participants to solve problems and make decisions under expert guidance.

Problem solving and decision making without using mental models is called "guesswork."

9

The Group Dynamics Strategy

Human Relations and Teamwork

*T*he record of team performance speaks for itself. Teams invariably contribute significant achievements in business, charity, schools, government, communities, and the military . . . In fact, most models of the "organization of the future" that we have heard about—"networked," "clustered," "nonhierarchical," "horizontal," and so forth—are premised on *teams surpassing individuals as the primary performance unit of the company.*[1]

—JON KATZENBACH and DOUGLAS SMITH,
The Wisdom of Teams

GROUP DYNAMICS STRATEGY OVERVIEW

BEST USE
Improving human relations and building skills needed for teamwork.

LEARNING THEORY
Group communication theory. Learning through group interaction or team activities.

HISTORICAL ROOTS
Post-World War II research on groups, particularly the pioneering work of Mayo, Lewin, Rogers, and Bion.

APPLICATIONS
Reexamining the emotional basis of opinions, attitudes, and beliefs, and developing abilities for projects in organizations that require collaboration.

PARTICIPANT ROLES
Involves participants at emotional as well as cognitive levels and requires self-disclosure and active listening skills.

NATURE OF MOTIVATION
Grows out of natural human need for personal growth, inclusion, and recognition and is supported by peer interaction that builds involvement, acceptance, and group cohesion.

PARTICIPANT FIT
Best for participants who enjoy social interaction, who have skills in speaking and listening, and who are willing to share feelings and perceptions.

FACILITATOR'S ROLE
Composes the groups, develops the instruments or tasks that set the group in motion, monitors the group at both task and process levels, and manages the overall arrangements.

STRENGTHS
Draws on collective contributions of all participants, involves them at emotional level, and fosters active participation and cooperation in learning. Provides for human social need for interaction and allows for flexibility and group ownership of the learning process.

WEAKNESSES
Can result in social loafing by some members, avoidance of individual responsibility, conflict, apathy, or groupthink. Can be slow, inefficient, and subject to breakdown at the process level. Presupposes willingness for self-disclosure and a minimal level of listening skills. Can get out of control.

Teamwork in Organizations

Many significant human accomplishments are the result of team-work. Making films, playing symphonies, designing skyscrapers, building bridges, performing heart transplants, conducting space flights, and finding the causes of exotic diseases all involve collabo-rative teams. Many businesses that have undertaken reengineering have turned to teams to design, produce, or deliver their products.[2] Most organizations now rely on some type of team collaboration to achieve their goals.

Alas, collaboration does not always come naturally to *Homo sapiens*. Although studies of bees, ants, and geese indicate that they work together instinctively, humans often need to be trained to collaborate. For teamwork and human relations training in orga-nizations, the Group Dynamics Strategy is widely used to teach collaboration, as illustrated in the following examples:

- Sokos Hotel Ilves in Tampere, Finland, takes the whole staff "orienteering" to build a sense of belonging.

- ABC Algar in Uberlândia, Brazil, teaches workers collaboration and teamwork through stimulating group activities.

- The American Red Cross tries to build empathy and understanding through its HIV/AIDS education programs.

- Merrill Lynch brings together financial planners to exchange their best ideas on locating and working with clients.

- The U.S. Foreign Service Institute trains families, including young children, in overseas safety.

- United Airlines conducts diversity training for flight attendants serving international routes.

- The Department of Social and Health Care Services in Tampere, Finland, trains volunteers who help clients adjust to grief and loss.

- Grupo Tampico in Tampico, Mexico, provides consciousness-raising for women employees.
- COBE Laboratories conducts teamwork training for its international marketing group.
- Lackland Air Force Base uses computers to network group members in logistics training.

In all of these examples, groups and teams are being used so that people will learn something new about themselves or the process of working together.

The Benefits of Groups

Why are groups used in organizational settings? There are four main reasons.

1. *Groups are used when individual effort is insufficient.* Some work requires only the sum of the outputs of each individual. In tasks where the total output is greater than the sum of individual efforts, there is an *assembly effect.* "The assembly effect bonus is productivity which exceeds the potential of the most capable member and also exceeds the sum of the efforts of the group members working separately."[3] Groups are used to accomplish work that requires collaboration.

2. *Groups are used to generate ideas.* Research has established that groups produce more ideas. People not only pool their ideas, but there is something about the process that generates more ideas. In an early review of studies of group problem solving, it was found that ideation is 60 to 90 percent higher for groups than for individuals.[4] Try this classic problem:[5]

> A man bought a horse for $60 and sold it for $70. Then he bought it again for $80 and sold it one more time for $90. How much money did he make in the horse-trading business?

For this problem, individuals tend to present far fewer options (they close down on a single solution), and their solutions are far less imaginative than when the same individuals discuss the options in a group. There is no guarantee that groups will come up with the best ideas but they will usually generate more ideas.

──Merrill Lynch USA ──────────────────

$\mathcal{M}$errill Lynch & Co., Inc., a large financial services company, brings financial consultants to its state-of-the-art training facility in Princeton, New Jersey, for face-to-face training activities. One of the most popular group activities involves a simple sharing of ideas called Idea Exchange. Small groups are given a focus topic, such as prospecting for clients or presenting financial recommendations, and are asked to generate as many good ideas as possible. Then they select their three best and present them to the participants from the other groups.

3. *Groups are used to bring about change in opinions, attitudes, and beliefs (OABs).* "Research shows that people hold OABs that are in harmony with their group memberships and identifications." OABs are rooted in group behavior and grow out of social contacts and group affiliations; they are not simply the product of individual thinking. It is not surprising to learn, therefore, that opinions, attitudes, and beliefs are not easily changed. In a summary of some of the earliest social science research on OABs, Berelson and Steiner report that "the more a person is emotionally involved in his [sic] beliefs, the harder it is to change him by argument or propaganda—that is, through an appeal to intelligence—to the point of virtual impossibility." Again, not surprisingly, "when OABs do change, it is through the influence of a reference group, perhaps a new affiliation."[6] Groups are used in organizations to help people overcome fears, work through their reservations, reconsider long-standing beliefs, and develop more positive attitudes. Groups,

therefore, are especially useful for examining matters of the heart, what psychologists refer to as *affective learning*.

— Foreign Service Institute usa

*T*he Foreign Service Institute of the U.S. Department of State trains families who will be living abroad about how to stay safe in its Security Overseas Seminar. For children, ages six to eighteen, small groups are used for part of the training. "Sometimes children don't have much of an idea about why they need such training," says Terri Williams, coordinator of the Overseas Briefing Center, "but more likely, for children, their imagination is unbounded, and their worries are worse than the reality. We use groups to address their feelings and get rid of their worries. We also try to develop some very practical skills on what to do. For example, for a child, the best self-defense is often a bloodcurdling scream, but odd as it may seem, children who scream all the time are often too scared to scream when they should. So we take them outside, and in small groups they practice a group scream and their individual scream. The facilitator critiques the scream, and the group members provide support and encouragement. Sometimes the screaming is also a good therapy for the worries," says Williams. "Then their whole attitude about going overseas changes."

4. *Groups are used to broaden participation and cultivate belonging.* The early work of Kurt Lewin demonstrated that there is a higher acceptance of outcomes when they are arrived at through a group process.[7] Members are more likely to accept an outcome (even if they don't agree with it fully) if they have had the opportunity to discuss it in a group. In recent years an outpouring of literature on management, leadership, and organizational change has stressed the importance of involvement (participation and inclusion) in bringing about acceptance of new ideas and change. Groups produce in the participants a sense of ownership over outcomes and a sense of belonging.

—Sokos Hotel Ilves FINLAND

Sokos Hotel Ilves is one of the Sokos hotels, the largest hotel chain in Finland, with 42 hotels, 6,380 rooms, and approximately 2,000 personnel working in 26 cities. The hotel chain plans some training centrally for a particular group—managers, for example—but at other times a single hotel will provide training for its whole staff. "A big hotel can have 150 employees, and sometimes we plan things for all the employees, and they are all welcome," says Arja Rajakaltio, manager's assistant. "Out in the forest we count off into teams of seven—cooks, housekeepers, managers, accountants, bellmen—all mixed together on the same team. The activity is *orienteering,* the popular activity of northern outdoors countries, in which groups find their way from spot to spot with minimal directions and a compass. "Of course, there is beer and sausage along the way at some of the stops." Is it just a game and a good time? "Well, yes and no," says Rajakaltio. "It's designed to create a spirit of belonging and cooperation that cuts across the whole staff. It is about participation."

Groups are used for these reasons in the day-to-day work of organizations, but groups have also become a favorite of trainers for certain kinds of learning. Clearly, the Group Dynamics Strategy can have positive benefits, but as with the other strategies, it helps when trainers know the theory behind what they are doing. Clever group activities may be fun, but what should a trainer know about using groups so that participants learn from those activities?

Origins of the Group Dynamics Strategy

For centuries human beings have assembled themselves into groups for a variety of purposes and have given their groups special names, such as guilds, councils, tribunes, communes, congregations, troupes, teams, and companies.[8] Groups have also been used for educational purposes, from the small bands that followed wandering scholars such as Confucius or Plato to the medieval guilds. In modern times, groups have been used in more explicit ways for educational purposes. When did the group movement start, and who were the key leaders in exploring, identifying, and exploiting the educational potential that resides in group processes?

Interestingly, the self-conscious use of groups for educational and therapeutic purposes has its origin in *employment settings*. A classic set of research studies conducted by Elton Mayo and his colleagues at Western Electric in the 1930s revealed the importance of human factors in the productivity of workers.[9] Although the factors being studied had to do with better working conditions, such as lighting, it turned out that the personal attention being given to the workers *as a group* by the researchers proved to be the most important consideration. This discovery gave birth to the Human Relations Movement.

The movement was advanced, somewhat by accident, in 1946 when Kurt Lewin and his associates were conducting group training for community leaders. Lewin, a professor at M.I.T. and already well known for his work in group dynamics, was joined by his colleagues each evening to discuss the processes that were taking place in the groups that day. Some of the workshop participants began attending these meetings in which their own behavior and its effect on the group was discussed and analyzed openly.[10] Lewin and his associates discovered that when group members were confronted objectively with interpretations of their behavior and were encouraged to think about these interpretations in a nondefensive way, meaningful learning could occur. The staff began to theorize about what they were observing and planned ways in which group experiences could be structured to heighten this kind of learning.[11] In the summer of 1947, shortly after Lewin's death, his associates met in Bethel, Maine, to sponsor the first formal group training programs in which trainers assisted the group in discussing its behavior.[12] This kind of group became known as a *T-group* or *basic skill training group.* In 1949, Lewin's former associates formed the National Training Laboratory (NTL) under the auspices of the National Education Association.[13]

Another important historical source for the Group Dynamics Strategy is the work of Carl Rogers. In 1946 and 1947—the same years that Lewin and his associates were working in the East—Rogers and his associates at the Counseling Center at the University of Chicago were training personal counselors at the Veteran's Administration. The goal was to train counselors to become effective in working with GIs returning from World War II. In Rogers's own words, "Our staff felt that no amount of cognitive training would prepare them, so we experimented with an *intensive group experience* in which the trainees met for several hours each day in order to understand themselves better, to become aware of attitudes which might be self-defeating in the counseling relationship, and to relate to each other in ways that would be helpful and could carry over into the counseling work."[14] The Chicago groups led by Rogers focused explicitly on personal growth and differed somewhat from the training groups developed by Lewin and NTL. Eventually Rogers moved to California and became involved with the encounter group movement there. In California another strand of the group movement developed under the banner of humanistic psychology, drawing on the work of Maslow, Reich, Jung, and various eastern religious traditions. In the 1960s an independent training center, The Esalen Institute, was established in northern California, where the encounter group reached its fullest expression.[15]

Another historical source is *group therapy.* Although the idea of therapy conducted in groups dates back as far as Freud and his followers, and although the term *group therapy* seems to have been coined by J. L. Moreno in 1920,[16] the widespread use of groups for explicitly therapeutic purposes is also a post-World War II phenomenon. Confronted with numbers of disruptive patients at a veterans' hospital and inadequate resources to treat each of these patients, a group of psychiatrists and psychologists led by W. R. Bion developed a theory for treating patients in groups. Bion's work at the Tavistock Institute in London became the basis for modern group therapy techniques.[17]

As groups began to be used widely in the 1960s and 1970s, they also came to be studied more seriously, and a vast literature on group processes eventually emerged.[18] Groups have been studied from many vantage points, but most of the literature that is valuable to trainers—insights about the underlying theory for the Group Dynamics Strategy—comes from the field of *human communication studies.*

What We Know About Groups

What is known today from the research on groups and teams? Have the years of studying group processes yielded general principles and theories about what takes place in groups? Here is what is known:

Groups Have Definable Characteristics

Because it is difficult to arrive at one definition of groups that is acceptable to all, it may be best to think instead of criteria. A collection of people is likely to be a group when it possesses the following characteristics:[19]

- *A definable membership*—a collection of two or more people identifiable by name and type.
- *Consciousness of membership*—the members think of themselves as a group, have a collective perception of unity, and have a conscious identification with each other.
- *A sense of shared purpose*—the members have the same object model of goals or ideals.

- *Interaction*—the members communicate with one another, influence one another, and react to one another.
- *Ability to act in a unitary manner*—the group can behave as a single organism.

Although each group will have its own particular qualities, most groups have the five general characteristics just listed.

A Team Is a Group with a Mission

All teams are groups, but not all groups are teams. When people get together on a Friday night for square dancing, we would call them a group, not a team. A group that has the responsibility for achieving or producing something, such as a heart transplant, we would call a team. Carl Larson and Frank LaFasto, in their provocative book, *Teamwork,* define teams as follows: "A team has two or more people; it has a specific performance objective or recognizable goal to be obtained; and coordination of activity among the members of the team is required for the attainment of the team goal or objective."[20]

Groups and Teams Go Through Various Phases or Stages

It takes a while for a group to become a group, to develop an identity and become productive. One classic formulation of these stages uses four catchy rhyming words:[21]

- *Forming*—a stage of testing and member independence with emphasis on defining the task.
- *Storming*—a stage of intragroup conflict and emotional expression.
- *Norming*—a stage of development of group cohesion and establishing the rules.
- *Performing*—a stage of functional role relatedness and emergence of solutions.

Most groups go through some stages, and when old members leave and new members join, the group has to adjust.

Group Communication Focuses on Task and Process Needs

Put people in groups and they will talk. Who talks and what do they talk about? How often do they talk? To whom do people talk? Whom do they look at when they talk—one person, the group, the floor or ceiling? Who talks after whom, and who interrupts whom?[22] What is all this talk about? Many scholars who have studied groups have noted that communication seems to be taking place at two levels, often simultaneously.[23] At one level, members are communicating about the *task* to be completed; at another level, they are dealing with the *process* needs (sometimes referred to as *social* or *maintenance* needs) of the group members.

The task is the activity that a group is required to perform. The task is is what people do, what they work on, or what they produce in and through groups.[24] If a group of trainees is asked to produce a marketing plan, that is their task. Other communication is about the process. When people participate in groups, they bring with them their individual needs for recognition, identity, status, power, visibility, competition, and inclusion. All of these factors can influence the social and emotional climate of the group and the group process.[25] These factors also affect the way in which the task is undertaken and completed. It is natural and expected that participants will not be focusing their attention exclusively on the task. In theory, one may single out task and process dimensions of group behavior, but in practice, task and process behaviors are inseparable.[26]

Groups Develop Cohesion

When the process needs of the group are being met in satisfactory ways, the group becomes *cohesive.* Cohesiveness refers to the ability of the group members to get along, their loyalty, pride, and commitment to the group. Or more simply, cohesiveness is the degree of liking that members have for each other.[27] When there is a high level of bickering in a group, when members express boredom or search for excuses to avoid group meetings or drop out, the group usually lacks cohesiveness. Something is going wrong at the process level. Cohesiveness is an output of an effective group process, but once established, it is an input to effective task activities.[28] As might be expected, cohesive groups are more productive, but only up to a point. As cohesiveness increases, productivity increases until cohesiveness reaches such a high level that productivity falls off. Why? When group members become too fond of each other, they spend too much time socializing and too little time on the task. They may have a reserve productivity that is much higher than their actual productivity, because they enjoy, perhaps too much, the process behaviors that make the group cohesive.[29]

Groups Have Structure

As groups mature, passing through various stages, they eventually develop a *structure*.[30] Just as a building has a structure—foundation, walls, roof, doors, windows—so a group also has a structure, where members take their places and serve particular functions. The group's structure is not always immediately obvious. Some people, because they have more to contribute, because they have more initial status, or because they have a strong personality, take a more central place in the group's structure, while others end up on the periphery. Groups also develop different kinds of communication networks that give the group structure. The composition of the group and its patterns of communication help to determine the group structure.

Group Participants Play Roles

The structure of a group also becomes clearer as one examines the roles that various group members begin to play. In groups, roles are the "set of expectations which group members share concerning the behavior of a person who occupies a given position in the group."[31] There are many different kinds of roles that members can act out in a group. The classic delineation of these roles was worked out by Kenneth Benne and Paul Sheets during the initial National Training Laboratory meetings in 1947.[32] We have reclassified, paraphrased, and eliminated some items on the classic list in compiling the roles that appear below.

Positive Task Roles

Initiator-contributor—suggests new ideas or procedures.

Information seeker—asks for clarification of ideas, facts, or evidence.

Opinion seeker—asks for agreement or disagreement by other group members.

Information giver—offers facts or relates own experience.

Elaborator—clarifies and explains further.

Coordinator—shows relationships among ideas and pulls things together.

Orientor—defines where the group is, summarizes, keeps things on track, evaluates progress.

Energizer—prods the group to a decision or action.

Recorder—writes down suggestions, takes minutes.

Positive Process Roles

Encourager—agrees with, praises, or accepts the ideas of others.

Harmonizer—resolves conflict, mediates differences, and reduces tension, often with humor.

Gatekeeper—keeps channels of communication open, encourages others to participate and be heard.

Standard setter—expresses standards for the group to reach.

Group observer—evaluates the mood of the group.

Follower—goes along with the group trend, accepts the ideas of others, serves as audience.

Negative Individual Roles

Aggressor—attacks others, or the group, in various ways to
  promote own status.

Blocker—opposes others' ideas beyond reason and refuses to
  cooperate.

Recognition seeker—calls attention to self by boasting, acting
  in unusual ways.

Self-confessor—engages in irrelevant discussion, uses the group
  audience for expressing personal problems.

Playboy—displays lack of involvement in group through humor,
  cynicism, or horseplay.

Dominator—monopolizes the group for personal ends by
  asserting authority, interrupting, giving directions.

Help seeker—calls forth sympathy from the group through
  unreasonable expressions of insecurity or inadequacy.

Special interest pleader—represents a group to others.

Not all groups will contain members who play out all of these roles,
but this list of task, process, and individual roles can be used as a
valuable checklist of what to look for in analyzing group structure.

Groups Establish Rules

Eventually, when the roles that people play within a group become
well established, and when the structure of the group becomes set,
the group can be said to have established group *norms*.[33] As certain
behavior patterns are repeated, they become endowed with normalcy. It becomes expected that a certain member will come into
the room, take the same seat, play the same role, and participate
in the same way each time. Norms will differ, of course, from
group to group, and what may appear to be a bold and abrasive
confrontation in one group may be viewed simply as open and
direct self-disclosure in another. Eventually, however, the behavior
is established as a rule for that group, and individual members will

internalize these norms and play by the group's rules. The skillful facilitator of a group learns how to assist the group in establishing and following useful rules.

Communication in Groups

Trainers who use groups become effective observers of the communication process within the group. They become good observers of what group members say and do, particularly the quality of the listening that takes place. When a person interacts with another person in a group, a *communication event* takes place that involves self-disclosure and feedback. Self-disclosure occurs when a person lets someone else know something about himself or herself that the listener wouldn't ordinarily know.[34] This disclosure need not be a deep, dark secret (though it may be) but can refer to any idea or feeling a person is expressing. The second half of the communication event occurs when someone else in the group, or several members of the group, make a response in return. Usually this response, if it is truly a response to what has been said, and is perceived by the sender as a response rather than simply as a new disclosure, is called *feedback*.[35]

In order for this transaction of self-disclosure and feedback to take place in an effective way, *active listening* needs to take place. Active listening is sometimes further differentiated as *deliberate listening* and *empathic listening*.[36] The deliberative listener is actively engaged in trying to understand ideas, standing ready to agree or disagree, criticize, summarize, or conclude. The empathic listener is focusing on feelings, trying to understand the speaker's emotions from the speaker's point of view. Both are needed, but when active listening is taking place the feedback is likely to be more appropriate and useful than when the quality of listening is poor. Poor listening occurs when the listener becomes prematurely involved emotionally (losing objectivity), is busy mentally preparing answers (before fully understanding the disclosure), is distracted, is set off by emotionally laden words, or allows personal prejudices to interfere with understanding. Good listeners try to concentrate on listening, avoid interrupting the speaker if possible, demonstrate interest and alertness, seek areas of agreement, search for meanings, avoid getting stuck on specific words, and demonstrate patience. They also try to provide clear and unambiguous feedback and repress the tendency to respond emotionally to what is said; they ask questions and withhold evaluation of the message until the speaker is finished.[37]

Usually trainers need to assist group members in becoming more skilled as active listeners.

Not all of the communication that takes place in a group occurs at the verbal level. In recent years, new importance has been given to *nonverbal communication* and the role it plays in the total communication process. Nonverbal communication occurs in a variety of ways in groups, and sophisticated group-watchers will look for the following:[38]

- *Proxemics*—the way group members arrange themselves in space (through seating arrangements, physical distance, and general body orientation).
- *Appearance*—overall physical appearance, dress, attractiveness, style, and mood.
- *Kinesics*—body movement, postures, gestures, and movements of the head, limbs, hands, and feet.
- *Facial expressions*—facial features, movement of the eyes and mouth.

All of these ways are used by group members to further communicate their ideas, attitudes, and feelings within a group. Nonverbal communication is especially important in activities that require group members to get out of their seats and do something.

Much can be learned about people by watching what they do as well as listening to what they say.

How does nonverbal communication relate to verbal communication? Sometimes directly, by repeating or elaborating a verbal message, for example, by using a gesture to accent an important point. At other times, however, a nonverbal message may contradict the verbal message—for example, an arms-folded, tense denial of anger—sending a visible clue throughout the group that what is being said is not what is being felt.[39] In some activities, the nonverbal message is the only communication. In a sense, then, group members are always communicating, whether they speak or not, through gestures, facial expressions, or the place taken in the group.

It is not possible to not communicate because people are always sending messages and making meaning, whether they are responding verbally or nonverbally, or are doing nothing.[40]

Problems in Groups

Trainers who use groups also know how to look for, spot, and deal with four common problems of group dynamics: *conflict, apathy, groupthink,* and *social loafing.*

Conflict

Some conflict in groups is normal and even necessary. Tension, at a low level, can be a productive force that holds the group together. But when tension exceeds an acceptable threshold, and open conflict breaks out, tension can pull the group apart. Signs of group conflict include:

- expressing impatience with each other
- attacking ideas before they are completely expressed
- taking sides and refusing to compromise

- making comments or suggestions with a great deal of vehemence, and attacking one another on a personal level in subtle ways[41]

Group-watchers also look beyond individuals for the sources of conflict. Sometimes conflict arises because the group does not have enough resources or time, lacks a well-defined task, or is being influenced by outside interests. In other words, conflict also can be generated by structural problems of the group.[42] If there are structural problems in the group, if the task is ambiguous, or if the resources or time allotted are too little, then these issues should be resolved, if possible. If the conflict is growing out of genuine individual differences of opinion, standard procedures for resolving the conflict include taking a vote, compromise, mediation, arbitration, or determined efforts to reach a consensus.

The key to the successful resolution of conflict within a group is to face it, identify it, and meet it head-on. Understandably, this may take some courage; but in the end, hopefully, the group that fights, unites!"[43]

Apathy

In some groups, the members do not appear to care enough about the group to get excited about anything. Members may do what they are told, but they have little commitment to the group's activity.[44] Apathy can be expressed through a low level of participation, a dragging conversation, frequent lateness and absenteeism, restlessness, hastily made decisions, failure to follow through on decisions, and reluctance to assume any further responsibility.[45] Apathetic groups can be made up of apathetic individuals, but more likely, apathy is the result of structural problems in the group. Often the task the group is working on is perceived as unimportant or is not as important as something else it could be working on. In other instances, the task may appear to be important, but the group is afraid to take it on because it may seem overwhelming, requiring too much effort or risk. Sometimes the group does not know how to go about the task, sensing that the members lack essential knowledge, skills, resources, or leadership. At other times the group may feel that its efforts will not be appreciated, that its recommendations will not be received, and that the task is merely a sham exercise because the real decisions are being made elsewhere. A prolonged fight or unresolved conflict may cause a group to become so discouraged that individual members withdraw.[46] All of these conditions, alone or together, can produce apathy.

Almost always, some major restructuring of the group—some new definition of the task and the conditions for achieving it—must be undertaken to counter apathy.

Groupthink

This is a term coined in 1972 by the social psychologist Irvin Janis to apply to "a mode of thinking that people engage in when they are deeply involved in a cohesive group, when the members' striving for unanimity overrides their motivation to realistically appraise alternative courses of action."[47] Janis studied the decision-making groups of selected United States presidents and concluded that there was a common pattern: An illusion of invulnerability and a lack of healthy disagreement led to such major fiascoes as Pearl Harbor, the Bay of Pigs invasion, and the escalation of the war in Vietnam.

Groups sometimes reach premature closure without considering alternatives because no one wants to disagree.

A good facilitator can spot groupthink and challenge the group to go further, reconsider, or generate better alternatives.

Social Loafing

Sometimes group members do not do their part or carry their own weight. Some old experiments with tug-of-war games showed that two do not pull twice as hard as one, and three do not pull three times as hard, and so forth. Social psychologists call this *social loafing,* and it usually occurs when it is difficult to distinguish individual contributions.[48]

In some groups, the facilitator and other group members need to confront loafing members who do not contribute what they should.

Group members collectively also tend to let the group take on risk that most people, at the individual level, would avoid.[49] Sometimes when everyone is responsible, no one is, and the entire group loafs.

Making Groups Work

Facilitators need to do six things to make groups work: compose the group, determine the size, provide the task, monitor progress, manage arrangements, and interpret the learning. Most of this activity is done behind the scenes, and it is a very different role from being a presenter.

Composing the Group

The facilitator should compose the group. One way to decide how to compose the group is to not decide, to let participants drift to whatever group they wish. Sometimes this is called *random assignment.* Occasionally this works, if the composition of the groups is not important, but usually the facilitator will want to have a method and some criteria for assigning participants to groups. The criteria arise naturally out of the purposes of the group. What does the group need to achieve, and who could best help the group achieve it? If the group needs some particular skill or background information, at least some of the members need to have it. If the task is going to generate conflict, maybe the group needs at least one keeper of the peace. If the task requires movement, the group needs some people with coordination; if it requires abstract conceptualization, the group needs at least one or two good thinkers. If some people are more experienced than others, perhaps the group needs a good mix of experts and novices.

Groups work best when they are composed of the right people to do the work.

Determining the Size

The facilitator also determines the size of the groups. When is a group too small or too big? Can the interaction of two people, commonly referred to as a dyad, be considered a group? Although dyads are widely used in training and are generally treated as groups, the interaction of two people has some characteristics that are different from the interaction of three people.[50] When two people interact, there is only one channel to connect the two; when a third party is present, there are multiple channels, an opportunity for a *network* or *system*, and, most important, the opportunity for the third party to observe and comment on the communication of the other two. A group, therefore, can be as small as two or three people but is usually larger.

The upper limit to size depends, once again, on the purpose of the group. Although some magic numbers have been proposed (seven or fifteen), the upward limit actually depends on the scope and difficulty of the task to be accomplished. Depending on the purpose, adding to the group size can make an important contribution. Some activities require a specific number of people. One useful rule for size is as follows: "A group needs to contain a number of people sufficiently small for each to be aware of and have some relation to the other."[51] If some members have no opportunity to interact because the group is too large, their contribution to the goal will be minimal or insignificant. Sometimes groups split themselves into subgroups.

A group needs to be large enough to accomplish its task and small enough so that everyone can participate.

Providing the Task

The task can be provided by the facilitator through verbal instructions, but usually it is better if the task is written down and spelled out. The written task, passed out to the group members, is called an *instrument*. The instrument may call for discussion or activity. The instrument always contains instructions but usually contains much more. A good instrument provides a strong stimulus—perhaps an interesting quotation, an activity, a short news item, or a simple problem—to get the group talking, moving, or doing something. Along with the discussion starter or description of an activity comes some specific instruction—discuss, react to, build, share, solve, create, criticize, or compare your views on. A good instrument usually provides an excuse for the members of the group to talk about or do something they ordinarily would not do, and it contains clear instructions about what is expected. Most trainers collect good instruments and activities, and they are usually willing to share these, but the key to using instruments is tying them to the desired learning outcomes. Too often instruments are chosen because they are clever or fun, and although fun is one of the by-products of group activity, the main purpose in using the Group Dynamics Strategy is *learning*.

Therefore, trainers need to begin with a purpose and find, adapt, or invent an instrument that serves that purpose. There is nothing worse—and most participants recognize it—than an instrument or activity in search of a purpose.

Here are several good examples of instruments used by a company in Brazil.

—ABC Algar BRAZIL

*A*lgar S.A. Empreendimentos e Participações (ABC Algar) is a holding company for twenty-four Brazilian companies, most noted, perhaps, for its farm equipment manufacture and dealerships but also increasingly known for communication technology. ABC Algar was founded by Alexandrinho Garcia, a poor immigrant from Portugal who owned nothing more than a gas station in the 1940s. His son, Alberto Garcia, was recently listed in *Forbes* magazine as the seventh richest person in Brazil, with a personal wealth of over $US 1 billion. Obviously, ABC Algar is heavily involved in training at many of its locations, but some of its most interesting work is in the use of groups in its farm equipment plant in Uberlândia.

"We were beginning to design more work around teams, and we wanted to make a deep impression on the participants about the importance of collaboration," notes Elizabeth Amaral Oliveira, human talent analyst. "It's a simple little task—building an origami-type paper boat—only no one knows at the beginning what they are building. Participants, arranged in rows and working alone silently, have the instructions for their step and that's all, so they make their fold—a little island of excellence—and pass it on to the next," says Oliveira. "The problem is, it is not built very well, it is not on time, and the person who does the last fold doesn't even recognize it as a boat. So we got in a circle and began to discuss the problem. Participants in prior groups said they did not like the isolation and not being able to talk. They were really upset about this. They recognized that being good at one particular task did not necessarily produce a good product. So we let them suggest how to reengineer this process. They began to talk about the best way to build the boat, how they could cooperate on some steps, and how they needed to see the big picture. They drew in their chairs and got quite animated as we wrote their good ideas on a flip chart. It is a simple instrument," says Oliveira, "but if you use it right, it really makes its point. They actually redesigned the boat project, and felt good about it at the end."

Oliveira has some other favorite instruments. "We use one to help think through the importance of planning. We break participants into small groups, and their task is to develop plans to build a kite, complete with instructions. The only catch is they don't build their own kite. They pass the instructions to another group who has to build the kite based on the written plan. We spend a lot of time, then, talking about the implications for planning. What happens when people don't follow the plan, is it the people or the plan?

"We also like instruments that can be used out of doors," says Oliveira. "We have a plastic barrel with twenty-four holes. Twelve people gather around the barrel and try to plug all the holes. Then we start filling the barrel with water. The goal is to get it filled, of course, and it takes a tremendous amount of cooperation." In another activity, Oliveira blindfolds the participants and gives them a rope to hang on to as they try to arrange themselves in a perfect square. "They all bunch up and it takes them some time to learn how to communicate well enough to compensate for the loss of their visual reference." Oliveira emphasizes the importance of finding the right instruments and adapting them to the desired learning outcomes. "Sometimes we end the day with something just for fun, like blindfold soccer," she adds with a sly smile, "and because we are Brazilian, naturally we are good at it."

Monitoring the Progress

Sometimes the facilitator will be a member of the group, especially if there is just one group, or if the group is a little larger, say twelve to fifteen members, and the facilitator wants to guide how the group proceeds with the task from time to time. In groups that are used to explore attitudes and rework feelings, where some sensitivities are involved, or where there is high potential for serious controversy, each group may need to have a facilitator to manage the group dynamics. The facilitator may reflect back to the group what the group is saying or doing or may comment on the progress of the group. Facilitators need to restrain their participation and, above all, avoid lecturing the group. On the other hand, most groups will manage themselves and may not need a facilitator. Groups that function on their own are called *leaderless groups,* although that is something of a misnomer because most groups, even after a brief time together, will generate someone who plays the role of leader. With leaderless groups, the facilitator usually visits the groups to see how they are progressing, to check whether they are clear about their tasks, to see how they are performing the activity, or to ask if they have questions. Sometimes the wandering facilitator will bring a new piece of information or provide a clue that helps the group get unstuck. By passing from group to group, the facilitator can see if the instrument is working and can tell how much time the group may need to complete the task. The skilled facilitator will monitor task and process behavior, note what roles people are playing, check the verbal and nonverbal communication, and watch for conflict, apathy, groupthink, and social loafing.

Effective facilitators set their groups in motion, but they also watch carefully what happens.

Managing the Arrangements

The total population of participants may be broken into small groups, then reassembled as a whole for reporting or sharing ideas. Sometimes groups are broken into participants and observers, with one group (the outer circle) watching the group behavior of the participants (the inner circle). Sometimes one group is set against another in a competitive race for the best solution. At other times groups are asked to cooperate with other groups by sending a messenger to share their ideas. Effective facilitators devise many creative ways to manage groups. Notice how skillfully groups are managed in the two examples in the following illustration.

—American Red Cross USA

At the headquarters of the American Red Cross, materials are developed to train the national faculty who then train instructors to work with volunteers in local communities on HIV/AIDS education. The program began in 1988 and emphasized information—knowledge gained through presentation of factual information. More recently there has been a shift toward emphasizing skills-based prevention education, attitudes, and feelings, and not surprisingly, more group techniques have been included. Within one of the many courses that make up the full program is an interesting activity on understanding a stigma. Having AIDS often carries with it a heavy stigma (a mark of disgrace), and to understand how people with AIDS might feel, it is important to understand the dynamics of a stigma more generally. In the group exercise, participants draw a stigma out of a hat and then share it with the group. The stigmas are things such as "I never finished high school," "I use drugs," "I've been married five times," or "I haven't filed my income tax in three years." "When the participants begin to share their stigma," notes Zora Salisbury, manager of HIV/AIDS educational development, "they have a sense that they are sharing a personal secret, and they are not so sure about how this secret is going to be received. What is going to be the effect of this stigma on them or on the group?" In this activity each group has a facilitator who plays an important role in helping the group talk about the stigma, and perhaps more important, about their feelings afterward. "They learn to generalize some lessons about stigma," notes Salisbury, "and then maybe they can have a better discussion of the stigma associated with AIDS."

In a more complex exercise for managers and supervisors, the groups are managed differently. Participants are given an instrument that describes a situation where a coworker, Larry, begins to present some behavior that his coworkers are questioning. Larry has been coming in late and has missed some days. They know he has a gay lifestyle. His coworkers are concerned, and rumors are flying. They have been hearing talk about AIDS in the news, and they think they have a right to know if Larry has AIDS. The facilitator divides the participants into three equal leaderless groups of about five people each, one group to be Larry, one to be the coworkers, and one to be managers. The task of each group is to identify their feelings, needs, and tasks from the perception of their roles. The trainer is busy listening to the different discussions. When sufficient time has passed, the trainer elicits from the groups their responses to the three tasks. "Much depends on the trainer's ability to orchestrate the three groups," notes Salisbury. "The goal is to help the participants develop an awareness of the viewpoints of the three workplace groups and to better understand how HIV infection challenges everyone in the workplace."

Interpreting the Learning

Perhaps the most important aspect of the facilitator's job is to interpret for the group at the end of the activity what learning occurred. Usually people have had fun, but they often miss the purpose. Some debriefing to drive home the point or get feedback from the group is usually necessary.

Participants may want to continue talking about a group experience long after it is over and may discover new meaning in the activity days later, but no facilitator should terminate a group activity without the participants knowing what they learned.

Consider how the meaning of the activity is drawn out in the following illustration.

—United Airlines USA ——————————————————

*T*o train flight attendants who work on international routes, United Airlines provides a course called World-Wise, with units on ethnocentricity, cross-cultural sensitivity, proper terminology, and nonverbal communication. To get participants involved at more than an intellectual level, United has developed a special cross-cultural activity. Participants receive some old-fashioned, 3-D eyeglasses, designated for the activity as cultural lenses. One group receives pink glasses; the other group gets blue. (The color has nothing to do with gender.) What the participants do not know is that those who wear blue can only see what is written on the chart in pink, and those who wear pink can only see what is written in blue. The trainer begins to discuss a series of body language gestures and illustrates each gesture by pointing to the chart, calling attention to the interpretations that appear there. Naturally, participants can see only the interpretation that their cultural lenses permit. For example, the pink group reads that the hand gesture with thumb and first finger together means okay, whereas the blue group gets a rather different interpretation. When the cultural lenses eventually come off, the groups see that they have been getting only one interpretation, whereas two (or many) interpretations may be possible. The trainer then facilitates a general group discussion of the meaning of the activity. "Students begin to ask about where these differing cultural interpretations come from," notes Heather Peterson, special assignment flight attendant, "and soon they get into a big discussion of how to interpret behavior. The participants begin to share examples of things they have seen people from other cultures doing. The cultural lenses activity is only the beginning; it's the interpretation of the activity where we spend most of our time."

Going Deeper

Groups are often used for diversity training or the exploration of other sensitive human relations issues. As noted earlier, groups are useful for bringing about changes in opinions, attitudes, and beliefs, and sometimes that kind of learning affects people deeply. Although trainers need to keep their work focused on learning, not therapy, the lines between the two are not always clear. The work of groups often goes deeper than entertaining games about teamwork. Very few trainers would think of themselves as leading anything like what were once called encounter groups, but knowing something about the methods and processes of these and other therapy groups, can be valuable to trainers who use the Group Dynamics Strategy.

As noted earlier, the principles that guide groups used for human relations training have their roots in T-groups, encounter groups, sensitivity training, training laboratories, and group therapy. Although those words may have an odd ring today and may bring to mind for those who lived through the late 1960s and early 1970s some of the excesses of these experiments, much was learned through these groups about how people change and develop new attitudes about themselves and others. T-groups were designed to provide a setting in which "participants work together in a small group over an extended period of time, learning through analysis of their own experiences, including feelings, reactions, perceptions and behavior."[52] It was discovered that groups such as these could provide a laboratory for learning that the real world often denies. What are the outcomes of learning in the classic encounter group? Outcomes will surely vary, depending on the purposes and composition of the group, but in the words of one of the founders, Carl Rogers:

> In such a group the individual comes to know himself and each of the others more completely than is possible in the usual social or working relationships. He becomes deeply acquainted with the other members and with his own inner self, the self that otherwise tends to be hidden behind his facade. Hence he relates better to others, both in the group and later in the everyday life situation.[53]

How does this occur? Although therapy groups tend to emphasize mental health—from the Greek *therapia,* meaning healing—the processes employed in group therapy can be modified and used for the more modest goals of human relations training. Irvin D. Yalom, the author of a definitive text on group therapy, *The Theory and Practice of Group Psychotherapy,* notes eleven *therapeutic factors* that make therapy in groups effective.[54] The factors and brief paraphrased descriptors are as follows:

- *Instillation of hope.* People who share a problem come to believe there is hope for resolving it.
- *Universality.* Participants realize they are not alone and that others have a similar problem.
- *Imparting information.* Members of the group share information about how they have dealt with the problem.
- *Altruism.* People discover that they can be helpful to others.
- *Recapitulation of the family.* Groups become like families and members rediscover how they have acted as family members.
- *Development of social skills.* Members become aware that they are perceived as shy, regal, tactless, or aggressive and learn new interpersonal skills.
- *Imitative behavior.* Participants imitate the positive behaviors of the facilitator and of other group members.
- *Interpersonal learning.* By reviewing critical incidents in their lives, members can have a corrective emotional experience where they relearn something about relationships.
- *Group cohesiveness.* A sense of good feeling among group members provides the therapeutic setting for acceptance and honest sharing of feelings.
- *Catharsis.* The group becomes a place where members can "get things off their chest," and this in itself can be therapeutic.
- *Existential factors.* Participants get a new sense of what life is all about and learn to live life more honestly.

Not all of these factors will be present in every group, but in general, these are the characteristics of therapy groups that promote growth and change. Consider how deep feelings are brought out in the training of volunteers in this example.

— Department of Social and Health Care FINLAND —

*I*n the Department of Social and Health Care in Tampere, Finland, small groups are used to train volunteers to work with those who are grieving. "We can't increase our number of employees," notes Seppo Prunnila, social services coordinator, "so we increasingly turn to volunteers to help us get our work done. We provide training, some presentations, and role plays, but the heart of the activity is a group process where we are teaching basic listening skills." The volunteers are specially selected on the basis of having had, themselves, some experience with grieving the loss of a loved one, and they want to be helpful to someone else in this situation. "We encourage them in the group to discuss their own situations, to get their own feelings out, and to revisit how they coped with their loss. By getting them to relive their own experiences, we draw out of them ideas about how they can be helpful to others. Sometimes the groups get into some very deep feelings."

What does the facilitator do with groups that go deeper? Ideally, the facilitator will have some additional special training and experience with groups, although generally the facilitator plays roles that are similar to the leader in other groups. In addition the facilitator does three other important things:

• *Deepens communication.* The facilitator sets guidelines to establish desirable norms for deeper communication, such as active involvement, nonjudgmental acceptance of others, extensive self-disclosure, desire for understanding, and motivation for change. The facilitator may give explicit instructions, comment on something that has taken place, provide an instrument or activity, raise questions, or reward members with praise for positive behavior—all with an eye toward deepening the level of communication. The facilitator may also model the behavior that is appropriate to the norms through nonjudgmental acceptance, interpersonal honesty, and spontaneity.

• *Deals with the here and now.* One of the most important parts of the facilitator's job in a training context is to encourage group members to talk about and deal with the here and now. Although many forms of psychotherapy are noted for dredging up the past—due in part to Freud's original emphasis on understanding the formative experiences of early childhood—one of the unique aspects of group therapy is its emphasis on the present. Members are expected to deal with the real problems of their present lives but, perhaps even more important, with real communication events taking place within the group at the moment. As the group experience develops, the group itself will realize that its task is to focus on the here and now.

• *Comments on the group behavior.* The facilitator also monitors the process that is ongoing in the group and provides for the group an illumination of what is taking place through process commentary. The commentary will focus on recurring themes, deeper meanings, and the relationship between outside problems that members may be having and the problems they are discussing at the moment within the group. The facilitator, without being judgmental, points out how a member's behavior makes others feel, how the behavior brings about reactions from others, and how, in the end, the behavior influences that member's own self-esteem. Sometimes the facilitator will give a group process commentary, that is, feedback to the group as a whole about its behavior.

—Grupo Tampico MEXICO

*O*n the Gulf Coast of Mexico, in the medium-sized city of Tampico, are the home offices of Grupo Tampico, a holding company for more than fifty industrial, commercial, and service firms serving several adjoining states. The first Coca-Cola bottling company in Mexico, Grupo Tampico, with eighty-three years of history, operates a series of gas stations, computer stores, automotive retailers, hotels, and radio stations, and they still distribute Coca-Cola but also now bottled water. With over 4,500 employees, many of whom are women, they developed a unique training program for women in the workplace.

Initiated in 1989 by the president, Henry Fleishman—the fourth generation of Fleishman family owners—the program was designed to help women employees affirm the importance of women's work in the productive life of Mexico and in Grupo Tampico and to enable women to develop their full capacity for productivity and creativity. Although the total program has many aspects—workshops, conferences, role models, recreational activities—and has focused on a different theme each year, one important aspect of the program has involved group activities. These group activities have provided an opportunity for women to "go deeper" into aspects of what it means to be a woman, particularly a woman in the workforce in Mexico.

Director of Human Resources Esteban Fuentes Salazar is proud of the program and has presented the idea at a training conference in the United States. "I can remember when female employees, really good workers, would come in and say, 'I've got to leave now because I am getting married.' This is the way it was. Today there is a new mentality, not only because of the changing status of women in Mexico but also because we have cultivated it in our company. We have many women working as professionals, secretaries, and nonprofessionals. They knew they needed to learn new habits, new skills, and new motivations—to cultivate a whole new mentality." Grupo Tampico's controller is a woman; she has been there twenty-five years and provides a positive role model, but the president wants more women at the executive level. Right now there are many women at mid-levels training for upper levels. "What we have been working on is cultural development and attitude change," notes Salazar, "and we have been using groups to facilitate that. We get into some fairly deep things."

"It was wonderful," notes Beatriz Aguilar Mijes, administrative assistant to the president. "We women all talked to each other on the phone all the time but there we were in training, face to face, talking about serious matters. We used roundtable groups with facilitators, and they were excellent. The first challenge was to get participation. Nobody wanted to talk at first. Then the facilitator got us to talk about why we didn't talk. We had to get the idea that we had a voice. Women aren't accustomed to speaking out in Mexico. Then we had to learn to express our views and learn how to defend them. If you haven't had any views, you certainly haven't learned to defend them. Then we had to learn how to respect the views of others and express that." Her eyes flashing with enthusiasm, Beatriz continues, "A lot of it was communications training, but it was more than that; it was raising our consciousness, getting our personal goals established, and finding ways to align them with opportunities in the organization. The roundtables were an important part of this, and we felt the support of the organization to do this in a familiar setting." The development of a new consciousness for women is no small training task in Mexico—almost a kind of therapy—and the Group Dynamics Strategy worked well because the facilitators were effective.

Should organizations get involved in this type of human-relations training, and can trainers learn to become effective facilitators of groups designed to provide deeper kinds of change and growth? Although the more serious mental health problems (substance abuse, deviance, violent behavior) are usually handled through employee assistance programs or outsourced to professionals, other, more general human-relations problems, particularly those relating to diversity issues—ethnicity, gender, and sexual preference—fall properly under the domain of training. If there are problems in human relations (or if problems are anticipated), they need to be addressed, otherwise, the organization suffers. If these issues are to be addressed, the Group Dynamics Strategy is the one to use. Presenting information or policies alone will not do the job unless people also have the opportunity to rework attitudes and feelings. That happens best in groups.

Using Groups to Train Teams

As noted earlier, many organizations are reengineering the basic processes for conducting business, and the result is that often more work is done by teams. Teams require *collaboration*, and sometimes team members need to learn teamwork.

After studying many types of teams in a variety of work settings, Carl Larson and Frank LaFasto developed a list of the characteristics of high-performance teams as follows:[55]

- clear and elevating goal
- results driven structure
- competent members
- unified commitment
- collaborative climate
- standards of excellence
- external support and recognition
- principled leadership

They also noticed, from their study of teams, that not all teams have the same type of purposes, nor do they function in the same way.[56] All teams need a results-driven structure, but the purposes and, therefore, the structure can be quite different. They identified three types of teams:

- *Problem-solving teams*—such as epidemic-identification teams sent out by the National Center for Disease Control

- *Creative teams*—such as the new-product team that created Chicken McNuggets at McDonald's
- *Tactical teams*—such as the Texas Heart Institute's heart transplant team

Sometimes group activities are designed expressly to help team members build collaboration, and often the collaboration must be of the particular type needed for the work of that team. For example, there is little place for creativity on a heart transplant team; they need to practice the routines and procedures that make them the perfect tactical team. Notice how this team discovered what type of team they most resemble.

──COBE Laboratories USA ──────────

COBE Laboratories, Inc., in Lakewood, Colorado, is part of the Swedish-owned Gambro Group and produces high-tech medical equipment for heart, blood, and kidney treatments and markets the equipment all over the world. The International Marketing Services Group wanted to improve its effectiveness as a team, and a number of group exercises were used initially to improve group communication. In subsequent training, the group's members began to explore the characteristics and differences among problem solving, creative, and tactical teams. They broke into groups and explored instruments with tricky problems and creativity activities and then threw tennis balls around a circle to test their tactical skills. They began to raise two critical questions: What kind of team are we? What kind of team should we be? After completing a careful analysis of their work patterns, with the help of an outside facilitator, they concluded that they were spending a large amount of their time being a problem-solving team, working patiently with all kinds of order-processing irregularities, when in fact they should be operating more as a tactical team. Now they are working on new forms of collaboration as they take steps to make the transition from problem-solving to tactical team.

When groups are used to teach teamwork, the instruments need to provide participants with activities that require collaboration. Sometimes the instrument is an apparatus or other specially designed piece of equipment that lends itself to activities that require teamwork. Note how Kodak provides a special environment for learning collaboration and teamwork.

—Eastman Kodak USA

*M*ost of the Eastman Kodak Company Learning and Development Center at its River Road site in Rochester, New York, is surrounded by the well-kept lawns of a typical suburban development. Behind the center, beyond the parking lot, is a thickly wooded area. What is in the forest? Two rustic training buildings and beyond that the Wild Woozy, the Catwalk, the Wall, the Pamper Platform, and Ships Passing in the Night—names given to the specific types of apparatus used by Kodak for training. With assistance from Project Adventure, in Hamilton, Massachusetts, Kodak has created a unique outdoor environment for learning. The Wall, for example, is a thirteen-foot-high wall with a catwalk on the back side. The goal is to get all the members of one's team up the wall and onto the catwalk by building human pyramids and then reaching back down some way to gather up the last person. To get to the Pamper Platform, participants climb on big staples high up into a tree; when they get to the small wooden platform, they are expected to jump off into space, hoping to grasp a trapeze bar suspended some eight to ten feet away. "It is all done with a safety harness, but some people really face their fears up on that platform," says Rick Tette, curriculum manager for outdoor based experiences and team development. The Catwalk is like a long balance beam, the kind used in gymnastics, only suspended thirty feet in the air. The team uses a belay system to support the walker, maximizing team roles and individual responsibility in this exercise.

"We use a model," says Tette, "where we assess group needs, design environments with initiatives and activities that will provide experiences that support the goals, help the group establish its norms for communication and behavior, then get the members involved in the concrete experiences. We put a major focus on the debriefing part of the cycle to help people reflect on what learning took place. We ask them to describe what they saw themselves doing and then build a bridge to the workplace to understand how they might be doing the same things there and decide what they might want to change."

At the time of the visit, a team of workers from the Eastman Color Print Division was struggling to send team members, one at a time and face down, across a 2 x 8 plank through an area bounded by cords—the object being to get every member through without touching any of the cords. If a cord is touched, the whole team has to start over from the beginning. "This is a great exercise to cultivate teamwork but also individual responsibility," notes Tette. "If you mess up, you have to own it and admit that there are consequences for the whole team. We happened to know that this is a team that is getting some new responsibilities and is a little ambivalent about whether they want them."

Useful Technologies

Although the power of the Group Dynamics Strategy derives primarily from face-to-face interpersonal encounter, there are some technologies that can be used to augment and extend that dynamic. The most obvious is the video recorder. At the simplest level, a video segment can be used as an instrument. A more sophisticated use involves taping a group process and showing it to the group. This video provides a good opportunity for individuals to see themselves as others see them and for the group as a whole to get a facilitator's eye view of the total group dynamic. The group can work on a task, view a video of its process, and then discuss how it worked on that task. Although videotaping may shut down some of the more spontaneous expressions of feeling, group members can grow accustomed to taping and learn to appreciate its advantages.

More recently, networked computers and specifically designed software have been used to enhance and facilitate group communication. Individual members of the group can seek and provide information to each other in a process that bypasses taking turns. Consider the following example.

— Lackland Air Force Base USA

*A*t Lackland Air Force Base (37th Training Group), in San Antonio, Texas, senior logistics officers are trained through group activities that require collaboration and teamwork by using networked laptop computers. Participants in the training are already field-grade specialists (majors and above) in one of the five career field specialties of Air Force logistics: supply, transportation, contracting, planning, and maintenance. In the Advanced Officer Logistics Course officers are trained to sit at the top of the pyramid in roles where they will need to coordinate all of these career fields of logistics. "What better way to get at this than to have the participants work together as a team, teaching each other their specialties," notes Fred Van Wert, chief of advanced training technology/flight. Most of the course is on the computer, including study materials, case scenarios, and information relevant to the case. Each scenario provides a set of embedded problems that the team needs to work on together. "The essence of the learning, however, is in the group process facilitated by the networked laptops," says Van Wert. The participants all sit in the same room, and their computers are all hooked together so that they can chat with each other and the instructor at any time. The instructor may facilitate by accessing information or questions on the large screen, and participants may send mail messages back to the instructor or to each other, at any time. "The discussion bounces back and forth across the room as in a live group," notes Van Wert, "but in some ways it is more efficient than a live group because, theoretically at least, everyone gets to talk at once." Participants can call up information, send mail messages or requests, make comments, ask each other for help, consult a glossary of acronyms, or access word processing to take notes. There is even the possibility of conducting two classes in separate rooms simultaneously. "The course is on a CD, and at the end of the training they take the CD with them," says Van Wert. "On their new assignment, either as senior coordinator or in an alternate field area, they can slip in the CD, look at their notes, and retrace the discussion that took place in the group."

THE BOTTOM LINE

Groups are used widely in organizations for many purposes. Groups are good for tasks where the sum is greater than the parts; for generating ideas; for changing opinions, attitudes, and beliefs; and for cultivating participation and a sense of belonging. Years of research on groups has established that

- Groups have identifiable characteristics.
- Teams have a mission.
- Groups go through phases and stages over time.
- Communication in groups is about both the task and the process.
- Groups develop cohesion and structure.
- Group members play roles and make rules.

Effective communication in groups requires active listening and awareness of body language.

Groups can develop problems: conflict, apathy, social loafing, and groupthink, but these problems can be addressed.

Effective facilitators

- compose the groups
- determine size
- provide the activities or instruments

- monitor progress
- manage overall arrangements
- interpret the learning that has occurred

Sometimes groups go deeper with feelings. Drawing on ideas from group therapy, the facilitator establishes ground rules for deeper communication, helps participants focus on the here and now, and offers process commentary on group behavior.

Teams can learn collaboration, but there are different types of teams.

Video (record and playback) and networked computers are useful technologies for supporting learning in groups.

The principles of group dynamics are well established through years of research in human communications studies, counseling, and psychotherapy.

In groups, not communicating is a form of communication, and it means something.

10

The Virtual Reality Strategy
Role Play, Dramatic Scenarios, and Simulation

*T*he difficulty is not in running the crane. Anyone can run it. But making it do what it is supposed to do, that's the big thing. It only comes with experience. Some people learn it quicker and there's some people who can never learn it. (Laughs.) What we do you can never learn out of a book . . . Maybe you're picking fifty, sixty ton, and maybe you have ironworkers up there 100, 110 feet. You have to be real careful that you don't bump one of these persons, where they would be apt to fall off . . . [1]

—STUDS TERKEL, "Interview with a crane operator
named Hub Dillard" in *Working*

VIRTUAL REALITY STRATEGY OVERVIEW

BEST USE
Developing confidence and competence in a simulated situation before going to a real-life situation where there could be financial loss, injury, or fatality.

LEARNING THEORY
Simulation and gaming theory, learning through role play, dramatic scenarios, and simulation games.

HISTORICAL ROOTS
Work of E. L. Moreno on psychodrama and sociodrama and the development of simulation theory from war games.

APPLICATIONS
Training where live experience is too dangerous or expensive and where practice is needed under controlled conditions.

PARTICIPANT ROLES
Engages participants in active practice of their real-life roles under circumstances of challenge, support, and safety.

NATURE OF MOTIVATION
High motivation comes from knowing that the real thing is just around the corner, and this is a sheltered opportunity to practice.

PARTICIPANT FIT
Best for participants who already have some level of proficiency and are not shy about getting up and acting out their roles.

FACILITATOR'S ROLE
Sets the scene, provides the scenarios or games, and intervenes or steps back as appropriate for role play, dramatic scenario, and simulation.

STRENGTHS
Provides opportunities to practice and fine tune, gets participants up and acting, creates the next best thing to live experience, or sometimes has advantages over live experience.

WEAKNESSES
Requires much preparation and working out of material and supporting materials, requires usually unfamiliar and difficult facilitation skills. Can get too real and potentially explosive or can fall flat by not enough reality.

Creating Virtual Realities

Some jobs are hard to learn in the actual setting where they are performed because making mistakes can cause big problems. We do not know how crane operators are trained because we never talked to one or anyone who trained one, but we know that there are many jobs like a crane operator's, where workers can make big, costly, and perhaps even life-threatening mistakes if they have not had a chance to practice first. Sometimes the job involves danger of physical harm, as in the case of mental health workers dealing with out-of-control patients. At other times, as in making investments, huge sums of money can be lost. For some kinds of work, such as training pilots, flying in a real plane for each training session is too expensive. One hopes never to use emergency preparedness training in a real-life situation. For these kinds of training, the Virtual Reality Strategy is a welcome alternative.

There are no old books on library shelves on the subject of *virtual reality*, only new publications classified under computer science. Although virtual reality as a technical term, and now a buzzword, is new, the concept is old. Storytellers create a type of virtual reality, a world of words constructed from experience and imagination, and they invite the reader to interact with that world through the reader's own mental pictures. When we look in the mirror we see what the field of optics has long called a virtual image—a flat surface, seemingly three-dimensional and backward, but lifelike. Films now enhanced by computer imaging can create the frightening virtual reality of a disaster at sea or the simulation of actual American presidents talking and shaking hands with characters in the film.

The newer and more technical use of the term *virtual reality*, however, refers to the relatively recent ability to combine visual images and computer programming capabilities to make it possible for people to experience a lifelike, created reality and to interact with it. L. Casey Larijani describes a simple example in *The Virtual Reality Primer:*

> Realistic, stereoscopic images are projected off tiny screens inside a helmet, and sounds are added to convince the wearer that he or she is in another world. Motion sensors in the glove and helmet of the wearer become the means of interacting with the new world . . . Wrapping pictures and sounds around us and immersing our senses in such a way that the line between the real and illusionary disappears are being done only through a dynamic convergence of many different technologies, each of which evolved and matured at its own pace. Computer speed and power have had to be combined with advances in image processing, tracking mechanisms and intuitive human-to-computer communication to converge into the experimental medium called virtual reality.[2]

Virtual, then, means existing in essence or effect, but not in fact.

When the Virtual Reality Strategy is used to facilitate learning, activities can include simple role plays, more complex dramatic scenarios, games, and simulations. Their common goal is to create a virtual reality training environment that is like the world where the actual work will be performed. Correspondence to the actual setting can be low or high, and the use of technology can range from nil to very sophisticated, but the goal in each case is to provide a safe and relatively inexpensive practice setting where workers can learn their roles comfortably and with increasing levels of proficiency.

In all of the following examples, some form of the Virtual Reality Strategy is used for training.

- American Express Financial Advisors, an American Express company, trains financial planners to conduct a Personal Money Management interview.
- VINFEN trains mental health workers to use personal safety techniques.

- United Airlines trains flight attendants to develop empathy for handicapped passengers.
- The American Red Cross teaches disaster relief volunteers what to do in a crisis.
- The Royal Canadian Mounted Police trains cadets for difficult assignments.
- United Airlines trains pilots to fly without using real airplanes.
- Eastman Kodak teaches production personnel to work on emulsion batch processing.
- The Foreign Service Institute trains high-level officials to understand complex foreign policy issues.
- Merrill Lynch trains brokers to be proficient in investment strategies involving large sums of money.
- Prudential Intercultural teaches cross-cultural awareness to business personnel going to work in a foreign country.
- The National Emergency Training Center trains community representatives in emergency preparedness.

Bridging Realities

Role plays, dramatic scenarios, games, and simulations are the most common techniques used for bridging the real world of the job and the virtual world created for training. The most important task, in the use of all of these techniques, is to select precisely those elements of the real situation that are most important for training. Exactly which aspects of the real-life situation are necessary to evoke the desired learning? How will these elements be re-created in the simulated situation? What will the participants actually do and how will they learn through their doing? Looking back on their doing, how will they develop a better understanding of their jobs, display the abilities actually needed to perform their roles, and gain insights about themselves as players of a role?

The primary challenge in using the Virtual Reality Strategy is to bridge the gap, as much as possible, between the training setting and the real world. The enormous advantage of the Virtual Reality Strategy is that it provides a good opportunity for actually bridging this gap.

In this respect, the Virtual Reality Strategy is far ahead of just telling people what they are supposed to do when a challenging situation arises. For trainees, there are great advantages to having walked through the job in a simulated situation.

Origins of the Virtual Reality Strategy

Viewed in one way, the origins of the Virtual Reality Strategy are general, deep, and old, going back to primitive efforts in every society to simulate reality. In all societies, it has been discovered, human beings have made what have come to be called *folk models* of how their environment works. Folk models have included, among other things, various types of games and activities designed to help the participants discover and adapt to that culture's view of the world. Thus, puzzles are created to explore the relationship of humankind and nature, games of chance to cope with randomness, games of strategy to act out relations with others, and various crafts and ceremonies to express the social and aesthetic values of the group. Serious games played by adults have existed in every culture for a long time, using the low technology of bits of wood, stones, feathers, and lines drawn in the dirt.[3]

Efforts to simulate the real world are also found widely in children's play. By the mid-twentieth century, scholars had recognized that play is children's work and that what takes place in children's play is the serious business of socialization, learning how to fit into the adult world. Through more formalized games, children learn to internalize rules, develop their self-image, try out or learn new roles, explore potential or future realities, have fun, and socialize.[4] Oddly enough, this list describes almost exactly what happens when the Virtual Reality Strategy is used in training.

Viewed in another way, the roots of the Virtual Reality Strategy, as a consciously employed method for education and training, are found in two specific sources that supplement the more general origins of folk models and children's play. These sources are the work of J. L. Moreno, with role play, psychodrama and sociodrama, and the efforts of the military with simulations and war games.

Jacob Levy Moreno (1889–1974) was an eccentric Viennese doctor who struggled for at least part of his life with a messiah complex.[5] He knew at an early age that he would do something important, and he did. He is the indisputable father of *psychodrama* and *sociodrama*. Moreno had the insight to see in the play of children the seeds of a fruitful educational and therapeutic device. As a medical student in Vienna, Moreno often spent his lunch hours in the public gardens, where children would gather around him at the foot of a tree to listen to his dramatic telling of fairy tales. Sometimes he moved up into the tree, taking on the role of director, giving the children roles, and urging them to take on new names or invent new characters. The children were captivated by his radical little dramas, but soon he was in trouble with teachers, parents, and the police, and he realized it was time to go work with adults. He started therapy groups for prostitutes, worked with refugees, and developed ingenious techniques for dramatizing the daily news. Along the way, he began to theorize and write about how dramatization could be used for learning and for therapeutic purposes. Was it Moreno's fate that he would become the founder of psychodrama? In his own words he describes an early experience, which, in retrospect, appears to have many of the elements of the actual psychodramas he would later conduct.

When I was four and a half years old my parents lived in a house near the river Danube. They had left the house on a Sunday to pay a visit, leaving me alone in the basement of the house with neighbors' children. It was empty except for a huge oak table in the middle. The children said: "Let's play." One child asked me: "What?" "I know," I said, "let's play God and his angels." The children inquired: But who is God?" I replied: "I am God and you are my angels." The children agreed. They all declared: "We must build the heavens first." We dragged all the chairs from every room in the house to the basement, put them on the big table and began to build one heaven after another by tying several chairs together on one level and putting more chairs above them until we reached the ceiling. Then all the children helped me to climb up until I reached the top chair and sat on it. There I sat pretty. The children began to circle around the table, using their arms as wings, and singing. Suddenly I heard a child asking me: "Why don't you fly?" I stretched my arms, trying it. A second later I fell and found myself on the floor, my right arm broken. This was, as far as I can recall, the first "private" psychodramatic session I have ever conducted. I was the director and the subject in one.[6]

Another historical source of the Virtual Reality Strategy is the use of simulations and games in the military services.[7] The first use of simulations is usually attributed to the Prussian army of the nineteenth century, not only for planning battlefield strategies but also for recruiting soldiers. The paper-and-pencil tests used for screening were not producing the officers they wanted, so they devised simulations to test how potential soldiers would actually cope with realistic command situations. The idea was taken up by the British army to test for different types of roles—officer, agent, engineer. Some simulations placed the candidates in situations where they had to act alone, but others involved interactions in teams. Soon the simulations were used in the training of soldiers as well as the selection process. Simulations were used in U.S. business and industry originally for recruitment but then more generally for training, eventually evolving into complex management simulations.

The other military source of the Virtual Reality Strategy is war games.[8] The original war games, played on boards, were developed by the Prussians; the first war game to be introduced at Schleswig in 1798 was called *Kriegspiel*. The boards were expanded to maps with grids and pieces that could be moved to represent and work out real military situations.[9] To develop the game, the nature of the conflict had to be analyzed, and the antagonists and their material resources had to be defined. Real-world constraints were agreed to, and chance elements, such as weather or surprise attacks, were noted. With crude sand tables to simulate the terrain, alternative war plans could be tested at low cost. During World War II, at the Japanese Naval War College, a war game was developed to simulate the time period from mid-1941 to mid-1943, to try out Japan's military intentions. Sophisticated war-gaming was used by the Allies to cope with packs of German submarines. Today, war games are simulated on computers or carried out through live military practice maneuvers. After World War II, what was learned about games in simulated war was adapted for the business environment to simulate complex management situations.

The first business game is usually credited to Frank Ricciardi of the American Management Association (AMA), who applied what he had learned about gaming at the Naval War College to the development of a business game.[10] After a year of development it was released by the AMA in 1957 as Top Management Decision Simulation. Interactive team play was made possible where rival managers competed for market share based on complete knowledge of their own companies, but less complete information about the market and competitors.

Gaming theory also owes a historical debt to the mathematician John von Neumann, who worked out the quantitative theory of decision making under conditions of competition and uncertainty. His classic work, *The Theory of Games and Economic Behavior*, published in 1944, provided the vocabulary for describing the characteristics of competition and the quantitative methods needed for using computers in gaming.[11]

The roots of the Virtual Reality Strategy are varied, but the sources all have in common the discovery of ways to create a simulated reality that can be used to learn something in a safe environment about a role, a situation, or oneself.

Role Playing

A role play is an activity where a limited number of participants, usually two or three, take on specifically assigned and well-defined roles and act out an encounter that involves some goal or problem.

In one of the classic role plays, for example, one participant takes on the role of a dissatisfied customer returning a defective shoe, while another plays the role of the clerk. The customer is told to gain some satisfaction, and the clerk is instructed to maintain a no-returns policy. The players act out their differences as they assume their roles and try to negotiate.

The concept of *role* comes from the field of sociology and denotes a cluster of culturally prescribed behaviors associated with particular social positions."[12] For example, being a trainer, supervisor, or manager is a role, and each carries with it certain *role expectations*. The expectations can vary from organization to organization and even country to country. Being a wife is a role, but being a wife in Jeddah, Saudi Arabia, is different from being a wife in Beverly Hills, California. Some jobs involve *role conflict*, where one is expected to carry out some activities that interfere with others, such as the manager who needs to discipline an employee but who wants to remain open and approachable when employees have problems. Some sociologists (functionalists) maintain that roles are set and prescribed by society, while others (interactionists) believe that roles are modified and played out differently by individuals with different personalities and varying interpretations of their roles. Sociology's best known role theorist, Irving Goffman (1913–1982), believed that all of life was, indeed, a stage, and that much of human behavior could be understood in the way roles are played out on that stage—sometimes in a sincere and realistic way, sometimes in an idealized manner, and sometimes cynically.[13]

Role plays employ the concept of social role and are used for various purposes in training, such as diagnosing and analyzing a particular role, teaching participants the content of the role, giving participants an opportunity for practicing a role, or evaluating how well participants can actually play the role.[14] The different purposes of role play are illustrated in the Personal Money Management (PMM) interview used at Investors Diversified Services, an American Express company, based in Minneapolis, Minnesota.

——American Express Financial Advisors USA ————

*T*rainers at American Express Financial Advisors Inc. are carefully schooled in how to do a PMM interview before they begin to do live financial planning with a client. After hearing detailed presentations, the trainee studies thoroughly an eight-page booklet and memorizes a typical script. A role play between an experienced planner and potential client is used to *demonstrate* a good interview. Later the trainee *practices* the interview through role play, and a trainer observes and provides feedback. When the trainee is ready, another interview is role-played, and the trainer confirms that the trainee is ready to perform with a real client. "We use what we call the DOC technique," notes Roger Rogos, district manager, "to demonstrate, observe, and confirm; and role play takes on different purposes as the trainee works through this."

Role plays can be used for different purposes, and it is important to gain some clarity about what the precise purpose of the role play is. Participants will be confused, for example, if they think the purpose is practice, when, in fact, they are being evaluated.[15]

Arrangements for Role Playing

Clarity of purpose helps guide a series of subsequent decisions about arrangements that need to be made:

• *Single or multiple plays.* Will one role play be acted out in front of several observers, or will several role plays be enacted simultaneously? Several role plays get more people involved, but one carefully enacted play provides an opportunity for more control, observation, and discussion.

• *High or low structure.* Will a general description of a situation be provided for participants to act out their roles spontaneously, or will the roles be carefully scripted? The scripted role play provides a highly focused demonstration, and the less-structured role play stimulates more involvement and allows for variations that may fit the real-world needs of the participants.

• *Number of roles.* How many roles will be presented at once? Will the players have alter egos or coaches they can consult about how to play their role and what to do next? Complications can arise when too many roles are being enacted at once, but there are advantages to getting more people involved as players or as alter egos.

• *Importance of nonverbal behavior.* Will emphasis be placed on the spoken lines or the nonverbal action? An emphasis on the content of the script provides more focus for ideas and language, but stressing nonverbal behavior may involve participants more in the emotional aspects of the role play. A role play could be entirely pantomime.

Important decisions need to be made about how to set up a role play, and the options are multiplied when important decisions about arrangements are combined. Choices about arrangements depend on goals for the role play.

Try to identify and categorize the types of arrangements in the following example of role play in the training of mental health workers at the VINFEN Corporation in Cambridge, Massachusetts.

─VINFEN USA

VINFEN Corporation trains over one thousand mental health workers for its more than 160 residential living centers (sometimes called halfway houses) in the metropolitan Boston area. These workers need to know how to protect themselves when upset patients are acting out. The first step, of course, is to de-escalate and avoid confrontation if possible. But sometimes patients get violent. In the case of physical attacks by out-of-control clients, however, there are a number of ways to extricate oneself, depending on the nature of the attack. It helps to know these safety techniques and to have practiced them before a crisis occurs. To teach the workers a set of releases—from hand grab, hair pull, front and back choke, and biting—the trainers use role play. Each worker has a partner, and the trainer uses one worker to demonstrate each release against the particular type of physical attack. In pairs, the workers then use simultaneous, multiple role plays to practice the technique, switching the roles of out-of-control aggressor and mental health worker until the techniques have been mastered. The trainer circulates among the role plays to provide feedback and demonstrate again as necessary. "We train the trainers in how to use role play for this," notes Karen Unger, director of research and training, "and we use some good materials. It gets the job done so our people can feel safe."

In the VINFEN example, multiple role plays are used with two roles and a high degree of structure for demonstrating and practicing each of the release techniques serially, in what is primarily nonverbal, physical role playing.

Materials for Role Playing

The materials used to initiate a role play have some of the properties of instruments used for group activities; for example, they set up a task and provide an excuse. Role play materials must, however, emphasize roles—what people will do in a particular situation and how their efforts to play their roles will become complicated as the action progresses. Materials should be thought of less as instructions and more as efforts to create a setting or state of mind.[16] The materials used to initiate a role play can be demonstrations, diagrams, short cases, memos, e-mails, capsule descriptions of characters, brief plots, or actual scripts.

Materials need to be brief enough to be read quickly, clear about what to do, and capable of generating a situation that can be acted out. The materials must also be related closely to purposes so that the situation developed provides a virtual reality of the expected real-world performance and has the potential to draw out the intended learning outcomes.

The Facilitator's Role

The facilitator plays an important part in making decisions about arrangements and in developing materials but is also the manager of the role play.

The facilitator chooses the appropriate participants for each role, makes sure that instructions are clear, assigns precise duties to

the observers, guides the role play as it unfolds, and leads the subsequent discussion of the meaning of the role play.

The facilitator often has (or seeks) inside knowledge about who would be good at or who could profit from a particular role. The facilitator knows how to get the role play started and when and how to stop it. The facilitator is sensitive to whether it is necessary to debrief the players, sometimes asking them to express how they were feeling during the role play. Above all, the facilitator needs to use the energy and motivation generated by the role play to explore the intended learning. Although the learning often comes in the process of the role play itself, it is usually valuable to discuss the role play so that the participants and observers can identify and put into words what was learned. Sometimes the role play sparks a discussion that moves on to other matters and extends the learning well beyond the issues portrayed in the role play. The facilitator carries the heavy responsibility of creating the virtual reality and relating it to the intended learning, always keeping in mind the real-world context where the participants will eventually use their learning.

A skillful facilitator knows that different aspects of a role can be emphasized in role plays.[17]

- *Role conflict*—when the player is asked to play two different roles that interfere, such as the Red Cross volunteer who is supposed to get victims to safety but also empathize with their loss.
- *New role*—when the role is full of puzzles and surprises, as with a new mental health worker facing a crisis on the first day at the community center.
- *Role relationships*—when the people one interacts with are difficult, such as a flight attendant relating to an intoxicated traveler.
- *Role fatigue*—when it becomes difficult to play the same role over and over again, always smiling, always pleasant.

- *Role confusion*—when one is unclear about his or her role, as with the police officer arriving on a domestic conflict scene after the couple has decided to make up.
- *Dual roles*—when the player has two roles, as with the financial planning consultant who ultimately wants to sell an investment product, but who also wants to maintain a long-standing friendship with the family's attorney.

Effective facilitators also know that some role enactments involve *role taking*, simply assuming the rigid parameters of a socially prescribed role; some involve *role playing*, where the participant renders the role with some freedom to interpret; and some actually requires *role creating*, where the participant has to improvise the role using a high degree of spontaneity and inventiveness. The facilitator also knows that most roles have a social aspect that emphasizes relationships and a *psychodynamic aspect* that emphasizes personality and the inner emotional life of the participant.

One of the favorite techniques of facilitators is role reversal, where two or more participants play a role and then are asked to switch and play the other person's role. Role reversal enables the participants to "walk in each other's shoes" and develop empathy for what it is like to be in the other role. Here is an interesting example of how role reversal is used to teach flight attendants about the needs of special travelers.

—United Airlines USA

*A*t the United Airlines Training Center near O'Hare Airport in Chicago, Illinois, flight attendants receive extensive human relations training in addition to their basic training on emergency procedures. Role play is used to teach attendants about the special needs of passengers who are blind, deaf, or in a wheelchair. "We give the trainees earplugs to make them deaf, blindfolds to make them blind, and we put them in a wheelchair," says Michele Manoski, manager of automation for flight operations. "They are not accustomed to being in these roles, and this gives them some experience in being disabled." Some of the trainees play the role of the attendant and some the role of the passenger. Then they switch. "After playing the role of the disabled they have a better idea about how to respond as an attendant," notes Manoski.

The variety inherent in differing types of roles offers the facilitator a good opportunity to guide the role play in a number of interesting directions. The skilled facilitator is aware of this variety and uses it appropriately to tailor the activity to desired learning outcomes.

The most frequently used technology to extend the power of role play is video. Facilitators often find it valuable to videotape the role play and replay sections of it, using the tape to focus on particular aspects of the role or specific behaviors. Participants usually enjoy the instant replay to analyze their own behaviors and consider what they might have done differently. Sometimes the role play is run again after watching the video. Occasionally a video is used to set up the environment of the role play, as in this example.

— American Red Cross USA

*A*merican Red Cross disaster mental health workers going into a disaster situation (hurricane, earthquake, bombing) often need skills in defusing and debriefing in an emotionally charged situation. Workers are taught the steps and are then asked to role play a partially scripted tense situation, as observers watch. "To get into the mood and simulate the environment of the disaster, we play a video with some strong scenes and noise—the next best thing to being there," says Christopher Saeger, senior training development associate. "It provides the context where the work will be done and creates the setting for the role play."

Role plays are a fairly simple, easy-to-manage form of the Virtual Reality Strategy, but they have great potential because there are so many ways to craft and adapt the basic technique.

Dramatic Scenarios

Dramatic scenarios are enactments of more complex situations, usually involving several characters and a problem that unfolds or evolves, much like a short scene from a play.

Dramatic scenarios—the term used in training settings—have their conceptual roots in *sociodrama* and *psychodrama*. Sociodrama tends to be concerned with social roles and relationships and is more often used for educational purposes. Psychodrama focuses more on the private concerns of individuals and is used primarily for therapeutic purposes. The techniques for both are quite similar, however, and both grow out of the work of their founder, J. L. Moreno.[18] Trainers can adapt the techniques used in sociodrama and psychodrama to enhance their work with dramatic scenarios in training settings.

Most dramatic scenarios also involve roles, so that everything that was said previously about roles in role playing also applies to dramatic scenarios. What makes a dramatic scenario different is the length of the action and the complexity of the situation.

Like a role play, the dramatic scenario needs something to get it started. There is a scene to be enacted, a little drama to be carried out, hence the term *scenario.* In some cases the scenario will be carefully worked out ahead of time, with scripts for each player, a description of the scene, a summary of the action, and perhaps even props and costumes. In other cases the preparations will be less formal, the actors will be given only general instructions, and the action will need to be invented, as in improvisational theater. For dramatic scenarios, the same three stages used in sociodrama apply:

• *Warming up* is used to help the participants make the transition from the life they have been living, full of its immediate concerns, to the world of drama. Participants need to be clear about their instructions, the content of the scenario, and the general goals of the activity. They need to get ready to play.
• *Enactment* is the actual portrayal of the situation. The portrayal needs to be taken with enough seriousness to create the virtual reality, but the emphasis should always be on the potential for learning, not the quality of the acting. Most of the learning should take place from the enactment itself.
• *Sharing* is useful for exploring the feelings and ideas of the participants retrospectively, as well as the observations of those who may have been watching.

The dramatic scenario, like sociodrama, should produce some *catharsis* (expressions of emotion), some new *insights* (fresh ideas), and some *role training* (new ability) for carrying out a role effectively in a particular situation.[19]

Facilitating Dramatic Scenarios

Several valuable techniques drawn from sociodrama can be used to facilitate the action of dramatic scenarios.[20]

• *Role reversal.* Players are shifted around to take other parts, either during the enactment or later in a rerun. Participants can be moved to another role to develop empathy and gain a new perspective and then be returned to their original role to complete the scenario.
• *Double.* A person is assigned to one of the actors to serve as an inner voice or alter ego. The double may interrupt the dialogue to

express the inner thoughts of his character or even act out body language that portrays his character's unexpressed inner feelings.

• *Mirror.* A double actually takes the player's place for a while, so that the player can step out and watch what has been happening. Sometimes the facilitator becomes the double or mirror, to provide support, to challenge, to question, or to magnify feelings.

• *Empty chair.* A place is assigned to an imaginary additional character, someone the players can vent their feelings on, experiment with, or turn to for advice.

• *Soliloquy.* This technique, often used in plays, provides a character the opportunity to emerge from the action and reflect on inner feelings—the most famous example being Hamlet's "to be, or not to be" soliloquy. In dramatic scenarios the facilitator may stand beside a player and call for a brief soliloquy on present thoughts or feelings.

• *Walk and talk.* The facilitator may ask the player to pace back and forth in a walk-and-talk soliloquy to reduce tension and get unstuck from a puzzling situation. Sometimes the facilitator will actually walk the player out of the scene and talk it over to find a new approach to the situation. A sensitive facilitator knows when a player wants to say "give me a minute," and will arrange for a brief time out as needed. After overcoming whatever it was the player was troubled about, the action can be resumed, and perhaps played out more productively.

• *Freeze frame.* The facilitator stops the action, as one might with a video. When the players hear the command to freeze, they are expected to stop where they are, and the facilitator can comment on body language, expressions, tone of voice, communication, or arrangement in space. Sometimes observers will be asked to comment on the freeze frame.

• *Concretization.* Abstract expressions like, "low man on the totem pole" or "bouncing off the walls," can be played out in concrete actions that represent feelings.

- *Sculpting.* A whole scene where relationships can be portrayed—for example, a dependent employee holding the supervisor around the knees, the supervisor turning to other employees for help—is enacted to shed light on a situation everyone knows but does not want to talk about.
- *Future projection.* The facilitator asks the players how they think this scene is going to play out sometime in the future.

The skilled facilitator not only sets the action in motion but knows how to use an array of techniques to structure the action as the drama unfolds so that learning is maximized.

Notice how dramatic scenarios are used effectively in the training of cadets at the Royal Canadian Mounted Police Training Academy in Regina, Saskatchewan, Canada.

Royal Canadian Mounted Police CANADA

When the curriculum for training cadets at the Royal Canadian Mounted Police (Gendarmerie Royale du Canada) Training Academy was shifted from a didactic tell-and-test approach to the current problem-based method, scenarios were introduced to create real-life situations illustrating typical problems faced in police work. Although some scenarios serve primarily as cases for discussion, others are adapted for dramatization, both for teaching and assessment. Dramatic scenarios may range from situations as simple as young boys stealing apples from a neighbor's tree, to domestic violence or a break-and-enter situation. The drama usually starts with the role play of a phone call that sets the action in motion. In one scenario, the scene then shifts to a restaurant where two young officers have gone to gather some information. Suddenly a situation develops: A patron gets nervous, his girlfriend freaks out, and the owner wants to know what is going on. The girl is lashing out. Does she need to be restrained? What is the role of the police now? "We have used paid actors in the past," notes Corporal Donna Morken, of the Canadian Law Enforcement Training Unit, "but now we tend to rely on retirees, students, and people from the community. We make it as realistic as possible with props, costumes, wigs, and weapons. The pairs of cadets are there with their batons, pepper spray, and dummy guns. We pose the situation, the actors rehearse it, and they all play it out." The dramatization can go in different directions, it can be stopped and started again; the facilitator can intervene, and it can be replayed with a new pair of cadets. Although the scenarios are used primarily for learning how to handle a real situation effectively, they are also used in the final assessment process with cadets along with a written final and oral panel. "The field supervisors are so impressed with the knowledge and confidence of our graduates in responding to scenarios," notes Gary Bell, officer in charge, training program support and evaluation, "that they want to send them out on the job directly. We know we've done a good job preparing the cadets for the real world with these scenarios, but we believe that the six-month, probationary assignment is still necessary."

Sharing the Learning

Participants usually will recognize when the scene has been played out, and the facilitator needs to end the enactment and begin the *sharing*.[21] Often the players will need an opportunity to express their feelings—frustration, embarrassment, confusion, satisfaction—and get out of their role. The observers, who have been patient in their observation, are eager to talk and want to comment. The facilitator can help set ground rules for sharing, such as nonjudgmental observation, acceptance of divergent opinions, honest disclosure, and minimization of the giving of advice and drawing of morals. Observers need to remember that the day will come when they will be the players, so they should present their observations in the form they themselves would like to receive them.

In training settings, sharing is very important to show how the dramatic scenario fosters learning that will result in improved performance in the workplace.

Once again, video is the preferred technology for extending the power of dramatic scenarios. Because the action is more complex than role play, it may be valuable to use more than one camera. A second camera can capture the nuances of dialogue or be used to zoom in on the activity of a primary player. In more sophisticated arrangements, a mixer can be used to edit and blend the input of multiple cameras. Videos can be replayed and can be used to focus on particular behaviors for the sharing session. Participants learning complex roles may wish to take their videotape home to study it closely or play it for someone else to further share and discuss the learning.

Although dramatic scenarios are more complex than role plays and demand more knowledge and skill from the facilitator, they offer great opportunities for creating a safe and inexpensive virtual reality for training.

Simulations and Games

Role plays and dramatic scenarios both have an element of virtual reality about them, but with simulations and games the virtual reality becomes even more important, and the complexity increases. The terms *simulation* and *game* are often used interchangeably in the writing about them, and sometimes the terms *simulation game* or *simulation/game* are used, adding confusion.

Simulations are representations of some aspect of the real world where abstract models are developed and then manipulated in dynamic ways to create learning.[22] Simulation involves abstracting elements of a social or physical reality so that a person can enter into it and learn.[23]

Simulations can lean in one of two directions: Either they are set up to explore, understand, or practice *social interactions* among individuals or groups; or they are arranged to explore, understand, or practice aspects of the *physical or mechanical world*.[24] Some simulations used in training, for example, are designed to explore aspects of organizational behavior, teamwork, or the provision of services; but other simulations establish a practice setting for production processes, using equipment, or mechanical support services. Note how these two simulations differ.

United Airlines USA

𝓕light attendants at the United Airlines Training Center use a simulated airplane cabin to practice serving procedures. "Flight attendants work in teams under conditions of limited time, space, and equipment," notes Michelle Manoski, manager of automation for flight operations. "How do you compensate when someone is too slow or too fast? We put them into the cabin and let them work it out." Interestingly, the simulation exercise takes its place between on-flight observation and mandatory supervised operating experience. In this case, simulation is an important bridge to the real world.

Eastman Kodak USA

𝓞ne wing of the Eastman Kodak Company Education and Development Center in Rochester, New York, contains a series of laboratories with equipment used to simulate real situations in various aspects of plant operations. For example, one lab contains a series of portable carts that contain all the equipment needed to simulate operations in an emulsion processing unit. "Emulsion," explains David Carlson, technical instructor, "is what makes film sensitive to light. Photographic film has multiple layers of emulsion. The portable labs have all the same equipment that employees will see on the job," notes Carlson. "They learn to control the flow rate, the mixing speed, the temperature or pressure, and how to prevent bubbles, and they learn this in a safe environment where they can't ruin a whole batch of emulsion. It's one small step in manufacturing film, but it has to be controlled precisely."

In the first example (United Airlines), the emphasis is clearly on simulating social interactions, but in the second (Eastman Kodak), a physical environment is being simulated.

A game is a type of simulation that stresses competition among adversaries, a contest with rules and a clear outcome.[25] Although in most games players or groups of players compete against each other, sometimes they work together against a common adversary or to control a natural event or destructive force. If we eliminate games that are played simply for entertainment, such as sports or board games, and if we also eliminate games that deal in abstractions and are designed primarily to stretch the mind or cultivate creativity, then we are left with serious games that simulate for educational purposes.

A good example is provided in the public policy games used at the Foreign Service Institute of the U.S. Department of State. Drawing on the earlier experience with war games and business games, foreign policy experts began to develop games "to simulate official decision making about world events in a controlled setting." Lincoln Bloomfield at M.I.T. and Harold Gutzekow at Northwestern University were leaders in this effort in the 1960s, along with the Rand Corporation, and today games are widely used to simulate foreign policy decision making.[26] Here is an illustration of how foreign policy games are used at the Foreign Service Institute.

— Foreign Service Institute USA

*I*n a foreign policy game used at the Foreign Service Institute of the U.S. Department of State, teams are usually assigned to represent different countries and other interested parties. For example, in the Caspian Oil Pipeline Game, developed and played out in 1995, teams were assigned for key countries—the United States, Russia, Turkey, Georgia, and Azerbaijan—and to the Azerbaijan International Operating Company (AIOC), a consortium of eleven oil companies developing offshore interests in the Caspian Sea. The goal of the game was to try to assist policy makers and analysts to think ahead on how the development of Caspian Sea oil reserves will affect key interests of the major countries in the region and U.S. policy. In games such as these, players are given an introduction that describes the central issue, the roles for the teams, the schedule, and the ground rules as well as a detailed scenario to frame background issues and introduce a problem that is likely to emerge in due time. The players first meet separately, as teams, to explore the *Taskers* (key questions) and *Action Options* provided for them and to begin to anticipate what issues will develop. The control group manages and monitors the game, providing input and sometimes altering the course of the game. The control group observes the process closely through one-way glass and sometimes introduces a scenario update, a news bulletin, or a television announcement to complicate the situation. Although the teams are competing against each other and, in a sense, against the control group, "the main value of the game," notes Fred Hill, director of special programs, "is to project ahead, to test various policies, to see how knowledgeable people react to these, and to identify effective options for dealing with the key issues, perhaps coming up with ideas or initiatives that will reduce or prevent conflict. The games simulate a real situation and bring forth issues and responses that even the experts haven't thought about, and they are used not so much to decide policies but to foresee issues that might arise and develop ways of responding creatively." Examples of topics used for other games include U.N. Security Council Expansion, NATO Enlargement, Environmental Security, and U.S. Balkan Policy.

This example shows some of the common elements of games: They usually have players set against each other as individuals or teams, they have an element of competition leading to conflict or negotiation, and they include a dynamic situation that is played out to some resolution over time. Not all simulations are games; some have no clear outcome or competitive element, and not all games are simulations because some games lack a component of virtual reality. Simulations and games that simulate are so close in spirit, however, that they can be treated as nearly the same— give or take the competitive element—within the Virtual Reality Strategy.

Simulations and games are made up of certain components, and understanding the components is important for the facilitators who wish to use this aspect of the Virtual Reality Strategy effectively. Although authors use a variety of terms to describe these components, we believe they can be reduced to a simple list of eight words that all begin with *R:*

• *Reasons.* There must be a clear purpose or set of reasons for the activity, such as economy, safety, exploration, or practice. The reasons will set the guidelines for other decisions and will give the activity a particular emphasis.[27] What learning is desirable? In what context will it be used? What is the fundamental purpose of the activity?

• *Reality.* Choices need to be made about what aspect of reality is to be portrayed. The simulation activity will incorporate some abstraction of reality as a model. What elements will be highlighted and which will be eliminated? How much and what kinds of reality will be drawn into the model?[28]

• *Roles.* Roles need to be defined and allocated and a scenario provided. Who are the players and what roles will they play? What will they do? How will the object of the activity get them into action? Where will the action carry them?

• *Rules.* The activity will have certain rules or procedures that set the parameters for the players. The rules actually drive the game and set up or limit possibilities. How will the rules be determined and communicated? Can the rules be broken or modified? How will rules be enforced? What will be the combination of personal choice and chance?[29]

• *Resources.* The activity will utilize certain resources, such as a simulated room or apparatus, graphic displays, problems, data banks, objects, videos, audiotapes, materials, supplies, implements for writing and recording, and so forth. What resources will this activity need, and at what times will they be needed?

• *Records.* The activity may generate information, data, scores, or possibly the need for calculations. What will be the accounting system for the activity? Who will keep track of the data that is generated and meet the needs for data analysis? Will a computer be used for computations or word processing, or perhaps both? What procedures will be set to establish the accounting system, and in what sequence will information be received and delivered?[30]

• *Running time.* The activity will have certain steps of play, phases, or sequences of activity.[31] Sometimes these are incorporated into directions or intermittent commands. What is the simulated time frame (day, month, quarter) for the activity, and what amount of real time will be allocated for the simulated time? What cycles will the activity have and how much time will be allocated for the various cycles? How much simulated time is represented in a cycle?

• *Results.* The activity will produce certain results, perhaps a successful or unsuccessful outcome, winners and losers, or a resolution of some type. To what extent is the resolution defined or open? How will the players know when the game is over? How will the activity be concluded?

Notice how choices about these eight *R*s have been made in a simulation used by Merrill Lynch for training investors.

─Merrill Lynch USA

*O*ne of many financial services offered by Merrill Lynch & Co., Inc., is capital markets investment. New York is the center for training for five regional offices—Chicago, Atlanta, Boston, Los Angeles, and Dallas— that specialize in capital markets. Capital markets involve big investments, not the small amounts that individuals put into mutual funds or stocks at the advice of their financial planners, but the huge sums invested by insurance companies, retirement funds, banks, or other financial institutions. These organizations with money to invest come to the market seeking good investments, and of course, there are institutions coming to the market looking for sources of money for debt financing, for expansion, and for capital development. The Merrill Lynch brokers who make these marriages are experienced investors, usually with M.B.A. degrees and high levels of confidence, so the training for them needs to have clear *reasons* and be challenging. One activity the brokers have enjoyed is the Investment Manager Game, developed expressly to simulate the *reality* of the financial environment in which they must make decisions. The participants work in teams of five and take on the *roles* of brokers, clients, and investors. Everyone is governed by the real-world *rules* for investing, and the object is to make a good match, meeting the varying needs of each client. The brokers have all kinds of *resources* at their disposal—background information on clients and investment possibilities, historical trends, news updates, and other general financial and market information. The computer is available to keep *records*, analyze the data, and simulate actual performance. The *running time* is four days, but in that real time, the simulated time of a whole year passes, one day representing a quarter. At the beginning of each new day, players are given the simulated *results* of how their investment decisions worked out, and based on performance, new decisions need to be made about how to adjust. At the end of the four days, the participants write a report analyzing their work, and five teams are selected to present their results and their rationale to the other participants, with as many as seventy trainees working on these simulations simultaneously. "The question we ask," notes Vice President Judith Swedek, director of training, institutional business group, "is how well did you do for your client based on what they wanted? The results can sometimes be humbling even for experienced investors. It is a good way to practice, because usually sizable sums of money are involved."

Facilitating Games and Simulations

As with the facilitator of the role play or the director of the dramatic scenario, the gamer has certain responsibilities in managing a simulation or game.[32] For simulations and games, *planning* takes a high priority because once set in motion, the simulation should run itself. Here is a planning checklist:

1. *Selection.* The facilitator plays an important role in the selection of the game or simulation. Because there are many off-the-shelf games available, the first step is to become aware of what the possibilities are. Although there are many classic games, some having been available for twenty years or more, new games with increasing levels of sophistication are being developed each year.

2. *Adaptation.* An existing simulation can sometimes be adapted (within the confines of copyright) to fit a particular purpose or time frame.

3. *Creation.* More work may be necessary for the creation of a simulation or game, but in the long run, a simulation or game may be more suited to specific training purposes, especially if the goal is to create a virtual reality.

4. *Participation.* Prior to taking on the facilitator role, it is desirable to participate as a player to gain complete familiarity with how the simulation works.

5. *Materials.* The materials need to be carefully developed and arranged for timely presentation.

6. *Role allocation.* Assignment to groups and to individual roles needs to be well conceived and carried out through a deliberate process involving either random assignment, selection and appointment, or seeking of volunteers.

7. *Space arrangement.* The location needs to fit the activities planned and may include more than one space, arrangements for media, one or more home bases for the participants, laboratory space as needed, or perhaps a specially designed simulated environment.

8. *Accounting.* Provisions need to be made when data banks are used or when quantitative information is generated and needs to be analyzed.

9. *Briefing.* Before the simulation begins, the facilitator holds a briefing to make assignments, give an overview of the activity, provide materials, explain the roles and rules, and alert the participants to the types of learning anticipated.

10. *Detached observation.* Once the simulation is underway, the facilitator usually cultivates an air of studied detachment. Unlike the director of a dramatic scenario, the facilitator of a simulation is more like a prop manager, trying to stay offstage, limiting visibility, restraining the urge to intervene, and generally maintaining a poker face devoid of an expression of either satisfaction or displeasure. There are several reasons for this: A well-planned simulation or game should be so well designed as to run almost unassisted; the participants should own their activity, and the mood should not be interrupted, thus heightening the semblance of reality.

11. *Time management.* The facilitator, therefore, is primarily a time manager, initiating the action, helping participants make transitions through cycles, letting the players know how much time they have left or what deadlines they must meet, and making decisions about when to stop or whether to rerun. Thus the facilitator

may circulate and observe, but not direct or intrude, because the action, growing out of the roles and rules, will take care of itself.

12. *Debriefing.* The facilitator gets back into a more familiar role during the debriefing when the participants are asked to describe their learning. The key challenge here is to get the participants to stop talking about the details of the activity and to extract from it the essence of the learning.

The emphasis on planning and the limited role of the facilitator are well illustrated in the following example.

—Prudential Intercultural USA

𝒫rudential Insurance of America, Inc., like many large companies, has several collateral interests, one of which is Prudential Resources Management, which provides, among other things, relocation services and cross-cultural training through Prudential Intercultural, located in Boulder, Colorado. One of its projects was to develop a simulation for a group of sales representatives doing business in the People's Republic of China. The trainees were experienced go-getters, but there was some concern that they were not being as effective as they could be because they lacked detailed understanding about how business is done in China. "The company wanted something very hands-on but also high level, confrontational, and compressed," notes Ann Wederspahn, director of consulting services, intercultural services. The training ran from noon on day one to noon on day three, long fourteen- to sixteen-hour days. The training began with presentations on history, geography, and culture as background. The simulation itself began at dinner, a formal banquet, on the first evening. "We hired ten Chinese to act assigned roles and provided ten hours of training for them," notes Wederspahn. "They were all given hidden agendas and were instructed to find out as much as possible about the Americans while revealing as little as possible about themselves. All of a sudden the Americans are at this banquet, with seating agendas, gift giving, and toasting, and they are fairly confused, to say the least." At seven-thirty the next morning, there is a debriefing by the facilitator and two of the Chinese, and the Americans gradually discover what was happening to them. The simulation continues through a second phase, where the Americans make a proposal; a third phase, where the Chinese respond; and a fourth phase of hard negotiation. There is debriefing after each phase, but the carefully planned simulations run themselves. Because everything for the simulations has been so well designed and carefully staged, the simulator's role is limited primarily to debriefing. The simulation ends with a protocol dinner at another restaurant, and by now the Americans are learning what to do, where to stand and sit, what to use, and what not to talk about. "At the end, we let the Chinese come out of their roles, so the Americans can learn who they really are. It's a real boot camp, tough and confrontative, but it gets great reviews," notes Wederspahn.

One advantage of simulations and games is that they can be run on any scale desired, ranging from the brief, focused game that lasts a few hours, to much longer, more elaborate arrangements of roles and activities that can become, indeed, quite complex. If the reality to be simulated is complex, then the virtual reality needed to simulate it may be difficult to create, consuming extensive time and resources. Notice the effort that goes into developing and carrying out a simulation that enables participants to practice their responses to a large-scale disaster.

—National Emergency Training Center USA

*D*isaster training is one of the main responsibilities of the National Emergency Training Center of the U.S. Federal Emergency Management Agency (FEMA). "Few people understand the level of risk for potential disaster that surrounds all of our lives," notes Bruce Marshall, preparedness training and exercises director. "Every state in the Union has tornadoes, 70 percent of all settlements are in river valleys, all of

New Orleans is below sea level, and the East and Gulf coasts are quite vulnerable to hurricanes. St. Louis and many other communities, not just L.A. and San Francisco, sit on potential earthquake sites, and who knows where an airplane will crash or a terrorist bomb will explode." The National Emergency Training Center provides an array of educational materials and training experiences through what has become the largest satellite training center in the world, but one of their most fascinating on-site activities is a complex simulation where local communities can practice and test their emergency preparedness. Teams of thirty to fifty people are invited for the Integrated Emergency Management Course—appropriate representatives of policy level groups, coordination agencies, and operations units. In a simulation done for Kansas City, Missouri, for example, fifty-two trainees participated, including, among many others, the assistant city manager; city council members; the chief of the fire department and chief of police and their several deputies; the Jackson County sheriff; police dispatchers; the director of technical services of Missouri Gas Energy; the associate superintendent of schools and the school security director; a legislator; a community psychologist; associate director of ambulance services; representatives from the Health Department, the National Guard, the Red Cross, and the Salvation Army; and the communications director from the Mayor's office. "We invite a broad cross section of players and we use their population, their topography, and their emergency plan. After several hours of lectures going over what we know about effective responses to disasters—and we know a lot now—we put them into the labs we have designed to simulate their work space. They have a regular Emergency Operations Center (EOC) (comparable to the 911 center in most communities), and they know who is supposed to be there and what roles they are to play. In the EOC they have phones, televisions, radios, computers—everything they need.

There is a second room for the mayor, council members, and city administrators—the policy people. And then there's us, the people who designed the simulation and who facilitate it, off in our separate room."

From still another room, the media control center, the facilitators can send out pretaped radio or TV announcements as the simulation progresses. The disaster unfolds—earthquake, flood, spill, terrorist activity, or maybe a combination—and the personnel in the EOC and the mayor's office have to manage it. The facilitators are all experienced in disaster work, and they know how to make it come alive. "We can play some real nasty tricks, right up to wiping out their whole infrastructure. We also know the little annoyances: For example, in many responses the relief vehicles get a lot of flat tires; so when you run out of tires, where do you get more?" The participants may make good or bad decisions, and they have to live with the consequences that keep piling up. "Is it realistic, we asked?" "The room temperature," says Marshall, "heats up to about 80° from the cool 65° we always start with. It runs for about 4 1/2 hours straight, and most people get very involved emotionally, because this could be their city. Once I saw a fire chief and police chief get in a fight and I thought punches were going to fly." There is a cooling off period and then an extensive two-hour debriefing for a serious examination of the adequacy of the plan and its method of implementation. "We hope that the participants will never need to use their plan, but if they do, we want them to be ready for anything. We had the folks from Oklahoma City here only two weeks before the bombing."

High-Tech Virtual Reality

The ultimate virtual reality is the high-tech simulator. Its virtual reality is so close to reality that it is hardly virtual. This kind of training environment can now be created by employing a broad range of sophisticated technologies and coordinating them with computers. What technologies are used in a simulator? Virtually all of them. Taped or filmed images are used with realistic, recorded or generated sounds. Controls can be made to feel completely real and give real responses. The entire environment can be lifted, tilted, leaned, and twisted. All of the media employed can be controlled by computers, communicating back responses to actions taken by the trainee. The simulator works as a manipulable cybernetic system, and can be programmed to do whatever the "real one" does. The instructor can use it to create any desired situation for training, moving forward or back, changing, repeating, or modifying the environment at will, until the trainee gets it right. Consider the flight training simulators used by United Airlines.

─ United Airlines USA

*N*ear the "old" Stapleton International Airport in Denver, Colorado, pilots are trained on the most up-to-date and sophisticated flight simulators that money can buy at the United Airlines Flight Training Center. Around 800 people work at the Center, including around 180 just to maintain the whole operation. Does it matter that the Flight Training Center is miles from the new Denver International Airport? Not really. There is no need for a runway, or even an airplane. "We call this zero-time airplane training," says Gene Yokomizo, manager of flight simulator services. "That means that the first time the pilot flies the new seat, it is an actual flight with passengers on board. The partner for that flight is a very experienced senior pilot with that aircraft, and there is a specified number of hours in that arrangement, but there is no training in an airplane at all. We used two to four hours of airplane training before, but it was far too expensive. It is much cheaper this way, and safer, too," notes Yokomizo. How much cheaper is it? It has to save a huge sum, for example, to pay for the new simulator for the Boeing 777, which comes in at around $16 million.

A pilot with enough seniority who bids on a new seat and gets it— a larger aircraft or an upgrade with more responsibility in the same aircraft—comes in for a month of training. Even new pilots are experienced and have 3,000 to 5,000 hours in the air; United is not spending its time teaching people how to fly, only how to fly its aircraft. The training begins with a two-week ground school, presentations and explanations coupled with significant amounts of computer-based training done independently. The pilot also spends four to eight sessions in a Flight Management and Systems Trainer, a "mini-simulator" that teaches and allows practice of the flight management system for a particular airplane. Then it is time for training in the simulator for the aircraft the pilot will be flying.

The Flight Training Center has thirty full-flight simulators. These are arranged in large bays of about five or six each, with two bays joined by a large computer room that serves both bays. The simulator looks exactly like (and for the most part is) the cockpit of a particular aircraft—727, 747, 777—and is approached up a long flight of stairs leading to a platform and entryway. Inside the simulator, just behind the seats for the pilots, is a third seat for a trainer, who sits in front of an impressive control panel that can be used to send the pilot anything from changes in visibility to engine loss or wind shear. Where the pilots look out the windshield of the cockpit, they see images produced either by a CRT with a collinating mirror for a three-dimensional effect with 75° vision, or a wide-screen projection system with 150° vision—both are used depending on the aircraft. The pilots' headsets provide the same radio control tower chatter they would hear, and the sound of the engines is simulated by sound systems exactly as it would be on the actual airplane. The controls do what they would normally do and feel like what they would feel like while doing it. The entire simulator is moved around by hydraulic and mechanical six-axis motion systems so that the nose rises on takeoff, and the cockpit rolls right or left when turning. All of the data from the simulated mechanical systems, such as cable systems to the wings, ailerons, and rudder is turned into digital data for the computer. "Is it a big computer?" we asked naively. "Well, it is actually sets of computers," replied Yokomizo, "for example, a total of eighteen computers guide the new 777 simulator."

Routine flying conditions can be simulated, such as a typical city-to-city flight, or landings at any of the airports where United flies that aircraft. Much of the training, however, focuses on emergency procedures, and that is why simulation is so important. Pilots need to be able to deal with any malfunction, such as a hydraulic leak or loss of power, and use advanced maneuvers to handle unusual conditions. Even a crash can be simulated, not just any crash, but a particular crash, such as the one in Sioux City.

Time in the simulator is preceded by a briefing and is followed up with extensive debriefing. For the final city-to-city simulation a camcorder in the cockpit records exactly what the pilots did, and the tape is played back later for discussion in the debriefing. "In the context of the total training program," notes Yokomizo, "the simulator is indispensable. It is actually better than a real airplane, because you can try things, like cutting out one engine, that you really wouldn't want to do in a flight. Take, for example, wind-shear training, where United has been a real pioneer in training; what would you do, fly around until you find some wind-shear conditions and then fly into them? No way! But we can simulate those conditions with the flick of a switch."

United is constantly gathering data on the effectiveness of the simulation training, trying to make little improvements wherever possible. All pilots also get three days a year of recurrent training, to sharpen up skills needed for unusual conditions. "It must be working," said Yokomizo, because to date United has had no accidents in eighteen years attributable to pilot error."

THE BOTTOM LINE

Some jobs need to be practiced before they are actually performed because making mistakes can cause big problems. Role plays, dramatic scenarios and games, and simulations provide a safe virtual reality where participants can learn to play their role comfortably and with increasing levels of proficiency.

Role playing requires careful choices among many options for arrangements, well-crafted roles, and a facilitator able to draw people into playing various types of roles and role relationships.

Dramatic scenarios require appropriate preparations to develop the script and set the scene, and an active job for the facilitator in directing the drama and helping participants to share their learning when it is over.

Simulations require extensive preparations because once set in motion they should run themselves, but the facilitator plays a key role in briefing and debriefing.

Sophisticated virtual realities may be high-tech or low-tech. High-tech virtual realities draw on many media coordinated by computers to simulate situations almost indistinguishable from reality. Low-tech virtual realities are clever in their use of people to simulate social systems.

The principles guiding the use of the Virtual Reality Strategy grow out of well-researched and long-established work in sociology, psychodrama, sociodrama, and simulation and gaming theory.

Some simulated realities are even better than reality.

II

The Holistic Strategy

Mentoring and Counseling

*H*umanity has survived for over three million years because of its many-sided powers of adaptation. Unlike the rest of the animal kingdom, human beings possess the power to reflect, to observe themselves, and to modify their encounters with the world in order to meet their needs. This encounter with the world is called experience. Experience has been the basis of learning from the first human appearance on earth.[1]

—PHIL GANG, "Experiential Learning" in
Holistic Education: Principles, Perspectives, and Practices

HOLISTIC STRATEGY OVERVIEW

BEST USE
Reflection on a potentially educative experience from which personal learning and self-discovery may derive.

LEARNING THEORY
Holistic learning and constructivist psychology. Experience-based learning and reflection on what has occurred under the guidance of a mentor or skilled helper who provides challenge and support.

HISTORICAL ROOTS
Recent studies of brain evolution and function. Counseling theory with its roots in Freud's talking cure and Rogers's client-centered therapy.

APPLICATIONS
Experience-based learning settings, such as cross-cultural, arranged, or natural work experience.

PARTICIPANT ROLES
Involves participants holistically in multichannel processing of experience and provides opportunities for reflection and expression about the meaning of the experience.

NATURE OF MOTIVATION
Grows out of the participants' initial involvement in selecting the experience and wanting to succeed in it and make meaning of it.

PARTICIPANT FIT
Best for participants who learn by doing, enjoy new experiences, have some ability to size up a situation, and possess an openness to self-examination.

FACILITATOR'S ROLE
Matches participants to appropriate experiences, devises adequate orientation, provides useful mechanisms for reflection, and engages in one-on-one interaction as a skilled helper who provides support and challenge.

STRENGTHS
Puts participants in real-world learning situations, which involve the total self and call for insight, action, and self-examination. Is often a welcome relief from more structured classroom learning. Is spontaneous, down-to-earth, and useful.

WEAKNESSES
Forgoes the benefits of more systematic input of new information and structured inquiry. Is subject to the hazards of vague goals, loose structure, and ambiguous outcomes. Includes many factors in the learning situation that may be beyond the control of the learner and the facilitator.

Experience-Based Learning

Everyone learns from experience, we say, but alas, we all know people who never seem to. But what is experience and how do we learn from it? We say of a new worker that he is inexperienced, and we say of the new manager that she is very experienced. We look back and say, "that was a painful experience, but actually it was a good learning experience." We often mention "learning" and "experience" in the same breath. What is the connection?

If there is one thing that organizations have plenty of, it is experience. Perhaps all this experience can be harnessed for learning. After all, colleges and universities use experience for learning; they send students off campus for cooperative education work experience in business and industry. Some professional programs want students to have internship experience. Many universities today encourage students to have a study abroad experience, a wilderness challenge experience, or a service learning experience. Some high schools also provide opportunities for out-of-the-classroom learning experiences. All of this is usually referred to as *experiential education.* The assumption behind these programs is that something can be learned from a structured experience that puts students in a new or challenging situation out of which various kinds of learning can arise.

Organizations also use experience for learning. They are, of course, often on the receiving end of cooperative education and internship placements, and they play an important role in the supervision of these experiences. Many organizations are also beginning to use experience as a basis of learning for their own employees or volunteers. Consider the following examples:

- Asea Brown Boveri (ABB) provides three internal rotations and an overseas placement to train first-year employees just out of college.

- United Airlines uses observation flights and practice runs as part of the training for flight attendants.
- J.D. Edwards sends translators overseas to learn how the technical language of their software products works in a specific setting.
- Employees at the Lai Lai Sheraton in Taiwan go out to observe the services at other hotels and return to discuss what they have seen.
- Promising actors at the Guthrie Theater track real people and then use these experiences to transform themselves into characters.
- New teachers at ELSI Taiwan Language Schools are mentored to ensure continuous improvement of their teaching of English.
- Route drivers at Coors Distributing learn to improve sales techniques from a trainer who rides their routes with them.
- The president of ARIEL Corporation mentors his son on the elegance of engineering design.
- Top managers at American Express Financial Advisors learn to reflect on their leadership experience through executive coaching.

In organizational settings, this type of learning is sometimes known as *action learning*. We prefer the term *experience-based learning* to describe these activities.

Experience-based learning refers to sponsored or guided experiences identified or established for the express purpose of bringing about learning. In most cases this involves procedures for selecting or assigning the experience, planning for it, supervising it, and making provisions for participants to reflect on the experience.

Experience-based learning is illustrated in the following two rather different examples.

—Asea Brown Boveri SWEDEN

*A*sea Brown Boveri AB, known around the world as ABB, is now the world's largest electrotechnical company and is capable of delivering entire atomic power plants to any place in the world. ABB is actually a federation of more than 1,300 companies in 140 countries. The home for ABB Atom AB is Västeras, Sweden, a small city west of Stockholm. ABB Atom AB has an impressive internship program for new recruits that draws heavily on experience-based learning. The best graduates of the Swedish universities are recruited, and they go through a battery of intelligence and academic tests, writing tests, group problem-solving tests, personality measures, and a psychiatric interview. "It's not easy to get in," says Reijo Palola, director of university relations, "because we invest a great deal in the successful candidates." The new graduates are involved in six months of experience-based learning on three different assignments for two months each. One of the former interns, Camilla Podowski, now an employee at the Nuclear Fuel Division, described her experience to us: "The first six months, we work at ABB Atom AB; but they also send us abroad for six months, so we end up with a cross-cultural experience and a network of international contacts. For each assignment we have a real project and a real boss, and we talk with them each day. At the end of the assignment, we write a report, not only on the work, but on what we learned from the experience. The boss makes a report, too. We also have an interview at the end of each two months with a person from human resource administration—I called her my extra 'mommy'—and she wants to know what we are learning, too. She asks about our experience and how we feel about what is happening. When we are ready for the international assignment, we may do intensive foreign language study or spend some time in the country polishing language skills. They also give us cross-cultural training to prepare us for the culture shock. We have the same conversations with our overseas boss, we write a report, and when we come back we have the debriefing with our 'mommy' again." At the end, ABB Atom AB has a very good idea of what a trainee has experienced and what they have learned.

—United Airlines USA

*A*lthough United Airlines conducts extensive classroom instruction for flight attendants, parts of the training involve learning from experience. Trainees are instructed on what to look for, sent on an observation flight, and debriefed afterward. They go on a supervised flight where they do the actual job but under supervision. There are also support rides where an experienced attendant goes with a new one. New attendants learn from experience during their final six months as a probationer and meet regularly with an assigned supervisor. "All of this involves learning from hands-on experience," notes Heather Peterson, special assignment flight attendant, "and it is a good follow-up to the formal training."

Learning Through Experience

How is it that raw experience becomes educative? The answer to this question is found in the work of David Kolb, a contemporary theorist of experiential learning. Drawing on the earlier work of Lewin, Dewey, and Piaget, Kolb sets forth a cyclical model of experiential learning, shown in Figure 11.1.[2]

Experiential learning begins in concrete experience. The learner has some experience to begin with and then reflects on what that experience means. As the reflection deepens, the learner formulates abstract conceptualizations about what has taken place, that is, how experience works. As the abstract conceptualizations are developed, they must be tested to see if they do indeed work. This testing is done through a process of active experimentation, which of necessity returns the learner once again to concrete experience. For Kolb, "ideas are not fixed and immutable elements of thought but are formed and reformed through experience." Understanding is a process of continuous construction,

Figure 11.1 Experiential Learning Cycle

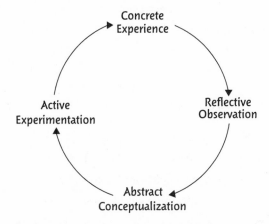

built on the interaction of ideas and experience. "Failure to modify ideas and habits as a result of experience is maladaptive. Therefore, one must engage in a continuous cycle of experience, reflection, abstraction, and testing, finally returning to experience once again." Kolb's work shows that experienced-based learning involves some steps, some phases, a going out and coming back, and above all, a process of reflection, as illustrated in the next two interesting examples.

— J.D. Edwards USA

*J.*D. Edwards World Source Company is a software producer based in Denver, Colorado, with more than 3,800 customers in ninety countries. J.D. Edwards relies heavily on people with high-level translation skills to translate its products into other languages. Although the company employs translators who are bilingual and native speakers, sometimes it is useful to send them overseas to experience how the software is being used in a particular setting and learn how the technical language works for the end user. "We customize the experience to the needs of a particular translator, so we send them out to visit one of our partners to see what the work is like there and how our product is actually used," notes

Susan Daly, manager of worldwide translations. "When they come back we want to know what they have experienced, and we ask them a lot of questions about what we should pay attention to and change. It is their native language, but they absorb a lot about technical usage in the software business by being there."

Lai Lai Sheraton TAIWAN, REPUBLIC OF CHINA

The Lai Lai Sheraton was one of the first five-star hotels in Taiwan. Privately owned, but affiliated with the chain, the Lai Lai identifies employees with the right talents and trains them to be trainers and facilitators. "They have a training club, a jacket, a logo, and a better shot at promotions," notes Abraham Folts, training supervisor. One important and successful part of the program at the Lai Lai has involved experience-based learning. "We go out and visit other hotels," says Folts. "Usually we make arrangements to cooperate on this, but if they don't want to, we can visit anyway as customers." Folts sends out teams of four to five employees to check out various aspects of the competitive hotel's services. "We don't just send them out; they know what to look for," observes Folts. "They have special areas of focus, checklists, and they know how to look at products, services, and attitudes." Sometimes, when the other hotel is cooperating, we get to talk to supervisors or even the general manager about what they are trying to improve." When the participants come back from this experience they have a lot to talk about, and this is where the training club people come in as facilitators. "They help the participants talk about the good points, the breakdowns in quality, the things they think need improvement." The program does not stop there. "Then we make a similar visit in our own hotel. We go into the restaurant, the bar, the lobby, and we have our standard operating procedure (SOP), but what we want to know is how it is working." The same discussion, facilitated by the trainers, follows the experience at the Lai Lai. "We train the employees to see service, and we want to know what their reaction to it is when it breaks down. How can the situation be corrected?" When this phase is done, the participants may go back through the Lai Lai for another visit with a supervisor who points out additional things they may have missed. "This isn't a factory," notes Folts, "this is a service industry, and you have to go out and see it as it happens, as the guests experience it."

What is the learning that takes place from this going out and coming back? Is it a mere application of knowledge learned elsewhere to a practical setting, or is there a new, perhaps qualitatively different, kind of learning that grows up out of experience? Some would argue that knowledge gained through experience in organizations is quite different from knowledge gained through formal training or study. This case has been made by Donald Schön in a stimulating book entitled *The Reflective Practitioner: How Professionals Think in Action*.[3] His argument is as follows:

• Professional education—the education of practitioners in law, medicine, theology, social work, engineering, and business—has been dominated by a model for training known as *Technical Rationality*. Technical Rationality stresses the development of a standardized body of knowledge—information, principles, theories—that can then be applied consistently to recurring professional problems.
• Most professional training involves an early disciplinary or basic science phase, an applied science (skill) or applications phase, and a professional phase. In other words, first you have to learn the theory, then you go out and apply it.
• The model of Technical Rationality has dominated professional education so completely that almost no one questions it.
• The world of professional practice today is not as neat and tidy as the model of Technical Rationality would suggest. The older model of more or less routine problems of practice to which standardized knowledge applies is no longer functional. There are too many cases that are not in the books, too many unique and unpredictable elements, too many unstable contexts for the old formulas to work.

• What is needed today is a new way of preparing professionals that goes beyond the incomplete model of Technical Rationality, a new way of knowing called *reflection-in-action*. Reflection-in-action, it turns out, is a way of knowing that grows out of experience. It is a kind of knowing that is in our action. Professional practitioners must think about what they are doing while they are doing it, and it is in this way that they learn from experience.

There is a commonsense resonance to the idea that we learn from experience—that knowing grows up rather naturally from action. The tightrope walker, for example, learns to walk the wire from walking the wire. Baseball pitchers speak of finding the groove, a process of getting a feel for the ball and adjusting to the mound, the stadium, and the succession of batters. Similarly, the jazz musician who improvises with others gets a feel for the music and the other musicians, varying the theme, making new combinations and contributions, evolving with the others a way of playing together. Knowing-in-action is the foundation of experience-based learning. Compare it with the way actors learn acting.

— Guthrie Theater USA

𝒯he Guthrie Theater in Minneapolis, Minnesota, is one of the country's great regional theaters and is deeply involved in the training and development of promising actors. In fact, Ken Washington occupies a new position, director of company development, created by Artistic Director Joe Dowling. Although actors can be developed by many methods, the method used by Washington involves *knowing-in-action*. What Washington and his colleagues do is set up experiences, invite participation, and then ask participants to put into words what they are learning. "One thing we do," says Washington, "is to get people to try to experience what another person thinks, feels, and believes. Washington assigns actors to go out and find people to observe over a period of time—to shadow their voices, speech, movements, and habits—and to talk with them. When the actors come to class he asks them to reflect on these observations. "Why do your people move like that? Why do they talk that way? Can you move and talk that way? How would you present your people?" Then he asks them to start playing the people they observed. They try a little acting and then talk about it. Next he asks them to get beyond mimicry and to transform those persons into characters. So they try some more acting, and then they discuss what they learned from this experience and how they learned it. "Then comes the tough question," notes Washington. "I ask the actors why they talk and move the way they do. Many admit they never thought about it."

One point is very clear from the examples of learning through experience: The learning doesn't happen automatically.

As with other forms of learning, learning through experience needs to be facilitated. It needs to be planned and arranged, settings need to be identified or selected, and participants need to be matched to the right setting and oriented to what learning from experience actually involves. Above all, someone needs to establish the reflection process, providing opportunities for the learner to reflect on the action and learn from the experience.

Origins of the Holistic Learning Strategy

Was all learning, before schooling, originally experience-based and holistic? The original emphasis on using experience for learning, as it developed over the years, appears to have been, more than anything, a revolt against certain aspects of formal education, a nostalgia for something lost through classroom instruction. Two famous philosophers who were "revolted" by this loss of the use of experience were John Dewey and Alfred North Whitehead. A constant theme in Dewey's writing was the reconstruction of experience, and he wanted to place more emphasis on the natural, present-moment experience of children in learning.

We always live at the time we live and not at some future time, and only by extracting at each present time the full meaning of each present experience are we prepared for doing the same in the future. This is the only preparation which in the long run amounts to anything.[4]

Dewey was joined in this point of view by Alfred North Whitehead, the great mathematician and philosopher. Whitehead expressed a deep concern for inert ideas, which he described as "ideas that are merely received into the mind without being utilized, or tested, or thrown into fresh combinations." He also said "there is only one subject-matter for education, and that is Life in all of its manifestations."[5] Dewey and Whitehead, perhaps more than any others, are the philosophical ancestors of experience-based learning, and some of their ideas became the foundation of the Progressive Education Movement.

Because experience-based learning takes many forms, it is not possible here to trace the origins of all of these, but the roots go deep. For example, cooperative education, the alternation of work and study, dates back to the University of Cincinnati in 1903. Adventure-based education grows out of the Outward Bound movement in England, with roots in the Gordonstoun School in the 1930s in Scotland, a training ground for survival and rescue techniques.[6] Mechanisms for using experience for learning have been in place for most of the century, but they were often seen as alternatives—or shall we say, offbeat exceptions—to the dominant trends of school-based classroom learning.

Holistic education is the name often given the various types of experience-based learning. Holistic Education is a national movement the United States. Its vision statement is contained in a document known as *Education 2000: A Holistic Perspective*, which elaborates principles that include education for human development, participatory democracy, environmental awareness, cultural diversity, and global citizenship. One of these principles, however, speaks to the importance of experience in learning:

> The goal of education must be nurture of natural, healthy growth through experience, and not to present a limited, fragmented, predigested "curriculum" as the path to knowledge and wisdom . . . Education should connect the learner to the workings of the social world through real-life contact with the economic and social life of the community.[7]

The most recent support for experience-based learning and holistic education grows out of current research on the brain. What advocates once knew by intuition is now receiving support in the emerging field of neuropsychology. The father of brain research is generally recognized to be Santiago Ramon y Cajal, who discovered and labeled different types of neurons.[8] Other researchers have focused on mapping functional areas of the brain or on brain evolution.[9] Neuropsychology suggests that human beings are efficient, multitrack simultaneous processors, which is a sophisticated way of saying holistic learners. Holistic learning also receives support from more recent developments in constructivist philosophy and psychology, particularly the later work of Piaget.

The idea of learning something about one's experience through reflection has its roots in counseling and psychotherapy. Freud's early methods of psychoanalysis were called the talking cure, and he was among the first to describe how people can achieve normalcy and personal growth through sustained reflection with a skilled listener.[10] If the origins of psychotherapy are in Freud, the roots of counseling are in Carl Rogers, and many of the techniques for enhancing personal growth, as opposed to the treatment of serious pathologies, have their foundations in counseling theory.[11] Counseling has American rather than continental roots and its origins were closely linked to the schools, providing the support services necessary for everyone to succeed in egalitarian Jeffersonian school systems. Thus, counseling and learning have natural ties, and one may even speak of *counseling-learning* as "a means by which the person teaches himself about himself through the counselor." These several strands of research and scholarship come together to provide a theoretical base for the Holistic Strategy.

Holistic Learning and Brain Research

Much of the current research on the brain supports the idea that human beings are especially well equipped to learn from experience and that our long history of adaptation favors a type of learning that might best be described as holistic.

Our use of the term *holistic* here refers to a manner of learning that involves the whole person—sight, sound, touch, taste, and smell, as well as mind, emotions, body, and soul—simultaneously. This type of learning is holistic because it reflects the capacity of the brain to take in and synthesize many aspects of experience at once.

In recent years there has been an outpouring of research on the human brain—how it has evolved, what it consists of, and how it functions. Classic summaries of that work are found in Paul D. MacLean's *A Triune Concept of the Brain and Behavior* and in the more popular work by the late Carl Sagan, *The Dragons of Eden*.[12] Recent brain research suggests a tripartite brain with three components functioning as a whole but not always in complete harmony. The evolution of the human brain, according to the most recent theories, is a story of "successive accretion and specialization of three further layers surmounting the spinal cord . . . after each evolutionary step, the older portions of the brain still exist and must still be accommodated. But a new layer with new functions has been added."[13] It is as if we look at ourselves and the world through three different mentalities, two of which have no speech. The three brains can be distinguished anatomically, functionally, and neurochemically.[14] These are the three areas:[15]

• *Reptilian.* The minimal type of brain, possessed by reptiles that evolved over 200 million years ago. In humans it plays an important role in aggressive behavior, territoriality, ritual, and social hierarchies—the more instinctual behavior related to our life in organizations.

• *Old mammalian.* The kind of brain that flourished in other, nonhuman, mammals about 60 million years ago. In humans, it is the base of emotions. The master gland, the pituitary, is an important part of this limbic region of the brain and plays an important role with feelings. Not only rage and anger reside here, but perhaps also the beginning of altruism.

• *New mammalian.* The cerebral cortex that evolved in humans as a new kind of brain to support language. The new mammalian brain is the site of most cognitive functions.

As with other aspects of anatomy, the human brain recapitulates its evolutionary development in the growth of the human fetus, which also develops the three areas of the brain in sequence.[16] Although not the largest overall, the human brain, which is roughly three pounds and a quart in size (1,500 grams and a liter), is the most developed and highly complex of animal brains, particularly in its new mammalian portion. If a giraffe might be thought of as a "neck freak" and an elephant as a "nose freak," human beings are "brain freaks."[17] Human brains are, on average, six times larger, relative to body weight, than the brains of other living mammals. (Dolphins are notable big-brain exceptions.) This process of brain enlargement, apart from the expected increase in size related to body size, is known as *encephalization*. The function related to encephalization is language—and ultimately the development of the capacity for intelligent behavior—not only the ability to communicate but to use linguistic images to map the territory of human experience.[18]

If the human brain is made up of different layers with specialized functions, in what ways are these "three brains" compatible and incompatible? It should be noted, of course, that the three components of the brain are not really three separate brains. The bad news about brain function is that the three parts of the brain do not always get along together. The good news is that the human brain is "well wired." It has great flexibility, many specialized places designated to conduct a multitude of functions, and an enormous number of neurons—tiny switches comparable to the circuits of an electronic computer—all standing ready to make connections.

A recent review of brain research provided as a special report by *Scientific American* outlines how complicated all of these functions are at the cellular, electrical, and chemical levels.[19] Apparently, basic nerve cells (neurons) in the brain are highly specialized and assume many odd shapes and sizes. Banks of them work together—100,000 of them in a slice one-tenth of a millimeter across—but the bottom line is that our 100 billion brain cells (about as many as there are stars in the Milky Way) are quite specialized. The key to their coordination is their high degree of networking. One of the reasons the cerebral cortex is so concentrated and convoluted—it would occupy 1.5 square meters if it were stretched out—is to facilitate the connections between brain cells. Neuropsychologists are beginning to develop something like ordered topographic maps to describe the connection pathways of the cerebral cortex.

Perhaps the most amazing aspect of the brain is its ability to serve as a central coordinator—a simultaneous communications processor—for so many different concurrent activities. Humans have a tripartite, highly interconnected, well-wired neurological system for dealing with experience.

The brain, of course, is not just a brain; it is connected to the world of experience and is able to relate to that world both as a receiver and sender through other sensory and motor organs. As Robert Sylwester notes in *A Celebration of Neurons: An Educator's Guide to the Human Brain:*[20]

> Imprisoned and protected within the darkness and silence of our skull, it depends on its sensory and motor systems for external access. Our sensory and motor systems developed to enhance survival, but our conscious brain also uses them to reach out and explore cultural interests and abstract diversions—to smell flowers, observe sunsets, thrill to thunder, run races, throw Frisbees.

Sylwester describes how all of the sense organs work independently, yet simultaneously, and how the three-part brain also allows for all kinds of sensory and motor activity, much of it automatic so that we do not even need to monitor it. Thanks to the basal ganglia and parts of the cerebellum, other parts of the brain are freed for simultaneous seeing, hearing, thinking, and communication activities.

Learning Beyond Classrooms

How does this awesome mechanism function in the process of learning from experience? Leslie Hart, in his fascinating book *Human Brain and Human Learning,* attempts to spell out the implications of brain research for learning.[21] Using the physical evidence and modern theories of brain evolution as a starting point, Hart speculates on how the brain was used in the earlier life of Homo sapiens, before the relatively recent development of civilization. As "brain freaks," humans developed a capacity for an unprecedented amount of learning that resulted in being able to breed, live, survive, and dominate where less-developed animals could not. The way humans learn, Hart contends, is not, however, in the logical, rational, linear mode of classrooms. The human brain operates in a multilinear way all at once, using all of the sensibilities, employing its many layers, going down many paths simultaneously. As Hart notes,

> We identify an object, for example, by gathering information—often in less than a second—on size, color, shape, surface texture, weight, smell, movement, any sound it may make, where it is found, what else is with it, any symbolic information within it (such as label or price sign), how other people are responding to it, and so on. All of these investigations by the brain to answer the question "What is this?" go forward along many different paths, and branching paths, among the brain's trillions of connections, at the same time. From the vast information stored, answers or tentative answers get pulled out, then assembled, compared and interpreted by, if possible, extracting a pattern. The whole miraculous procedure bears no relationship to linear processing.

Hart argues that logic, conceived of as a step-by-step, linear, sequential way of thinking, did not appear for millions of years and that most of what humans developed as the broad foundations of society and culture—clothing, tools, weapons, utensils, housing, dance, music, language, religion—did not require logic, but rather this more multidimensional, holistic kind of learning. What the brain does, and is best at doing, is to write and retrieve programs—to recognize, store, and utilize the patterns that emerge from experience. The brain's strength is in its holistic, multipath ability to make sense of the world by generating, storing, and calling forth programs to deal with experience.

Instead of imprisoning people in classrooms, Hart argues, where they are forced to engage in linear, step-by-step learning (predetermined subject fragments arranged in fixed sequences that seem logical to somebody), learners should be given the opportunity to engage experience in their own personal, individual, mostly random ways. To illustrate the point, Hart provides the example of young children learning to play baseball, a process not characterized at all by logical sequence.

> Watch Little Leaguers play baseball, and you can marvel at their skill and grasp of an intricate game, and related knowledge, picked up over years in random fashion, mostly by participation as opportunity offered. If the game were to be taught logically, there would be a unit on its origins and history, on terminology, on the playing-field geometry, on hitting, on fielding, on base-running, and so on down the list. Obviously, none of the players learned this way. They "picked-up" the game by exposure over many years, in an utterly random, unplanned way—perhaps with no formal teaching at all. If they do get coaching, it will likely be on a purely individual basis, as the need is seen.

Human beings, both children and adults, seem to pick up learning in a somewhat random, happenstance manner from all kinds of exposure to experience.

The Terror of Formal Learning

Usually the newer brain is capable of monitoring the whole in a kind of executive oversight, drawing on the functioning of all parts of the brain and keeping them in delicate balance. But sometimes the older brain takes over, particularly when the organism is under threat. Hart calls this *downshifting*. Sometimes the action of the new cerebral brain is suspended in favor of the faster-acting simpler brain resources of the older brain. Hart observes,

> It becomes plain that *absence of threat is utterly essential to effective instruction.* Under threat, the cerebrum downshifts—in effect, to greater or lesser extent, it simply ceases to operate. To experienced

teachers, this shutting down of the newest brain is an old story and a familiar frustration. The threatened (student) . . . "freezes," and seems unable to think, stabs wildly at possible answers, breaks into tears, vomits, or acts up, perhaps to the point of violence. Since language exists almost wholly in the new brain, downshifting leaves us speechless, quite literally.

The triune brain seems to work fairly well in its natural environment, but under pressure, such as the pressure of classrooms, something can "snap." Consider how holistic learning avoids threat and pressure.

— ELSI Taiwan TAIWAN, REPUBLIC OF CHINA

ELSI Taiwan Language Schools is a proprietary English language school with eight sites in Taipei but a growing number of branches in other cities. As in many countries today, Taiwan residents are scrambling to learn English, and they will put forth considerable effort to do so. The schools depend heavily on good instructors, and they are hard to find, especially native speakers. When new teachers arrive, they are given ninety minutes of formal orientation and two hours of instruction, but most of their training is one-on-one with teacher trainers. "They learn by actually teaching and from their peers in the work room," notes Kenneth Hou, president and chief executive officer, "but we rely heavily on the teacher trainers to serve as mentors. Inexperienced people can feel very insecure, and the experienced ones can be resistant when confronted with formal training." The trainers make observations of classes and then hold conferences with the new teachers. "Instead of offering criticisms and suggestions," notes Hou, "it's more like a counseling process, a dialogue about what they are doing and why. It is a nonthreatening process of nudging them in whatever is the right direction for that teacher." Hou believes they get the best performance improvement by working toward gradual changes via direct experience.

Learning as a Natural Process

Frank Smith, a Harvard-educated psycholinguist, the author of many books on literacy and a well-known text on reading, describes in his book, *To Think,* how learning should be a natural commonplace process, the normal business of the brain.[22]

> The brain picks up huge amounts of "information" on our journey through life, but only incidentally, the way our shoes pick up mud when we walk through the woods . . . If learning is normally so easy, why should it sometimes be so difficult? Learning is easy when it is part of the flow of events in which we are involved, when we can make sense of what we are doing, when the brain is in charge of its own affairs. Just like remembering and understanding, learning is easy when it is not a particular focus of attention, when it happens to us in the course of doing something else. We learn best when we are engaged in an activity that is interesting and meaningful to us, where our past experience is relevant. On the other hand, learning is difficult when it is a deliberate intention, undertaken against the flow of events and made the specific focus of attention . . . learning is difficult when it is contrived.

Consider how a trainer works with the natural flow of events as he rides the route with one of his distributors.

——Coors Distributing USA ————————

*O*f six hundred distributors of Coors beer nationally, four are owned directly by the Coors Brewing Company, partly to keep in direct contact with customers through the distribution process. Robert Jiron is sales training specialist for seventy-two people at Coors Distributing Company, and one of the things he does is to ride the route with salespeople. "We do classes and we show videos, but a big part of the learning comes through the experience of being out there." Jiron arranges for a convenient date, sends a memo that stresses two or three things to focus on, and then rides along as an observer. He is watching for a lot of things: Are they organized? Do they make a complete, fact-based presentation to the customer? Are they seeking good shelf space (favorable adjacencies), and are they talking dollars and cents? "So I will ask them, 'How did that go?' Then they need to talk to me, and we discuss what they are doing. It is all very relaxed and natural." Maybe on the next stop Jiron teams up with them on the presentation. "By the end of the day, they are doing a lot better. They usually thank me, and sometimes they will say, 'Nobody taught me how to do that before.' I tell them they just need experience."

Learning as Constructing Meaning

Smith argues that the primary function of language is not communication but thinking. Thinking involves the creation of the meaning that helps us interpret experience. This process of making meaning of experience occurs in many ways—through the fine arts and music, through the creation of scientific mathematical symbol systems, through the finding and making of patterns (as Hart also emphasized)—but especially in the creation of stories.

> Language enables us to put together and express the stories that make our lives meaningful, in whatever cultures we live. If we had no stories, we would not have the kind of thought we have . . . Language enables us to create the stories we need to make sense of experience and to share experience.

What Smith develops in his book is an image of thinking that is "a single, continual, all-embracing operation of the mind, powered by an imagination that never rests, not a collection of disparate skills, some of which may be absent or deficient until taught." It is not surprising, therefore, that Smith sees learning "as less a matter of instruction than of experience and opportunity."

Holistic learning also receives support from a new group of philosophers and psychologists known as *constructivists*. Constructivists begin with the proposition that whatever knowledge is, it is not a copy of reality. Rather, we construct the meaning of the phenomena in our experience. Stated in its more radical form, "knowledge does not exist outside a person's mind."[23] As Jacqueline and Martin Brooks explain in *The Case for Constructivist Classrooms:*

> It sounds like a simple proposition: we construct our own understandings of the world in which we live. We search for tools to help us understand our experiences . . . Each of us makes sense of our world by synthesizing new experiences into what we have previously come to understand . . . We either interpret what we see to conform to our present set of rules for explaining and ordering our world, or we generate a new set of rules that better account for what we perceive to be occurring. Either way, our perceptions and rules are constantly engaged in a grand dance that shapes our understanding.[24]

Brooks and Brooks provide a provocative illustration of a young girl whose concept of water has been shaped only by her experience of a bathtub and a swimming pool. Water is calm and moves when she moves. But when she goes to the ocean and experiences the waves throwing her about and crashing on the shore, she has to construct a new meaning for water. "In this instance," the authors note, "the interactions of the child with the water, and the child's reflections on those interactions, will in all likelihood lead to structural changes in the way she thinks about water."[25] Note also that "knowing" in this instance is a holistic enterprise, involving not just some abstract concept of water, but the experience of being in the ocean.

Constructivist psychologists attempt to explain the process of knowing set forth by the philosophers. They describe in more detail, for example, what happens when the young girl with a limited experience of water encounters the ocean. Drawing on the later writings of the Swiss philosopher and psychologist, Jean Piaget, they have elaborated a theory of how people learn by constructing meanings.[26] As we go through life, we gather a set of meanings and perceptions from our experiences. As we encounter new experiences, three things can happen.

• *Assimilation.* If the experiences more or less fit our previous meanings, we absorb them into our already established framework for interpreting that experience. This provides a way of assimilating new experiences into existing interpretations.

• *Accommodation.* At other times, however, the new experiences do not fit, and in fact, they may create a perturbing state of disequilibrium, contradiction, tension, and stress. Something has to change, so we change our interpretation and assign a new meaning to that experience. This provides a way of accommodating existing interpretations to new experiences by changing the interpretations.

• *Differentiation and integration.* Sometimes two sets of interpretations do not fit and they both need to be readjusted. Consider the image of someone looking out of a moving train at a person who is walking beside the train. When the train was at rest and the person was not moving, one set of interpretations worked, but now with both the train and the person moving, two sets of interpretations need to be unified into some larger meaning. This provides a way of adjusting two subsystems of meaning into a larger system of meaning.

Piaget called this whole process of adjusting meanings to experience *equilibration.* Learning, according to constructivist psychology, is about this process of equilibration. Learning in organizations often involves experiences that are the equivalent of being thrown in the ocean.

Some experiences can be assimilated to current interpretations, others require changing those interpretations or acquiring a new big-picture perspective.

The Reflection Process

Learning from experience does not occur automatically just from immersion in something different; it involves *reflection in action*. There are a number of ways to facilitate the reflection process, including lists of what to look for, initial discussion about what to anticipate, goal setting for desired learning outcomes, logs and diaries, a postexperience reflection report or presentation, or a follow-up project. Along with these activities, it is valuable to engage in ongoing, serious, one-on-one dialogue between a facilitator and the participant in the experience.

Sometimes this conversation occurs after the experience and is brief, perhaps occurring only once. At other times this conversation is ongoing throughout the experience and may occur several times while the learner is immersed in the experience. In this case the dialogue is not only about what is happening but also what the learner might do about what is happening. In this situation a more structured conversation becomes appropriate and is used to work with the learner over time to get the most out of the experience. What is this structured conversation about, and how does the facilitator help the learner reflect on experience?

Facilitating reflection is a form of helping. A valuable resource for reflecting on reflection is the popular text, often used in basic counseling courses, Gerard Egan's *The Skilled Helper: A Systematic Approach to Effective Helping.*[27] Egan notes that *helping* (his more general and preferred term for counseling) provides a context not only for solving problems but also for engaging "missed opportunities and unused potential," occasions to deal more creatively with our work, ourselves, and others. This is an especially useful resource, therefore, for trainers who hope to facilitate reflection on experience. People in the midst of an experience often find themselves in a predicament, and they need to reflect on the problematic aspects of their experience, but just as often, perhaps more often, they find themselves in an experience where they are at a loss to know what they can learn from it.

The facilitator, as skilled helper, helps the learner reflect on the experience not only to address problems but to capitalize on opportunities for learning.

To make this happen, Egan suggests dividing the helping process into three stages.

The Present Scenario

The persons to be helped focus on *telling their stories,* that is, to describe their experiences and begin making initial assessments of them. The facilitator provides a safe setting for a learner to tell his or her story and uses active listening skills to draw out perceptions and feelings. The first step in facilitating reflection is to understand the story. Sometimes at this stage, however, the learner may be so immersed in the experience that he or she does not have much insight about it or may be reluctant to talk openly about it. *Resistance* may develop when the learner lacks trust, is uncomfortable with the potential intensity of the helping exchange, worries about what might be uncovered, or is anxious about change in general.

Helpers regard resistance as normal, recognizing it in themselves from time to time, and are skillful at providing challenge to the learner (within a climate of support) to reflect more deeply on the experience. If the facilitator sees the world only as the learner sees it, the facilitator has little to offer.

What needs to be challenged? Egan lists "failure to own the problems; failure to define the problems in solvable terms; faulty interpretations of critical experiences, behaviors, and feelings; evasions, distortions, or game playing; failure to identify or understand the consequences of behavior; and hesitancy or unwillingness to act on experience." Challenging, of course, needs to be done in an overall context of *support* and *acceptance* and is usually better received when there is empathy (understanding of feelings); appropriate self-disclosure from the facilitator ("I've been there, too"); more immediacy of exchange ("I notice that right now you and I . . ."); occasional humor ("Maybe you shouldn't have taken this assignment"); or presentation of an observation as a hypothesis ("Perhaps what is happening is that . . .").

Once the experience has been set forth, understood, and challenged, the facilitator tries to help the learner *gain leverage* by making an initial assessment of the situation, deciding how important the issues are, looking for what is missing, and exploring whether anything needs to be done.

The Preferred Scenario
The facilitator and participant try to arrive at a description of what the situation will look like if the problems and lost opportunities in the experience are to be managed successfully. What are the possible scenarios for this situation? This phase of the reflection is aided when the facilitator asks *future-oriented questions* such as, How would you like things to be? What could be happening that is not happening now? What accomplishments would you like to see? What current behavior would need to be changed to make this experience better? The major goal at this stage is to help the learner *construct the future* by becoming aware of either possible futures and managing the current experience as part of a more successful future. To do this, the learner is encouraged to craft

productive agendas and *commit to these agendas* by setting goals and finding concrete actions to take within specified time frames.

Preferred Scenarios Linked to Action Strategies

The focus now is on implementation. If we know now where we are in this experience, and we are clear about where we would like to be, how do we get there? The facilitator becomes a partner in generating *action strategies* by asking questions that begin with phrases such as: Have you considered . . . ? What if . . . ? What do you need to do to . . . ? Who could help you to . . . ? This discussion is aimed at getting to the preferred scenario and involves helping the learner to *formulate plans.*

When a structured reflection process is used, the learner is no longer just having an experience but is actually learning from and growing through the experience.

The reflection process makes all the difference because the learner is challenged to think about the experience realistically, put feelings and ideas into words, formulate preferred scenarios, and put plans into action. Far from being soft or fuzzy, learning from experience is challenging and demanding. A skilled facilitator will quickly end the games of a chronic complainer but will also provide an opportunity for a timid person to discover his or her hidden potential.

The Role of the Facilitator as Mentor, Counselor, and Animator

As we can see, the role of the trainer in experience-based learning is sometimes like a *mentor* and at other times like a *counselor.* Both terms need further definition. Chip Bell provides this humorous and informative background on the term *mentor* in his book *Managers as Mentors.*

The word "mentor" comes from *The Odyssey,* written by the Greek poet Homer. As Odysseus ("Ulysses," in the Latin translation) is preparing to go fight the Trojan War, he realizes he is leaving behind his one and only heir, Telemachus. Since "Telie" (as he was known to his buddies) is only in junior high, and since wars tend to drag on for years (the Trojan War lasted ten), Odysseus recognizes that Telie needs to be coached on how to "king" while Daddy is off fighting. He hires a trusted family friend named Mentor to be Telie's tutor. Mentor is both wise and sensitive—two important ingredients of world-class mentoring.[28]

Mentoring is about being a partner but also a role model, and a mentor may or may not be a supervisor. A mentor is usually older (as Mentor was) or at least more experienced, and provides opportunities for inducting (socializing) someone less experienced into the ways of the organizations. Usually there is an ongoing but unstructured relationship, perhaps even a friendship, over a period of time. Facilitating experience-based learning is partly mentoring, but the focus is on what the mentor does to ensure that real learning occurs from particular experiences.

Consider this example where facilitation of experience-based learning is like mentoring.

——ARIEL USA

ARIEL Corporation, a medium-sized manufacturer of high-quality gas compressors, had its beginnings, literally, in the basement of a dwelling in the quiet town of Mount Vernon, Ohio. Jim Buchwald, president and chief executive officer, purchased and then taught himself to run the machine tools needed to build a small gas compressor. He designed the first one; someone liked the prototypes; he built some more, sold some, and the rest is history. ARIEL may be one of the last examples of the American dream where one man's genius for design became a highly successful company. Now it is time, however, for Buchwald to think about retirement. All of the members of the family have been involved in ARIEL in different ways, and Jim would like to pass on to his son, Kurt, some of the things he has learned about design. An outsider might think that designing compressors is a fairly routine and mechanical process but not to Jim Buchwald. "You can learn the mechanical stuff in an engineering school or in some books," Buchwald notes. What he is concerned about passing on to Kurt are the "secrets," and these are not so easily transmitted. When you ask Jim Buchwald about what he hopes Kurt will learn about design, interesting words begin to surface, such as *elegance, flow, coherence,* and *aesthetics.* "A good design has a visible flow of energy and strength. It also has the qualities the customer likes, such as quality, longevity, and reasonable price. A good designer also has a sense of what's possible for the people who build it, what the castings will look like, how it will be machined, how to make it doable. Jim concludes, "You hope that it won't look like something that was designed by a committee. It has to make sense."

Jim is fairly sure that he can not teach design directly to Kurt. "Kurt is simply going to have to try his hand at some designing. I will work with him, we will work together on some things, and we will reflect as we go along on what we are designing." In short, Kurt will have to experience the design process and reflect on what he is doing with his dad. It is a type of mentoring, but it goes beyond that. To the extent that Jim and Kurt can systematize the mechanisms for reflection—taking stock, analyzing what has been produced, projecting implications, considering alternatives—the process will probably be more conducive to learning. "I know there will need to be a lot of drawing and a lot of talking," says Buchwald.

Counseling, as opposed to mentoring, is generally a more formal relationship in which the counselor often has a clearly defined role. Formal counseling focuses on personal growth and development of an individual seeking help voluntarily, and if it is an HRD function it is frequently provided as a separate service or outsourced. Counseling is usually associated with normal developmental challenges, as opposed to psychotherapy, which may deal with deeper disturbances. Counseling is more often short-term, whereas psychotherapy usually goes deeper and takes longer. Counselors have the skills to provide a setting where people can work on aspects of themselves that need to be changed or at least understood better.

Facilitating experience-based learning is partly counseling (but certainly not psychotherapy) and may draw on some of the abilities of a skilled helper. The focus is on the personal growth that is learned through particular experiences.

Consider this example where facilitation of experience-based learning involves helping that is more like counseling.

——American Express Financial Advisors USA ——

*I*DS Financial Services, known formally since January 1, 1995, as American Express Financial Advisors Inc., was formed in 1894 by John Tappan with $2,500. Now with more than $100 billion in owned or managed assets, American Express Financial Advisors also invests heavily in training. In 1994, the company established for forty-five group vice presidents (GVPs) an experience-based learning program called Action Learning. Notes Katherine Tunheim, director of leadership development, "We have a long tradition of using experience for learning." More recently, American Express has been focusing efforts on self-awareness for leaders through executive coaching, a kind of one-on-one dialogue that gets fairly close to counseling. Executives bring some aspect of their management experience to the once-a-month session, and all of a sudden they find they are talking about the family origins of their behavior, their parents, their home relationships, and so on," notes Tunheim. Although American Express has been outsourcing most of its executive coaching, it is planning to do more of it in-house.

In addition to *mentoring* and *counseling,* we also like the term *animating,* suggested by David Boud and Ned Miller in their book *Working with Experience: Animating Learning.*[29] They suggest that words like *teacher, trainer,* or *coach* emphasize too much the role of authority, and they find *experience worker* or *worker with experience* too clumsy and awkward. Therefore, they note, "We propose to refer to the function of working with the experience of others as 'animation,' and to refer to the person who works to promote others' learning as 'animator.'" They like these words because they have "connotations which include 'give life to,' 'quicken,' 'vivify,' 'enliven,' 'inspire,' 'encourage,' 'activate,' or 'put in motion.'"

The facilitator of experience-based learning, therefore, is half mentor and half counselor, but superimposed on both of these roles is the function of animator, the person who helps the experience come alive for the learner.

Although these roles are significant, it is important not to forget that the facilitator of experience-based learning also has many other duties, including arranging for potentially educative experiences and orienting the learner to ways of learning from them. Above all, the facilitator is aware of how the Holistic Learning Strategy works and strives to maximize learning through reflection on experience.

Technologies to Support Experience-Based Learning

Although the human brain is well suited to absorbing learning in a natural environment, its marvelous capabilities can be further supported and extended by various media. The best devices for helping to record the experience are a camera, a tape recorder, a video camera, and a laptop computer. Cameras and video cameras are good for recording various aspects of the experience, including close-ups that provide detail that might be lost. Tape recorders are good for interviews or live conversations with people otherwise involved in the experience and may also be used for making on-the-spot observation notes to save what could be forgotten. A laptop computer is valuable for taking notes, keeping logs and diaries, or recording data. Telephone and e-mail are good for arranging the experience and following up with after-the-fact questions.

All of these media used to record and keep track of the experience may produce material that later can be used by the learner in presentations. A difficult task in any presentation about an experience is helping others understand the experience at a deep enough level to know why the experience is valued and why it is being interpreted as it is. The presentation is enhanced by media that animate the experience, ranging from the simple use of slides or video to a full-fledged multimedia presentation.

The use of various technologies to record and present experience-based learning not only enhances the learning for the participant but also provides a means of sharing the experience with others who were not able to participate directly. Using media also further involves the participants in constructing meanings for the experience and reflecting on what was learned.

THE BOTTOM LINE

When organizations are rich in experience with potential for learning, or have access to experiences outside, the Holistic Strategy provides a natural way of learning, sometimes called "reflection-in-action."

Although many people learn things from experience informally, they will probably learn more from carefully selected experiences, where the learning is planned for and supervised and where the learner has structured opportunities for reflecting on it. Experience-based learning

- is a process of going out and coming back—a cycle that moves through stages of concrete experience, reflective observation, abstract conceptualization, active experimentation, and then back to concrete experience again.
- is holistic because it draws on all the senses and reflects the capacity of the brain to take in and synthesize many aspects of experience at once.
- is maximized through formal opportunities for reflection, particularly through one-on-one conversations with a skilled helper, such as a mentor, counselor, or animator.

The Holistic Strategy is based on theory and research findings about how the brain functions as a three-part, highly interconnected, well-wired neurological system for dealing with experience.

The facilitator finds or designs good experiences, matches them with the participant's needs, and sets in motion a reflection process that involves challenge, support, opportunities to design preferred scenarios, and encouragement to take action.

The brain is designed for natural learning and picks up information from experience like our shoes pick up mud when we walk through the woods. You can pick up more mud if you know where to walk and someone helps you to see that it is not just mud but soil.

PART THREE

Maximizing Learning

*A*T THE END of the Introduction we suggested that the promise of this book is to maximize learning through the use of Training Strategies. If people within an organization (trainers, managers, supervisors) and those from outside (consultants and other training providers) are willing to learn about theory-based Training Strategies and then practice what they know, there is the promise, or at least a greatly increased probability, of maximizing learning. Maximizing learning, however, depends not only on understanding Training Strategies but also on using them effectively.

Although we have tried to make clear within each chapter what the facilitator does within the framework of each Training Strategy, the facilitator also plays an important role in selecting the right strategies, sequencing and arranging the strategies, and managing the overall impact of the strategies.

Thus, someone responsible for the learning that is to occur must also take on the job of managing the overall approach to learning. This role is described in Chapter Twelve, "Choosing and Using Training Strategies." The people who facilitate learning need to understand and be good at facilitating Training Strategies, but they, or some other designated person, must also be able to step back from the situation, analyze what is needed, make critical choices about employing strategies, and manage their use.

In addition, the selected Training Strategies need to be adapted to the participants. Theories are transformed in practice, and the sensitive facilitator knows what adaptations need to be made for a particular audience. Individual learners and groups of learners differ with regard to several dominant characteristics, and these usually have important implications for learning.

All of the strategies can work for any set of participants, but for the strategies to work well, to maximize learning, they must be adapted to the important characteristics of the participants as learners.

Anyone who facilitates learning must consider the learners and adapt to them. How to do this is explained in Chapter Thirteen, "Adapting Strategies to Participants."

Finally, it is important to know whether actual learning took place, and if so, how much. This task of finding out about the outcomes of learning is often called evaluation. We prefer the broader term *assessment*. Assessing the effects of training is a difficult and complicated task with many vital parts. Ultimately, trainers want to know whether there is a change in performance or capacity in the people being trained. Before that can be known, the trainer must find out what type of learning took place, if any. Most of the people we interviewed, with some promising exceptions, admitted that this was an area where they needed to do better, and where they could use some help.

Assessment should be closely linked to the Training Strategies used. If there are many kinds of learning, and if each strategy is

especially useful for a particular kind of learning, then the assessment needs to be directed toward that kind of learning.

These assessment techniques are discussed in Chapter Fourteen, "Assessing Outcomes."

Maximizing learning in organizations depends on finding good answers to five key questions:

1. How do I know which strategy to choose?

2. What is the proper way to arrange and sequence the strategies?

3. How can the strategies be managed to create the greatest impact?

4. What do I need to do to adapt the chosen strategy to the characteristics of the participants as learners?

5. How can I assess the type and amount of learning that is occurring?

Guidelines for answering these questions are provided in the chapters in Part Three.

12

Choosing and Using Training Strategies

IN THE PREFACE to *The Reforming of General Education,* Daniel Bell recounts the old story of a rabbi confronted with the conflicting accounts of two women in the midst of a heated controversy.[1] The rabbi listens intently to the story of the first woman and after having heard her through, responds, "You are absolutely right!" The rabbi's wife, who is listening in, says to her husband, "Wait a minute, you have only heard one side of the story. Listen to the other woman." The rabbi listens just as intently to the second woman, and when she has finished her story, the rabbi responds, "You are absolutely right!" The rabbi's wife, quite astonished, turns to him and says, "Just a moment, they can't both be absolutely right." The rabbi scratches his head and tugs on his beard, then turning to his wife says, "You are absolutely right!" The differences in the Training Strategies pose a problem for the trainer similar to that confronted by the rabbi: All of the Training Strategies are different, but they all seem to be "right." Which theory is right?

Theories provide valuable insights, but they are also limiting. They provide a consistent outlook and a set of rules for investigation, but they also have assumptions. Their power derives from seeing the world in a certain way, but this vision is sometimes narrow, and often conflicts with other perspectives. Advocates of different

399

learning theories make different assumptions about what learning is, choose different phenomena to study, and suggest different applications for their results. They see learning through the lenses of their own research, training, and practice. Behaviorists and cognitive psychologists reach different conclusions about learning because they make different assumptions and choose to study and elaborate things differently. Thus, there is always some disagreement and often some fierce battling among those who are committed to different theories. Advocates of holistic learning, for example, will surely have a hard time understanding the behaviorist who wants to build skills systematically and efficiently by breaking everything into predetermined steps. Neither side wants to grant the other's assumptions. Both want to be right, so they tend to generate many criticisms of each other's theories. These battles are not easily resolved, and sometimes they are ugly. It is important to recognize, therefore, that learning theories are different, that they describe learning in different ways, that those who use them to conduct research will go about their investigations in unique ways, and that those who employ them as a basis for Training Strategies will practice their art, at least to some extent, in different worlds.[2]

There are a number of ways of resolving this dilemma of difference. One common way is to say that one strategy is the super-strategy since it tells us the most about learning and the other strategies can be incorporated into it or subsumed under it. We have made an effort in this book to present the Training Strategies as parallel, separate, and equal. We do not think that any one of the strategies is either the patriarch or poor cousin of one of the others. One strategy doesn't need to own the others. The differences among strategies are real, and at many points simply unresolvable.

Although we believe that the strategies, and the learning theories on which they are based, are different, they are not absolutely different. Sometimes they overlap a little, and sometimes it is possible to see a little of one theory operating within the framework of another. It may be possible to see how group dynamics are at work when the Inquiry Strategy is used or how reinforcement shows up in the Group Dynamics Strategy. The boundaries between the strategies are not absolute.

A better solution, and the one advocated here, is to take an eclectic approach—to recognize the differences in the Training Strategies and their theories and to draw on them selectively as needed according to their strengths for achieving different purposes. Each theory captures and expresses something important about learning. Each provides a different way of managing the processes involved in maximizing that kind of learning. As Joseph Schwab noted years ago,

> Nearly all theories in the behavioral sciences are marked by the coexistence of competing theories. There is not one theory of personality but many ... There is not one theory of learning but half a dozen ... It will remain the case, then, that a diversity of theories may tell us more than a single one.[3]

The diversity of learning theories provides an intellectual base for a broad range of Training Strategies. The array of Training Strategies available to us provides a richness of options from which to choose. We leave decisions about "absolutely right" to philosophers, kings, and rabbis with the wisdom of Solomon.

To ask which theory or Training Strategy is right is to ask the wrong question. The right questions are, Which strategy should be used when? How should we go about choosing and using the Training Strategies? What is the right match?

Reading this chapter will help you answer these questions.

Choosing the Appropriate Strategy

Maximizing learning involves choosing the appropriate Training Strategy, using it effectively, and assessing the results. Choosing the most appropriate strategy requires careful thought and sound professional judgment, but the selection is made easier by following this simple four-step process:

1. *Consider the organizational context.* Go back to the very beginning of the planning process described in Part One and ask those important questions that frame all decisions about learning. How is training defined? What are the characteristics of the organization, and how do those determine the goals and arrangements for learning? What is the philosophy of learning? Remember, the answers to these questions provide the context for the way other questions about learning are asked and answered.

2. *Review general plans.* Note again the goals that emerged from the plans that were made. Focus on the descriptions of the training need and the desired learning in the rational planning models. Make sure the right decision makers were brought together to negotiate power and interests and focus on their priorities. What learning should occur, and how will it be used?

3. *Focus on learning outcomes.* Consider the subject matter, and then analyze the situation very carefully to determine what specific learning outcomes are desired. Return to the questions at the end of Chapter Four, "Planning for Learning." These questions will lead you quite naturally to the kind of learning for which the Training Strategies are best suited.

4. *Compare the strategies systematically.* The Training Strategies presented in Part Two all have their strengths and weaknesses. They are meant to be placed side by side in a matrix and compared systematically. The Strategy Overview at the beginning of each

chapter in Part Two provides not only an overview but also a useful summary of the characteristics of each strategy. Also check the end of each chapter in Part Two for the Bottom Line summary of key points. Consult the chart in Figure 12.1 for a systematic comparison of the chief characteristics of all seven strategies.

Although it is tempting to select a Training Strategy that feels comfortable for the facilitator ("I'm good at this") or is the preference of participants ("this looks like fun"), a trainer should make a rational choice of the strategy that best fits the desired learning outcomes. It may take time and require effort for facilitators and participants to become accustomed to a new strategy, but both can do so.

The selection of Training Strategies involves seeking the right match between what the situation calls for and what each strategy has to provide. The matrix in Figure 12.1 reveals vividly their strengths and weaknesses and makes their selection, if not obvious, at least fairly clear. If there is some confusion about the right match, it usually grows out of an incomplete analysis of what the training situation calls for, not the strategy itself, because the central strength and power of each strategy is clear when they are placed side by side for comparison. As a rule of thumb, if there is confusion over choice and match, it has to do with understanding organizational goals, philosophy, the subject, and desired learning outcomes, not the strategy.

To maximize learning, choose the Training Strategy that matches the organization's needs and philosophy, the subject matter to be addressed, and the desired learning outcomes.

One Strategy or Several?

Sometimes the goals of training are simple, and one set of learning outcomes is easily identified. In this case, the choice of Training

Figure 12.1 The Seven Training Strategies: Side-by-Side Comparison

Strategy	Best Use	Theory	Participants	Facilitator
1. Behavioral	• beginning or advanced skill development	• behavioral psychology • operant conditioning	• exploring actively • adjusting to feedback	• setting objectives • determining present performance level • performing task analysis • providing feedback
2. Cognitive	• presentations and explanations	• cognitive psychology	• attending to, processing, and remembering information	• selecting, ordering, and presenting information
3. Inquiry	• critical, creative, and dialogical thinking	• philosophical and psychological studies of critical thinking and creativity	• responding to questions • analyzing arguments • generating creative ideas • understanding opposing viewpoints	• establishing climate • asking questions • probing assumptions • examining assertions • asking for evidence • seeking new ideas
4. Mental Models	• problem solving • decision making	• basic problem-solving models • expected utility theory	• appropriate mental models	• providing information about problem-solving and decision-making techniques • guiding discussion of case monitoring progress on projects

5. Group Dynamics	• examination of opinions, attitudes, and beliefs • collaboration and working in teams	• group communication theory	• speaking and active listening process and task-behavior teamwork	• composing groups • developing and using instruments • monitoring groups • facilitating deeper communication
6. Virtual Reality	• development of competence and confidence in a simulated environment	• psychodrama • sociodrama • gaming and simulation theory	• practicing real-life roles through role play, dramatic scenarios, and simulations	• setting the scene • designing the scripts and scenarios • intervening or stepping back • debriefing
7. Holistic	• personal learning and self-discovery through experience	• holistic learning • constructivist philosophy and psychology • brain research	• simultaneous multi-channel processing of experience • reflection	• identifying experiences • matching experiences to participants • providing useful mechanisms for reflection • providing skilled help as mentor, counselor, animator

Strategy is easy. The focus is on one particular kind of learning. The following illustration provides a good example of how one organization is able to focus on one type of training and do an excellent job with one strategy.

—Gates USA

Gates Rubber Company, based in Denver, Colorado, and recently acquired by a British firm named Tomkins, is a large manufacturer of rubber automotive products. Gates has a number of training programs worldwide, but now a major focus of much of its training is on team building. "Almost all of our work is done in teams," notes Kathy Kimmens, manager of education and training, "and it is part of our philosophy." Gates identified promising team leaders and trained them in how to use a series of fifteen carefully worked out team-building modules. "We now have a questionnaire that helps us to identify where people are in the team-building process, and we can tell which modules to use based on responses to the survey. The team facilitators go back to their units and train others in use of the modules. What we do in training is focused mostly on team building, and we have become quite expert at it," notes Kimmens.

Obviously, the nature of the company, philosophy of learning, type of work, subject matter, and learning outcomes greatly affect the selection of the Group Dynamics Strategy in this setting.

At other times, especially in larger organizations, multiple goals and complex philosophies exist so that many types of learning are desirable. Sometimes a complex array of experiences is designed for participants, and these often require rotation through several Training Strategies. Sometimes, even within the two- or three-hour span of a single workshop, several types of learning are desired.

Can more than one strategy be used for a course, workshop, or extended program? Obviously, yes, but we recommend using

the strategies serially—one at a time—rather than mixing them together.

The blending of Training Strategies often causes confusion, and when that happens, they lose their power as strategies. A carefully worked out training program will probably call for many kinds of learning. The challenge is to define each type of learning and then select and manage exactly the right progression of strategies to meet the goals of the training in order to maximize learning.

Consider how these two organizations sequence an array of Training Strategies.

——Mercedes-Benz GERMANY

$\mathcal{M}$ercedes-Benz in Stuttgart, Germany, sponsors a special vocational academy (*Berufsakademie*) that prides itself in the use of a wide range of Training Strategies. An idea that began in Stuttgart as the cooperative efforts of BOSCH, Siemens, IBM, and Mercedes-Benz, the vocational academy, sometimes known as the *Stüttgarter Model*, provides an alternative to the standard six-year university degree with a three-and-a-half-year work-and-study diploma program. It is based in the companies and is an intense form of training. "Something must be working right," notes Martin Scherzinger, one of the academy coordinators, "because 1,300 students apply for forty spots, and at the end of the program only 4 percent exercise their option to leave Mercedes-Benz."

Scherzinger showed us a Wheel of Methods Model used throughout the training and described several of the methods in detail. Some of the general studies take place in classrooms where traditional lectures and explanations are given. Sometimes guests from other fields are invited for informative discussions and inquiries. Cohort groups are used for various projects and problem-solving tasks. Computer-aided training is used, as is behavioral training for learning basic skills and communication. A simulation game involving four companies in competition is used, as well as a macroeconomics game developed by a professor at Göttingen University. Participants are assigned to project groups to work on problem-solving techniques for personnel problems. They learn creative thinking at the *Ideenhaus,* the Daimler-Benz think tank for new ideas. They have regular interviews with counselors to review their past experiences and lay out future plans, and older program peers provide mentoring and support (particularly on computer skills) through a program called Multipliers. Student-planned excursions are arranged at other plants, and when participants return, each gives a short report.

As we listened to the description of the Wheel of Methods, we thought we heard all of the Training Strategies mentioned (if sometimes by other names), and we were impressed by both the variety of methods and the good sense used in matching methods to desired outcomes. "We keep rotating the apprentices through different learning experiences throughout the three years," notes Scherzinger, "and they come out with a very well-rounded background for many different kinds of opportunities they will have at Mercedes-Benz."

Here is another example in a radically different setting.

─Wilderness Inquiry USA ─────────────

Wilderness Inquiry, based in Minneapolis, Minnesota, is a not-for-profit organization that arranges for and conducts high-quality outdoor adventure experiences for mixed groups of disabled and nondisabled youth and adults. With roots that go back to the 1970s, Wilderness Inquiry now serves over six thousand people a year with various types of adventures of differing durations, primarily canoe and kayak trips, but also Northwoods dogsled trips, horsepacking in the Colorado Rockies, Grand Canyon rafting, and others. A typical trip will include people who use wheelchairs, people who ambulate with canes or crutches, and people with other impairments such as deafness or blindness, epilepsy, or mental retardation, as well as a minimum of 50 percent of the participants without disabilities. The staff who serve as leaders for these trips need to be and are well trained. Some of them also have disabilities.

Nine days of training for the summer staff is based in Minnesota. "We use every approach we can think of," notes Erik Wrede, accessibility specialist. A lecture format is used to relay important points about the history and philosophy of Wilderness Inquiry, to go over safety information, and to present rules. Small groups are used for "icebreakers" and team-building activities. Teamwork exercises are used for learning to deal quickly and efficiently with equipment and gear. Out in the field, trainees experience a three- to five-day river trip with campfire reflection sessions. A dramatic rescue scenario is presented—usually as a surprise overturned canoe—and various role plays of typical difficult interpersonal situations are offered. Brief written cases are presented with "what-if" problems (safety, weather, morale) embedded in them, and trainees are asked how they would respond. Some deep sharing goes on in groups around questions that people are often afraid to ask.

Corey Schlosser-Hall, director of training, and Jeff Liddle, director of operations and logistics, have now developed a computer bank of over 150 curriculum lessons for training, including outlines, activities, overheads, handouts, presentation notes, cases, and related materials, with information about when the unit was last used or modified. "We have a good materials bank on the computer, and we are getting good at drawing on just the right kind of training for the outcomes we want."

Many different types of Training Strategies are used in these programs, and each one is carefully tailored to the intended goals and learning outcomes. Some organizations have a high level of consciousness about selecting the differing strategies they use for training, and they organize these into an overall plan and keep track of the materials they use.

Managing the Strategies

In addition to selecting and sequencing the strategies appropriately, what else can be done to maximize learning? Training Strategies do not work miracles, and there is nothing magical about their use. They need to be employed rigorously, often enough, and over a long enough period of time to bring about the desired outcomes.

A man went to his doctor—so the story goes—and asked if there was any truth to the suggestion that stewed prunes will relieve constipation. The doctor replied in the affirmative. The man then asked the doctor how many prunes to eat. With a sly smile the doctor asked, "What kind of results do you want to get?" In prescribing medicine, physicians are accustomed to using three familiar guidelines: intensity, frequency, and duration. *Intensity* refers to the level of dosage—the number of milligrams of the particular chemical in the pill. *Frequency* refers to how often the pills are taken, for example, three times a day. *Duration* refers to the length of time of the course of administration, for example, one month. These terms—intensity, frequency, and duration—are useful for thinking about how to maximize learning through Training Strategies.

Intensity is sacrificed when a Training Strategy is used half-heartedly or ineptly. Whatever the strategy selected, it needs to be used in a strong and focused way to achieve the highest impact. For each Training Strategy there is a different way of being intense, and, alas, for intensity to break down. There are dangers, for example, in using only pieces of the Behavioral Strategy, hazards in selecting poor instruments for the Group Dynamics Strategy, and liabilities in selecting an inappropriate experience as the basis for the Holistic Strategy. The Training Strategies, as approaches to learning based on consistent theories, provide their own ground rules for intensity. In general, intensity involves paying attention to all of the component parts of the strategy and carrying out the facilitator's role as skillfully as possible.

Frequency refers to how much time is allotted for the strategy, how much it is practiced, and how many different applications might be needed for real learning to occur. It is unlikely, for example, that participants will learn much about problem solving and decision making from solving only one problem or working through one decision. Frequency is sometimes hard to achieve in training because time means money, and it is often difficult to involve people in long enough blocks of time to get the training done. Trainers often agree to shorter time frames than are actually necessary for the frequency needed. Unfortunately, one-minute training doesn't exist, and trainers might be better off to give up an entire project than to agree to time frames that prevent a frequent enough use of the strategy for learning to occur.

Duration refers to how often the Training Strategy is used over an extended period of time, how often the learning can be revisited, and whether a sequence of learnings can be built one upon the other. Most learning takes time to process and absorb. Some kinds of learning require repeated efforts over time. Many organizations are beginning to use a pattern of training where participants learn ideas, go back to implement them, then return for more training. For certain kinds of tasks, training needs to be cyclical. Creative thinking, in particular, requires time for preparation and for spontaneous moments of insight. Experience-based learning often plays out over several weeks or months or may require several experiences in different settings. Problem solvers need time to generate and choose among solutions.

Learning is like taking medicine; you need to take a strong dose often enough and long enough to get well.

Notice how intensity, frequency, and duration are illustrated in the next example.

—— Denver Museum of Natural History USA ————

The Denver Museum of Natural History relies heavily on more than two thousand volunteers for its ongoing programs and exhibits. When the museum learned that it would receive the Imperial Tombs of China exhibit, a massive volunteer recruiting program was begun, including twenty-four meetings at various companies and community agencies, not to mention mass mailings and media spots. As part of the recruitment meetings, volunteers were asked to fill out a commitment form to indicate that they understood what was expected. Four months before the exhibit was to open, the pool for the four hundred interpreter positions was filled and the position had to be closed. It was time for training.

For interpreters, that was eight two-and-a-half-hour training sessions, a lot of reading, and a written, take-home, final exam. "It was like a university course in Asian studies," notes Beth Steinhorn, anthropology educator. The training, in addition to including carefully developed slide lectures on background history, aesthetics, and specific objects in the exhibit, was supplemented by sessions on techniques for communicating with visitors and problem-solving role plays. A virtual walk-through of the entire exhibit was developed on video from the exhibit's previous location, and later a general museum orientation and an actual walk-through were held when the full exhibit was in place. Volunteers also received many written training materials: a *General Volunteer Handbook,* an *Interpreter Training Packet,* and a *Volunteer Handbook for the China Exhibit.* A question-and-review session was presented on the lectures and reading assignments before the take-home exam. On one of their four-hour shifts, the volunteers were observed and given feedback. As if this were not enough, after the exhibit was in progress, volunteers were expected to enroll in at least one more continuing education course to learn more about the other exhibits of the museum. "We used several different Training Strategies," notes Steinhorn, "but the key to our success is that we treat these volunteer jobs as if they were regular paid positions. We once calculated that volunteers are the equivalent of two hundred full-time staff that would cost $4–5 million in the budget."

Without question, the success of this training depends on the clear agreement about high-intensity expectations, the length and frequency of sessions over an extended period of time, the materials, the tests, the walk-throughs, and the observations. This is a total program designed for maximizing learning.

THE BOTTOM LINE

Training Strategies are all different, and they are all attractive. Each has its strengths and weaknesses and none is absolutely right.

Choosing the most appropriate Training Strategy requires sound professional judgment, but the task is made easier by following four steps:

1. Consider the organizational context.
2. Review general plans and goals.
3. Focus on subject-matter needs and learning outcomes.
4. Compare the strategies systematically.

Reexamine the questions in Chapter Four, "Planning for Learning" that help focus learning outcomes. Review the Strategy Overview and Bottom Line of each chapter in Part Two. Study the two-page matrix in this chapter (Figure 12.1) for a side-by-side comparison of the seven Training Strategies.

Do not select a strategy just because the facilitator is comfortable with it or participants will enjoy it.

When more than one strategy is needed, use them serially, one at a time.

Use appropriate Training Strategies with intensity, frequency, and duration to maximize learning.

13

Adapting Strategies to Participants

$\mathcal{A}$LTHOUGH IT IS NOT appropriate to select Training Strategies on the basis of participant preferences, it is important to consider the learners when *using* a particular strategy. How can the strategies be adapted to the needs and abilities of the participants in order to maximize their learning?

Notice the different kinds of people participating in training in the following example. How are they different from each other?

—Volunteers of America USA

$\mathcal{V}$olunteers of America, founded in 1896, is a large, nationwide, not-for-profit agency that trains and organizes volunteers for a host of tasks, depending on local community needs. Best known, perhaps, for its senior citizen program, Meals on Wheels, Volunteers of America trains a wide diversity of volunteers. "We screen people," notes Linda Dee, director of volunteer services for the Colorado branch, "to make sure we are not recruiting volunteers who will later be problems, but we work with essentially anyone over age sixteen, whatever their backgrounds. In any one training session we might have, side by side, a Ph.D. and a high school graduate, a housewife and the executive of a company."

Participants in training bring with them a wide range of human characteristics that influence how they will respond as adult learners. At times, when training is done one-on-one with an individual, it is important to know the *individual characteristics* of that particular participant. At other times, by necessity, the learning will take place in groups, and it becomes important to identify, if possible, the *dominant characteristics of the group members,* while remaining sensitive and open to individual differences.

Much has been written about adult learning. Perhaps best known is the work of Malcolm Knowles in which he sets forth the concept of *androgogy.*[1] He describes how adults are more self-directed and less dependent, more experienced, more oriented toward their developmental needs, and more focused on immediate applications. The concept of androgogy provides a useful framework for thinking generally about adults as learners and serves as a valuable reminder that adults are not children. Instead of making generalizations about adults as learners, we prefer to examine them as individuals.

In this chapter we provide a set of rules for adapting the Training Strategies to the learners, several examples of how to consider the learners for selected strategies, and a checklist of the right questions to ask when considering the learners. We have identified and presented what we believe are the human characteristics most likely to influence the way participants will respond as learners. Reading this chapter will help you understand adults as learners and will provide you with ideas and guidelines for adapting the Training Strategies to the populations you serve.

Life-Stage Development

Rule 1. Adapt the selected Training Strategy to the life-cycle developmental needs and interests of the learners.

Developmental psychologists have demonstrated how people at different life stages tend to have different preoccupations, called *developmental tasks.*[2] Thanks to the pioneering work of Freud,

Piaget, and Erikson, psychologists have been able to chart the stages of life-cycle development by observing very carefully what people appear to be working on at different times throughout their lives.[3] Erik Erikson was the first to recognize that this process, though more obvious in childhood, continues into adulthood.[4] What interests people at age twenty-one may not interest them at age forty-three. Consider this example of training with families.

── Foreign Service Institute USA ──────

The Foreign Service Institute of the U.S. Department of State trains families for overseas assignments. "We have all the family members in our training," notes Terri Williams, Training Coordinator for the Overseas Briefing Center, "and we recognize that we have people of all ages. Sometimes we pull the children out separately to work with them as youngsters or adolescents. At other times we work with the intact family group, but we always have to adapt the training to the age level and needs of the participants."

Although many psychologists have set forth outlines of life stages and done research to establish them, one of the best and most thoroughly documented is provided by the late Daniel Levinson.[5] He divides the life cycle into three basic eras, early (17–45), middle (40–60), and late (60+) adulthood. Each of the eras is marked by a transition period, early-adult transition (17–22), midlife transition (40–45) and late-adult transition (60–65). Within the eras, people work on particular tasks and build life structures that fit those eras. For example, early adulthood is a season for "forming and pursuing youthful aspirations, establishing a niche in society, and raising a family," whereas people in middle adulthood "are becoming 'senior' members" of their particular worlds, are advancing in their work, and "are responsible for their own work and the work of others."[6] Gail Sheehy, in *New Passages* suggests that the life cycle may need some revision, that age 50 today is more like what 40 was a few years back, and age 60 is more like 50. She suggests that many older adults today have the opportunity to create a "second adulthood."[7] Knowing where a person is in the adult life cycle provides information about where learning fits in the larger scheme of that person's development. Here are some examples of how to consider the learners in adapting selected Training Strategies.

Considering the Learners

• *Group Dynamics Strategy.* Early adults may be more caught up in process needs, whereas middle adults may be better at focusing on the task.

• *Inquiry Strategy.* Early adults may not be as well prepared to engage in critical, creative, and dialogical thinking, whereas middle adults may excel because they have more experience, but may be more rigid.

• *Holistic Strategy.* Early adults may relish experience-based learning but may need more help with reflection, whereas late adults may be naturally more reflective but may resist having new experiences.

Cognitive Development

Rule 2. Adapt the selected Training Strategy to the level of complexity in thinking demonstrated by the learners.

Adults also vary in their stages of cognitive development, that is, in the way they go about thinking. In a fascinating book entitled *Developing Reflective Judgment,* Karen Kitchener and Patricia King explain how people tend to think about ill-structured problems, issues about which there is no one, simple right answer.[8] They have developed seven categories (stages) that describe how people move from simpler to more complex ways of thinking. At the *pre-reflective stages,* people tend to see issues in more black-and-white, right-or-wrong, dualistic terms. At the *quasireflective stages*, people become more relativistic in their thinking, that is, they recognize that there is uncertainty in knowing and that issues have their historical and cultural context. They are more likely to say "it depends" at this stage. At the *reflective stages*, people have learned what to make of authorities, how to value and handle evidence, and what to do about relativism, and they are more willing to craft their own argument and make a commitment to it. Here is an example of how training and development activities are adapted to complex thinkers at the reflective stages of cognitive development.

—University of Minnesota USA

The Twin Cities campus of the University of Minnesota, with about 30,000 employees, has the unusual arrangement of a unified personnel office for all employees that guides and keeps track of nearly all of the training for faculty, administration, and staff. One of its successful training programs is for department chairs, a difficult but important role in most universities, and a job that few people are willing to do because it has become so onerous. "How do you help intellectuals become educated in subjects they typically abhor?" asks Tim Delmont, coordinator of the administrative development program. The program was customized for the intelligence level and capability of the participants as thinkers. "We used focus groups to define the content and then provided a familiar seminar format and dinner from five to eight in the evening," notes Delmont. "These are very bright people, and they are highly skeptical of nonacademics, so we worked hard to find the very best minds within the university for leaders. We said to ourselves, let's find our smartest people—former chairs, deans, and others who are wise in the ways of academic administration—and let's have them lead cases or answer questions." Because the participants were taught by their intellectual peers in a manner that fit their own complex ways of thinking about administration, the role of department chair became more understandable. No simple right-wrong formulas were presented.

Knowing about stages of cognitive development provides important information about how learning will be affected by the capacity for complex thinking.

Considering the Learners

• *Inquiry Strategy.* People who think in fairly rigid, dualistic ways will have trouble analyzing and constructing arguments and will probably struggle with dialogical thinking.

• *Holistic Strategy.* Some people may reflect on experience in a relativist pattern, being content to grant differences but giving them little significance. More complex thinkers may have a lot to say about assimilation and accommodation of new experiences and may want to work out new commitments.

Trainers do not simply adapt the strategy to where participants are but recognize the stage where participants appear to be and often provide opportunities that will nudge them in the direction of more complex thinking.

Intelligence, Aptitude, and Achievement

Rule 3. Adapt the selected Training Strategy to the ranges of intelligence, types of aptitudes, and previous achievements of the learners.

Intelligence is regarded by some trainers as a taboo subject. It has played a major role in schooling, particularly test taking, and has shaped the way we often think about ourselves; thus, intelligence always seems to be a personal topic. We all know also that members of minority groups have often been "burned" by intelligence testing and also by supposedly well-credentialed researchers in the treatment of the topic. But intelligence really cannot be ignored as a characteristic of adult learners, and some types of training need to be adapted to the intelligence of the participants. Although this is a broad field with many points of view, there is one theory that makes good sense for trainers, Howard Gardner's theory of multiple intelligences set forth in his book *Frames of Mind*.[9]

According to Gardner's theory, intelligence involves the ability to manipulate symbol systems (for example, linguistic, musical, mathematical), some of which differ widely enough to be regarded as unique domains of intelligence. Support for the theory of multiple intelligence comes from the study of child prodigies, who can be very bright and precocious in one area but rather average in another, and from recent efforts to map the brain, which have shown that the abilities to use different symbol systems reside in specific, localized areas of the brain. Gardner describes six different types of intelligence:

• *Linguistic*—special ability to deal with the semantic (meaning), phonetic (sound), syntactic (ordering), and pragmatic (useful) properties of words. This intelligence is highly developed in novelists, poets, critics, philosophers, and historians.

• *Musical*—special ability to hear and generate pitch, melody, tone quality, rhythm, and harmony. This intelligence is highly developed in musicians, performers, conductors, and composers.

• *Logical-mathematical*—special ability to manipulate numbers and other abstract symbols in long and complex chains of logical reasoning involving deduction and proof. This intelligence is highly developed in mathematicians, statisticians, and computer scientists.

• *Spatial*—special ability to perceive the world visually, to produce visual images and geometric forms, to mentally rotate or otherwise manipulate those forms in space in order to perceive them from other angles or in different contexts. This form of intelligence is highly developed in scientists, inventors, engineers, architects, and artists.

• *Bodily-kinesthetic*—special ability to project, carry out, and receive feedback on gross and fine movement. This intelligence is highly developed in actors, athletes, dentists, surgeons, and other people who use tools.

• *Personal*—special ability to access and act on one's own feelings (intrapersonal skills) and to notice and make distinctions among the feelings and behaviors of others (interpersonal skills). This intelligence is highly developed in political and religious leaders, teachers, therapists, and others in helping professions.

Although some would say that the theory does not address intelligence, but rather classifies different kinds of human intellectual competencies—a phrase Gardner himself uses occasionally—the trend in thinking about various mental abilities, classically known as intelligence is toward a greater, rather than lesser, inclusion of abilities. Unfortunately, the distribution of various mental powers is spread out somewhat unequally throughout the population. Although we need to be careful in defining intelligence and jumping to conclusions about where it resides, we also need to be sensitive to certain variations in the amounts and types of intelligence found in participants. Motorola has successfully taken into account various kinds of intelligences in the adaptation of certain aspects of its training.

—Motorola USA

At Motorola, Jim Frasier, manager of educational research at Motorola University, The Americas, has developed a keen interest in intelligence theory, in particular the work of J. P. Guilford on the Structure of Intellect Model. At various sites around the world—Dublin, Manila, Guadalajara—Motorola has done testing of its workers to gain a better understanding of their abilities. In Mexico, Motorola discovered that many workers were not very good verbal (semantic) learners, but they were much stronger with symbolic representations. "At first we thought it might be cultural," notes Frasier, "but then we began to see the difference in other places, including the United States. As we thought about it, we began to realize that these were factory workers, many of whom were not very good at the verbal learning emphasized so much in schools." Motorola took a look at the training materials they used and realized how much they were dependent upon verbal intelligence. Frasier pulled from his bookshelf two big ringbinder notebooks and began to leaf through the training materials, comparing them page by page. One book contained the usual text, mostly long paragraphs full of long sentences. The other notebook, which paralleled the text almost completely, contained almost all pictures, diagrams, tables, and graphs. "We realized we were dealing with symbolic learners," notes Frasier. "Now we do in two and a half hours what before took six to eight hours, and people are actually getting it."

Aptitude is a somewhat related, but perhaps even more slippery, concept than intelligence.[10] General aptitude might be thought of as the overall ability to succeed in learning. Special aptitude involves the projected ability to learn in a specific field. Trainers are not likely to have much access to formal information about the specific aptitudes of participants. It is useful, nonetheless, to keep a watchful eye out for clues about general and specific aptitude. We have all known participants who seem to be bright and generally successful but without much aptitude for a particular job. On the other hand, we want to be alert to our misuse of low aptitude as an excuse for ineffective training.

—Safeway USA

A large foodstore chain, Safeway Inc. screens potential new hires for checkout positions for aptitude. "They are given tests for hand-eye coordination, a math abilities test, and tests of memory ability," notes

Linda Hawkins, training instructor. "We need to know first if they have the basic abilities to be able to profit from training."

Achievement, the third ability measure, relates to the previous learning the participant brings to training. It is more directly connected to the skills and content of the subject matter.

Intelligence, aptitude, and achievement are interlocking characteristics of adult learners, and learning can be affected deeply by all three.

Considering the Learners

• *Behavioral Strategy.* Aptitude and previous achievement can greatly affect the learning of skills as will the match between the skill and the level and type of intelligence needed to perform it.

• *Cognitive Strategy.* People with more limited verbal intelligence may have difficulties processing an explanation that relies only on the spoken word but may do much better when visuals call into play their spatial intelligence. Their ability to understand the presentation may also be related to their aptitudes for and previous achievements with the subject matter.

Motivation and Emotional Intelligence

Rule 4. In using the selected Training Strategy, take into account the motivation and overall emotional control of the learners.

Adult learners involved in training also vary in terms of motivation and what has recently been described as emotional intelligence. Any experienced trainer knows that not all participants come to training opportunities with the same desire to learn or equal ability to manage their feelings about learning. Consider how this company considers motivation in its training.

—ARIEL USA

"*I* think you need to begin," notes C. G. "Skip" Parker of the ARIEL Corporation, "by recognizing that on the shop floor you are working with people in the lower 50 percent of their high school class, if they graduated. Most of them hated education. So the first thing they think is, 'Oh, no, not school.'" So ARIEL does a lot of subtle things to work on motivation. "When they look skeptical about training we say, 'Someone thought you would be good at this.' We try not to flunk anyone. We give them the calculator they've been using at the end of the course. But mostly we teach about 'real stuff' that they are going to see out on the shop floor. We get them to wonder about why things work the way they do. Then they get hooked." In short, ARIEL does not assume motivation, the company builds it in to the way it goes about training.

Motivation is a factor, and facilitators of learning are sensitive to the varying degrees of motivation that participants bring to any proposed learning.

The key aspects of a theory of motivation have been presented by Raymond Wlodkowski in *Enhancing Adult Motivation to Learn.*[11] He notes that at the beginning of the learning process, motivation will be affected by the attitudes the learner brings about the learning environment, instructor, subject matter, and self and also by the number and intensity of needs that the participant has for learning. During the learning process, motivation is affected by the stimulation that comes from (or does not come from) the learning experience and from the kind of emotional experience the learner is having. Toward the end of the process, motivation is influenced by the degree to which the new learning is valued by the learner and the reinforcement that comes from learning new things. Thus, motivation is seen as complex, not just something the learner has or lacks, but as a combination of initial needs and attitudes as well as factors during and after training that influence learning. In some settings, the motivation of the participants is very important.

──American Red Cross USA ──

*T*rainers at the American Red Cross are sensitive to the motivations of the volunteers they are training. "When you are working with a volunteer audience," notes Christopher Saeger, senior training development associate, "you need to be aware that they can leave at any time." Designing learning experiences that motivate as well as train is very important in organizations that depend on volunteers.

Motivation is also illuminated by the recent work of Daniel Goleman who suggests that emotional intelligence can matter more than IQ. What he is referring to in his book, *Emotional Intelligence,* is a series of domains that affect not only general effectiveness in life but especially learning.[12] These involve issues such as knowing ones emotions, managing emotions, motivating oneself, recognizing emotions in others, and handling relationships." One form of emotional intelligence, labeled the *master aptitude,* is impulse control. Because learning often involves deferring—or patiently sitting through—some things to get to others, impulse control becomes a very important factor in learning, and, of course, people vary in the amount of impulse control they bring to a learning situation.

Considering the Learners
• *Mental Models Strategy.* Problem solving and decision making assume reasonably high levels of motivation as well as persistence and patience. When these are in short supply, people may regress to "let me out of here" responses.

• *Group Dynamics Strategy.* People with less awareness of their feelings or less experience in expressing and managing emotions may find it difficult to be a participant in a group.

Knowing about the motivation of participants—and it will vary—can help the person responsible for learning to tailor the strategy to the participants' motivations or, through the careful use of the strategy, heighten that motivation. Sometimes participants may need persistence training.

Learning Styles

Participants in training may also vary in what has come to be called in recent years *learning style.* Although the concept has enjoyed enormous popularity, the ideas have remained somewhat fuzzy with only limited backing in research. Learning style theories can be grouped into three basic categories: those that deal with brain functions, those related to personality, and those addressing differences in sensory modalities.

One group of learning-style theorists has stressed the importance of differences in *left-brain* and *right-brain* functions.[13] It has been argued that the left hemisphere of the brain is predominantly involved with analytical, logical thinking, especially in verbal and mathematical functions, while the right hemisphere is specialized for orientation in space, artistic endeavor, body image, recognition of faces, and holistic and rational thinking. When students appear to exhibit pronounced individual differences in their preferences for linear (analytic) thinking as opposed to holistic (artistic) thinking, these differences are often referred to as a learning style preference. The preferences may indeed be there, but whether they are related to the way the brain hemispheres function is open to question. The three-part brain has many lobes and is surely too well wired to be thought of as left and right. As Carl Sagan noted in the conclusion of his study of the evolution of the human brain, "The coordinated functioning of both cerebral hemispheres is the tool Nature has provided for our survival."[14] Perhaps the best way to think of left-brain/right-brain learning style theory is as a metaphor for preferences. Which side of the brain is more important? We vote for the inside!

In training settings, the two most prominent learning-style theories based on *personality types* are David Kolb's Learning Style Inventory and the learning-style theory growing out of the Myers-Briggs Type Indicator. Kolb notes that most people differ along two dimensions in their learning preferences, from Abstract to Concrete and from Reflective Observation to Active Experimentation.[15] Kolb has used these two sets of polarities to develop the Learning Style Inventory, a nine-item self-description questionnaire that asks the respondent to rank, in order, four words (in each item) that describe his or her learning style. Because all people fall somewhere on both dimensions, scores will cluster in one of four quadrants. The four learning styles, made up of the combined emphases of the two dimensions, are summarized briefly as follows:

• *Convergent.* Problem solving, decision making, conducting practical applications of ideas, finding a single correct answer or solution, and working on technical tasks are preferred.
• *Divergent.* Organizing many specific relationships into a meaningful gestalt, generating alternative ideas and implications, brainstorming, and using imagination are preferred.
• *Assimilative.* Reasoning, creating theoretical models, integrating explanations, and working with ideas, concepts, and sound and precise theories are preferred.
• *Accommodating.* Doing things, carrying out plans, seeking opportunity and risk, taking action, fitting the theory to the facts, and relying on other people for information are preferred.

The four learning styles establish preferences that grow out of personality characteristics. The implication is that different people will prefer to approach learning in different ways.

A second prominent learning style theory is based on the Myers-Briggs Type Indicator. The dedicated work of a mother-daughter team, Kathleen Briggs and Isabel Briggs-Myers, the personality inventory is based on categories developed by the famous psychoanalyst Carl Jung.[16] The personality theory includes Jung's familiar categories of *Introvert* and *Extrovert,* as well as polarities relating to sensing, intuition, thinking, feeling, judging, and perceiving. The learning-style theory is extrapolated from the personality theory, the idea being that people with certain personality characteristics will have related orientations to learning as follows:[17]

• *Extrovert.* Learns best in situations filled with movement, action, talk. Enjoys discussion groups, cooperative projects. May have trouble sitting still, reading books, writing.
• *Introvert.* Learns best alone in periods of concentrated study. Is teacher-centered, enjoys lectures, may not like discussion. May not share what is known. Thinks before speaking.
• *Sensing.* Likes to focus on the here-and-now, concrete facts and details, putting knowledge to use, learning skills and procedures, being precise and accurate.
• *Intuition.* Likes to gain general impressions, the entire gestalt, concepts, theories. Dislikes structured and mechanical approaches to learning, prefers open-ended assignments, opportunities for imagination. May be careless about details.
• *Thinking.* Prefers performance criteria, wants to know how learning will lead to a deeper understanding of how things work. Likes rule-based reasoning.
• *Feeling.* Wants to know how learning will affect people, is interested in process of learning, is motivated by learning that touches convictions and values.

• *Judgment.* Prefers structured learning environments, goals, deadlines. Enjoys accomplishment, completing assignments, achievement.

• *Perception.* Prefers more freewheeling learning environments, working on several things at once, delaying closure until the deadline. May feel imprisoned in highly structured classrooms.

Although these personality types appear to be measurable by the Myers-Briggs Type Indicator and although a logical connection appears to exist between personality type and learning-style preference, the trainer may not always know how to respond to this information.[18] Unfortunately, most of the concepts used in such theories are very broad and unspecified. What does it mean to be more of a thinking person than a feeling person, when most people do both frequently and usually simultaneously? Moreover, because personality is so complex, trainers need to be careful about typing and labeling participants and treating them as if they were forever a certain way ("Here comes my intuitive learner"). On the other hand, different people do have different personalities, and personality is one of the variables to consider in adapting Training Strategies for participants.

One very successful adaptation of training to learning styles has been conducted at the Foreign Service Institute of the U.S. State Department.

Foreign Service Institute USA

The Foreign Service Institute of the U.S. Department of State provides training in some 65 languages and has been experimenting for some time with the adaptation of language training for learning-style differences. "We use a number of questionnaires, such as the Myers-Briggs, the Hartmann Boundary Questionnaire, and the Modern Language Aptitude Test, to gain a better understanding of our learners," notes

Madeline Ehrman, director of research, evaluation, and development and author of *Understanding Second Language Learning Difficulties*. "We evaluate student learning styles, and then we assign learning consultants who serve as mediators between the teacher and student. They help teachers understand better the way that a student likes to learn. For example, some learners are more random, and they like to design their own path; others are more sequential and like to follow a lesson book. Some are very analytical, and they like grammar; others don't. We try to take these factors into account."

A third category of learning styles involves *sensory modalities*, the preferred sense for learning. Of the five senses—taste, smell, touch, sight, and sound—the last two, sight and sound, are very important in most training settings. Of course, various forms of musical, dramatic, athletic, and artistic expression draw on other senses, but in the vast majority of training tasks, participants take information in through their eyes and ears and express what they have learned through writing, speaking, or doing. Participants vary significantly, however, in their sensory capacity for input and output, in what educators call their *sensory modalities*.

Building on the earlier work of the famous preschool educator Maria Montessori, Walter Barbe and Raymond Swassing have used the idea of sensory modalities as the basis of a learning style theory.[19] The styles are categorized as auditory, visual, and tactile-kinesthetic. *Auditory learners* (more precisely, those who prefer using auditory channels) like to use their voices and ears, and they learn best by talking and listening. They like to talk about ideas and enjoy presentations and discussions. Silence can be disturbing for them. *Visual learners* like to see words, pictures, charts, diagrams, graphs, time lines. They like their assignments written out, and they enjoy doing written assignments. *Tactile-kinesthetic learners* like doing projects—building, handling materials, acting out. They do not want to be told about the computer; they want to try it. When they *do* a task, they learn it and remember it. They hate sitting still.

There is a commonsense validation for the idea of learning styles based on differences in sensory modalities. Consider the situation of participants with serious physical disabilities. Some have speech and language disorders; some are deaf; some are blind; others have learning disabilities. Increasingly, people who have been identified and served through special education programs in elementary and secondary schools are finding their way into training settings. It is helpful, therefore, to recognize that all participants vary in their sensory modalities (and in their compensating preferences) and that Training Strategies need to be adapted to these learning styles.

Considering the Learners

• *Virtual Reality Strategy.* Extroverts and accommodating learners will happily enter into role plays, dramatic scenarios, and games, but introverts and assimilative learners may need coaxing and encouragement.

• *Mental Models Strategy.* Convergent learners and people with personalities that tend toward thinking and judgment may enjoy problem solving and decision making as will visual learners, but those who prefer tactile-kinesthetic learning may not like sitting still.

Our view of the frenzy of interest in learning styles is that they have been much overrated in their relative significance for training and that Training Strategies based on well-researched learning theories are far more important. Nonetheless, Training Strategies need to be adapted to differences in personality and sensory modalities, just as they need to be adapted to other characteristics of the participants in training. The role of learning styles in training offers a promising area for further research. For some organizations, such as the Foreign Service Institute, where the adaptation has been done carefully and with good judgment, sensitivity to learning styles has made a big difference in maximizing learning.

Gender, Ethnicity, and Social Class

There are many groupings we all belong to—many ways to say "we." Our social belonging also affects our learning.

One of the great debates in education today is about the role of gender in learning. Although there is not much evidence that women learn differently, there is considerable evidence that they have been treated differently as learners. Research suggests that elementary school teachers tend to talk more to boys, ask boys more higher-order questions, and give boys more instructions in how to complete a task. Teachers also tend to praise boys for the content of their work while paying more attention to the form and neatness of work done by girls.[20] Patterns established in primary and secondary schools persist in college—overall, male students just tend to get more attention.[21] Effective trainers are aware that many women have had a different experience in their schooling, and sensitive trainers make special efforts to free themselves of the everyday inequities that may creep into the training setting. They also recognize that women may need some special encouragement in participation, as in this example.

──Grupo Tampico MEXICO ─────────────────

Sometimes training needs to be done separately by gender. The training done at Grupo Tampico in Tampico, Mexico, described earlier under the Group Dynamics Strategy, was held just for women because the subject was about women's roles in the organization. The Group Dynamics Strategy had to be adapted to the situation as participants discovered how reticent they were to speak up in groups, even groups composed only of women. "It really took some time for them to learn how to participate in the groups," notes Esteban Fuentes Salazar, director of human resources.

In one of the more revealing studies of women and learning, entitled *Women's Ways of Knowing*, the authors demonstrate that many women must find or recover their voice as learners, that is, they must discover that they have something to say and how to say it.[22]

——Iittala Finland FINLAND

*A*t Iittala Finland, a glass products company, special efforts are made to adapt training to women applicants. "Glassblowing has been an all-male profession," notes Harri Jokinen, a trainer for Iittala. "More women are beginning to be attracted to the work, especially in Sweden, and special efforts are being made to adapt the training. It is hot work and the physical requirements are quite demanding, even for some men, but women can work on some of the smaller, less difficult pieces," notes Jokinen with a smile, "just as some of the smaller men do." Women entering this profession need a lot of encouragement.

In a similar way, ethnic background may influence learning. Although the United States has often been described as the great melting pot, most sociologists today would agree that not much melting occurred. Many people are members of ethnic subcultures that determine key values and behavior related to learning. Increasingly, training also occurs in a cross-cultural or multicultural context, and it becomes important to ask how ethnicity may influence the learning process. This example from Japan provides a vivid example of how cultural differences and gender interact.

——SHARP JAPAN

*C*ultural training and cross-cultural training is important at SHARP Corporation, a large electronics company with offices in Osaka. There is a strong cultural element in many Japanese companies, and it is important to learn about things such as dress, grooming, bowing politely, and for women employees, the serving of tea. Employees are trained in the culture, so training must also fit the culture. On the other hand, in addition to the 23,000 employees in Japan, there are 60,000 in other countries. "Every country has its culture," notes Asanori Fujita, manager of overseas personnel, "and when we do training we have to take into account where we are."

Ethnicity is one of those catchall terms used to designate many things, but sociologists would generally include race, language, religion, and cultural traditions as the components of ethnicity. To the extent that people identify strongly with these components of ethnicity (or have no choice about identifying), these factors can influence the learning process. Trainers are aware of differences and walk the fine line between ignoring ethnic differences that may be important and overresponding to differences that may not be important. They avoid racial and ethnic stereotyping and will not permit this from other participants, but they also try to encourage legitimate expressions of ethnic difference and draw upon these differences in creative ways to enrich the cultural awareness of all participants.

─ American Red Cross USA

*T*he American Red Cross adapts some of its basic HIV/AIDS training materials and techniques for Hispanic and Afro-American populations. "Some materials are put into Spanish," notes Zora Salisbury, manager of HIV/AIDS educational development, "but we also adapt materials to take into account different family structures and views of authority and autonomy. Naturally, the illustrations are also different." Volunteers who serve as trainers learn to use these materials and to adapt the training to different populations.

Similarly, social class, sometimes referred to as socioeconomic status (SES), determines who we are and is likely to affect learning. In the United States—the land of professed equal opportunity— social class is another taboo subject, but like intelligence, whether discussed openly or not, it is one of the characteristics that participants bring to the training environment. The chief determinants of SES are occupation, educational attainment, and income; and these factors determine, in turn, where people live, what they spend on housing and cars, their memberships, patterns of consumption, and attitudes about and opportunities for learning. Differences in SES have important impacts on what resources are available for books and magazines, lessons, cultural experiences, travel, and so forth. Some participants have had very few opportunities in their lives for enriching experiences with a high educational impact, while others have had many. SES can affect language usage, ways of behaving, attitudes toward learning, and the value placed on training. In many studies, social class and educational attainment are highly correlated. Effective trainers are aware of the relative wealth or poverty of participants and how extensive or limited previous exposure to good learning experiences may influence their behavior as learners.

Considering the Learner

• *Group Dynamics Strategy.* Gender, ethnic background, and social class may all become important factors in group participation and teamwork, especially when the groups are composed of people where differences in background are great.

• *Holistic Strategy.* Learning from experience can take participants into a strange new world, and the amount of reflection may need to be increased for some participants.

Using Professional Judgment

We offer, as a summary, a checklist of characteristics of adult learners that are important in training and may affect how Training Strategies are used. There is no magic formula for the successful adaptation of each of the strategies because this is a matter of thoughtful and sensitive professional judgment.

With experience and good sense, trainers can learn to consider the background characteristics of the participants and adapt the Training Strategies accordingly to maximize learning.

The checklist of appropriate questions in Figure 13.1 provides a set of useful reminders for considering the learner.

Keep in mind that the checklist only provides a reminder of things to consider. What the facilitator does about these characteristics requires a considerable amount of professional judgment. The word *adapting* does not imply reducing to the common denominator, lowering aspirations, watering down goals, spoonfeeding, dumbing down, or any of the other crude accusations frequently made when facilitators are asked to consider the learners. The point of this book is *maximizing* learning, not minimizing or diminishing it!

The reason for considering the learners is to target the strategies to what the participants can reasonably be expected to do, to provide a good fit, and to present just the right level of challenge. The goal is for participants to get the most out of the learning experience, and this is more likely to occur when the Training Strategies have been tailored to their key characteristics as learners.

If the training provided for the learners is beneath them, it is insulting; if it is over their heads, it is more than likely unattainable. Either way they may lose interest and withdraw. If it is a good fit but not challenging, they might like it, but little learning will result. Maximizing learning involves providing just the right levels of challenge and support, and the only way to do that is to consider very carefully the characteristics of the participants. The rest is professional judgment.

Figure 13.1   Checklist of Characteristics of Participants as Adult Learners

❑ **Life Stages and Developmental Tasks**

At what life stage or transition point are the learners?

What developmental tasks are they addressing?

How does their life stage influence their overall attitude about training?

What can be done in employing the strategies to adapt to or respond
to the developmental needs of the participants?

❑ **Cognitive Development**

How do the participants think about thinking?

Do they appear to be dualistic or relativistic in their thinking patterns,
or are they accustomed to thinking in more complex ways?

How are they inclined to treat authorities, and how sophisticated are
they about identifying or using evidence?

Does the training fit their way of thinking?

Can anything be done to nudge the participants toward more complex
patterns of thinking?

❑ **Intelligence, Aptitude, and Achievement**

What kinds of intelligences are most prominent in the participants?

How do differences in types and amounts of intelligence influence
their abilities to learn?

What aptitudes do the participants have for the subject matter or
the learning outcomes?

What is their previous level of experience and achievement with the
subject matter?

What adaptations need to be made in light of these variations?

❏ **Motivation and Emotional Intelligence**

What level of motivation do the participants bring to the training, and
what steps does the facilitator need to take to enhance motivation
through the training?

What attitudes are surfacing?

What needs are being met?

What is the level of emotional intelligence or maturity of the
participants?

To what extent are they willing or able to delay gratification or maintain
persistence when learning is demanding?

❏ **Learning Styles**

What personality characteristics of the participants may enter into or
influence learning?

Do certain personality factors result in preferred ways of learning?

In what ways do participants differ in their strengths and uses of
their senses?

Do they have preferences for visual, auditory, or kinesthetic learning?

Does the training require recognition of and adaptation for these
preferences?

❏ **Gender, Ethnicity, and Social Class**

How might the participants be described in terms of gender, ethnicity,
and social class, and how are these various ways of belonging likely
to influence readiness for and manner of participating in learning?

To what extent should these differences be recognized or used for
enriching the learning experience?

What special forms of encouragement may be necessary?

What should be avoided?

THE BOTTOM LINE

To maximize learning, it is important to adapt Training Strategies to the needs and abilities of the learners.

Although adult learners are different in certain ways from younger learners, the most important point to notice about adults as learners is how they are different from each other.

The human characteristics that are most likely to influence learning are

- life stage and developmental tasks
- cognitive development
- intelligence, aptitude, and achievement
- motivation and emotional intelligence
- learning styles
- gender, ethnicity, and social class

In using Training Strategies it is important to consider the learners, and take into account how they might react to the strategies and what might need to be done to maximize their learning through the strategies.

Decisions about adapting Training Strategies to fit the learners requires professional judgment.

It helps to ask the right questions in considering the learners.

Learning is maximized when there is a good fit, the right challenge, and proper support.

There should be no dumbing down.

14

Assessing
Learning Outcomes

YEARS AGO, John Dewey, the most famous American philosopher of education, wrote, "Teaching may be compared to selling commodities. No one can sell unless someone buys. But perhaps there are teachers who think they have done a good day's teaching irrespective of what pupils have learned." It is difficult to imagine anything less rewarding than a good day of training where no one learned. If no one is learning, how could it be a good day? In business, selling is a visible transaction; you know what was sold by counting up what was bought. The learning transaction is not so easily measured. How do you know if the learners are buying?

What results does training produce? Does training result in learning and does learning make a difference in the organization? Everyone wants the answers to those questions. Interestingly, however, different organizations have quite different ideas about what results are, the importance of getting results, how to measure results, and how much to worry about measuring results.

At Lackland Air Force Base in San Antonio, Texas, the 37th Training Group has a high level of concern about getting results. Training Administrator Robert Koger notes:

> Much of our training is technical training where people need to perform a skill, so it is not so difficult to track results because we

know where people go, and we get feedback from supervisors. Our first concern is always effectiveness, but we are also deeply concerned about efficiency because we are dealing with large numbers. Let's say it costs $450 a day for a person to come in for training. It has been taking four days, but what if we did it in three? When we save one day and multiply that by the thirty thousand people in that program each year, we have saved a lot of money. We had been required to examine time, results, and efficiencies of all training programs annually. Now we do it quarterly.

Consider another, rather different view on measuring results. James Buchwald is founder and chairman of the board of the ARIEL Corporation, a medium-sized gas compressor manufacturer in Mount Vernon, Ohio. For ARIEL the benefits of training seem so obvious from other data they gather that they do not spend a lot of time worrying about measuring results. Notes Buchwald:

> The cost is tiny compared to the benefit. It is a huge payoff in skill, professionalism, and knowledge about the company. To tell the truth, we don't try to measure it because it is so damn obvious. We can look at scrap and remachine rates, downtime, turnover, and number of inspectors on the payroll. All the indicators improve from the training we do. We want to have a good product and a good place to work, and we aren't going to spend our time running around mother-henning the system.

Obviously, results are different for different kinds of training, but results are also viewed differently in different types of organizations. Results may be very specific outcomes related to performance and expertise, or results may be an improved general capacity, an ability to move on to more responsibility, an ability to handle an emergency if it should occur, the skills to do a different job, or to do a job differently. In any case, getting results involves at some point, learning. No buying, no selling!

The Context of Assessment

Perhaps the best known and most widely used framework for thinking about the outcomes of training is what has come to be known as the Four-Step Model, set forth in Donald Kirkpatrick's *Evaluating Training Programs*.[1] Although there are criticisms of the Kirkpatrick Model and counterproposals—see especially Richard Swanson's Performance-Learning Satisfaction Evaluation System[2]—Kirkpatrick's work provides a starting point for understanding the broader context for the assessment of learning.

Kirkpatrick suggests that the systematic evaluation of training involves four levels: reaction, learning, behavior, and results.[3] *Reaction* is focused on measurements of "how those who participate in the program react to it." It is "a measure of customer satisfaction." The measurement of satisfaction is important—participants who are extremely unhappy with the process may not learn much or want more—but there are two problems with the measurement of satisfaction. One is that there is not a very high correlation between satisfaction and learning. As Richard Swanson notes, "Contrary to the practitioner's myth, the research shows that participants most satisfied with a program are not necessarily those who learned most. High or low satisfaction can be found among low, medium, and high achievers."[4]

Some training is difficult and challenging and may not draw high satisfaction scores. Understanding satisfaction provides useful feedback on facilities, schedules, attitudes, and materials, but measures of satisfaction are not likely to have much to do with learning.

The other problem with measuring satisfaction, what Kirkpatrick calls "the evaluation of reaction through happiness sheets,"[5] is that there is a tendency to stop there, that is, to confuse the measurement of satisfaction with the assessment of learning.

Trainers would often confess to us that they rely too much on "smile sheets." It is wrong to assume that if participants liked the experience, they must have learned something.

For many training programs, the measurement of reaction is all that is done. Smile sheets measure reaction, not learning, and assessment requires going well beyond gathering up reactions.

The second level of evaluation in the Four-Step Model is *learning*.[6] Although Kirkpatrick provides several suggestions for evaluating knowledge, skills, and attitudes, this part of the model is quite underdeveloped. We focus on the assessment of learning in the rest of this chapter and provide suggestions for assessing the learning related to each of the Training Strategies. Reading this chapter can help you to design assessments appropriate for each Training Strategy. This level of evaluation is pivotal because without adequate assessments of learning it is difficult to go to the other levels of the model—behavior and results.

The evaluation of *behavior* focuses on the transfer of knowledge, skills, and attitudes to the workplace and is concerned with "what change in job behavior occurred because people attended a training program."[7] The evaluation of behavior gets tricky because many other variables come into play besides learning. In recent years much attention has been given to the other factors that influence performance, and those who study these matters now see performance improvement as a system of variables, of which learning is just one. As Richard Swanson notes, in his valuable book *Analysis for Improving Performance,* "pit a good performer against a bad system, and the system will almost always win."[8] It may be a difficult lesson for trainers to learn, but new learning— even when real learning has occurred—does not necessarily result in improved performance, precisely because so many other variables can and do enter in.

The relationship between learning and behavior, therefore, is seldom direct and linear, and someone needs to pay attention to the other factors that also affect performance.

It is reasonable to conclude, however, that behavior is not likely to change, even when other factors have been considered, unless learning has occurred. Logicians would say that learning is a necessary but not sufficient condition for the change of behavior. Evaluation of behavior is an important aspect of any thorough examination of the outcomes of training and has been written about elsewhere. Our focus is on assessing learning.

The fourth level in the Kirkpatrick Model is *results*. According to Kirkpatrick, the final results of training include such things as "increased production, improved quality, decreased costs, reduced frequency and/or severity of accidents, increased sales, reduced turnover, and higher profits and return on investment."[9] Results are the longer-term impacts of training, but as Kirkpatrick points out, results are often the main reason for having training programs. At the fourth level, even more variables begin to enter the process, such as equipment, resources, nature of the product, marketing, competitive advantage, and so forth. As was the case with behavior, a tidy relationship no longer exists between learning and results. A relationship does exist, as Kirkpatrick was able to see, among learning, behavior, and results, but it becomes an increasingly complex relationship as other factors enter in.

One might, at this point, want to give up in despair about measuring results, but there has been some valuable progress in this domain in recent years. Consider, for example, the book, *Forecasting Financial Benefits of Human Resource Development* by Richard Swanson and Deane Gradous.[10] They develop a HRD Benefit Forecasting Model that gets down to the difficult job of calculating the dollar value of various types of performance. They show

how the costs of training can be calculated and compared with the dollar value of improvements in a cost-benefit approach to training. Although everything they say can be applied to evaluating training after it has occurred, they stress the value of forecasting costs and benefits up front to guide choices about training before programs are selected and implemented. Predicting the results of training is not impossible, only difficult and time consuming.

Notice how the four levels—reaction, learning, behavior, and results—are illustrated in this fascinating example from rural Brazil. What would happen if no learning occurred?

— COPASA MG BRAZIL

Companhia de Saneamento de Minas Gerais (COPASA MG), a large public sanitation company, provides safe drinking water for the State of Minas Gerais. Providing high-quality water supplies in remote rural areas is still a challenge not only in Brazil but the world over. In developing countries, 500 million people a year still get sick from water-related diseases, and over 10 million per year die, mostly children.

Daniel Adolpho Cerqueira, a biologist at COPASA's central laboratory, invented a clever, easy-to-use device for testing the quality of the water supply in rural areas, but he also had to develop the training to use the device and a means of assessing the training. Picture a very remote area with a small town and a water supply vulnerable to contamination. In the past an inspector took a water sample, sent it by bicycle, bus, or truck to a regional testing center where tests were performed and results were sent back—maybe! As one might guess, the system often broke down. "We had to develop a simple, on-site testing procedure that could be learned and used by people with very limited education," notes Cerqueira.

The device is ingenious—a small box for incubating bacteria overnight. A powder of salts and substrates provides food for the bacteria. As the bacteria release enzymes, there is a noticeable change of color in the water sample that indicates trouble. The local contact for the company is a man with perhaps a fourth- or fifth-grade education. "He *is* COPASA in that town," says Cerqueira, "not only testing water but collecting fees and operating the system." Five to ten such persons come to a regional center (the next biggest town) for training. After passing a basic color-acuity test, the participants are taught to take water samples, mix and add the powder, place the samples in the box, and read the sample for coloration. The training is infused with assessment.

What is the *reaction* of the participants? They like the training. It builds their pride, gives them a valued sense of autonomy, and provides a sense of satisfaction in being able to do the test perfectly. "One man actually cried when he passed the training," notes Cerqueira, "because he was so pleased he could play this important role in his community." But assessing reaction is surely not enough in this situation. To assess *learning,* a written test with multiple choice, true/false, and fill-in-the-blanks is provided. To get the participants ready for the test, many of the questions are interspersed with the explanations. Learning from the practical training is assessed by demonstration—individuals are picked randomly to perform the process while participants comment on and correct any mistakes to avoid negative modeling. At the end of training, each participant must be 100 percent effective in both the written and practical test. To assess *behavior,* a technician visits trainees one or two months later and uses a checklist to see if they are still performing accurately. Every three months a parallel sample is sent in by a technician to compare test results with the local sample. The technician always carries a positive sample and asks, "What do you do when it looks like this?" The trainee also returns to a regional center quarterly for continuing education on problem-solving techniques with positive samples. To assess *results,* COPASA keeps records on the incidence of contamination and reduction of disease. COPASA improves water quality and (even with the training costs) saves money through just-in-time quality control. Cerqueira, who is now presenting the results of his work at international meetings, sums up the benefits of the new system with a comment on quality from a proud trainee, "It starts with me, and it ends with me. Instead of waiting for results that may never come, I give the outcomes."

This example and summary of ideas about evaluating training show that learning is crucial to the other levels of outcomes.

Learning may be temporarily overshadowed by a host of other influential variables, but it remains the indispensable factor in training—no learning, no change of behavior or long-term results.

The assessment of learning, therefore, is essential in the larger undertaking of evaluating training programs and has a high priority in this broader context. Our focus and contribution is in making suggestions about assessing the learning that should result from using the Training Strategies presented in this book.

Purposes of Assessment

Assessment is somewhat like research, but its purposes are different. Assessment and research are both about finding out, but people who conduct research are interested in addressing a general theory or problem and adding to a body of knowledge. Usually assessment is directed toward finding out whether learning occurred from a particular experience that was designed to produce learning within the context of an organizational setting. Assessment is designed to answer the question, Did it work here? Developing effective assessment is largely a matter of thinking carefully about the goals of the desired learning and developing systematic methods to find out if those goals have been or are being achieved.

The primary purpose of assessment, of course, in training settings is to provide evidence about what was learned. Those responsible for the desired learning—someone besides the facilitator or participant—must know if learning took place. Because training usually involves learning some subject matter, it is important to make sure that the content of the learning is addressed. On the other hand, most carefully designed training also involves learning outcomes that go beyond the subject matter content, such as certain skills and abilities or changes of attitude.

Effective assessment addresses subject-matter content and learning outcomes.

Another purpose of assessment is to provide useful feedback about learning *for the facilitator* and *for the learner.* The facilitator wants and needs to know if participants are learning, but the participants also need to know if they are learning. Comprehensive assessment will provide feedback on learning for both the facilitator and the learner. The feedback for participants may also provide useful information for the facilitator, but sometimes the facilitator wants to know and needs to know more. Thus, feedback to the learner and the facilitator may or may not be the same thing.

Another purpose of assessment not to be overlooked is to increase learning. The concrete feedback provided by assessment improves learning but so does the expectation of being assessed. If assessment is built into training and participants know it will occur, that awareness itself can help to maximize learning. It is human nature to take learning activities more seriously—whatever Training Strategy may be used—if participants know that they (individually or as a group) will be held accountable for their learning. Most people learn more if they know someone is checking. Assessment sends a message that helps to maximize learning.

Types of Assessment

Because several different types of assessment can be used, professional judgment needs to be exercised in making rational choices.

- *Formal or informal.* Formal assessment usually involves methods agreed to in the planning process, prepared materials, and systematic sampling of the learning and the participants at a designated time. Informal assessment may take place more spontaneously, may involve only a few available participants, and usually does not require special materials.

- *Quantitative or qualitative.* Quantitative methods often produce data (answers to tests, reports from questionnaires, frequency counts from observations) that can be quantified, that is, put into numbers—hence the name *quantitative.* Qualitative approaches often produce information that can be used to describe the qualities of something (attitudes, responses, observations, reactions)—hence the name *qualitative.*

- *Observing or asking.* Some learning is observable. It is possible to observe participants and see whether what they do now is different from and better than what they did before. Other assessment involves asking participants, either through written surveys, tests, or interviews, what they know or how they feel. Many sophisticated methods are available for conducting assessments, but they all boil down to observing or asking.

- *Before, during, or after.* Most trainers are familiar with pretests and posttests and are skilled at using these and comparing the results. Sometimes follow-up assessment comes long after the instruction has been completed to see how much participants have retained or can use later. At other times, assessment is done during the instruction to get feedback on what students are learning so that adjustments in the use of the Training Strategy can be made before the instruction has been completed.

Assessment need not be limited, therefore, to one or two old standby methods. Many techniques can be used, and in some organizations a true research orientation toward assessment develops.

—Lockheed Martin Astronautics USA ——————

"*M*any organizations admit that they don't do a good job of measuring the outcomes of training," notes Carol North, director of human resources support services at Lockheed Martin Astronautics. "We try to select the best assessment methods for the particular kind of learning. Some assessment, as with our Systems Engineering Course, involves end-of-course evaluations to gain insights about what value was added through the course and how it might be updated. In the production area the old pretest/posttest model still works. At other times, an interview process is used with supervisors to get their views of why training may or may not be working out in the work setting. We also get a lot of unsolicited feedback," notes North, "and we pay attention to that, too. People in this industry love to learn—they are learning-oriented—and that helps. Training is a wonderful area for research on outcomes. Let's say for example, ten thousand people get training on sexual harassment—what is the positive measure?"

Strategy-Driven Assessment

Three events typically occur with the assessment of learning:

1. *Assessment is not done.* An assumption is made that the measurement of reaction (satisfaction) is enough or that the measurement of behavior change or long-term results is so important that learning can be inferred from these results. This leaves the facilitator, and often the participants, with no feedback on whether and how much learning occurred.

2. *Assessment is a ritual.* Assessment methods may be drawn from the general well of research and evaluation techniques—primarily quizzes and questionnaires—and may not serve well the particular strengths of the strategy being used or the intended learning outcomes.

3. *Assessment is inappropriate.* A particular assessment technique that may be appropriate for one strategy is ripped out of context and applied to another strategy, usually missing important aspects of the learning that occurred or providing a distorted view of it.

We want to recommend Strategy-Driven Assessment—where assessment efforts grow naturally out of the particular Training Strategy used. If each Training Strategy is especially good for bringing about a particular kind of learning, then assessment efforts need to be focused on that type of learning.

In the summaries that follow we provide a brief discussion of the assessment techniques that are most appropriate for each Training Strategy. We make no claim to providing an exhaustive list (so keep thinking of other techniques), but the examples we provide should set in motion a way of thinking about assessment that can be expanded and developed with experience and experimentation. For each strategy we return to some of the illustrations from organizations that were presented with that strategy, but please note that the types of assessment we discuss are what we have imagined or would recommend but do not represent necessarily what was actually done.

The Behavioral Strategy

If the Behavioral Strategy is especially good for building cognitive and psychomotor skills, then the assessment needs to measure how well those skills can be performed. If the learning outcome is an observable behavior, then the best assessment technique is observation, watching the participant in training actually perform the task. If the task is not observable—psychologists would call it covert—then it becomes necessary to get the task out of the head and into some form of behavior that is observable. In this case, a written test that reflects well the mental operations would be useful, such as describing the steps of the task, ordering the steps, or identifying a missing step.

In the examples provided, the rigging of doors at Boeing is assessed by having a certified door rigger watch the trainee actually rig a door. The observational assessment is supplemented by written tests that call for descriptions of the steps and the reasons for the steps. The assessment for glassblowers at Iittala Finland would be primarily observational; one can see the quality of the product and the appropriateness of the steps used to produce it. There probably is not much benefit to written testing. On the other hand, written testing on the skills related to basic telecommunications at TELEBRÁS lend themselves to stepwise, item-by-item testing via well-developed computer frames. CAI to teach and CAI to test.

The Behavioral Strategy, therefore, calls out for observation or very focused quizzes and is well suited to the common pretest/posttest design to measure present performance level and gains in learning. Obviously, some observation must also take place along the way to see if crucial substeps are also being mastered. The Behavioral Strategy lends itself to frequent testing, unit-by-unit, and is often self-paced, so that the participant can get regular and timely feedback. Thus, in the Behavioral Strategy, assessment is closely related to the feedback process itself and is crucial for the participant as well as the facilitator. Assessment for learning where the Behavioral Strategy is used is also usually quantifiable in some way. Criteria for acceptable performance are usually set, and the percent of correct responses can be accumulated. Observations may range from an informal "yes, he or she can do it" to a carefully worked out observation checklist. Obviously, qualitative measures are not very useful here. We do not want to ask participants if they think they can perform or how they feel about performing when actual performance is the issue.

The Cognitive Strategy

The Cognitive Strategy is used for communicating information through presentations and explanations. The desired learning outcome is to understand and remember the information. Because understanding and remembering are covert mental processes, the assessment will need to be designed to pull the learning out of the learner and get it on paper. The remembering part is not so difficult to assess. Paper-and-pencil or computerized quizzes on the essential information can be developed. It is important to design the quizzes in a systematic way so that the questions and problems used on the quizzes reflect the most important information and an adequate sampling of it. Thus, testing must correspond precisely to the information that was actually presented. Assessing understanding is not as easy. Often an explanation is used to describe a process, explain how something works, or recount how something came to be. Understanding also can be assessed through carefully developed quiz questions (such as multiple choice) with the focus of the questions shifting from recall of information to understanding concepts, theories, processes, and progressions. Open-ended production items, where the participant is asked to describe or recount a process, are also useful for assessing understanding.

Sometimes participants will be asked to apply their new information as the ultimate test of their knowledge, but this is reasonable and fair only when they have been taught about applying and have some familiarity with the new situation. Actually, learning to apply may require other strategies and additional training, so when the Cognitive Strategy is used, it may be best to confine assessment to remembering and understanding and to do a good job with these.

The training conducted at Paychex involves a host of technical information, and participants need to be able to remember that information. On the other hand, the training is also about a process, a payroll process, which is the essence of the business. Participants must be able to show that they understand that process. Participants in training on project management conducted through the Air Force Institute of Technology must learn new terminology and information, but they also must be able to describe the process of project management. Trainees at Merrill Lynch, using the lessons transported to their desktop computer, must soak up the information needed to pass the General Securities Representative Examination (Series 7). In all of these cases, we would want to avoid assessments that stress how people will solve problems, perform skills, or assess how they feel about what they are learning.

The Inquiry Strategy

The Inquiry Strategy involves three types of thinking—critical, creative, and dialogical—and the type of assessment for each will vary somewhat. Assuming that the participants have not just been told about thinking but have been given opportunities to practice it, either as individuals or in groups, the appropriate assessment is to see whether and how well they can engage in one or more types of thinking. Almost always, critical thinking involves either the analysis of writing (someone else's) or producing writing. Thus, an appropriate assessment would involve the analysis of what someone else has written, such as a report or proposal, or the generation of a similar work. Naturally, what one hopes for in a critique is sound analysis—analysis that identifies some of the problems in thinking, the way the argument is being made, the evidence, the assumptions, and of course, the fallacies. If the assessment is of writing produced by a participant, then, of course, all of these same criteria would be used to judge the product. Likewise, creative thinking can be assessed in both of these ways—by the participant's ability to analyze something that has been set forth as creative or by the ability to produce something creative themselves. Dialogical thinking can be assessed by asking the participants to generate counter arguments, to compare and contrast arguments, or to take an unfamiliar or perhaps uncomfortable position and defend it. All of these techniques, however, suggest the production of either a critique or a product on the part of the participant, usually written, but this type of assessment could be done orally as well, as a focused dialogue. The focus is not on remembering information but on how well the participant thinks.

Although thinking is usually done by individuals, and the assessment will often be on an individual basis, more often than not, thinking in organizations is done by groups, and it may be important to assess the capacity of a particular group to engage in critical, creative, or dialogical thinking. These assessments will almost always involve group reports or projects, something that all of the members contribute to that measures their collective effort. Recall particularly the training at Norsk Hydro in Norway, where selected employees are asked to develop creative new business ideas or where the unemployed in Sweden were asked by KRESAM to create a business plan for a new enterprise.

The assessment of thinking does not lend itself well to the pretest/posttest model, to quizzes, or to the descriptions of feelings. What one hopes to be able to find are modest but accumulating signs of improvement—clues, examples, and indicators that participants are becoming better thinkers.

The Mental Models Strategy

The Mental Models Strategy is used to cultivate abilities in problem solving and decision making. What one hopes to assess is increased ability in those areas, and the assessment needs to provide opportunities, therefore, for actually solving problems and making decisions. These opportunities may be provided as individual exercises or, as we have suggested, as cases or projects for group action. Assessment of problem solving and decision making also is structured in such a way as to find out not only what answers or decisions people arrive at but how they arrive at them. The instruments should include not only a problem or need for a decision but also the opportunity for expressing the response in a way that shows how the response is being framed and the reasoning processes that are being used. The response to a case, for example, would include a careful case analysis, a consideration of various options, the selection of the best options, and the reasons for selecting those options. To the extent possible, the assessment should involve the real problems and decisions of the organization, just as the training does. As with the Inquiry Strategy, the learning and its application sometimes takes place in groups, and the assessment may employ a case or project worked on by a group.

The assessment, for example, of problem solving at Ford Motor Company would not be a written quiz on problem-solving principles (although this might be used as a preliminary check on information about problem solving) but rather on the use of the Global 8D Model on a specific problem. The proof is in the application, the way in which participants go about using the model and the kind of results they get with it. Similarly the results of problem-solving training with the market cells at USIMINAS are in the concrete suggestions that come forth for increasing sales. The assessment of decision making in the training of military police at Lackland Air Force Base is carried out with the very sophisticated laser equipment used to practice the training so that the assessment is really an extension of responding to scenarios similar to those used for practice. Although most assessment for problem solving or decision making will result in a product that can be evaluated, important feedback also may be gained from observing the process—watching carefully how participants respond within the process—or asking participants afterward to explain their thinking and defend their solutions.

The Group Dynamics Strategy

The Group Dynamics Strategy is used for exploring opinions, attitudes, and beliefs, for building team skills, and sometimes for probing deeper into personal issues. Where opinions, attitudes, and beliefs are involved, beginning with a standardized measure or, more likely, devising a simple attitude scale to measure initial and posttraining attitudes about particular issues may be useful. Because most attitudes are slow to change, several sessions over a period of time may be needed for measurable change to take place when a scale is used.

It is valuable, of course, to watch what people do and say in their groups and to see if observable changes occur in body language, participation, and feelings expressed. Another valuable procedure is to ask people what they learned from the group experience and to inquire directly about any changes they see in themselves or in other group members. Videotaped sessions can be used to analyze group behavior and may be used as a before-and-after comparison to assess how the group or individuals in the group may have developed over time.

If the emphasis is on teamwork, additional group activities may be given to see how the group works as a team after they have had some practice. Participants may also be able to express how they see themselves differently as a result of team training, what they learned about themselves, and what they need to work on to improve.

The results that come from the Group Dynamics Strategy are usually less tangible than those from other strategies and usually need to be "teased" out by observation or self-report. Usually people who have been involved in a group or team experience can tell what they think they have learned, and the best assessment may simply be to ask them.

The group activities used by ABC Algar in Brazil all had a point, and a significant amount of time was spent in debriefing participants on the message. Most were able to describe quite fully what the message was and how it applied to their work. The diversity training used by United Airlines was striking enough in the points it made that participants could go on to describe other similar experiences and situations they had encountered. Assessment for the Group Dynamics Strategy often involves waiting for the participants to understand—as with the women in training at Grupo Tampico—and listening to their ability to elaborate on the experience, generating their own examples and applications. For teams, the test may be to give them the same instrument before and after training and observe how they perform after they have had some practice or to give them a new instrument to see if they can transfer some of their teamwork skills to a new task.

The Virtual Reality Strategy

The Virtual Reality Strategy is used for learning about or practicing tasks that might otherwise have high risk in real life. Role plays, dramatic scenarios, and simulations are used, and to the extent that these reflect the larger reality, assessment involves seeing how close the participants can come to a live performance. The assessment is primarily through observation. If the learning has been about roles, and role play was used to teach about roles, then role play is a good way to test what was learned. After learning about the role and having a chance to practice it, a new role play is presented as a test to see how the participant responds. The same principle applies to dramatic scenarios and simulations. The test is, "Well, let's run that one more time." Usually the test is not an exact repetition of what was done before but is a similar situation in a new setting with different players. Although observation is the key to this assessment, conversation with the participants is also important to discern the reasons and motives for their actions. Sometimes they can explain what went well or wrong and what they might do differently.

The trainees at VINFEN in Boston must be able to perform certain physical maneuvers to protect themselves. The assessment is to see how they handle themselves in as close to a real-life situation as can be provided. The cadets in training at the Royal Canadian Mounted Police Academy are given a dramatic scenario as part of their final exam. Experienced Mounties are brought in to sit on a panel that observes and comments on the cadets' performance. The final assessment for the United Airlines pilots in the flight simulators is very simple: Don't crash! The trainer is literally sitting behind the pilot in training, watching every move and checking the outcomes.

The Holistic Strategy

The Holistic Strategy is used to draw learning out of experience. All of the senses and the amazing multitrack processing capabilities of the brain are brought to bear on an identified experience to produce reflection-in-action. We are now a long distance from the behavioral pretest/posttest design keyed to operationalized objectives. Assessment, when the Holistic Strategy is used, depends to a large extent on the learner's self-report of learning. The learner has ventured out into a new experience. In coming back, the learner reports on and makes meaning of the experience with a mentor or counselor. Assessment, in this case, relies very heavily on what the learner says about the learning; in fact, the learning and words used to describe the learning are almost inseparable.

The assessment, however, is not just the participant's report. The mentor or counselor listens to this report, makes certain interpretations, and sometimes offers challenges. Thus, the assessment is really what the mentor or counselor thinks about what the participant has said. The person who facilitates the reflection is also the monitor of the whole experience and is able to step back and reflect on the learner's reflection, thus, drawing conclusions about whether the participant learned much, little, or nothing from this experience. With the Holistic Strategy the assessment is an evaluation of what the learner appeared to glean from the experience. To supplement this verbal report, the mentor or counselor can also examine the logs, diaries, letters, or reports the participant has kept to aid reflection.

The wise "mom" at Asea Brown Boveri who counsels the interns, is by now, no doubt, very perceptive about what the interns are actually learning from their experience. On one hand, she offers support and challenge, but she also assesses what kind of learning (what quality and how much) has occurred through the internship experience. She may occasionally talk with a supervisor or call a colleague to do some further checking, but she is in a position to know what was learned through the intern's experience. Similarly the mentor to the hotel employees at the Lai Lai Sheraton knows from the discussion of visits to other hotels what is being brought back from that experience, and the supervisor at Coors Distributing who rides the route knows at the end of the day what the driver learned because he asks the driver what he learned, and the supervisor can tell from the responses to his questions what was learned. Assessment of experience-based learning depends heavily on the participant's ability to put the experience into words and the mentor or counselor's ability to hear through those words what learning did or did not occur.

Four Principles

Four principles emerge from this discussion of assessment of learning.

• *Assessment flows from the strategy.* Assessment is not some mysterious technique, a separate field, or a discipline apart from learning. Appropriate assessment techniques flow naturally from the strategy; they are not something external brought to the strategy. The place to begin, in thinking about assessment, is with the learning that the strategy is most likely to generate. What learning is likely to take place? How can it be captured and described?

• *Assessment is embedded in planning.* As planning for training is undertaken, the approach to assessment needs to be made part of that planning. Assessment is not an afterthought, something that gets tacked on to training after it is finished, the guess-we-ought-to-do-some-assessment approach. The issue of assessment ought to surface in the very beginning, and it is, in fact, already there in most rational planning models.

• *Assessment is part of the learning.* Assessment usually plays an important role in bringing about learning. It is not only something done later to see if learning occurred but is part of the learning itself. A good question to ask is, Is this assessment dispensable, or do I really need it as an integral part of the feedback provided for the learner? Effective assessment is so embedded in the learning that participants would miss it if it were not there.

• *Assessment is the window that lets the facilitator see and share the joy of learning.* Assessment lets the facilitator know that there was learning. It provides the primary opportunity for satisfaction in what is often a difficult and challenging process. If there is learning, there can be rejoicing.

These four principles provide the guidelines for developing the appropriate means for assessing learning. Appropriate assessment is an essential factor in maximizing learning.

Add "effective assessment" to "intensity, frequency, and duration" as the keys to maximizing learning.

The Joy of Learning

We expressed a concern early in this book that too much training might be taking place without learning, that on the way to the professionalization of training, learning got left out. Too much training, we said, is devoid of theory. We also noted that too much training operates at the level of tactics without appropriate use of strategies. We focused on elaborating seven effective Training Strategies and illustrated these with concrete examples. We also expressed a concern that too much training takes place without appropriate levels of intensity, frequency, and duration, and without appropriate means of assessment. All of these are factors that affect the promise of maximizing learning. We want to add now one additional concern: Too much training takes place without joy.

Learning ought to be joyful. When training becomes a ritual, a matter of going through the motions, studying something that someone else thinks would be good for you, or learning to recite someone else's answers to someone else's questions, it just is not joyful. It is a pain. To relieve the anticipated pain—most facilitators have some sense of when they are getting into a painful situation—trainers turn to fun. How often have you heard the question, "What can we do to make this fun?" Fun, as we should know, is not the antidote for pain. An already badly bruised body will not take much pleasure in the fun of downhill skiing. Pain is relieved not by fun but by going to the sources of the pain, by healing. Many of the sources that make training a pain can be alleviated by planning—by patiently working through goals, by involving participants in planning, by designing experiences that truly meet a need. One would hope (every trainer's dream) that participants will come eager, motivated, and ready to learn and in that sense, free of pain. Now there is hope.

If the goal of training is learning, the outcome ought not to be fun so much as joy. Joy, the dictionary reminds us, is the emotion of great delight or happiness caused by something good or satisfying. The "something good or satisfying" ought to be learning, and the "great delight or happiness" ought to be the joy of learning.

The joy of learning is what participants experience when real learning takes place. The facilitator's joy is watching learning happen and being a part of it.

The joy of learning should be visible while the Training Strategies are being employed, but a deeper joy comes at the end when appropriate assessment techniques demonstrate that real learning occurred. We get joy from families, friends, and leisure activities, but there is also a deep and satisfying joy to be derived from maximizing learning in organizations.

THE BOTTOM LINE

The assessment of learning takes place in the wider context of reaction, learning, behavior, and results.

Assessment is designed to answer the question, Did it work here?

Assessment provides feedback for the learner and the facilitator, and information about subject-matter content and learning outcomes.

Assessment lets participants know that someone is checking.

Assessment can be

- formal or informal
- quantitative or qualitative
- done by observing or asking
- carried out before, during, or after

Strategy-driven assessment uses methods that grow naturally out of the particular Training Strategy being used.

The most effective assessment flows from the Training Strategy used, is embedded in planning, is part of the learning, and lets the facilitator see and share the joy of learning.

The very bottom, bottom line, is the joy of learning.

APPENDIX
Directory of Organizations

The following organizations are mentioned in the text as examples and illustrations. Because the interviews were done over a period of three years, some personnel, titles, and phone numbers may have changed, but we have done our best to provide an accurate list.

Algar S.A. Empreendimentos e
  Participações (ABC Algar)
Av. Industrial, 2689
Caixa Postal 212
38405-323 Uberlândia, MG, Brazil
tel.: (55-34) 218-3068
fax: (55-34) 235-1818
Contact person: Elizabeth Amaral Oliveira,
  Analista de Talentos Humanos

American Express Financial Advisors Inc.
T7 / 88
IDS Tower 10
Minneapolis, Minnesota 55440
tel.: (612) 671-3752
fax: (612) 671-2302
Contact person: Katherine A. Tunheim,
  Director-Leadership Development,
  Leadership & Organization
  Effectiveness

American Red Cross
8111 Gatehouse Road
Falls Church, Virginia 22042
tel.: (703) 206-8696
fax: (703) 206-8849
Contact person: Christopher E. Saeger,
  Senior Training Development
  Associate, Disaster Preparedness/
  Disaster Services

ARIEL Corporation
35 Blackjack Road
Mount Vernon, Ohio 43050-9482
tel.: (614) 397-0311
fax: (614) 397-3856
Contact person: James Buchwald,
  President and Chairman

ARLA Group
Örebromejeriet
Box 2007
S-700 02 Örebro, Sweden
tel.: (46-19) 611-9070
fax: (46-19) 611-7160
Contact person: Ingrid Bäckman-Persson,
  Agronomist, Training Manager for
  Members and Elected Members

Asea Brown Boveri AB (ABB)
721 83 Västerås, Sweden
tel.: (46-21) 32 50 04 / 32 50 00
fax: (46-21) 32 50 12
Contact person: Reijo Palola, Director,
  University Relations

Blue Cross Blue Shield of Massachusetts
100 Summer Street
Boston, Massachusetts 02110-2190
tel.: (617) 832-4409
fax: (617) 832-4414
Contact person: Sandra Casey Buford,
  Manager, Employee Relations

The Boeing Company
The Boeing Commercial Airplane Group
Center for Leadership and Learning
P.O. Box 3767 M.S. 20-28
Seattle, Washington 98124-2207
tel.: (206) 662-7445
fax: (206) 666-7463
Contact person: Nancy Birdwell, Course
  Developer and Instructional Designer

COBE BCT, Inc.
1201 Oak Street
Lakewood, Colorado 80215-4498
tel.: (303) 231-4662
fax: (303) 231-4311
Contact person: Kathe Burke, Director of
  Human Resources

COBE Laboratories, Inc.
1185 Oak Street
Lakewood, Colorado 80215-4498
tel.: (303) 231-4145
fax: (303) 231-4949
Contact person: Ellen Cohig, Marketing
  Services Manager/Office Manager

Companhia de Saneamento de Minas
  Gerais—COPASA MG
BR-040 km 446
Trevo de Nova Lima-Belvedere
30950-640 Belo Horizonte, MG, Brazil
tel.: (55-31) 250-2382
fax: (55-31) 250-2355
Contact person: Daniel Adolpho
  Cerqueira, Biólogo, Responsável pelo
  Controle Microbiológico da Água

Companhia Vale do Rio Doce (CVRD)
Av. Graça Aranha, 26-2° andar
20005-900 Rio de Janeiro, RJ, Brazil
tel.: (55-21) 272-4345 / 272-4607
fax: (55-21) 272-4587
Contact person: Virgínia de Abreu,
  Gerente Treinamento/Rio

Coors Distributing Company
1280 W 47th Avenue
Denver, Colorado 80211
tel.: (303) 964-5544
fax: (303) 964-5553
Contact person: Robert O. Jiron, Sales
  Training Specialist

Dallah Group Co. (Dallah Albaraka
  Group)
P.O. Box 2618
Jeddah 21461, Saudi Arabia
tel.: (966-2) 671-0000
fax: (966-2) 671-0412
Contact person: A. Hakim Al-Shafei,
  Executive Director of Global Group
  for Training and Development

Deloitte & Touche Consulting Grup
10 Westport Road
Wilton, Connecticut 06897
tel.: (203) 761-3159
fax: (203) 834-2254
Contact person: Katie Weiser, Director of
    Education

Deloitte & Touche Consulting Group
Pilestredet 75 C
P.O. Box 5945 Majorstua
0308 Oslo, Norway
tel.: (47-22) 464770
fax: (47-22) 467004
Contact person: Anders Stang,
    Management Consulting Partner

Denver Museum of Natural History
2001 Colorado Boulevard
Denver, Colorado 80205-5798
tel.: (303) 370-6419
fax: (303) 331-6492
Contact person: Volunteer Services
    Department

Department of Social and Health Care
P.O. Box 98
FIN-33201 Tampere, Finland
tel.: (358-3)
fax: (358-3) 219-7791
Contact person: Seppo Prunnila, Planning
    Manager

Eastman Kodak Company
343 State Street
Rochester, New York 14650-0811
tel.: (716) 724-9588
fax: (716) 724-0826
Contact person: Susan M. Connolly,
    Director, Education and Development

ELSI Taiwan Language Schools
6F, #9, Lane 90, Sung Chiang Road
Taipei, Taiwan, R.O.C.
tel.: (886-2) 581-8511
fax: (886-2) 581-0907
Contact person: Kenneth Hou, President

FIAT Automóveis S.A.
BR 381-km 429 (Rodovia Fernão Dias)
32501-970 Betim, MG, Brazil
tel.: (55-31) 529-2235
fax: (55-31) 529-2198
Contact person: Roberval Brandão Nunes,
    Diretor de Relações Industriais-
    Formação e Treinamento

FMC Corporation
Executive Offices
200 East Randolph Drive
Chicago, Illinois 60601
tel.: (312) 861-5819
fax: (312) 861-5902
Contact person: William P. O'Brien,
    Director Organization Excellence

Ford Motor Company
Fairlane Training and Development Center
P.O. Box 6055
19000 Hubbard Drive
Dearborn, Michigan 48121-6055
tel.: (313) 323-2763
fax: (313) 390-1237
Contact person: Paul F. Day, Program
    Manager-North American Education
    and Training

Foreign Service Institute (U.S. Department
    of State)
4000 Arlington Blvd.
Arlington, Virginia 22204-1500
tel.: (703) 302-7178
fax: (703) 302-7181
Contact person: Barry L. Wells, Associate
    Dean of the Senior Seminar

The Gates Rubber Company
Mail Code: 50-1-2-A2
990 South Broadway
P.O. Box 5887
Denver, Colorado 80217-5887
tel.: (303) 744-5257
fax: (303) 744-4905
Contact person: Kathy Kimmens,
    Manager, Education & Training

General Mills, Inc.
Number One General Mills Blvd.
Minneapolis, Minnesota 55426
tel.: (612) 540-3377
fax: (612) 540-7224
Contact person: Scott A. Weisberg,
    Director Employee & Organization
    Development

Grupo Tampico
Ejercito Mexicano 708
Col. Primavera
Tampico, TAM. 89130, Mexico
tel.: (52-12) 137677
fax: (52-12) 130071
Contact person: Esteban Fuentes Salazar,
    Director de Recursos Humanos

The Guthrie Theater
725 Vineland Place
Minneapolis, Minnesota 55403
tel.: (612) 347-1128
fax: (612) 347-1188
Contact person: Ken Washington,
    Director of Company Development

Iittala Finland
Lasimestarintie 2 A 6
FIN-14500 Iittala, Finland
tel.: (358-917) 676-5493
fax: (358-917) 535-6232
Contact person: Harri Jokinen,
    Näytöspuhaltaja

INLAN-Indústria de Componentes
    Mecânicos, S.A.
Circular Poente
Apartado 40
7401 Ponte de Sôr Codex, Portugal
tel.: (351-42) 26153 / 26742
fax: (351-42) 26942
Contact person: António Pinheiro,
    Director Recursos Humanos

J.D. Edwards World Source Company
8055 East Tufts Avenue
Denver, Colorado 80237
tel.: (303) 334-4000
fax: (303) 334-1679
Contact person: Susan Daly, Manager of
    Worldwide Translation

KRESAM
Ångåsen 60, S-683 92
Hagfors, Sweden
tel.: (46-5) 632-4080
fax: (46-5) 632-4080
Contact person: Bengt Gustavsson,
    Edutrainer & Edutainer

Lackland Air Force Base (37th Training
    Group)
950 Voyager Drive
Suite # 3 (Lackland AFB)
San Antonio, Texas 78236-5724
tel.: (210) 671-2261
fax: (210) 671-3370
Contact person: Fred Van Wert, Chief
    of Advanced Training Technology/
    Flight 37 TRSS/TTFT

Lai Lai Sheraton (Vandyke Hospitality
    Support)
6F, # 9, Lane 90, Sung Chiang Road
Taipei, Taiwan, R.O.C.
tel.: (886-2) 581-8511
fax: (886-2) 581-0947
Contact person: Abraham Folts, General
    Manager

Lockheed Martin Astronautics
P.O. Box 179
Denver, Colorado 80201-0179
tel.: (303) 971-8420
fax: (303) 971-3324
Contact person: Carol L. North, Director,
   Human Resources Support Services

Martins, Comércio e Serviços de
   Distribuição Ltda.
Av. Floriano Peixoto, 2300
38406-900 Uberlândia, MG, Brazil
tel.: (55-34) 218-1122
fax: (55-34) 218-1340
Contact person: Ricardo Rezende, Gerente
   de Recursos Humanos

Massachusetts General Hospital
75 Blossom Court
Boston, Massachusetts 02114
tel.: (617) 726-2232
fax: (617) 726-6972
Contact person: Kathy A. Rice, Assistant
   Director of Human Resources

Mercedes-Benz
Karl-Bentz-Platz 1
Stuttgart-Untertürkheim
Mercedes-Benz AG
T 101
70322 Stuttgart, Germany
tel.: (49-711) 17-23546
fax: (49-711) 17-53928
Contact person: Martin Scherzinger,
   Personnel Development

Merrill Lynch & Co., Inc.
Merrill Lynch Capital Management
Merrill Lynch World Financial Center
North Tower
New York, New York 10281-1303
tel.: (609) 282-0883
fax: (609) 282-2739
Contact person: Michael L. Quinn,
   Managing Director

Motorola
Motorola University, The Americas
1303 East Algonquin Road
Schaumburg, Illinois 60196-1097
tel.: (708) 576-0650
fax: (708) 576-8591
Contact person: Brenda B. Sumberg,
   Director of Motorola University,
   The Americas

Museo del Prado
Calle Ruiz de Alarcon, #12
28014 Madrid, Spain
tel.: (34-1) 522-2588
Contact person: José Manoel Hernando,
   Jefe de Area de Organización y Medios

National Emergency Training Center
U.S. Federal Emergency Management
   Agency
16825 South Seton Avenue
Emmitsburg, Maryland 21727
tel.: (301) 447-6771
fax: (301) 447-1112
Contact person: Bruce Marshall, Chief
   Support Systems Branch, Preparedness
   Training & Exercises Directorate

Norsk Hydro a.s.
Bygdøy allé 2
N-0240 Oslo, Norway
tel.: (47-2) 243-2100
fax: (47-2) 243-2555
Contact person: Sigbjørn Engebretsen,
   Vice President Human Resources
   Organisational Development

NOVA Corporation
645 Seventh Avenue S.W.
P.O. Box 2535, Station M
Calgary, Alberta T2P 2N6, Canada
tel.: (403) 261-5355
fax: (403) 261-5230
Contact person: Joy Halvorson,
   Organizational Effectiveness Specialist

Paychex Inc.
911 Panorama Trail South
Rochester, New York 14625-0397
tel.: (716) 383-3100
fax: (716) 383-3159
Contact person: Roberta Goheen, Training
Director

Prudential Intercultural
Flatiron Park West
2555 55th Street, Suite 201D
Boulder, Colorado 80301-5729
tel.: (303) 546-1006
fax: (303) 449-1064
Contact person: Ann Wederspahn,
Director, Consulting Services-
Intercultural Services

The Quaker Oats Company
P.O. Box 049001, Suite 16-1
Chicago, Illinois 60604-9001
tel.: (312) 222-7476
fax: (312) 222-2733
Contact person: Angie Karesh, Senior
Manager of Training and Development

QUANTUM Corporation
333 South Street
Shrewsbury, Massachusetts 01545
tel.: (508) 770-2597
fax: (508) 770-3738
Contact person: Henry Tarby, Director of
Training

ReliaStar Financial Corporation
20 Washington Avenue
South #1512
Minneapolis, Minnesota 55401
tel.: (612) 342-3213
fax: (612) 342-3066
Contact person: Dean H. Hoppe, Second
Vice President of Human Resources

Robert Bosch GmbH (BOSCH)
Further Education Feuerbach
Postfach 30 02 20
70442 Stuttgart, Germany
tel.: (49-711) 811-4694
fax: (49-711) 811-5011
Contact person: Peter Gutzan, Training
Director

Royal Canadian Mounted Police
(Gendarmerie Royale du Canada)
"Depot" Division, Training Academy
P.O. Box 6500
Regina, Saskatchewan S4P 3J7, Canada
tel.: (306) 780-8197
fax: (306) 780-3473
Contact person: D.L.M. (Donna) Morken,
Corporal, Canadian Law Enforcement
Training Unit

Safeway Inc.
6900 South Yosemite
Englewood, Colorado 80112-1412
tel.: (303) 843-7622
fax: (303) 843-7673
Contact person: Linda Hawkins, Training
Instructor

The Savola Company
Al-Meena Centre-Al-Meena Street
P.O. Box 14455
Jeddah 21424, Saudi Arabia
tel.: (966-2) 647-7333
fax: (966-2) 648-1508
Contact person: Mahmoud M. Khan,
Senior General Manager Human
Resources

SHARP Corporation
22-22 Nagaiko-Cho, Abeno-Ku
Osaka 545, Japan
tel.: (81-6) 625-3013
telex: LABOMET A-B J 63428
Contact person: Asanori Fujita, Manager-
Overseas Personnel

Sokos Hotel Ilves
Hatanpään valtatie 1
FIN-33100 Tampere, Finland
tel.: (358-31) 212-1212
fax: (358-31) 213-2565
Contact person: Arja Rajakaltio, Assistant

Sumitomo Metal Industries
5-33, Kitahama, 4-Chome, Chuo-Ku
Osaka 541, Japan
tel.: (81-6) 220-5515
fax: (81-6) 223-0194
Contact person: Hiroshi Tsubouchi,
Personnel Dept. No. 3 Personnel
Section
tel.: (81-6) 466-6150
fax: (81-6) 466-6231
Contact person: Atsushi Hamazaki,
General Manager of Automotive
Materials

TELEBRÁS—Telecomunicações
Brasileiras S.A.
Centro Nacional de Treinamento
SAIN-Via L-4, Quadra 6, Lote 4
70800-200 Brasília, DF, Brazil
tel.: (55-61) 212-7373
fax: (55-61) 212-7387
Contact person: Luiz F. B. Peres dos
Santos, Gerente da Seção de
Tecnologia em Capacitação

United Airlines
United Airlines Flight Training Center
Flight Center
7401 Martin Luther King Blvd.
Denver, Colorado 80207
tel.: (303) 780-5920
fax: (303) 780-5860
Contact person: Gene T. Yokomizo,
Manager Flight Simulator Services

United Airlines
United Airlines Training Center
P.O. Box 66100
Chicago, Illinois 60666
tel.: (847)700-3022
fax: (847) 700-4850
Contact person: Michele Manoski,
Manager of Automation for Flight
Operation

The United Methodist Church
P.O. Box 840
Nashville, Tennessee 37202-0840
tel.: (615) 340-7179
fax: (615) 340-1724
Contact person: Timothy E. Moss, Director in the Discipleship Ministries Unit
of the General Board of Discipleship

University of Minnesota
200 Donhowe Building
314 15th Avenue S.E.
Minneapolis, Minnesota 55455-0106
tel.: (612) 624-4307
fax: (612) 625-2574
Contact person: Timothy J. Delmont,
Programs

U.S. Air Force Institute of Technology
(AFIT)
AFIT / LSE
2950 P Street
Wright Patterson AFB, Ohio 45433-7765
tel.: (513) 255-6863
fax: (513) 476-7622
Contact person: Phillip J.-L. Westfall, Director, Center for Distance Education

U.S. Army Special Forces–Ft. Carson
95 A Watch Hill Drive
Colorado Springs, Colorado 80906
tel.: (719) 524-1838
Contact person: Captain David Bruce,
Special Forces–Airborne Operations

Usinas Siderúrgicas de Minas Gerais,
    S.A.—USIMINAS
Rua Professor José Vieira de Mendonça, 3011
Engenho Nogueira / Caixa Postal 806
31310-260 Belo Horizonte, MG, Brazil
tel.: (55-31) 499-8423
fax: (55-31) 499-8204
Contact person: Jarbas de Almeida Krauss,
    Analista-Gerência de Seleção e
    Treinamento-Sede

VINFEN Corporation
950 Cambridge Street
Cambridge, Massachusetts 02141-1001
tel.: (617) 441-1800
fax: (617) 441-1758
Contact person: Karen V. Unger, Director
    of Research & Training

Volunteers of America
1865 Larimer Street
Denver, Colorado 80202-1493
tel.: (303) 297-0408
fax: (303) 297-2310
Contact person: Linda Dee, Director of
    Volunteer Services

Wilderness Inquiry
1313 Fifth St. SE, Box 84
Minneapolis, Minnesota 55414-1546
tel.: (612) 379-3858
fax: (612) 379-5972
Contact person: Corey C. Schlosser-Hall,
    Director of Training

NOTES

PART ONE: Preparing for Learning

1. Robert H. Waterman, Jr., *What America Does Right* (New York: Norton, 1994), p. 65.
2. Warren Bennis and Burt Nanus, *Leaders: The Strategies for Taking Charge* (New York: Harper & Row, 1985), pp. 190–194.
3. Ibid., p. 191.
4. Peter Senge, *The Fifth Discipline: The Art and Practice of the Learning Organizations* (New York: Currency Doubleday, 1990), p. 14.
5. Ibid., p. 14.
6. Calhoun W. Wick and Lu Stanton León, *The Learning Edge: How Smart Managers and Smart Companies Stay Ahead* (New York: McGraw-Hill, 1993), p. 22 and p. 19, respectively.
7. Lester Thurow, *The Future of Capitalism* (New York: William Morrow, 1996), p. 68.

CHAPTER ONE: The New Importance of Learning

1. Peter Drucker, *Post-Capitalist Society* (New York: HarperBusiness, 1993), pp. 32–47.
2. Ibid., p. 42.
3. Lester Thurow, *The Future of Capitalism* (New York: William Morrow, 1996), p. 67.
4. Robert Reich, *The Work of Nations* (New York: Vintage Books, 1992), pp. 174–180.
5. Paul Kennedy, *Preparing for the Twenty-First Century* (New York: Vintage Books, 1993), p. 51.
6. Lester Thurow, *Head to Head: The Coming Economic Battle Among Japan, Europe, and America* (New York: Warner Books, 1992), p. 14.
7. Ibid., p. 30.
8. Rosabeth Moss Kanter, *World Class: Traveling Locally in the Global Economy* (New York: Simon & Schuster, 1995), p. 41.
9. Ibid., p. 52.
10. William Davidow and Michael Malone, *The Virtual Corporation* (New York: HarperBusiness, 1992), p. 73ff.

473

11. Rosabeth Moss Kanter, *The Change Masters* (New York: Simon & Schuster, 1983), p. 31 and p. 61, respectively.

12. Thomas J. Peters and Robert H. Waterman, Jr., *In Search of Excellence* (New York: Harper & Row, 1982), pp. 9–11 and pp. 13–16, respectively.

13. Michael Hammer and James Champy, *Reengineering the Corporation: A Manifesto for Business Revolution* (New York: HarperBusiness, 1993), pp. 31–32 and p. 70, respectively.

14. John Naisbitt and Patricia Aburdene, *Megatrends 2000* (New York: William Morrow, 1990), p. 153.

CHAPTER TWO: Reframing Training

1. Richard Swanson and Richard Torraco, "The History of Technical Training" in L. A. Kelley (ed.), *ASTD Technical and Skills Training Handbook* (New York: McGraw-Hill, 1994).

2. Wendy Ruona and Richard Swanson, "Foundations of Human Resource Development" in H. C. Hall (ed.), *Human Resource Development* (Columbia, Mo.: UCVE, 1997); Vincent Miller, "The History of Training" in Robert L. Craig (ed.), *Training and Development Handbook: A Guide to Human Resource Development,* 3rd ed. (New York: McGraw-Hill, 1987).

3. In chronological order: Patrick Pinto and J. Walker, *A Study of Professional Training and Development Roles and Competencies,* 1978; Patricia McLagan and R. McCullough, *Models for Excellence,* 1983; Patricia McLagan, *Models for HRD Practice,* 1989; N. Dixon and J. Henkelman, *Models for HRD Practice: The Academic Guide,* 1991. All are published in Alexandria, Virginia, by the American Society for Training and Development.

4. Patricia McLagan, *Models for HRD Practice: The Models* (Alexandria, Va.: American Society for Training and Development, 1989), p. 6.

5. Richard Swanson, "The Theoretical and Disciplinary Foundations of Performance Improvement" in Richard Torraco, *The Research Agenda for Improving Performance* (Washington, D.C.: ISPI Press, 1998), pp. 10–14.

6. McLagan, *Models for HRD Practice,* p. 7.

7. William Rothwell, *ASTD Models for Human Performance Improvement* (Alexandria, Va.: American Society for Training and Development, 1996), p. 11 and p. 5, respectively.

8. Richard Swanson, *Analysis for Improving Performance: Tools for Diagnosing Organizations and Documenting Workplace Expertise* (San Francisco: Berrett-Koehler, 1996), p. 8.

9. Richard Swanson "Human Resource Development: Performance Is the Key," *Human Resource Development Quarterly* 6:2 (Summer 1995), p. 208.

10. Peter Vaill, *Learning as a Way of Being: Strategies for Survival in Permanent White Water* (San Francisco: Jossey-Bass, 1996), pp. 20–21.

CHAPTER THREE: Learning in Organizations

1. Edward Gross and Amitai Etzioni, *Organizations in Society* (Englewood Cliffs, N.J.: Prentice-Hall, 1971), pp. 5–6 and p. 11, respectively.

2. Rosabeth Moss Kanter, *The Change Masters* (New York: Simon & Schuster, 1983), pp. 60–61.

3. Thomas J. Peters and Robert H. Waterman, Jr., *In Search of Excellence* (New York: Harper & Row, 1982), p. 42 and pp. 14–15, respectively.

4. Thomas J. Peters, *Tom Peters Seminar* (New York: Random House, 1994), p. 5ff and p. 29ff, respectively.

5. Peter Vaill, *Learning as a Way of Being* (San Francisco: Jossey-Bass, 1996), p. 4.

6. J. Eugene Haas and Thomas Drabek, *Complex Organizations: A Sociological Perspective* (New York: Macmillan Publishing, 1973), pp. 23–93.

7. Robert Heilbroner and Lester Thurow, *Economics Explained* (New York: Simon & Schuster, 1994), pp. 44–47.

8. Susan Mohrman and Allan Mohrman, Jr., "Organizational Change and Learning," p. 87ff, and Jay Galbraith and Edward Lawler III, "Effective Organizations: Using the New Logic of Organizing," p. 285ff, in Jay Galbraith and Edward Lawler III, *Organizing for the Future: The New Logic for Managing Complex Organizations* (San Francisco: Jossey-Bass, 1993).

9. Jay Galbraith and Edward Lawler III, "Effective Organizations: Using the New Logic of Organizing" in Galbraith and Lawler, *Organizing for the Future*, p. 285ff.

10. Paul Hersey and Kenneth Blanchard, *Management of Organizational Behavior* (Englewood Cliffs, N.J.: Prentice-Hall, 1988), p. 414ff.

11. Rensis Likert, *The Human Organization* (New York: McGraw-Hill, 1967).

12. Kanter, *The Change Masters*, p. 178.

13. Peters and Waterman, *In Search of Excellence*, p. 75.

14. Kanter, *The Change Masters*, p. 93.

CHAPTER FOUR: Planning for Learning

1. Cyril Houle, *The Design of Education* (San Francisco: Jossey-Bass, 1972); Malcolm Knowles, *The Modern Practice of Adult Education* (Chicago: Follett, 1980).

2. Jerald Apps, *Problems in Continuing Education* (San Francisco: Jossey-Bass, 1979), as cited in Ronald Cervero and Arthur Wilson, *Planning Responsibly for Adult Education: A Guide to Negotiating Power and Interests* (San Francisco: Jossey-Bass, 1994 [originally published 1979]), p. 3.

3. Rosemary S. Caffarella, *Planning Programs for Adult Learners* (San Francisco: Jossey-Bass, 1994), pp. 19–22, 23–24, 10, respectively.

4. Cervero and Wilson, *Planning Responsibly for Adult Education*, pp. 4, 28, 29, 30, 137ff, respectively.

5. The concepts for analyzing the curriculum—scope, breadth, depth, and so on—are found scattered about in the basic standard curriculum texts. Our list is a composite developed from William H. Schubert, *Curriculum: Perspective, Paradigm, and*

Possibility (New York: Macmillan, 1986); Daniel Tanner and Laurel Tanner, *Curriculum Development* (New York: Macmillan, 1975), and Paul Dressel, *College and University Curriculum* (Berkeley, Calif.: McCutchan, 1968). The concept of the hidden curriculum comes from Benson Snyder, *The Hidden Curriculum* (New York: Alfred Knopf, 1971), and the idea of the null curriculum is derived from Elliot Eisner, *The Educational Imagination,* 2nd ed. (New York: Macmillan, 1985).

6. Thomas R. Phillips, *Roots of Strategy: A Collection of Military Classics* (Harrisburg, Pa.: Military Service Publishing Co., 1940), p. 18.

7. Ralph Sawyer, *Unorthodox Strategies for the Everyday Warrior* (Boulder, Colo.: Westview Press, 1996). The ideas are from the introduction to a translation of a Sung Dynasty classic attributed to Liu Chi.

8. John Etting, *The Super-Strategists* (New York: Scribner, 1985), p. 2.

PART TWO: Understanding Training Strategies

1. B. D. Slife, and R. W. Williams, *What's Behind the Research: Discovering the Hidden Assumptions* (Newbury Park, Calif.: Sage, 1995), p. 235.

2. Alfred Morrow, *The Practical Theorist: The Life and Work of Kurt Levine* (New York: Basic Books, 1969), p. viii.

3. S. B. Merriam, *Case Study Research in Education: A Qualitative Approach* (San Francisco: Jossey-Bass, 1988).

CHAPTER FIVE: The Behavioral Strategy

1. Lester Thurow, *Head to Head: The Coming Economic Battle Among Japan, Europe, and America* (New York: Warner Books, 1992), pp. 51–52.

2. The shaping process is described by B. F. Skinner in *Science and Human Behavior* (New York: Free Press, 1953).

3. The model for shaping is borrowed from Joel Macht, *Teacher, Teachim* (New York: Wiley, 1975), p. 177.

4. The discussion of behaviorism is based on the writings of B. F. Skinner. Most textbooks on educational psychology summarize his work. The clearest introductory explanation of behavioral learning theory is found in the work of his student Fred S. Keller, *Learning: Reinforcement Theory,* 2nd ed. (New York: Random House, 1969). The most accessible work by Skinner is *About Behaviorism* (New York: Knopf, 1974).

5. E. L. Thorndike, *The Psychology of Learning* (New York: Teachers College, 1921), p. 237. Thorndike understood the relationship between consequences and learning and referred (p. 17) to "associative learning," "connection forming," and "laws of habit." The Law of Effect is explained in *Human Learning* (New York: Century, 1931), pp. 58–61. See also Thorndike's *The Fundamentals of Learning* (New York: Teachers College, 1932).

6. B. F. Skinner was an enormously productive scholar. The basic principles of behaviorism are outlined in *The Behavior of Organisms* (New York: Appleton-Century-Crofts, 1938). The relationship between behavior and reinforcement is described in *The Contingencies of Reinforcement* (New York: Appleton-Century-Crofts, 1969). The effects of various systems of rewards and punishments are spelled out in *Sci-*

ence and Human Behavior (New York: Free Press, 1953) and in *Schedules of Reinforcement,* coauthored with C. Ferster (New York: Appleton-Century-Crofts, 1957). Skinner's essays on education are collected in *The Technology of Teaching* (New York: Appleton-Century-Crofts, 1968). His article "Why We Need Teaching Machines" appeared in the *Harvard Educational Review* 31 (1961), pp. 377–398. His texts on operant conditioning are *About Behaviorism* (New York: Knopf, 1974) and *The Analysis of Behavior,* coauthored with J. Holland (New York: McGraw-Hill, 1961). For his work on languages, see *Verbal Behavior* (New York: Appleton-Century-Crofts, 1957), *Walden Two* (New York: Macmillan, 1948), and *Beyond Freedom and Dignity* (New York: Knopf, 1971). The "outside interests" appear in *Cumulative Record* (New York: Appleton-Century-Crofts, 1959). A collection of Skinner's essays appear in *Upon Further Reflection* (Englewood Cliffs, N.J.: Prentice-Hall, 1987). For Skinner's thoughts on old age, see *Enjoy Old Age: A Program of Self-Management* (New York: Norton, 1983), coauthored with M. E. Vaughan.

7. R. Burns, *New Approaches to Behavioral Objectives* (Dubuque, Iowa: Brown, 1972), p. 5.

8. Robert F. Mager, *Preparing Instructional Objectives* (Palo Alto, Calif.: Fearon, 1962), p. 11.

9. The discussion of task analysis is based on Chapter 5 of Robert H. Davis, Lawrence T. Alexander, and Stephen L. Yelon, *Learning System Design* (New York: McGraw-Hill, 1974).

10. R. M. Gagne, "Learning Hierarchies," Educational Psychologist 6:1 (1968), pp. 1–6.

11. The classic research on modeling and modeling effects is presented by Albert Bandura, *Principles of Behavior Modification* (New York: Holt, Rinehart and Winston, 1969).

12. David Premack, "Toward Empirical Behavior Laws: 1. Positive Reinforcement," *Psychological Review* 66 (1959), p. 219.

13. Skinner discusses punishment in *The Technology of Teaching* (New York: Appleton-Century-Crofts, 1968), p. 96. For a review of forms of corporal punishment, see A. Maurer, "Corporal Punishment," *American Psychologist,* (August 1974), pp. 614–626.

14. G. Walters and J. Grusec, *Punishment* (San Francisco: Freeman, 1977).

15. B. F. Skinner, "Why We Need Teaching Machines," *Harvard Educational Review* 31 (1961), pp. 377–398.

16. L. Stolurow, "Programmed Instruction" in R. Ebel (ed.) *The Encyclopedia of Educational Research* (London: Macmillan, 1969), pp. 1017–1021.

17. J. Taber, R. Glaser, and H. Schaefer, *Learning and Programmed Instruction* (Reading, Mass.: Addison-Wesley, 1965).

18. C. Thomas, I. Davies, D. Openshaw, and J. Bird, *Programmed Learning in Perspective* (Chicago: Educational Methods, 1964).

19. Neill Graham, *The Mind Tool: Computers and Their Impact on Society* (St. Paul, Minn.: West Publishing, 1986).

20. P. McCann, "Learning Strategies and Computer-Based Instruction," *Computers and Education* 5:3 (1981), pp. 133–140.

21. For models of a systems approach to instructional design, see Davis, Alexander, and Yelon, *Learning System Design,* and W. Dick and L. Carey, *The Systematic Design of Instruction* (New York: Scott Foresman, 1978).

22. K. Johnson and R. Ruskin, *Behavioral Instruction: An Evaluative Review* (Washington, D.C.: American Psychological Association, 1977); Ohmer Milton, *Alternatives to the Traditional* (San Francisco: Jossey-Bass, 1972). Keller's own description of PSI can be found in "Good-Bye Teacher," *Journal of Applied Behavioral Analysis* 1 (1968), pp. 79–88.

CHAPTER SIX: The Cognitive Strategy

1. Bill Gates, *The Road Ahead* (New York: Viking, 1995), p. 9.
2. Ibid., pp. 20–21 and p. 9, respectively.
3. Many of the models of cognitive processing are based on a classic chapter by Atkinson and Shiffran that sets forth the basic concepts of "sensory register," "short-term store," and "long-term memory." See R. C. Atkinson and R. M. Shiffran, "Human Memory: A Proposed System and Its Control Processes" in K. W. Spence and T. W. Spence (eds.), *The Psychology of Learning and Motivation*, vol. 2 (New York: Academic Press, 1968).
4. R. E. Meyer, *The Promise of Cognitive Psychology* (San Francisco: Freeman, 1981); William James, *The Principles of Psychology* (New York: Holt, 1890); F. L. Bartlett, *Remembering: A Study in Experimental and Social Psychology* (New York: Macmillan, 1932).
5. For a brief history of how cognitive psychology came into being as a field of study, see Ulrich Neisser, *Cognitive Psychology* (New York: Appleton-Century-Crofts, 1967). For more detail, see also Howard Gardner, *The Mind's New Science: A History of the Cognitive Revolution* (New York: Basic Books, 1985).
6. In an interesting twist of fate, Noam Chomsky, a young linguist, was asked to review B. F. Skinner's *Verbal Behavior*. The result was more than a book review. Chomsky emerged as a leading psycholinguist. See Noam Chomsky, "A Review of Skinner's Verbal Behavior," *Language* 35 (1959), pp. 26–58.
7. R. Lachman, J. L. Lachman, and E. C. Butterfield, *Cognitive Psychology and Information Processing: An Introduction* (Hillsdale, N.J.: Erlbaum Associates, 1979).
8. A. Newell, J. C. Shaw, and H. A. Simon, "Elements of a Theory of Human Problem Solving," *Psychological Review*, 65 (1958), pp. 151–166. Other landmark works are D. E. Broadbent, *Perception and Communication* (London: Pergamon Press, 1958); G. A. Miller, E. Galanter, and K. H. Pribam, *Plans and the Structure of Behavior* (New York: Henry Holt, 1960); N. Chomsky, *Aspects of the Theory of Syntax* (Cambridge, Mass.: M.I.T. Press, 1965); and Ulrich Neisser's classic textbook, *Cognitive Psychology*.
9. C. Cherry, *On Human Communication* (New York: Wiley, 1957).
10. D. E. Broadbent, *Perception and Communication* (London: Pergamon Press, 1958).
11. P. Lindsey and D. Norman, *Human Information Processing: An Introduction to Psychology* (New York: Academic Press, 1972).
12. A. M. Triesman, "Contextual Cues in Encoding Listening," *Quarterly Journal of Experimental Psychology* 12 (1960), pp. 242–248. Anthony J. Sanford, *Cognition and Cognitive Psychology* (New York: Basic Books, 1958). This text is used as a general source for understanding the basic concepts of cognitive psychology explained in this chapter.

13. R. M. Shiffran and N. Schneider, "Controlled and Automatic Human Information Processing II. Perceptual Learning, Automatic Attending, and a General Theory," *Psychological Review* 84 (1977), pp. 127–190.

14. The description of the human "scanning process," including the template theory and Selfridge's "Pandemonium Theory" are drawn from Sanford, *Cognition and Cognitive Psychology*, pp. 39–43.

15. The following discussion of "top-down processing" draws heavily on the excellent summary of research in Sanford, *Cognition and Cognitive Psychology*, p. 51ff. Some of the ideas for the illustrations are drawn from the basic psychology text by Phillip Zimbardo, *Psychology and Life* (Glenview, Ill.: Scott, Foresman, 1985), p. 196ff.

16. See Sanford, *Cognition and Cognitive Psychology*, p. 203ff, for schema theory. The story is adapted from E. Charniak, "Toward a Model of Children's Story Comprehension," Technical Report 266, Artificial Intelligence Laboratory, Massachusetts Institute of Technology, 1972.

17. The source on "scripts" is R. Schank and R. Ableson, *Scripts, Plans, Goals and Understanding: An Inquiry into Human Knowledge Structure* (Hillsdale, N.J.: Erlbaum, 1977). The concept of "frames" is elaborated in M. Minsky "A Framework for Representing Knowledge" in *The Psychology of Computer Vision* (New York: McGraw-Hill, 1975).

18. Sanford, *Cognition and Cognitive Psychology*, p. 104ff. William James (1890) called the two forms of memory "primary" and "secondary."

19. L. R. Peterson, "Short-Term Retention of Individual Verbal Items," *Journal of Experimental Psychology* 58 (1959), pp. 193–198.

20. G. A. Miller, "The Magical Number Seven, Plus or Minus Two: Some Limits on Our Capacity for Processing Information," *Psychological Review* 63 (1956), pp. 81–97.

21. Lachman, Lachman, and Butterfield, *Cognitive Psychology and Information Processing*, p. 52.

22. E. Tulving, "Episodic and Semantic Memory" in E. Tulving and W. Donaldson (eds.), *Organization of Memory* (New York: Academic Press, 1972).

23. E. F. Loftus and G. F. Loftus, "On the Permanence of Stored Information in the Human Brain," *American Psychologist* 35 (1980), pp. 409–420.

24. E. Loftus, *Memory* (Reading, Mass.: Addison-Wesley, 1980).

25. R. C. Oldfield and A. Wingfield, "Response Latencies in Naming Objects," *Quarterly Journal of Experimental Psychology* 17 (1965), pp. 273–281.

26. R. Lachman, "Uncertainty Effects on Time to Access the Internal Lexicon," *Journal of Experimental Psychology* 99 (1973), pp. 199–208.

27. Sanford, Cognition and Cognitive Psychology, p. 107ff.; S. K. Reed, *Cognition: Theory and Applications* (Pacific Grove, Calif.: Brooks/Cole, 1982).

28. R. N. Shepherd, "Recognition Memory for Words, Sentences and Pictures," *Journal of Verbal Learning and Verbal Behavior* 6 (1967), pp. 156–163.

29. L. Standing, "Learning 10,000 Pictures," *Quarterly Journal of Experimental Psychology* 25 (1973), pp. 207–222.

30. H. Lorayne and J. Lucas, *The Memory Book* (New York: Stein & Day, 1974), pp. 25–27.

31. Loftus, *Memory*, p. 181.

32. Chomsky, *Aspects of the Theory of Syntax.*

33. K. F. Pompi and R. Lachman, "Surrogate Processes in the Short-Term Retention of Connected Discourse," *Journal of Experimental Psychology* 75 (1967), pp. 143–150.

34. Zimbardo, *Psychology and Life,* p. 327ff.

35. Raymond S. Nickerson and Marilyn J. Adams, "Long-Term Memory for a Common Object," *Cognitive Psychology* 11 (1979), pp. 287–307.

36. The shot put/Frisbee metaphor is borrowed from a colleague, Professor Alton Barbour, Professor of Human Communication, at the University of Denver.

CHAPTER SEVEN: The Inquiry Strategy

1. Edward De Bono, *De Bono's Thinking Course* (New York: Facts on File, 1994), p. 71.

2. Richard Paul, *Critical Thinking* (Santa Rosa, Calif.: Foundation for Critical Thinking), p. 113.

3. Diane Halpern, *Thought and Knowledge: An Introduction to Critical Thinking* (Hillsdale, N.J.: Erlbaum, 1984), p. 3.

4. Robert Ennis, "A Taxonomy of Critical Thinking Dispositions and Abilities" in Joan Baron and Robert Sternberg (eds.), *Teaching Thinking Skills* (New York: Wilt Freeman, 1987), pp. 12–15.

5. Barry Beyer, *Practical Strategies for the Teaching of Thinking* (Hillsdale, N.J.: Erlbaum, 1985), p. 19.

6. Joanne Kurfiss, *Critical Thinking* (Washington, D.C.: Association for the Study of Higher Education, 1988), p. 2.

7. Beyer, *Practical Strategies,* p. 33.

8. Ibid., p. 27.

9. Raymond Nickerson, David Perkins, and Edward Smith, *The Teaching of Thinking* (Hillsdale, N.J.: Erlbaum, 1985), pp. 90–92.

10. Richard Paul, "Dialogical Thinking: Critical Thought Essential to the Acquisition of Rational Knowledge and Passions" in Baron and Sternberg, *Teaching Thinking Skills,* p. 128.

11. Denise Dellarosa, "A History of Thinking" in Robert Sternberg and Edward Smith (eds.), *The Psychology of Human Thought* (New York: Cambridge University Press, 1988), p. 1.

12. Paul, *Critical Thinking,* p. 39.

13. J. P. Guilford, *Creative Talents* (Buffalo, N.Y.: Bearly Limited, 1986) and E. Paul Torrence, *Why Fly* (Norwood, N.J.: Ablex, 1995).

14. Paulo Freire, *Education for Critical Consciousness* (New York: Seabury Press, 1973).

15. Neil Postman and Charles Weingartner, *Teaching as a Subversive Activity* (New York: Delacorte Press, 1969).

16. Nickerson, Perkins, and Smith, *The Teaching of Thinking,* p. 44.

17. Beyer, *Practical Strategies,* pp. 20, 25.

18. Nickerson, Perkins, and Smith, *The Teaching of Thinking,* p. 45.

19. Louis Raths, Selma Wasserman, Arthur Jones, and Arnold Rothstein, *Teaching for Thinking,* 2nd ed. (New York: Teachers College Press, 1986), pp. 164–167.

20. Postman and Weingartner, *Teaching as a Subversive Activity,* pp. 34–37.

21. Raymond Nickerson, *Reflections on Reasoning* (Hillsdale, N.J.: Erlbaum, 1986), p. 35.
22. Ibid., p. 20.
23. Sharon Schwarze and Harvey Lape, *Thinking Socratically* (Upper Saddle River, N.J.: Prentice-Hall, 1997), pp. 49–50.
24. Nickerson, *Reflections on Reasoning*, p. 68.
25. Ibid., p. 69.
26. M. Neil Browne and Stuart Keeley, *Asking the Right Questions* (Englewood Cliffs, N.J.: Prentice-Hall, 1994), p. 16.
27. Ibid., p. 13.
28. Nickerson, *Reflections on Reasoning*, p. 36ff.
29. Ibid.
30. Edward Corbett, *The Elements of Reasoning* (New York: Macmillan, 1991), pp. 11–46.
31. Ibid., p. 23ff.
32. Ibid., p. 21ff.
33. Ibid., p. 23.
34. Ibid., p. 42ff.
35. Ibid., p. 45.
36. Nickerson, *Reflections on Reasoning*, p. 4.
37. Halpern, *Thought and Knowledge*, p. 27.
38. Corbett, *The Elements of Reasoning*, p. 112.
39. Ibid., p. 113.
40. Nickerson, *Reflections on Reasoning*, p. 115.
41. Ibid., pp. 114–115.
42. Ibid., p. 118.
43. Ibid., pp. 116–117.
44. Ibid., p. 127; Browne and Keeley, *Asking the Right Questions*, p. 77.
45. Corbett, *The Elements of Reasoning*, pp. 116–117.
46. Ibid., p. 110.
47. Ibid., p. 115.
48. Browne and Keeley, *Asking the Right Questions*, p. 76.
49. Ibid., p. 119.
50. Ibid.
51. Nickerson, *Reflections on Reasoning*, p. 112.
52. Ibid., pp. 112–113.
53. Ibid., p. 113.
54. Ibid., p. 126.
55. Ibid.
56. Browne and Keeley, *Asking the Right Questions*, p. 80.
57. Nickerson, *Reflections on Reasoning*, p. 122.
58. Frank Barron, "The Psychology of Creativity" in Albert Rothenberg and Carl Hausman (eds.), *The Creativity Question* (Durham, N.C: Duke University Press, 1976), p. 190. Originally published by Barron in *Creative Person and Creative Process* (Holt, Rinehart and Winston, 1969).

59. E. Paul Torrence, "Educational Creativity" in Rothenberg and Hausman (eds.), *The Creativity Question*, p. 217. Originally published by Torrence as "Scientific Views of Creativity and Factors Affecting Its Growth," *Daedalus* (Summer 1965).

60. Henri Bergson, "Creation as Unpredictable" in Rothenberg and Hausman (eds.), *The Creativity Question*. Originally published by Bergson as "The Possible and the Real" in *The Creative Mind* (New York: Philosophical Library, 1946).

61. Albert Rothenberg, "The Process of Janussian Thinking in Creativity" in Rothenberg and Hausman (eds.), *The Creativity Question*, p. 313. Published earlier by Rothenberg with the same title in *Archives of General Psychiatry* 24 (1971), pp. 195–205.

62. John Feldhusen, "A Conception of Creative Thinking and Creativity Training" in Scott Isaksen, Mary Murdock, Roger Firestein, and Donald Treffinger (eds.), *Nurturing and Developing Creativity: The Emergence of a Discipline* (Norwood, N.J.: Ablex, 1993).

63. Mihaly Csikszentmihalyi, *Creativity: Flow and the Psychology of Discovery and Invention* (New York: HarperCollins, 1996), pp. 25–26.

64. Ibid., p. 42.

65. Robert Weisberg, *Creativity: Beyond the Myth of Genius* (New York: Freeman, 1993), p. 246.

66. Ibid.

67. John Baer, *Creativity and Divergent Thinking: A Task-Specific Approach* (Hillsdale, N.J.: Erlbaum, 1993). The theory is presented by S. A. Mednick in "The Associative Basis of the Creative Process," *Psychological Review* 69 (1962), pp. 220–232. The RAT is from 1969.

68. Guilford, *Creative Talents* (Buffalo, N.Y.: Bearly Limited, 1986), pp. 41–50.

69. Baer, *Creativity and Divergent Thinking*, p. 14.

70. Ibid., p. 15. The reference is E. P. Torrence and J. Presbury "The Criteria of Success Used in 242 Recent Experimental Studies of Creativity," *Creative Child and Adult Quarterly* 9 (1984), pp. 238–243.

71. Ibid., pp. 15–16.

72. Guilford, *Creative Talents*, p. 21, citing R. Wallas, *The Art of Thought* (London: Watts, 1945).

73. Alex Osborn, *Applied Imagination* (New York: Scribner, 1957).

74. Csikszentmihalyi, *Creativity*, Chapter 4, "The Work of Creativity."

75. Ibid., pp. 79–80.

76. Ibid., pp. 80–81.

77. Ibid., p. 102.

78. Ibid., p. 104.

79. Ibid., pp. 58–76.

80. Ibid., p. 57.

81. Tudor Richards, "Creativity from a Business School Perspective" in Csikszentmihalyi, *Creativity*, p. 162.

82. Laura Kaplan, "Teaching Intellectual Autonomy: The Failure of the Critical Thinking Movement" in Kerry Walters (ed.), *Rethinking Reason* (Albany: State University of New York Press, 1994), p. 213.

83. Paul, *Critical Thinking,* p. 258.

84. Ibid., pp. 263–265.

85. Richard Paul, "Dialogical Thinking: Critical Thought Essential to the Acquisition of Rational Knowledge and Passions" in Baron and Sternberg (eds.), *Teaching Thinking Skills,* pp. 132, 134.

86. Ibid., p. 259–262.

87. Ibid., p. 292.

88. Ibid., pp. 138, 140.

89. Paul, *Critical Thinking,* p. 240.

90. Ibid., p. 297.

91. Matthew Lippman, *Thinking in Education* (Cambridge, U.K.: Cambridge University Press, 1991), pp. 232–233.

92. J. T. Dillon. *The Practice of Questioning* (London: Routledge, 1990), pp. 14–15, 131–134, 137–142, 142–144.

CHAPTER EIGHT: The Mental Models Strategy

1. Peter Vaill, *Learning as a Way of Being: Strategies for Survival in a World of Permanent White Water* (San Francisco: Jossey-Bass, 1996), pp. 11–12.

2. Min Basadur, "Impacts and Outcomes of Creativity in Organizational Settings" in Scott Isaksen, Mary Murdock, Roger Firestein, and Donald Treffinger, *Nurturing and Developing Creativity: The Emergence of a Discipline* (Norwood, N.J.: Ablex, 1993), p. 279.

3. Diane Halpern, *Thought and Knowledge: An Introduction to Critical Thinking* (Hillsdale, N.J.: Erlbaum, 1984), p. 160.

4. Ibid.

5. Vincent Ruggerio, *The Art of Thinking: A Guide to Critical and Creative Thought* (New York: HarperCollins, 1991), pp. 104–105.

6. Thomas Ward, Ronald Finke, and Steven Smith, *Creativity and the Mind: Discovering the Genius Within* (New York: Plenum Press, 1995), p. 53.

7. Ibid., p. 55.

8. Sam Glucksberg, "Language and Thought" in Robert Sternberg and Edward Smith (eds.), *The Psychology of Human Thought* (New York: Cambridge University Press, 1988), based on work by S. M. Kosslyn, *Ghosts in the Mind's Machine* (New York: Norton, 1983).

9. See also David Strauss, *Tools for Change* (San Francisco: Interaction Associates, 1971). The quotation is from *Process Notebook,* same author and publisher, cited in James Adams, *Conceptual Blockbusting* (New York: Norton, 1979), p. 76. The different names are from Chapter 5, "Intellectual and Expressive Blocks."

10. John Dworetzky, *Psychology,* 2nd ed. (New York: West Publishing, 1985), pp. 237–238.

11. Denise Dellarosa, "A History of Thinking" in Sternberg and Smith (eds.), *The Psychology of Human Thought,* pp. 9–10.

12. George Polya, *How to Solve It,* 2nd ed. (Princeton, N.J.: Princeton University Press, 1957).

13. Raymond Nickerson, David Perkins, and Edward Smith, *The Teaching of Thinking* (Hillsdale, N.J.: Erlbaum, 1985), p. 74.

14. Allen Newell and Herbert A. Simon, *Human Problem Solving* (Englewood Cliffs, N.J.: Prentice Hall, 1972).

15. Ibid., p. 315–316.

16. Scott Plous, *The Psychology of Judgment and Decision Making* (New York: McGraw-Hill, 1993), p. 80.

17. John Bransford and Barry Stein, *The Ideal Problem Solver: A Guide for Improving Thinking, Learning, and Creativity* (New York: Freeman, 1993), pp. 8–9.

18. Alan Lesgold, "Problem Solving" in Sternberg and Smith (eds.), *The Psychology of Human Thought*, pp. 207–208.

19. Bransford and Stein, *The Ideal Problem Solver*, pp. 20–37.

20. Vincent Barry and Joel Rudinow, *Invitation to Critical Thinking*, 2nd ed. (Fort Worth, Tex.: Holt, Rinehart and Winston, 1990), p. 366.

21. Min Basadur, "Impacts and Outcomes of Creativity in Organizational Settings" in Isaksen, Murdock, Firestein, and Treffinger, *Nurturing and Developing Creativity*, p. 284.

22. Newell and Simon, *Human Problem Solving*, pp. 53–63, 787–791.

23. Norbert Jausovec, *Flexible Thinking: An Explanation for Individual Differences in Ability* (Cresskill, N.J.: Hampton Press, 1994), p. 10. The author refers to the distinction between problems and tasks made by the well-known German psychologist Doerner.

24. The discussion here is based on Wayne Wickelgren, *How to Solve Problems: Elements of a Theory of Problems and Problem Solving* (San Francisco: Freeman, 1974), pp. 10–17.

25. Ian Mitroff and Harold Linstone, *The Unbounded Mind: Breaking the Chains of Traditional Business Thinking* (New York: Oxford University Press, 1993), pp. 49–50.

26. Kathy Yohalen, *Thinking Out of the Box* (New York: Wiley, 1997), p. 5ff.

27. Wickelgren, *How to Solve Problems*, p. 63.

28. Jausovec, *Flexible Thinking*, pp. 10–11.

29. Ibid., pp. 12–14.

30. Barry and Rudinow, *Invitation to Critical Thinking*, p. 363.

31. Jonathan Baron, *Thinking and Deciding* (New York: Cambridge University Press), p. 17.

32. Halpern, *Thought and Knowledge*, p. 189.

33. Wickelgren, *How to Solve Problems*, pp. 46–47.

34. Baron, *Thinking and Deciding*, p. 68.

35. Halpern, *Thought and Knowledge*, pp. 182–184.

36. Ibid., pp. 184–185.

37. Ibid., pp. 192–193.

38. Wickelgren, *How to Solve Problems*, p. 124–126.

39. Ibid., p. 26.

40. Ibid., pp. 109–110.

41. M. Burns, "Teaching 'What to Do' in Arithmetic Versus Teaching 'What to Do and Why,'" *Educational Leadership*, pp. 43, 34–38. Cited in Robert Marzano and Associates, *Dimensions of Thinking* (Alexandria, Va.: Association for Supervision and Curriculum Development, 1988).

42. Halpern, *Thought and Knowledge*, pp. 167–174. The babysitting problem originates here but has been adapted considerably, although the table is still very much like Halpern's.

43. Keith J. Holyoak and Richard Nisbett, "Induction" in Sternberg and Smith (eds.), *The Psychology of Human Thought*, pp. 82–83. The experiments are reported in M. L. Gick and Keith J. Holyoak, "Analogical Problem Solving" in *Cognitive Psychology* 12 (1980), 306–355.

44. Wickelgren, *How to Solve Problems*, p. 63.

45. Halpern, *Thought and Knowledge*, pp. 199–201. The problem about the socks comes originally from J. F. Fixx, *Solve It* (New York: Doubleday, 1978).

46. Anthony J. Sanford, *Cognition and Cognitive Psychology* (New York: Basic Books, 1958), p. 357ff.

47. Glucksberg, "Language and Thought," p. 225.

48. Bransford and Stein, *The Ideal Problem Solver*, p. 4.

49. John Feldhusen, "A Conception of Creative Thinking and Creativity Training" in Isaksen, Murdock, Firestein, and Treffinger (eds.), *Nurturing and Developing Creativity*, p. 45. Based on unpublished dissertation research by S. M. Hoover, Purdue University, West Lafayette, Indiana, 1988.

50. Sanford, *Cognition and Cognitive Psychology*, p. 309, cites a study by D. A. Hinsley, J. R. Hayes, and H. A. Simon, "From Words to Equations: Meaning and Representation in Algebra Word Problems" in P. A. Carpenter and M. A. Just (eds.), *Cognitive Processes in Comprehension* (Hillsdale, N.J.: Erlbaum, 1977).

51. Nickerson, Perkins, and Smith, *The Teaching of Thinking*, p. 69.

52. Halpern, *Thought and Knowledge*, pp. 225–226.

53. Ibid., p. 5.

54. Ibid., p. 11.

55. Ibid., p. 1–5.

56. Ibid., p. 57.

57. Ibid., p. 55. The diagram has been expanded to include values.

58. Ibid., p. 55.

59. Ibid., pp. 63–66.

60. Ibid., pp. 62.

61. Baron, *Thinking and Deciding*, p. 315. The language has been paraphrased and adapted slightly.

62. Ibid., p. 196.

63. Halpern, *Thought and Knowledge*, pp. 221–22.

64. Nickerson, *Reflections on Reasoning*, p. 32.

65. Halpern, *Thought and Knowledge*, p. 222ff.

66. Baron, *Thinking and Deciding*, pp. 346–349.

67. Ibid., pp. 382–384.

68. Ibid., pp. 375–376.

69. Halpern, *Thought and Knowledge,* p. 123. See also Baron, *Thinking and Deciding,* pp. 229–230.

70. Ibid., p. 23ff.

71. Paul Pigors and Faith Pigors, "Case Method" in Robert L. Craig (ed.), *Training and Development Handbook: A Guide to Human Resource Development,* 3rd ed. (New York: McGraw-Hill, 1987), p. 415.

72. Louis Barnes, C. Roland Christensen, and Abby Hansen, *Teaching and the Case Method* (Boston: Harvard Business School Press, 1994), p. 41.

73. Ibid., p. 38.

74. Ibid., p. 34.

75. Michiel Leenders and James Erskine, *Case Research: The Case Writing Process* (London, Ontario, Canada: The University of Western Ontario, 1973), p. 11.

76. Pigors and Pigors, "Case Method" in Craig (ed.), *Training and Development Handbook,* p. 415.

77. Ibid.

78. Ibid., pp. 418–419.

79. Ibid., pp. 422–423. We have used the basic categories as lead words, but we have greatly modified the descriptors; we want to give credit to the Pigorses for the good list.

80. Barnes, Christiansen, and Hansen, *Teaching and the Case Method,* p. 46.

81. Ibid., pp. 48–49.

CHAPTER NINE: The Group Dynamics Strategy

1. Jon Katzenbach and Douglas Smith, *The Wisdom of Teams* (New York: HarperBusiness, 1993), p. 19.

2. Michael Hammer and James Champy, *Reengineering the Corporation: A Manifesto for Business Revolution* (New York: HarperBusiness, 1993), p. 65ff.

3. Barry E. Collins and Harold Guetzkow, *A Social Psychology of Group Processes for Decision Making* (New York: Wiley, 1964), p. 58.

4. Irvin Lorge, "A Survey of the Studies Contrasting the Quality of Group Performance and Individual Performance, 1920–1957," *Psychological Bulletin* 55 (1958), pp. 337–372.

5. The example was used originally in research performed by H. H. Johnson and M. M. Torcivia and is referred to in Charles Pavitt and Ellen Curtis, *Small Group Discussion* (Scottsdale, Ariz.: Gorsuch Scarisbrick, 1990), p. 43.

6. Bernard Berelson and Gary Steiner, *Human Behaviour: An Inventory of Scientific Findings* (New York: Harcourt, Brace & World, 1964), p. 557ff.

7. Kurt Lewin, "Forces Behind Food Habits and Methods of Change," *Bulletin of the National Research Council* 108 (1943), pp. 35–65.

8. Alvin Zander, *The Purposes of Groups and Organizations* (San Francisco: Jossey-Bass, 1985). The examples presented below are drawn from Chapter 2, "Functions Served by Groups," p. 14ff.

9. A. Paul Hare, Handbook of Small Group Research, 2nd ed. (New York: Free Press, 1976), Appendix 2, "The History and Present State of Small Group Research," pp. 388, 392.

10. Robert T. Golembiewski and Arthur Blumberg (eds.), *Sensitivity Training and the Laboratory Approach* (Itasca, Ill.: Peacock Publishers, 1970), p. 4.

11. Alvin Goldberg and Carl Larson, *Group Communication* (Englewood Cliffs, N.J.: Prentice-Hall, 1975), pp. 162–163. For more detail, see Kenneth Benne, "History of the T-Group in the Laboratory Setting" in Leland Bradford, Jack Gibb, and Kenneth Benne, *T-Group Theory and Laboratory Method* (New York: Wiley, 1964).

12. Goldberg and Larson, *Group Communication,* p. 163.

13. Thomas R. Verny, *Inside Groups* (New York: McGraw-Hill, 1974).

14. Carl Rogers, *Carl Rogers on Encounter Groups* (New York: Harper & Row, 1970), pp. 3–4.

15. Hare, *Handbook of Small Group Research,* pp. 413–414.

16. Verny, *Inside Groups.*

17. W. R. Bion, *Experiences in Groups and Other Papers* (New York: Basic Books, 1959).

18. For an overview of the research on group processes, see Goldberg and Larson, *Group Communication.* One of the early classics in the field is James H. McBurney and Kenneth G. Hance, *Discussion in Human Affairs* (New York: Harper Brothers, 1939). A well-known study of groups from a sociological viewpoint is George C. Homans, *The Human Group* (New York: Harcourt, Brace & World, 1950).

19. Malcolm Knowles and Hulda Knowles, *Introduction to Group Dynamics* (New York: Association Press, 1959), pp. 39–40.

20. Carl Larson and Frank LaFasto, *Teamwork: What Must Go Right, What Can Go Wrong* (Newbury Park, Calif.: Sage, 1989) p. 19.

21. Bruce W. Tuckman, "Development Sequence in Small Groups," *Psychological Bulletin* 63 (1965), pp. 384–399. Described in B. Aubrey Fisher, *Small Group Decision Making: Communication and the Group Process* (New York: McGraw-Hill, 1980), p. 140.

22. Golembiewski and Blumberg (eds.), *Sensitivity Training,* p. 87. The questions are borrowed from a larger checklist for observing group communication.

23. Goldberg and Larson, *Group Communication,* p. 46. The distinction goes back to some of the earlier work of George C. Homans. See also Fisher, *Small Group Decision Making,* p. 37ff.

24. Larry L. Barker, Kathy J. Wahlers, Kittie W. Watson, and Robert J. Kibler, *Groups in Process: An Introduction to Small Group Communication,* 3rd ed. (Englewood Cliffs, N.Y.: Prentice-Hall, 1987), p. 37.

25. Michael Burgoon, Judee K. Heston, and James McCroskey, *Small Group Communication: A Functional Approach* (New York: Holt, Rinehart and Winston, 1974), p. 10.

26. Fisher, *Small Group Decision Making,* pp. 38–39.

27. Ibid., pp. 39–43.

28. Pavitt and Curtis, *Small Group Discussion,* p. 64.

29. Fisher, *Small Group Decision Making,* p. 42.

30. Barker, Wahlers, Watson, and Kibler, *Groups in Process,* p. 53ff, provides a good discussion of group structure from which we have drawn extensively.

31. Hare, *Handbook of Small Group Research,* p. 131.

32. Kenneth D. Benne and Paul Sheets, "Functional Roles of Group Members," *Journal of Social Issues* (Spring 1948), pp. 4, 41–49.

33. Fisher, *Small Group Decision Making*, pp. 183–184, contains a good discussion of group norms.

34. Fisher, *Small Group Decision Making*, p. 29.

35. Ibid., p. 70.

36. Charles M. Kelly, "Empathic Listening" in Robert S. Cathcart and Larry A. Samovar (eds.), *Small Group Communication: A Reader* (Dubuque, Iowa: Brown, 1970), pp. 350–351.

37. Barker, Wahlers, Watson, and Kibler, *Groups in Process*, p. 83.

38. John E. Baird, Jr., and Sanford Weinberg, "Elements of Group Communication" in Cathcart and Samovar, *Small Group Communication*, p. 296. The list is shortened, adapted, and paraphrased.

39. Ibid., p. 297.

40. Lawrence Rosenfeld, "Nonverbal Communication in the Small Group" in Cathcart and Samovar, *Small Group Communication*, p. 306.

41. Leland Bradford, Dorothy Stock, and Murray Horowitz, "How to Diagnose Group Problems" in Golembiewski and Blumberg (eds.), *Sensitivity Training*, p. 142.

42. Ibid., pp. 142–143.

43. Fisher, *Small Group Decision Making*, pp. 57–59.

44. Ibid., p. 54.

45. Bradford, Stock, and Horowitz, "How to Diagnose Group Problems," p. 145.

46. Ibid., pp. 146–147.

47. Irvin Janis, *Victims of Groupthink: A Psychological Study of Foreign-Policy Decisions and Fiascos* (Boston: Houghton Mifflin, 1972); quoted in Barker, Wahlers, Watson, and Kibler, *Groups in Process*, pp. 68–69.

48. Pavitt and Curtis, *Small Group Discussion*, pp. 38–40.

49. Fisher, *Small Group Decision Making*, p. 61.

50. Ibid., pp. 24–26 for information on group size.

51. John K. Brilhart, *Effective Group Discussion* (Dubuque, Iowa: Brown, 1967), pp. 20–21.

52. Charles Seashore, "What Is Sensitivity Training?" in Golembiewski and Blumberg (eds.), *Sensitivity Training*, p. 14.

53. Rogers, *Carl Rogers on Encounter Groups*, p. 9.

54. Irvin D. Yalom, *The Theory and Practice of Group Psychotherapy*, 3rd ed. (New York: Basic Books, 1985). The listing of therapeutic factors and their paraphrased descriptions are drawn from Chapters 1–3, pp. 3–69. Each factor corresponds to a section heading in those chapters, except for the discussion of catharsis, which is found on p. 84ff, and the discussion of existential factors, found on p. 92ff.

55. Larson and LaFasto, *Teamwork*, p. 26.

56. Ibid, p. 42ff.

CHAPTER TEN: The Virtual Reality Strategy

1. Studs Terkel, *Working: People Talk About What They Do All Day and What They Think of While They Do It* (New York: Avon, 1972), pp. 49–50.

2. L. Casey Larijani, *The Virtual Reality Primer* (New York: McGraw-Hill, 1994), p. 1 and p. ix, respectively.

3. Omar Moore and Alan Anderson, "Some Principles for the Design of Clarifying Educational Environments" in Cathy Greenblatt and Richard Duke (eds.), *Gaming-Simulation: Rationale, Design, and Applications* (New York: Wiley, 1975), pp. 49–50.

4. Betsy Watson, "Games and Socialization" in Greenblatt and Duke (eds.), *Gaming-Simulation*, pp. 42–43.

5. Rene Marineau, *Jacob Levy Moreno, 1889–1974: Father of Psychodrama, Sociometry, and Group Psychotherapy* (London: Tavistock/Routledge, 1989), pp. 25–49.

6. Jacob Levy Moreno, *Psychodrama*. Vol. 1. (New York: Beacon House, 1946), p. 2.

7. Ken Jones, *Simulations: A Handbook for Teachers and Trainers* (London: Kogan Page, 1987), pp. 19–20. The following section relies on the treatment by Jones, drawing here and there on expressions and ideas set forth in his brief history of the origin of simulations.

8. Alice Gordon, *Games for Growth* (Palo Alto, Calif.: Science Research Associates, 1970), pp. 4–6.

9. Kalman Cohen and Eric Rhenman, "The Role of Management Games in Research" in Greenblatt and Duke (eds.), *Gaming-Simulation*, pp. 233–235.

10. Thomas C. Keiser and John H. Seeler, "Games and Simulations" in Robert L. Craig (ed.), *Training and Development Handbook: A Guide to Human Resource Development*, 3rd ed. (New York: McGraw-Hill, 1987), pp. 457–458.

11. John von Neumann and Oskar Morgenstern, *The Theory of Games and Economic Behavior* (Princeton, N.J.: Princeton University Press, 1944).

12. Caroline Persell, *Understanding Society: An Introduction to Sociology* (New York: Harper & Row, 1989), pp. 58–61.

13. R. P. Cuzzort and E. W. King, *Twentieth Century Social Thought*, 4th ed. (Fort Worth, Tex.: Holt, Rinehart and Winston, 1989), pp. 272–284.

14. M. E. Shaw, R. J. Corsini, R. R. Blake, and J. S. Mouton, "Role Playing" in J. E. Jones and S. W. Pfeiffer (eds.), *The 1979 Annual Handbook for Group Facilitators* (San Diego, Calif.: University Associates, 1979), pp. 182–193.

15. Phyliss Cooke, "Role Playing" in Craig (ed.), *Training and Development Handbook*, pp. 430–431. The section on arrangements that follows is adapted from Cooke, as well as other ideas for the remainder of this section.

16. Norman F. Maier, Allen Solem, and Ayesha Maier, *The Role-Play Technique* (La Jolla, Calif.: University Associates, 1975), p. 12.

17. Patricia Sternberg and Antonina Garcia, *Sociodrama: Who's in Your Shoes?* (New York: Praeger, 1989), pp. 48, 50, 53, 104 and 105. The concepts are from this source; the examples are ours. This is an excellent source on role play and sociodrama and is recommended for further reading.

18. Ibid., pp. 4–7.

19. Ibid., pp. 15–24.

20. Ibid., Chapter 6, "Structuring the Action," pp. 55–69.

21. Ibid., Chapter 9, "Mastering Directing Skills," pp. 89–100.

22. Richard Barton, *A Primer on Simulation and Gaming* (Englewood Cliffs, N.J.: Prentice-Hall, 1970), pp. 4–7.

23. Richard Dukes and Constance Seidner, *Learning with Simulations and Games* (Newbury Park, Calif.: Sage, 1978), p. 15.

24. Dennis Adams, *Simulation Games* (Worthington, Ohio: Charles A. Jones, 1973), pp. 4–5.

25. Clark Abt, *Serious Games* (New York: Viking Press, 1970), pp. 6–7.

26. Bloomfield, Lincoln, "Reflections on Gaming" *Forum ORBIS* (Winter 1984), pp. 783–790.

27. Cathy Greenblatt, "Gaming-Simulation and Social Science: Rewards to the Designer" in Greenblatt and Duke (eds.), *Gaming-Simulation,* pp. 92–93.

28. Cathy Greenblatt, "Basic Concepts and Linkages" in Greenblatt and Duke (eds.), *Gaming-Simulation,* pp. 10–13.

29. Allan Feldt and Frederick Goodman, "Observations on the Design of Simulation Games" in Greenblatt and Duke (eds.), *Gaming-Simulation,* pp. 170–171.

30. R.H.R. Armstrong and Margaret Hobson, "Introduction to Gaming-Simulation Techniques" in Greenblatt and Duke (eds.), *Gaming-Simulation,* p. 85–86.

31. Barton, *A Primer on Simulation and Gaming,* p. 29.

32. Jones, *Simulations,* pp. 65–90.

CHAPTER ELEVEN: The Holistic Strategy

1. Phil Gang, "Experiential Learning" in Carol Flake (ed.), *Holistic Education: Principles, Perspectives and Practices* (Brandon, Vt.: Holistic Education Press, 1993), p. 53.

2. David Kolb, *Experiential Learning: Experience as the Source of Learning and Development* (Englewood Cliffs, N.J.: Prentice-Hall, 1984), pp. 22–23 for diagram and quotations.

3. Donald Schön, *The Reflective Practitioner: How Professionals Think in Action* (New York: Basic Books, 1983), pp. 3–69. See also Donald Schön, *Educating the Reflective Practitioner* (San Francisco: Jossey-Bass, 1987), pp. 3–22.

4. John Dewey, 1963, quoted in Phil Gang, "Experiential Learning."

5. Quoted in Brian Hendley and Russell Dewey, *Whitehead: Philosophers as Educators* (Carbondale: Southern Illinois University, 1986), p. 85.

6. James Kielsmeier, "Growing with the Times: A Challenge for Experiential Education" in Richard Kraft and James Kielsmeier (eds.), *Experiential Learning* (Dubuque, Iowa: Kendall Hunt, 1995), p. 3.

7. "Education 2000: A Holistic Perspective," Appendix A in Flake (ed.), *Holistic Education* (Brandon, Vt.: Holistic Education Press, 1993), p. 240.

8. Gerald Fishbach, "Mind and Brain," a *Scientific American Special Report* (1994).

9. Carl Sagan, *The Dragons of Eden: Speculations on the Evolution of Human Intelligence* (New York: Ballantine Books, 1977).

10. Peter Gay, *Freud: A Life for Our Times* (New York: Anchor Books, 1989) pp. 65, 71, 103.

11. Charles Curran, *Counseling-Learning: A Whole-Person Model for Education* (London, U.K.: Grune & Stratton, 1972), p. 25 and p. 12.

12. Paul D. MacLean, *A Triune Concept of the Brain and Behavior* (Toronto, Canada: University of Toronto Press, 1973) and Sagan, *The Dragons of Eden*.

13. Sagan, *The Dragons of Eden*, p. 53.

14. Ibid., p. 57.

15. Leslie Hart, *Human Brain and Human Learning* (New York: Longman, 1983).

16. Sagan, *The Dragons of Eden*, p. 60.

17. Ibid., p. 35.

18. Harry Jerison, "Evolution of the Brain" in M. C. Wittrock (ed.), *The Human Brain* (Englewood Cliffs, N.J.: Prentice-Hall, 1977), p. 42ff.

19. Fishbach, "Mind and Brain," 1994.

20. Robert Sylwester, *A Celebration of Neurons: An Educator's Guide to the Human Brain* (Alexandria, Va.: Association for Supervision and Curriculum Development, 1995), p. 55 and pp. 59–68.

21. Leslie Hart, *Human Brain and Human Learning*, p. 46ff. Quotations are from pp. 52, 60, and 109, respectively.

22. Frank Smith, *To Think* (New York: Teachers College Press, 1990), pp. 12, 49, 112–114, 124, and 126, respectively.

23. Catherine Twomey Fosnot (ed.), *Constructivism: Theory, Perspectives, and Practice* (New York: Teachers College Press, 1996), p. 3 and p. 5, respectively.

24. Jacqueline Grennon Brooks and Martin G. Brooks, *In Search of Understanding: The Case for Constructivist Classrooms* (Alexandria, Va.: Association for Supervision and Curriculum Development, 1993), p. 4.

25. Ibid., p. 5.

26. Catherine Twomey Fosnot "Constructivism: A Psychological Theory of Learning" in Fosnot (ed.), *Constructivism*, pp. 13–14. We have elaborated the ideas presented here.

27. Gerard Egan, *The Skilled Helper: A Systematic Approach to Effective Helping*, 4th ed. (Pacific Grove, Calif.: Brooks/Cole, 1990). The outline of stages presented here is found in Chapter 2, and more detailed concepts are drawn from chapters 7, 8, and 10–16. Material has been paraphrased and simplified, hopefully without damaging what is a very carefully worked out process. Those interested in a basic model for counseling should read the entire book.

28. Chip Bell, *Managers as Mentors* (San Francisco: Berrett-Koehler, 1996), p. 7.

29. David Boud and Ned Miller, *Working with Experience: Animating Learning* (London, U.K.: Routledge, 1996), p. 7.

CHAPTER TWELVE: Choosing and Using Strategies

1. Daniel Bell, *The Reforming of General Education* (Garden City, N.Y.: Anchor Books, 1968), p. xiii. Although retold here in different words, the essence of the story has been retained.

2. Thomas Kuhn, *The Structure of Scientific Revolutions*, 2nd ed. (Chicago: University of Chicago Press, 1970), p. 35. Kuhn makes many of these points with reference to paradigms.

3. Joseph Schwab, "The Practical: A Language for Curriculum," *School Review* (November 1969), reprinted in Martin Lawn and Len Barton, *Rethinking Curriculum Studies* (New York: Wiley, 1981), p. 311 in reprinted version.

CHAPTER THIRTEEN: Adapting Strategies to Participants

1. Malcolm Knowles, "What Is Androgogy?" in Malcolm Knowles, *The Modern Practice of Adult Education* (Chicago: Follett Publishing, 1980), pp. 43–44.
2. Robert Havighurst, *Developmental Tasks and Education* (New York: Longman, 1972).
3. David Brodzinsky, Anne Gormly, and Sueann Ambron, *Lifespan Human Development* (New York: Holt, Rinehart and Winston, 1986).
4. Erik Erikson, *Identity and the Life Cycle: Selected Papers* (New York: International Universities Press, 1959) and *Identity, Youth, and Crisis* (New York: Norton, 1968).
5. Daniel F. Levinson, *The Seasons of a Woman's Life* (New York: Ballantine Book, 1996).
6. Ibid., pp. 19–20.
7. Gail Sheehy, *New Passages: Mapping Your Life Across Time* (New York: Random House, 1995).
8. Patricia King and Karen Kitchener, *Developing Reflective Judgment* (San Francisco: Jossey-Bass, 1994).
9. Howard Gardner, *Frames of Mind: The Theory of Multiple Intelligences* (New York: Basic Books, 1983).
10. American College Testing Program, "Assessing Students on the Way to College," *Technical Report for the ACT Assessment Program* (Iowa City, Iowa: ACT Publications, 1973), pp. 13–28.
11. Raymond Wlodkowski, *Enhancing Adult Motivation to Learn* (San Francisco: Jossey-Bass, 1993), pp. 60–62.
12. Daniel Goleman, *Emotional Intelligence* (New York: Bantam Books, 1995), pp. 43–44 and p. 80, respectively.
13. Robert Ornstein, *The Psychology of Consciousness* (New York: Viking Press, 1972).
14. Carl Sagan, *The Dragons of Eden: Speculations on the Evolution of Human Intelligence* (New York: Ballantine Books, 1977), p. 248.
15. David Kolb, *Experiential Learning* (Englewood Cliffs, N.J.: Prentice-Hall, 1984), pp. 67ff. The category descriptions have been paraphrased and condensed. For the full description see pp. 68–69.
16. John B. Murray, "Review of Research on the Myers-Briggs Type Indicator," *Perceptual Motor Skills* 70 (1990), pp. 1187–1202.
17. George Jensen, "Learning Styles" in Judith Provost and Scott Anchors (eds.), *Applications of the Myers-Briggs Type Indicator in Higher Education* (Palo Alto, Calif.: Consulting Psychologists Press, 1987). The descriptions are condensed and paraphrased from Jensen's presentation of the categories, p. 183ff., and from Figure 1, p. 186.
18. Ibid., pp. 188–189. Jensen raises important questions about responding to identified learning styles.

19. Walter Barbe and Raymond Swassing, *Teaching Through Modality Strengths: Concepts and Practices* (Columbus, Ohio: Zaner-Bloser, 1979). There is a Swassing-Barbe Modality Index to test modality strengths.

20. Roberta Hall (with assistance from Bernice Sandler). *The Classroom Climate: A Chilly One for Women* (Washington, D.C.: Association of American Colleges, 1982), p. 5. The research on elementary teachers cited is Myra Sadker and David Sadker, *Sex Equity Handbook for Schools* (New York: Longman, 1982), pp. 107–109.

21. Isaiah Smithson "Introduction: Investigation Gender, Power, and Pedagogy" in Susan Gabriel and Isaiah Smithson (eds.), *Gender in the Classroom: Power and Pedagogy* (Urbana: University of Illinois Press, 1990).

22. Mary Belenky, Blythe Clinchy, Nancy Goldberger, and Jill Tarale, *Women's Ways of Knowing: The Development of Self, Voice, and Mind* (New York: Basic Books, 1986).

CHAPTER FOURTEEN: Assessing Learning Outcomes

1. Donald Kirkpatrick, *Evaluating Training Programs: The Four Levels* (San Francisco: Berrett-Koehler, 1996).

2. Richard Swanson, *Performance-Learning Satisfaction Evaluation System* (St. Paul: University of Minnesota Human Resource Development Research Center, 1996).

3. Kirkpatrick, *Evaluating Training Programs*, p. 21ff.

4. Swanson, *Performance-Learning Satisfaction Evaluation System*, p. 3. The conclusion is based on G. M. Alliger and E. A. Janak, "Kirkpatrick's Levels of Training Criteria: Thirty Years Later," *Personnel Psychology* 42 (1989), pp. 331–340.

5. Kirkpatrick, *Evaluating Training Programs*, p. 27.

6. Ibid., p. 42ff.

7. Ibid., p. 52ff.

8. Richard Swanson, *Analysis for Improving Performance: Tools for Diagnosing Organizations and Documenting Workplace Expertise* (San Francisco: Berrett-Koehler, 1994), p. 51.

9. Kirkpatrick, *Evaluating Training Programs*, p. 25.

10. Richard Swanson and Deane Gradous, *Forecasting Financial Benefits of Human Resource Development* (San Francisco: Jossey-Bass, 1988).

NAME INDEX

SUBJECT INDEX

THE AUTHORS

James R. Davis is professor of higher education and adult studies at the University of Denver. He holds degrees from Oberlin College and Yale University and the Ph.D. degree from Michigan State University in higher education administration. Jim teaches courses on characteristics of adult learners, training, teaching adults, program planning and administration, leadership, and the uses of technology in instruction. He has served in numerous administrative posts, including assistant to the provost, director of the center for academic quality, director of the school of education—all at the University of Denver—and as academic dean at the historically black college, Wilberforce University, Wilberforce, Ohio.

Jim is the author of four other books, the more recent being *Better Teaching, More Learning: Strategies for Success in Postsecondary Settings* (1993) and *Interdisciplinary Courses and Team Teaching: New Arrangements for Learning* (1995). Both are part of the American Council on Education's Higher Education Series and are published by The Oryx Press in Phoenix, Arizona. As a result of this writing, Jim has served as a consultant to organizations, an invited presenter at conferences, and a workshop leader across the United States and around the world. "I love to help people learn about learning," says Jim, "and I try to model the strategies as we discuss them and get participants involved in their own learning."

Adelaide B. Davis served as a training analyst to COPASA MG, a government-sponsored public water and sanitation company in Brazil. She taught human resource management at the Universidade Federal de Minas Gerais in Belo Horizonte, where she also earned her masters degree in administration with a specialization in human resource management. She planned and facilitated numerous training workshops for her company and spoke at several conferences and annual meetings in Brazil.

Adelaide has created a second profession for herself since moving to the United States in 1991, consulting regularly as a software translator and editor for J.D. Edwards World Source Company (Denver) and Sykes Enterprises, Inc. (Boulder). She teaches Portuguese at University College, University of Denver, and is an adjunct Professor of Portuguese at the Colorado School of Mines. "The ultimate training and travel experience for me," notes Adelaide, "was to present (in English) a workshop on teamwork to women faculty members in the college of business at King Abdulaziz University in Jeddah, Saudi Arabia."

Jim and Adelaide like to work together. *Effective Training Strategies* is their first joint venture as authors, but they have collaborated before as workshop planners and presenters, the most challenging being a bilingual presentation on training strategies for FIAT in Belo Horizonte, Brazil, and a similar arrangement on the topic of teamwork in Brasilia.

"Collecting the examples for this book from around the world was a great learning experience for us," notes Adelaide, "and we enjoyed learning about other cultures, but the most important thing we noted was not differences but similarities—the world-wide importance being given to learning in organizations and the common language used in talking about it." Jim and Adelaide hope to focus their time and energies now on consulting with organizations on training. "Our hope," notes Jim, "is to spread the word about training strategies around the globe." Their main interest is to help people in organizations to think through their own particular training needs, to assist them in developing appropriate organizational structures and philosophies, to guide them in planning for and designing programs and courses, and to provide consultation on selecting and using training strategies in ways that are most effective for the goals of the organization and the needs of the participants.

Another joint venture is underway. Jim and Adelaide have another book under contract with Berrett-Koehler Publishers on the topic of mananging one's own learning. A companion volume to *Effective Training Strategies,* this book will focus on the aspects of learning that people need to be aware of and understand in order to be able to take charge of and maximize their own learning.